The Theory of Taxation and Public Economics

LOUIS KAPLOW

The Theory of Taxation
and Public Economics

PRINCETON UNIVERSITY PRESS
PRINCETON AND OXFORD

Second printing, and first paperback printing, 2011

Paperback ISBN 978-0-691-14821-2

The Library of Congress has cataloged the cloth edition of this book as follows

Kaplow, Louis.

The theory of taxation and public economics / Louis Kaplow.

p. cm.

Includes bibliographical references and index.

ISBN 978-0-691-13077-4 (cloth : alk. paper)

1. Finance, Public. 2. Taxation. 3. Income tax. 4. Welfare economics.

5. Distributive justice. I. Title.

HJ141.K36 2008

336.2001—dc22   2007044141

British Library Cataloging-in-Publication Data is available.

This book has been composed in Minion.

Printed on acid-free paper. ∞

Printed in the United States of America

3 5 7 9 10 8 6 4

For Leah, Irene, and Jody

Summary of Contents

PART V: DISTRIBUTIVE JUSTICE AND SOCIAL WELFARE

Contents

🦗

PART V: DISTRIBUTIVE JUSTICE AND SOCIAL WELFARE

Preface

༝

The purpose of this book is to offer a unifying conceptual framework for the normative study of taxation and related subjects in public economics. Such a framework necessarily begins with a statement of the social objective, taken here to be the maximization of a conventional social welfare function, and then asks how various government instruments are best orchestrated to achieve it. The structure is built on the foundation provided by the fundamental theorems of welfare economics. The key deviation is due to the infeasibility of redistribution by individualized lump-sum taxation. Because of this limitation, the fiscal system relies significantly on income taxation, which gives rise to the basic tradeoff between distribution and distortion.

My motivating premise is that the analysis of various forms of taxation and of many other topics must be grounded explicitly in this framework. As a matter of a priori theory, this assertion seems self-evident. Its importance is reinforced by two considerations. First, the optimal use of any one instrument depends on which others are available and how they are employed. In the present context, the pivotal role of the income tax is particularly significant, and analysis that focuses on other instruments in isolation may be problematic. Second, in complex, second-best settings, failure to examine all the effects of a policy in terms of social welfare can be dangerous. For example, a reform that is found to reduce labor supply distortion may seem desirable on that account, but the reform may concomitantly reduce redistribution, perhaps to such an extent that overall welfare is lower. Examining only one set of effects can be misleading, especially when the omitted effects may systematically run in the opposite direction.

The most direct way to meet the challenge would be to optimize all instruments simultaneously. This task, however, is quite daunting even with only a few instruments and minimal complicating assumptions— all the more so when one piece of the problem includes optimal deployment of a nonlinear income tax. An alternative strategy, developed and frequently applied in this book, is to use a construction that makes it possible to (legitimately) set aside much complexity and examine a few elements at a time. Specifically, in order to analyze a given policy—such as a modification to commodity taxes, transfer (estate and gift) taxation, public goods provision, or some means of regulating externalities—the policy is combined with a distributively offsetting adjustment to the income tax. The net result is a reform package that is distribution neutral, which, as will be seen, holds much constant and leaves in play the distinctive effects of the policy instrument under consideration, ones that can then more readily be evaluated.

In most areas of economics, it is standard practice to relate analysis to a paradigmatic setting, often one closely related to the simplified world of the two welfare theorems. This methodology enhances rigor, economizes on effort, generates benefits from cross-fertilization, and facilitates understanding and communication. For taxation and many other public economics questions, the same advantages can be realized by adopting such an approach, although, as noted, the benchmark scenario should be the second-best one in which an income tax is present and redistribution is accomplished imperfectly and at a cost. My goal is to pursue this line of inquiry systematically in order to enhance our understanding of the theory of taxation and of public economics more broadly.

The ambition of this project is similar in spirit to that of Musgrave in *The Theory of Public Finance* and of some of his predecessors, including Pigou and Vickrey. The closest modern incarnation is Atkinson and Stiglitz's *Lectures on Public Economics,* which builds importantly on Mirrlees's seminal paper on optimal nonlinear income taxation. There has been a tremendous growth in research since these works, which is reflected in texts and surveys such as those in the four volumes of the *Handbook of Public Economics.*

This book is meant to be complementary to these more recent efforts. Most of them are rather specialized, presenting often-subtle developments on particular topics but attending less to interactions among the various pieces. It is inevitable and appropriate that most research and even most syntheses of research are of this nature. Nevertheless, it is useful from time to time to step back and reflect carefully and precisely on the whole enterprise and to trace directly the relationships among each of its constituent parts. Such an exercise ought to produce payoffs along a number of dimensions. Existing results may be solidified, better understood, and extended; solutions may emerge for previously intractable problems; and, in some instances, seemingly sound conclusions may be overturned. In addition, research agendas, both analytical and empirical, may be initiated, refined, or redirected in light of what is learned. Having undertaken this mission, it is my belief that the experience yields all of these rewards. Readers, of course, will judge this for themselves.

⋅   ⋅   ⋅

I began work on this book in earnest during the mid-1990s, producing hundreds of pages of manuscript that I aired to some extent. Upon resuming work five years later, after completing other projects, I decided to scrap my existing draft and begin afresh. Further reflection and interim research had produced new ideas, refined my thinking, and ultimately shifted my focus. Moreover, I wished to create a text more uniform in depth and rigor, with a scope more finely tailored to my central theme. In the intervening years, my work frequently alternated between this book and spin-off articles (including a *Handbook* survey, Kaplow 2007g). While working on particular chapters, I often discovered important gaps or deficiencies that required independent, sustained attention. In the end, it is hard to say which articles came from the book and which chapters or sections of the book came from articles. In every case, however, book chapters have been written from scratch in order to optimize their fit with the current project.

Although the first keystrokes for this venture were made in 1995, its intellectual origins are much earlier. During my economics training, Hugo Sonnenschein and Michael Spence were most responsible for inculcating in me the virtue of rigor, the value of tracing problems to their foundations, an appreciation of elegance, the importance of extracting and communicating core intuitions, and an understanding of welfare economics and the economics of information that underlies this endeavor. My interest in public economics, and taxation in particular, was sparked at an early stage by Martin Feldstein, Richard Musgrave, Stanley Surrey, Alan Auerbach, and Lawrence Summers. Subsequently, my thinking has been notably advanced and revised in reaction to lively discussions at regular meetings of the public economics group at the National Bureau of Economic Research and tax workshops at Harvard.

I received comments on the book manuscript and on related articles from participants at many additional workshops and conferences and in other, more individualized settings. Joel Slemrod, Steven Shavell, and David Weisbach have supplied the most extensive input. In addition, over the course of two decades I have benefited from countless conversations with David Bradford; even since his untimely death, I find myself contemplating how he might have reacted to new directions I have pursued. At various points, additional reactions were provided by Alan Auerbach, Peter Diamond, James Hines, Daniel Shaviro, Alvin Warren, referees and journal editors, university press reviewers, and additional individuals too numerous to mention.

I am also grateful to a large and unusually skilled supporting cast. Matt Seccombe and various individuals at Princeton University Press provided excellent editorial and related assistance; Molly Overholt and the late Regina Roberts offered secretarial and administrative support; staff at the Harvard Law School library assembled materials; and many research assistants over the years helped review literature and checked the text, notes, derivations, and references. This latter group includes (with apologies to any accidentally omitted) Susan Amble, Mary Bear, Elizabeth Bell, Clifford Chen, Ivan Chen, Eun Young Choi, Vicki Chou, Derek Colla, Ryan Copus, Shelley de Alth, Nicholas Degani, Sameer Doshi, Stephanie Gabor, Ryan Gavin, Yehonatan Givati, Thomas Gremillion, Zachary Gubler, Gregory Hannibal, Jeffrey Harris, James Hileman, Alexander Hooper, Anna Joo, Jasi Kamody, Lisa Keyfetz, Summer Sung Eun Kim, James Kvaal, Stacy Lau, Jonathan Lin, Richard Lin, Edward Locke, Daniel Lyons, Kenneth Moon, Kevin Mosher, Jesse Panuccio, John Rackson, Manoj Ramachandran, Daniel Richenthal, Kathleen Saunders, Brian Sawers, Amy Sheridan, Moshe Spinowitz, Andrew Steinman, Eric Sublett, Kevin Terrazas, George Wang, Tzung-bor Wei, Gregory Weston, and Jeremiah Williams. Finally, I appreciate receiving substantial financial support from the John M. Olin Center for Law, Economics, and Business and from Harvard Law School, as well as the encouragement of Deans Robert Clark and Elena Kagan.

The Theory of Taxation and Public Economics

1

Introduction

This book develops and applies a unifying framework for the analysis of taxation and related subjects in public economics. Its two central features are explicit attention to the social objective of welfare maximization and direct examination of how various government instruments should be orchestrated to achieve that objective. Consistent application of this approach solidifies and extends some familiar results and intuitions, overcomes seemingly intractable obstacles regarding other issues, and overturns several important settled understandings.

Mirrlees (1971), although most remembered for pathbreaking technical analysis of optimal nonlinear income taxation, also provides the seminal modern articulation of this research agenda. Concerns about distribution and distortion and the tradeoff between them, the key issues in his article, arise in connection with many topics in public economics, ranging from all forms of taxation to public goods and the regulation of externalities to social insurance. Nevertheless, literatures vary widely in the extent to which analysis is related to a social welfare function and connected to the backbone of modern fiscal systems: some form of labor income taxation (or consumption taxation equivalents). Even though optimal income tax writing has hewed closely to the course of inquiry suggested by Mirrlees and adopted here, work on the taxation of capital income, transfer programs, public goods, regulation, social insurance, and other subjects often has not done so, and research on other topics such as transfer (estate and gift) taxation and the tax treatment of different family units only rarely attempts the necessary linkages.

It is worth pausing to emphasize the pivotal role of the income tax in studying different types of taxation and many other problems in public economics. The truism that the optimal use of any policy instrument generally depends on what other ones are feasible is particularly apt when one of the available instruments is the income tax. Consider optimal commodity taxation, explored more fully in chapter 6. The familiar Ramsey (1927) result for the basic case with no demand interdependencies is that commodity tax rates should vary inversely with own-demand elasticities; if heterogeneity is introduced so that income distribution matters, luxuries should be taxed more heavily than necessities, ceteris paribus. But these results assume that no income tax is feasible. When an income tax is employed and set optimally, Atkinson and Stiglitz (1976) show that, with weak labor separability in the utility function, no differentiation in commodity tax rates is optimal; indeed, this is so regardless of own-price elasticities and income elasticities. Yet much research ignores the income tax—presumably due to the complexity of optimal income tax analysis—and builds models like Ramsey's, which may well yield conclusions that are inapplicable to an economy with income taxation, such as most developed economies today.

This book relates the analysis of all of its subjects to the income tax and attends to how both distribution and distortion influence social welfare. In many settings, it proves useful to accomplish this mission by employing a procedure that constructs distribution-neutral (and revenue-neutral) reform packages. Specifically, the income tax is adjusted to offset the distributive incidence of the modification to the policy instrument directly under consideration, whether it be commodity taxation, transfer taxation, public goods provision, or some means of regulating externalities. This method disregards neither the income tax nor important aspects of social welfare. Yet the complexities of optimal income tax analysis are largely moot because the initial income tax need not be optimal and the optimum need not be determined in order to implement this procedure. Moreover, as will now be explained, many second-best complications are successfully moved into the background.

When the entire reform package is distribution neutral, it obviously is appropriate to ignore distributive effects since there are none. Furthermore, distribution-neutral reform packages will be shown to have no effect on labor supply in a benchmark case, indeed, in the same case of weak labor separability noted by Atkinson and Stiglitz (1976). In other words, under the proposed approach both distribution and labor supply—the elements of the tradeoff at the heart of the optimal income tax problem—can legitimately be set to the side. As a consequence, all that remains to examine are what may be viewed as the distinctive effects of the original policy instrument under consideration. These effects may accordingly be assessed on efficiency grounds alone because any standard social welfare function will favor a reform package that increases efficiency while leaving distribution unaffected.

In this setting, it is correct to follow simple first-best commands like the Samuelson cost-benefit test, the Pigouvian prescription to set pollution taxes and subsidies equal to marginal external costs and benefits, and public sector pricing at marginal cost. This is so (subject to qualifications that will be explored) despite second-best concerns about distribution and labor supply distortion that have occupied increasingly complicated literatures, work that often does not incorporate the income tax and that frequently attends only to distribution or only to distortion—which is quite dangerous given the inevitable tradeoff between the two and, relatedly, the failure to apply a social welfare function. By comparison, the method adopted here enables analysis that is more streamlined and intuitive and, at the same time, more rigorous and reliable.

Furthermore, because the same technique can be utilized for such a wide range of seemingly disparate problems—from commodity taxation to transfer taxation to public goods to regulation—there are substantial economies of effort. In addition, greater specialization is facilitated because inquiries into specific subjects, properly framed using distribution-neutral income tax adjustments, can confine attention to distinctive features. Studies of cigarette taxation can concentrate on the merits of discouraging smoking, evaluations of transfer taxation on the virtues of encouraging consumption by donors rather than by donees, assessments of infrastructure projects on their effects on productivity, and appraisals of environmental measures on the direct costs of different modes of regulation and their environmental consequences. Other researchers can focus on the distribution-distortion tradeoff itself, which is done most directly in the context of the original optimal income tax problem, one that would benefit from greater attention to a number of little-explored yet important variations. There are, of course, interactions in some instances, but it will be seen that these, too, are clarified by the proposed approach.

As the foregoing discussion indicates, the methodological focus of this book is conceptual and normative. Therefore, only occasional attention will be given to the extensive empirical work that bears importantly on ultimate policy recommendations but not as much on how analysis should be structured. Additionally, macroeconomic and political considerations are largely ignored. Finally, except for occasional illustrative purposes, specific policy proposals are not examined. The purpose here is to enhance understanding of how analysis should be conducted and of what research agenda is implied thereby. It will nevertheless be apparent throughout the book that this approach has substantial and sometimes unconventional policy implications.

•   •   •

The framework for analysis is presented more fully in Part I. Chapter 2 discusses the case for an integrated view of various forms of taxation and associated subjects in public economics and begins to explore what this view entails. Substantial attention is devoted to how distribution-neutral income tax adjustments can be utilized to facilitate the analysis of tax, expenditure, and regulatory policies. Chapter 3 further develops the need for making the social objective explicit, presents the standard formulation of the social welfare function that will be employed throughout the book, and discusses a range of social judgments about redistribution and how differences among them relate to subsequent analysis.

Part II begins application of the framework by examining the optimal income taxation problem and related issues. Chapter 4 presents standard models and results for linear and nonlinear (labor) income taxation that will be drawn upon in subsequent chapters. Even readers already conversant with this work will likely find some nuances of interest. Chapter 5 elaborates and extends the classical analysis along a number of dimensions. Some matters are familiar, like the relevance of administration and enforcement, whereas others have received less attention, such as ability-based taxation, the complication that income may signal different preferences rather than just abilities, and the implications of interdependent preferences. Many of these topics warrant further research; in some instances, preliminary lines of inquiry are sketched.

Chapter 6, on commodity taxation, is especially important for this book because it presents the most elemental formalization of much of the integrative theme. Using the distribution-neutral approach, Atkinson and Stiglitz's (1976) aforementioned result on the inefficiency of differential commodity taxation is extended to the more general case in which the initial income tax is arbitrary rather than optimal and to cases involving partial reforms. A direct implication is that luxury taxes as well as widely employed exemptions, such as those from a VAT for expenditures on necessities, are inefficient tools for achieving distributive objectives. Qualifications to this analysis and its precise relationship to the assumptions and well-known principles associated with Ramsey taxation are discussed. The results of this chapter form a centerpiece for much of the subsequent analysis in the book because the method of distributively offsetting income tax adjustments is a generic one. Accordingly, the logic is not restricted to commodity taxation and thus can be used to reach important and sometimes unexpected conclusions regarding public goods, regulation, and other forms of taxation (such as of private transfers). As will be discussed at various points in the book, many policy instruments are formally quite similar to commodity taxation, so the unity of analytical approaches to these disparate subjects and the similarity of results should not, upon reflection, be viewed as surprising.

Part III completes the integrated framework by taking account of government expenditures. Chapter 7 examines transfer payments, supplementing the simplified treatment in standard optimal income tax analysis. Much study of transfer programs and of taxation is undertaken in isolation, which results in a deceptive picture regarding redistribution and the incentives faced by lower-income individuals. More broadly, existing views about optimal treatment at the bottom of the income distribution have conflicting elements: Extremely high effective marginal tax rates (largely from phase-outs of transfer payments) are widely condemned, whereas optimal income tax analysis suggests that high marginal rates at low income levels are attractive even though they lead the lowest-ability individuals not to work. These competing elements are reconciled, and the results are used to determine the optimal form of categorical assistance, that is, how levels of assistance and marginal tax rates (including phase-outs) should differ across groups, such as the disabled and those capable of work. It appears that groups that are typically subject to high (low) marginal rates should optimally face low (high) rates. In addition, increasingly popular work inducements are considered, and it is revealed that most existing and proposed schemes may deviate, perhaps substantially, from optimality.

Chapter 8 addresses government expenditures on goods and services. A proper view of distribution requires attending to how government expenditures are financed and how the combination of expenditure and finance affects distribution and distortion. Using the distribution-neutral income tax adjustments introduced in chapter 2 and analyzed in chapter 6, it is demonstrated that concerns about both distribution and the fact that finance involves income taxation with its associated labor supply distortion can largely be ignored in determining the optimal provision of public goods. In addition, the feedback (if any) of public goods provision on optimal redistributive taxation is examined; that is, it is determined how changing the level of public goods affects the optimal extent of redistribution. The analysis of these issues also elucidates—and in some cases dissolves—challenges that confront attempts to measure the distributive incidence of public policies, and it offers a new perspective on debates about conceptions of benefit taxation. Finally, the analysis of public goods is modified to produce analogous results regarding all manner of government regulation, such as that of the environment, which raises similar concerns regarding distributive effects and labor supply distortion. Again, the results depart, sometimes substantially, from those in the pertinent literature.

Part IV considers other forms and dimensions of taxation. Chapter 9 moves beyond the implicitly static, one-period model used in classical optimal income taxation analysis—actually, the analysis of optimal labor income taxation—to consider the taxation of capital income. Use of the distribution-neutral approach of chapters 2 and 6 to compare different levels of capital taxation serves to clarify and elaborate the point originally advanced by Atkinson and Stiglitz (1976) that capital taxation is equivalent to differential commodity taxation, in this instance of commodities in different time periods, and thus is inefficient in the basic case. A range of qualifications to this result are explored, including the possibility that individuals' savings decisions do not reflect neoclassical maximizing behavior. The conclusions are used to illuminate the choice between income and consumption taxation, wealth taxation, and corporate income taxation, and the results are extended to address uncertain capital income, capital levies and certain tax regime transitions, and the taxation of human capital. As suggested earlier, the analysis and some of the results in this chapter differ markedly from much of the existing literature on capital taxation because such work employs Ramsey-type models that assume (often implicitly) the infeasibility of income taxation.

Chapter 10 analyzes the taxation (or subsidization) of private transfers between individuals. Although transfer taxation is often understood as a revenue source and an important redistributive supplement in the fiscal system as a whole, these views are misconceived if one joins such taxation with a distributively offsetting income tax adjustment. Then the question becomes: Regarding individuals at a given level of income (say, very high), should their overall tax burden be relatively higher or lower if their marginal dollar is given to descendants rather than spent on themselves to live more opulently? This formulation immediately suggests an entirely different orientation toward the taxation of voluntary transfers. The analysis is complicated by two sets of factors: First, gifts directly affect two individuals, donor and donee, in a manner that qualitatively differs from expenditures on ordinary consumption; this feature gives rise to two species of externalities and has subtle distributive implications that are qualitatively distinct from those usually contemplated. Second, gifts are induced by a wide array of motives that may have diverse implications for behavior and welfare. The distribution-neutral approach neutralizes what many consider to be the most pertinent considerations and brings into view these important factors that previously have been largely hidden. The analysis is also applied to additional subjects, including determination of the optimal policy toward charitable giving, a problem that is also cast in a new light.

Chapter 11 examines aspects of social insurance that are related to the issues addressed elsewhere in the book. First, purely redistributive aspects of social security are noted. It is observed that ordinary redistribution through social security can generally be assimilated to redistribution under the income tax. Then attention turns to more distinctive redistributive dimensions, notably that social security retirement schemes depend on lifetime income (with consideration of how marginal tax rates optimally vary over the life cycle and whether this pattern is reflected in the ordinary operation of typical income and social security tax schemes), that intergenerational redistribution may be involved, and that different family types are often treated differently. Second, the forced-savings dimension of social security is analyzed, focusing on myopia and other factors that are central to some justifications for the existence of social security schemes. Emphasis is placed on how social security taxes paid during working years may affect labor supply in light of the fact that individuals may be myopic and thus excessively discount benefits paid in the distant future. Some of the results are initially surprising: Notably, in most respects a social security system does not have the effects of an additional tax on top of an existing tax on labor income (the income tax). The sign of the labor supply effects of social security reverses under certain variations of assumptions and parameters, and as the forced-savings constraint just begins to bind there is no first-order effect in one case but a positive effect in the other, yet one that declines rather than rises as the constraint tightens. Finally, more purely insurance-like features of social security are briefly considered.

Chapter 12 addresses the heterogeneity among family units that is central in setting income tax policy, designing transfer programs, and producing descriptive measures of the overall distribution of well-being. Previously, many of the issues have proved intractable and others controversial. Substantial redirection and illumination is provided by the present approach, both by insisting that analysis be explicitly related to the social welfare function and by employing distributively offsetting income tax adjustments to focus on distinctive aspects of the problem. The chapter first analyzes the optimal relative treatment of different family types—single individuals versus couples, and those with varying numbers of children—while abstracting from incentive considerations. Relative allocations may depend on inequality of sharing, economies of scale, different motives that underlie intrafamily sharing, and differences in how resources are translated into utility (notably, by adults compared to children). In each case, depending on traits of utility functions and the social welfare function, optimal results may differ qualitatively from standard views. For example, economies of scale could favor more generous rather than less generous per capita allotments to families, and optimal allocations might favor families with children to such an extent that the parents are enabled to consume more resources than are made available to adults without children. Then the chapter considers how these principles of allocation may require modification because of incentive considerations involving labor supply, marriage, and procreation.

Part V revisits issues of distributive justice and social welfare that are raised by the standard welfare economic framework initially introduced in chapter 3 and by some of its applications in subsequent chapters. Chapter 13 examines welfarism, the view that the social assessment of policies should depend exclusively on how they affect individuals' well-being. Because this approach is controversial, particularly among moral philosophers and some welfare economists—and more particularly because certain prominent tax equity norms, upon examination, conflict with welfarism—a defense is sketched. It is explained that all nonwelfarist approaches violate the Pareto principle, and further attention is devoted to reconciling the welfarist paradigm with moral intuitions that underlie competing normative criteria. This chapter also elaborates on the concept of well-being that is central to the welfarist approach and assesses a variety of issues that have been raised with regard to crediting individuals' preferences that might be viewed as mistaken or otherwise objectionable. Alternatives to welfarism involving capabilities and primary goods, associated with Sen and Rawls respectively, are shown to be problematic because, among other reasons, they transgress the Pareto principle.

Chapter 14 considers the choice of social welfare function within the welfarist paradigm. Specifically, should the welfare function be utilitarian or more egalitarian? Powerful arguments developed primarily by Harsanyi and further analysis that draws on the Pareto principle and the requirement of time consistency all favor a utilitarian social welfare function. Some standard concerns are addressed, namely, about the possibility of interpersonal comparisons of utility and the sufficiency of the weight given to equality. In choosing a social welfare function, it is also necessary to articulate who should be considered a member of the society whose welfare is to be maximized. Should the focus be local, national, or international? What about future generations? And how should society evaluate policies that affect the size of the pertinent population, and thus may raise total welfare while reducing average welfare? The discussion of these issues will be brief and speculative.

Chapter 15 presents and criticizes other normative criteria for the assessment of tax policy. Consideration is given to various approaches to the measurement of inequality, poverty, progressivity, and redistribution; the concept of horizontal equity; and classical doctrines, notably sacrifice theories, the benefit principle, and the notion of ability to pay. Many of these alternative evaluative precepts are incomplete. Others are redundant, which renders them of little normative use. Of greater concern is that some are in conflict with the Pareto principle. Accordingly, when policy analysis gives weight to these criteria, as is sometimes done, prescriptions may be perverse in ways that are unrecognized. It is suggested that the appeal of these various criteria lies in their tendency to serve as proxies for aspects of social welfare; hence, some may have instrumental value in certain settings, even though they do not constitute ultimate normative objectives.

Following Part V, concluding remarks are offered in chapter 16. The discussion focuses on the central virtues of the unifying conceptual framework that is developed and applied throughout the book. Examples are drawn from different chapters to illustrate the various benefits that are generated by the sort of systematic investigation pursued here. These payoffs arise particularly from use of the distribution-neutral construct, examination of the lessons that can be derived from optimal income tax analysis, and explicit reference to a social welfare function. Implications for research agendas, both analytical and empirical, are also noted.

PART I: FRAMEWORK

2

An Integrated View

Ideally, policy analysis attempts to consider completely specified policies, take a comprehensive view of the problem at hand with regard to potentially useful instruments, and present and assess alternatives in a comparable manner. These features are particularly important in developing a theory of taxation and in examining related subjects in public economics.

Completeness means that a policy must be fully articulated in all pertinent respects. An important requirement in the present setting is budget balance.[1] In spite of its familiarity, its dictates are sometimes forgotten, which can lead analysis astray—for example, by omitting income and substitution effects of expenditures that in many cases are in opposition to those of the taxes that finance them, and also by ignoring distributive consequences of expenditures. Furthermore, when examining any given tax or expenditure policy, there exists a variety of ways to make the specification complete, each of which may have different implications for the extent of redistribution and other welfare-relevant considerations. Hence, additional guidance in choosing how to complete the system is necessary.

Comprehensiveness indicates the need to consider all pertinent policy instruments. One would not ordinarily want to use a screwdriver or a knife to pound nails if a hammer were available. Likewise, in considering how one might employ estate and gift taxation to raise revenue or increase redistribution, the availability of the income tax should be kept in mind.

---

[1] See, for example, Musgrave's (1959, pp. 212–215) discussion of "differential tax incidence," and consider also the broader notion of "balanced-budget incidence."

It is usually best to use the tool that is most directly suited to the task at hand. Moreover, when other mechanisms are also in use, one must attend to interactions that may be overlooked when focusing on a single policy instrument. Notably, many policies interact with the income tax with regard to effects on labor supply and income distribution. For these and other reasons, we should, for example, hesitate to prescribe policy for the Earned Income Tax Credit without regard to the current state of welfare programs and possible reforms in them, and we cannot assess the taxation of capital income independently of other tax instruments that raise revenue from individuals in the same part of the income distribution.

Comparability refers to the idea that it is easier to assess choices among different types of apples than between apples and oranges (or, worse, apples and elephants). In evaluating a given policy, it is often most helpful to focus on one dimension at a time and, furthermore, to distinguish intrinsic from incidental characteristics. When shopping for an automobile, it is not very helpful to compare a white, high-end, over-sized SUV to a red, economy, subcompact car. For buyers on a tight budget to pick the SUV because they hate the color red or because it comes with a free microwave oven that happens to meet a current need would be foolish. Instead, it is more illuminating to undertake a series of comparisons of vehicles that are similar on all but one dimension, for example, to investigate subcompacts in other colors if one hates red and to visit a home appliance store if a new microwave oven is desired.

This commonsense notion of comparability has received too little attention in the theory of taxation. Comparability is in fact an extremely powerful idea, as much of this book will demonstrate. In particular, it turns out that in a surprisingly wide range of instances, comparability is sharpest when one completes the system—say, a luxury tax plan or a proposed expenditure on parks—by using a particular technique: *an adjustment to the income tax (and transfer) system that achieves an overall result that is distribution neutral.* Indeed, the availability of the income tax as an instrument casts a different light upon the analysis of such policies as commodity taxes, dividend and capital gains taxes, estate and gift taxes, social insurance, public goods provision, and economic regulation. It turns out that it is not generally sensible to use various indirect forms of taxation, expenditure policies, or regulations to redistribute income if an income tax is available, as it generally is in developed economies.

Among the many policy instruments typically thought of in distributive or revenue-raising terms, the income tax has a special place, and because of this role the others need to be analyzed differently from how they often are.[2]

Together, completeness, comprehensiveness, and comparability are essential aspects of an integrated view of taxation, government expenditures, and redistribution. One can only understand each policy instrument—each piece of the puzzle—if the others are also on the table and the relationships among them are understood. Most analysis is far more specialized, focusing on one particular policy, indeed, often a single aspect of a particular policy, and there are good reasons for this division of labor. However, research is best guided and its results are most effectively employed by policy-makers if the broader, integrated framework of which they are a part is well understood and kept clearly in view.

A. Completeness of Policy Specification

The idea developed in this section, as noted previously, is that one cannot properly analyze the redistributive character of a policy unless that policy is fully articulated in certain respects. Begin by considering a gasoline tax increase. Supposing that this tax is moderately regressive, the increase may well be opposed on distributive grounds.[3] Next, consider improvements to public parks. Supposing that these improvements are

---

[2] As will become apparent in chapters 4–6, it is not so much an income tax per se as a personalized tax system under which the taxes paid by individuals can be varied according to their level of well-being. In most developed economies, it is the income tax (combined with transfer programs) that plays this role; as subsection 9.B.1 indicates, this role could also be filled by a personal consumption tax.

[3] Such an objection presupposes that there is too little redistribution: Because redistribution is generally costly, due to labor supply distortion, there is an optimal degree of redistribution (see chapter 4). If that degree of redistribution were exceeded, then a regressive change would be desirable, not objectionable, on redistributive grounds. Where convenient, however, this preliminary discussion will follow convention in referring to greater redistribution as desirable, which should be understood as crediting the benefits of further redistribution while abstracting from the costs.

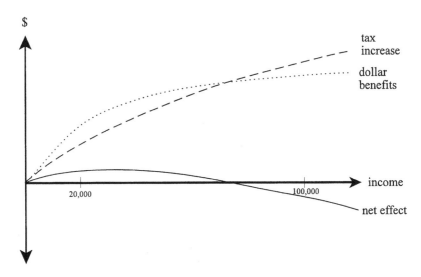

Figure 2.1. Park Improvements Financed by Gasoline Tax Increase

worth somewhat more (measured in dollars) to high-income individuals, this plan also might be opposed on distributive grounds.[4] If, however, these two proposals are combined into one, the distributive effect may well be favorable to the poor, as depicted in figure 2.1. Although lower-income individuals pay a somewhat higher proportion of their income in additional gasoline taxes, their payment is still a smaller absolute amount. Perhaps individuals earning $20,000 pay an additional $20 in gasoline taxes (0.1%) and those earning $100,000 pay an additional $60 in gasoline taxes (0.06%). Regarding the expenditures on parks, suppose that the dollar-equivalent benefit to those earning $20,000 is $30 and the benefit to those earning $100,000 is $50. Netting these amounts, the lower-income individuals gain by $10 per capita and the upper-income individuals lose by $10 per capita.

The possibility that two seemingly regressive policies, when combined, increase the extent of redistribution is readily explained by a fairly common although inconsistent use of baselines: proportionality for the tax

---

[4] In chapter 8, more will be said about the relationship between benefits measured in utility and in dollars.

and equal dollar benefit for the expenditure.[5] For taxes, there is a long tradition of assessment by reference to a standard of proportionality.[6] For government expenditures on goods and services, few would describe a project that benefits millionaires by $1000 per capita and the poor by $50 per capita as "progressive," even when the benefit to the poor is a far higher percentage of their income than is the benefit to the rich.

The main lesson of the illustration is that viewing a particular change in a tax or an expenditure as increasing or decreasing redistribution is problematic. If a tax increase is involved, one must ascertain how the revenue will be spent; if taxes are cut, how the revenue shortfall will be addressed. For any given tax change, one can imagine combining a wide range of expenditure policies or other adjustments to the system. Thus, the hypothesized gasoline tax increase might fund park improvements, welfare programs, police protection, income tax reductions, or many other actions. Likewise for expenditures.

The problem with incomplete depictions of policies is well illustrated by the debate over flat tax proposals. Consider the question: How progressive, or redistributive, is a flat tax?[7] The conventional answer is "not at all" because, as just noted, the standard benchmark is proportionality and a flat tax is perfectly proportional. But this response is seriously deficient. Take a pure flat tax: a linear income tax (a form of "negative income tax") wherein the uniform marginal tax rate is t and the proceeds are used to finance a grant of g to each individual.[8] (To simplify the present discussion, ignore both incentive effects and the need to

---

[5] This observation has also been made by Steuerle (2003).

[6] There exists a substantial, often technical literature measuring the progressivity and redistributiveness of taxes by reference to proportionality, most of which does not attend to the problems discussed in the text. See, for example, the surveys and analysis in Lambert (1999, 2001). Such measures are examined in section 15.A.

[7] Progressive, proportional, and regressive taxes are ordinarily defined as ones whose *average* rates rise, are constant, or fall with income. Occasionally, these terms are associated with *marginal* rates, but that usage will not be followed here. A motivation for focusing on average rates is that "progressive" taxes are often associated with redistributive taxes. In any event, the concept of progressivity is of limited importance because policies should be assessed by using the pertinent social welfare function, not by measuring how they fare under some index of progressivity (see section 15.A).

[8] This tax is formally analyzed in subsection 4.B.1.

finance government expenditures on goods and services.) If t is set at 0%, in which case g must be $0, no redistribution takes place, consistent with the standard view of a proportional tax. If t is set at 100%, in which case g would equal mean income, everyone's after-tax (and transfer) income is fully equalized. In other words, in this hypothetical world with no incentive effects, both an entirely nonredistributive tax and the most redistributive possible tax are flat taxes. For levels of t between 0% and 100%, intermediate degrees of redistribution are possible.

This example, by illustrating the importance of attending to the expenditure of tax revenue, illustrates the more general notion that an incomplete, unintegrated view can be highly misleading.[9] Actually, the problem with incompleteness is worse. In the example, it was specified that all revenue financed a particular sort of expenditure, namely, a uniform grant to each individual. But for any given flat tax rate t, one could instead assume that the revenue finances public goods with benefits proportional to income, in which case there would be no redistribution

---

[9] The specific lesson that the flat tax cannot be characterized with regard to the degree of redistribution involved independently of the level of the tax remains true, although in less extreme form, even if comparisons are limited to graduated and flat rate taxes, with revenue held constant and transfers through the tax system ruled out (or held constant). The reason is that adjusting the exemption level under a flat tax—essentially using the revenue raised by a higher tax rate to finance a more generous exemption—allows the degree of redistribution to vary substantially. Thus, for a given graduated income tax, an equal-revenue flat tax with the same level of exemption will be unambiguously less redistributive. (Those with income below the exemption pay nothing under both schemes, those with low incomes above the exemption have a higher average tax rate under the flat tax, and those with very high incomes have a lower average tax rate under the flat tax.) An equal-revenue flat tax with a sufficiently high exemption (and correspondingly higher tax rate, in particular one at least equal to the top graduated tax rate), however, would be unambiguously more redistributive. (Those with incomes moderately above the graduated tax's exemption would pay nothing under the flat tax; those with somewhat higher incomes would pay something under the flat tax but still less than under the graduated tax, and those with the highest incomes would pay more under the flat tax.) For intermediate levels of the exemption, middle-income taxpayers would pay more under the flat tax, while the rich and the near-poor (those with income high enough to pay some tax) would pay less. Whether such a state of affairs under the flat tax is viewed as more or less redistributive depends on whether greater importance is associated with the poor paying less or with the rich getting off easier. For more technical characterizations, see Davies and Hoy (2002).

regardless of the level of t (since tax payments and benefit receipts would be offsetting in their incidence). Or the revenue might finance public goods worth disproportionately more to the rich, in which case a higher level of the flat tax would increase inequality. Or the revenue might target the poor, producing even more redistribution than when the revenue finances a uniform grant. Thus, in the abstract it is precarious to associate any distributive assessment with the use of purely proportional taxation, even if the level of the tax is known.[10] More broadly, particular forms of taxation—ranging from taxes on dividends and capital gains or on estates and gifts to taxes on consumption—as well as expenditure policies are often assessed, in terms of distributive effects, in a vacuum and thus without regard to how the system as a whole might be brought into balance. Such problems will be identified and addressed throughout this book.

B. Comprehensiveness of Instruments Considered

The most pertinent tools for the present investigation include the main mechanisms by which governments do or could raise revenue and the various ways in which such funds are spent.[11] Accordingly, it is necessary

---

[10] Nevertheless, in policy debates it is generally believed that a flat tax would be less progressive. The Economic Report of the President (1996, p. 91) bluntly states that "[t]he prototypical flat tax would be less progressive than the current income tax." A major rationale for the USA tax proposal in the mid-1990s, a form of graduated consumption tax, was to overcome what was understood to be the inherent limitations of the flat tax with regard to redistribution (see, for example, Seidman 1997). This (mis)understanding of proportional versus graduated taxes has a distinguished lineage, including Blum and Kalven's (1952, 1953) famous discussion of "The Uneasy Case for Progressive Taxation," which argues as though undermining justifications for redistribution implies that a proportional income tax is superior to a graduated one. Critiques of Blum and Kalven include Bankman and Griffith (1987). Some in the debate may believe that the rates in most flat tax proposals are sufficiently low that they would raise significantly less revenue than the graduated tax schemes they would replace, which would make the proposals less redistributive if one adds particular assumptions about the incidence of the resulting expenditure cuts (on which see section 8.E).

[11] This statement is incomplete, for there exist other tools, such as wage regulation, that are potential means of redistribution. See also section 8.G on the distributive effects of regulations more generally.

to consider income taxes, commodity taxes, corporate taxes, estate and gift taxes, and payroll taxes as well as transfer programs, income security programs for retirement, disability, and unemployment, and direct public expenditures, whether on education, police, roads, or any other governmental program.

The advantages of taking a comprehensive view are illustrated by the application of economic analysis to the control of externalities, notably, environmental pollution. Economics provides a useful framework for defining the problem—the very concept of an externality constituting a significant contribution—and for assessing interventions—through the application of cost-benefit analysis. Additionally, and most relevant at this point, economics has offered significant insights into the choice of instruments for controlling externalities. In addition to command-and-control regulations, Pigou (1920) introduced taxes and subsidies, Coase (1960) emphasized the possibility of private bargaining, and Dales (1968) suggested the potential virtues of tradeable permits. Arguably the greatest modern contribution of economics in this field has been to broaden the focus with regard to the available tool set and to offer incisive analysis that indicates which tool or combination of tools is best depending on the particular characteristics of a given setting, such as the quality of the government's information.

The benefits that flow from a comprehensive view of instruments and an explicit attempt to determine their comparative advantages, however, have not been fully realized in the analysis of taxation and related subjects in public economics. For example, it is common to assess the redistributive effects of specific forms of taxation and types of government expenditure without simultaneously contemplating the alternatives and examining which policies are superior under various conditions. Thus, a study may consider what adjustments to a sales tax or VAT—perhaps exemptions for food—would best meet some distributive target without inquiring whether some combination of food stamps (vouchers), cash transfers, and income tax adjustments might better achieve the objective and involve less distortion. Or a study may assess modifications to transfer (estate and gift) taxation without comparing income tax adjustments that would have similar effects on revenue and distribution.

It is usually best to use instruments that are most directly related to the matter in question. In the case of redistribution, the income tax system (including cash transfers) is that instrument. Furthermore, in identifying the core role of the income tax system, the revenue-raising function of taxation should also be included because, were it not for differences among individuals that give rise to distributive concerns, revenue would optimally be raised instead through uniform lump-sum taxation, without causing any distortion.[12] Policy tools other than the income tax system tend to be advantageous in pursuing distributive and revenue objectives only when they are able to address particular shortcomings of a more direct approach, such as by mitigating evasion or reducing the labor-leisure distortion in various subtle ways. Accordingly, throughout this book, the income tax will always be kept in focus, and other forms of taxation as well as government expenditure policies will be related explicitly to it.

Although administrative and political considerations often require substantial deviations from what would otherwise be ideal, it is difficult to reach a sensible accommodation without first obtaining a reasonably comprehensive view of the relevant options. An additional problem is that a single instrument or a particular reform package—such as park improvements financed by a gasoline tax increase—often affects multiple margins simultaneously, which complicates the task of determining what combination of instruments is best when addressing multiple objectives. This challenge brings us to the third component of the proposed integrated view.

---

[12] That is, the distributive objection to uniform lump-sum taxation when individuals' income-earning abilities vary substantially is the primary justification for reliance on distortionary taxation, such as an income tax, which allows tax obligations to reflect individuals' circumstances. As a consequence, much analysis of the efficiency of taxation is intimately related to distribution, even if this connection often remains unrecognized or implicit. For further related discussion, see section 6.D on how the presence of an income tax and the problem of income distribution bear on the Ramsey tax problem and chapter 8 (especially subsection 8.D.3) on the relationship between redistribution and the need for revenue to finance government expenditures on goods and services as part of the optimal income tax problem.

C. Comparability of Proposals under Assessment

Section A explains the need to specify a policy completely in order to analyze it properly. But completeness, notably the requirement of budget balance, can be achieved in many ways. Some means of doing so better facilitate comparability than others. Moreover, the artful choice of policy combinations can take advantage of the range of available tools, as suggested in section B, while also addressing the difficulty of achieving multiple objectives simultaneously.

The most successful methods of meeting these demands will generally be ones that enable apples-to-apples comparisons, thereby permitting separate examination of each dimension of a policy, which in turn allows identification of the policy's intrinsic features. In the present setting, this result often is best achieved by postulating adjustments to the income tax and transfer system that yield distribution neutrality (and not merely revenue neutrality). Specifically, such an approach is useful whenever the policy in question is not purely redistributive (which it is in the case of a labor income tax or cash transfers). The result of this analytical technique is to separate redistributive effects of a policy, along with whatever distortion is caused by the act of redistribution itself, from other effects of the policy. The reasoning underlying this view will now be presented more fully, followed by further discussion of why this approach to comparability is so powerful in providing an integrated understanding of taxation, government expenditures, and redistribution.[13]

1. The Problem

To make the analysis concrete, consider whether luxury taxes should be imposed. Such taxation appears on its face to be redistributive, and that attribute is a likely motivation for implementing luxury taxes in particular.[14] As we know from section A, however, this characterization

---

[13] The approach presented in this section was initially articulated in Kaplow (1996d) and was further elaborated in Kaplow (2004).

[14] Similarly, one could consider subsidies to necessities, such as are implicitly provided by the common practice of exempting expenditures on food from sales taxes and VATs.

is premature because the policy description is incomplete. For example, if the revenue were spent deepening a harbor so it could handle larger yachts, the net effect might even be favorable to the rich.

This section focuses on what manner of completing the system best facilitates comparability. A common approach to analyzing taxation is to keep expenditures fixed (in level and composition) so that attention is confined to different ways of raising a specified amount of revenue.[15] To focus analysis further, adjustments to the income tax schedule are often considered. Even with this amount of refinement, however, there still are many degrees of freedom, because there exists an infinite variety of ways in which the income tax may be adjusted to meet a given revenue target, in our example, to reduce tax collections by the amount of funds raised by the proposed luxury taxes. Regarding redistribution, virtually any outcome—netting the effects of the luxury tax scheme and the as-yet-unspecified income tax reduction—is possible.

At this point, certain seemingly neutral yet essentially arbitrary focal points are usually invoked. For example, it may be hypothesized that everyone's marginal income tax rate is to be reduced by the same amount or percentage or that everyone's tax payments are to be reduced by the same amount or percentage. Even this incomplete list, however, allows for a great range of distributive effects. For example, reducing everyone's tax payments by the same amount would provide an equal dollar benefit to everyone; reducing payments by the same percentage would benefit higher-income individuals substantially more. Accordingly, two analysts of a proposed luxury tax scheme could provide very different assessments of the distortion, degree of redistribution, and effect on overall welfare that it would produce even if they agree on their empirical assumptions and other relevant factors. And when the underlying source of all the disagreement—different income tax adjustments—is mentioned only in passing, perhaps amid many other technical details

---

[15] This formulation is problematic because many sorts of expenditures, including transfers, can be made within some tax systems, notably as part of an income tax, such as is done in the United States through the Earned Income Tax Credit. More broadly, there is no clear theoretical distinction between taxes and expenditures (see Green and Kotlikoff 2007 and Shaviro 2004). The approach presented later, involving distribution-neutral finance, provides a determinate resolution to the issue raised in the text without relying on any such distinction.

of the analysis, it becomes difficult for other analysts—and virtually impossible for less technically sophisticated policy-makers—to decipher the results.

Furthermore, even if all assessments were by reference to a commonly agreed benchmark adjustment to the income tax schedule, it would remain difficult to interpret researchers' findings. The resulting composite reform—introducing luxury taxes combined with a particular income tax reduction—will in general (that is, except by coincidence) entail some redistribution of income. The extent and character, indeed even the direction, of the net redistribution will depend on the relationship between the policy in question and the benchmark that is chosen.

When the completely specified policy under consideration—that is, the original policy and the manner of tax adjustment—involves redistribution, two problems arise. First, it is difficult to interpret results because intrinsic effects of the policy are entangled with the effects of redistribution. Any measure of distortion or of aggregate welfare will have two separate sources. A policy that intrinsically reduces distortion, for example, might be characterized as increasing total distortion if the composite policy entails sufficiently greater redistribution. Likewise, a policy that raises distortion might appear to reduce it if the complete reform package reduces redistribution.

Second, when two analysts reach conflicting conclusions, it often will be difficult to discern whether their disagreements reflect different modeling and empirical estimates concerning the target policy or differences regarding redistribution. Analysis of redistribution is particularly difficult to untangle because a welfare assessment of its effects will depend on three factors that may vary across studies (or only two factors if a common benchmark tax adjustment is accepted): the assumed income tax adjustment; the analysis of redistributive effects, which is influenced by modeling assumptions as well as empirical estimates, such as of the labor supply elasticity; and the choice of social welfare function. For example, the analysis and estimation associated with luxury taxes per se might be identical between two investigations, but the analysts may stipulate different means of maintaining budget balance or use different estimates of the labor supply elasticity or different social welfare functions to evaluate redistributive effects and thereby yield conflicting assessments of the overall reform. Alternatively, divergent conclusions may be entirely attributable to differences in the analysis of luxury taxes themselves.

In all, even after a number of studies of luxury tax schemes have been undertaken, it will not be easy to articulate points of emerging consensus or to identify true underlying sources of disagreement. The problem is one of comparability. Because multiple dimensions are being varied simultaneously, it is harder to learn about any single dimension and to develop the best understanding of the whole. This difficulty is exacerbated because each dimension under consideration—here, luxury taxation and income redistribution—is itself complex.

It is worth emphasizing that these problems are not merely hypothetical. To foreshadow chapter 8, decades of analysis of public goods and of environmental regulation have often used simple adjustments to a proportional income tax as if it was a neutral benchmark. However, this tax adjustment is then combined with underlying projects whose incidence may well not be proportional to income. In fact, the benefits measured in dollars commonly are a falling proportion of income, yet it usually remains unrecognized that redistribution results. Moreover, this redistribution, rather than the public goods or regulations per se, is frequently the primary source of identified effects, notably, on labor supply. In addition, such work may present measures of social welfare that consist exclusively of deadweight loss, which is incomplete and misleading when redistribution is present.

2. Distribution-Neutral Income Tax Adjustments as a Solution

This section elaborates a solution to this problem of comparability that is applicable to all policies that are not purely redistributive (that is, other than the income tax and simple transfers). The method is to postulate that the income tax and transfer system is adjusted in a manner that produces a composite policy—the target policy combined with the income tax adjustment—that is distribution neutral. This income tax adjustment will be the one that not only has the requisite budget-balancing effect on revenue but also mirrors the distribution of the policy under consideration so that the net distributive incidence of the complete package is nil. It should be emphasized that this proposed income tax adjustment, viewed in isolation from the target policy, is not distribution neutral but rather is distribution offsetting. Hence, "distribution-neutral income tax adjustment" is used here as a shorthand, referring to the income tax adjustment that results in the entire policy package under consideration being distribution neutral.

The distribution-neutral income tax adjustment for the case of luxury taxes would achieve budget balance by reducing income tax rates more for the rich; the amount of reduction at any income level would be determined roughly by the fraction of income (at that income level) spent on taxed luxuries times the proposed luxury tax rate. To illustrate, suppose that a 10% luxury tax was to be imposed. If the taxed luxuries are a negligible (say, zero) percentage of consumption for lower-income individuals, their income taxes would stay the same; if luxuries are 5% of income for upper-middle income individuals, they would be charged 0.5% less of income in taxes; if luxuries are 30% of income for the super-rich, they would be assessed 3% less of income in taxes. In this manner, the entire income tax schedule would be adjusted to reflect the incidence of the policy in question so that individuals at each income level would in the aggregate be situated as they were before.[16]

Observe that one difference between the proposed method of adjustment and a fixed benchmark approach is that the particular adjustment to the income tax schedule depends not only on the amount of revenue to be raised or rebated but also on the distributive incidence of the particular policy under consideration. Different sorts of target policies will be associated with different income tax adjustments. Customization of the tax adjustments, however, results in a uniformity of certain effects, and this feature of the proposed method of tax adjustments greatly facilitates analysis.

---

[16] Rigorous statements of how the adjustment is carried out (taking into account that tax adjustments in this case actually must refer to reductions in disposable income rather than to pre-tax income and also that the target policy affects behavior and thus has further effects on individuals' utility) appear in chapters 6 and 8, where the approach is fully articulated in the cases of differential commodity taxation and public goods, respectively. (Regarding the feasibility of downward adjustments for individuals with incomes below the exemption level of an existing income tax, it should be kept in mind that transfers, through the income tax system or otherwise, are understood to be included in references to the "income tax schedule.")

Consideration of a complete policy—a target policy combined with an income tax adjustment—that is not merely revenue neutral but also distribution neutral has the obvious virtue that no redistribution results. Because any other tax adjustment entails redistribution, distributive effects inevitably confound analysis both of distortion (redistribution, after all, generally distorts behavior) and of overall welfare because of the simultaneous consideration of multiple dimensions, as described in subsection 1. By definition, distribution-neutral analysis avoids these problems, and uniquely so.

The recommended approach hardly renders policy analysis a simple exercise. Redistribution must still be analyzed; it is the focus of chapters 4 and 5 on optimal income taxation and also of chapter 7 on transfer programs.[17] And particular policies, stripped of their distributive and revenue effects, may still be difficult to untangle. Indeed, further decompositions are often useful. For example, when analyzing dividend taxation, it is useful to distinguish (by holding constant) the overall effect of a pure, uniform tax on capital income or savings from the specific effects due to differential taxation of particular forms of investment returns. Nevertheless, the proposed distribution-neutral approach to comparability greatly facilitates the analysis of most subjects in this book. The proof lies in later chapters, but it is useful to elaborate at the outset some of the generic benefits and implications of this method of analysis.

A distribution-neutral approach usefully reframes and focuses our understanding of many policies. Thus, with luxury taxes, instead of thinking primarily or even substantially about the rich, we instead are led to ask such questions as whether an individual with a given (let us suppose high) income should pay more tax as a greater proportion of purchases are shifted to the luxury category. This sort of inquiry is

---

[17] The proposed approach to comparability, under which distribution is held constant, obviously is useless when analyzing the pure effects of redistribution, which explains the previous qualifications limiting the approach to policies other than labor income taxation and simple transfers. However, many policies widely deemed to be redistributive—taxes on dividends and capital gains, estate and gift taxes, luxury taxes, and so forth—are not purely redistributive; indeed, this framework will be useful with regard to all tax, expenditure, and regulatory policies except a few, notably, a pure income tax-transfer scheme (considered in a one-period model) or a pure wage or personal consumption tax in certain multi-period models.

qualitatively different from the question of whether the rich should pay more tax.

How would one answer this type of query? In-depth analysis appears initially in chapter 6, but for the present consider two common features of the responses. First, efficiency will often be the central concern. As individuals are led to purchase more of some things and less of others, their utility will be affected; ordinarily, it will be reduced as distortions are introduced. When there are other distortions, such as externalities associated with certain purchases, the welfare assessment may differ. In addition, luxury taxes may involve different administrative costs or evasion opportunities than those associated with raising the income tax revenue that they replace. In any event, such analysis is in the realm of efficiency rather than equality. Indeed, this is so by definition when distribution is held constant. Second, an equity issue may also arise in the present setting when individuals have different tastes. Among those at a given income level, individuals with champagne tastes will fare worse under luxury taxation than those with more pedestrian desires. Such effects, often subtle, are of a different sort than standard distributive considerations because, by definition, this equity issue involves heterogeneity among individuals at the same income level rather than the distribution between individuals at different income levels.

These aspects of luxury taxation illustrate what are usefully deemed to be the intrinsic or inherent features of the policy instrument. The resulting effects will tend to arise whenever luxury taxes are implemented, independently of whether the overall set of reforms is distribution neutral; hence, these effects must be understood regardless of the particular circumstances. And, as the earlier discussion explains, they—as well as the effects of redistribution per se—can best be analyzed one dimension at a time.

Sometimes there is a further analytical payoff from holding distribution constant, namely that simple, familiar, first-best economic principles may be applicable (at least approximately so). For example, under certain assumptions, including the absence of externalities, there should be no differential commodity taxation; introducing luxury taxes, preferentially low rates for food purchases, and so forth will all increase distortion and have no other redeeming virtue. If instead there are standard externalities, Pigouvian taxes or subsidies set equal to the marginal external harm or benefit are optimal. Furthermore, even when more subtle second-best considerations, including ones pertaining to redistribution itself, complicate the story, it remains true that the lessons of distribution-neutral analysis often carry over fairly directly.[18]

3. Applicability

Does it make sense to think in terms of income tax adjustments that achieve distribution neutrality when many policies may not be implemented in ways that are in fact distribution neutral?[19] The foregoing analysis of the benefits of examining policies one dimension at a time suggests an affirmative answer to this question. To pursue the matter further, it is useful to begin by offering a simple two-step decomposition of actual policy packages that are not distribution neutral.

For any target policy and any associated (revenue-neutral) method of income tax adjustment, imagine implementing the tax adjustment in two steps:

1. *Distribution-Neutral Income Tax Adjustment:* Assume that initially the policy is implemented and is accompanied by precisely the income tax adjustment set forth in the preceding subsection.
2. *Purely Redistributive Income Tax Adjustment:* Assume that immediately after step one there is a further enactment wherein

---

[18] For example, as discussed in section 6.C, the argument that it may be desirable to (relatively) tax complements of and to subsidize substitutes for leisure, in order to help offset the distortion caused by redistributive labor income taxation, applies when the level of redistribution is held constant and can more readily be comprehended in such a setting.

[19] It should be noted that other tax adjustments often postulated by policy analysts are not particularly likely to be the actual ones implemented. Given the variation in analysts' assumed adjustments, this is necessarily true in many instances. Moreover, it is difficult to link particular tax adjustments to specific reforms even in the short run because many reforms will be implemented and it may be hard to know which components would be different if others were omitted or amended. Furthermore, in the long run, a tax adjustment used to finance one program may well have been used instead to finance another program if the original one had not been enacted. And any tax adjustment made today may be modified tomorrow. Later discussion in this subsection addresses these issues in part.

the initially distribution-neutral income tax adjustment is transformed into whatever is the actual income tax adjustment associated with the policy.[20]

This two-step decomposition is merely a concrete way of making the earlier conceptual point about isolating different dimensions of a reform package in order to enhance comparability. Analysis of the first step, which isolates what has been referred to as the intrinsic features of a target policy, is as described previously. Because the policy has been stripped of any distributive effects, analysis and comparability of results across studies is greatly facilitated. In particular, specialization by researchers is fostered. Experts on education, environmental regulation, health care policy, and other subjects need not master all aspects of redistribution policy, including the modeling and empirical analysis of labor income taxation and the determination and application of social welfare functions.[21] Instead, they can focus on factors peculiar to their specialty.

To complete the analysis of the entire reform, the effects of the second step would then be added. It should be emphasized that the method of analysis at this stage is generic because this step involves pure redistribution, regardless of the sort of policy involved in step one. Researchers can develop the best analysis of purely redistributive tax adjustments (the best models, the best estimates of parameters such as the labor supply elasticity), and this analysis can then be applied across the board, both to all purely redistributive reforms (for which this analysis must be undertaken in any event) and to the redistributive dimension of reform packages that have other features. For the infinite array of possible policy combinations, the approach in step two will be essentially

---

[20] The description of step two assumes that the postulated method of finance is an adjustment to income tax rates. One could extend this approach to other methods of finance— other sorts of taxes or other changes to the income tax (for example, closing a loophole)—by adding further steps to the decomposition that isolate any other dimensions of change.

[21] One could add the field of political economy, in which one must engage to make predictions of what redistributive tax adjustment is likely in the long run as a consequence of other policy changes.

the same.[22] Hence, in addition to enhanced conceptual clarity, use of the proposed two-step decomposition produces tremendous economy of analytical effort.[23]

Although the focus of this book is conceptual, it is worth noting some practical features of the use of distribution-neutral income tax adjustments and the related two-step decomposition just described. First, it often is possible to vary each of these two dimensions independently. In fiscal systems with an income tax and transfer scheme, which includes most developed economies, the income tax, with its redistributive flexibility, is in fact available, so a net distribution-neutral policy package can indeed be formulated.[24]

Second, it will often make sense to implement one of the steps in isolation. When considering any composite policy as an inseparable whole, implementation is sensible if and only if the net effects of the entire package are desirable. But sometimes this will be true when the net consequences from one step are positive and those from the other are negative. For example, the intrinsic effects of the policy may be highly

---

[22] This statement is not literally true because the effect of a given degree of redistribution, from a given starting point, may differ as a result of the reform in step one, notably, when there are interactions between the nonredistributive aspects of the target policy and redistribution. See, for example, note 18. Even then, however, the main impact will generally be in step one itself, for such interactions will tend to be applicable to the entire preexisting redistributive apparatus and not merely to what often will be relatively small adjustments entailed in step two.

[23] Furthermore, if the preexisting regime were at the distributive optimum and if the adjustment in step two were small, no additional analysis would be required because of the standard property of an optimum, which in the present setting means that the impacts on social welfare of slightly more (less) redistribution and of the accompanying increase (decrease) in distortion are offsetting.

[24] Practical policy analysis in economies that do not have an income tax and transfer scheme (or close substitutes thereto), such as many developing economies, is considerably more complex. The proposed approach should still be conceptually illuminating. Moreover, similar constructions, designed to isolate different dimensions of policies, might usefully be employed to focus on tax instruments other than the income tax. Qualitatively different policy prescriptions are likely to emerge. For example, if a government is capable of taxing only a handful of commodities and nothing else, higher taxes on luxuries may well have the attractive distributive properties conventionally ascribed to them.

desirable whereas the distributive consequences are, all things considered, modestly detrimental. In such cases, it would be preferable to implement only the first step. Likewise, sometimes the net effects of the entire package will be negative even though those of one component are positive, in which case implementation of that component (alone) would be appropriate.

Put another way, it makes sense (and may well be politically feasible) to implement step one if and only if it is beneficial. When it is, since the policy is by construction distribution neutral, everyone will tend to gain. Likewise, if step one would be detrimental, every income group will tend to be losers; even if the package as a whole garnered support, it is plausible that removal of step one could also occur. Similarly, if more or less redistribution is believed to be desirable overall or in any event has political support, step two can be implemented or forgone independently of whether step-one policies are enacted. In particular, whatever extent of redistribution is desired, it might be accomplished in the most efficient manner rather than being tied to whatever policies with incidental distributive effects happen to be proposed. (The foregoing political diagnosis is highly oversimplified and overly optimistic, but there nevertheless is some force to these claims.) Of course, for policy-makers to implement step one or step two in isolation, depending on which is desirable and which is not, it is necessary that analysts present results separately, by employing distribution-neutral income tax adjustments, making use of the two-step decomposition.

Third, as a matter of political reality, there is some gross plausibility to the distribution-neutral approach to policy-making. There may exist a sort of political equilibrium regarding the extent of redistribution. Thus, there may be a tendency for policies—perhaps not individually, but taken as a whole over a period of time—to be implemented in a distribution-neutral fashion. Consider, for example, the 1986 Tax Reform Act in the United States, in which a vast array of tax changes, many primarily affecting particular income groups, were combined in a package, one that also included income tax rate adjustments, that purported to be both revenue neutral and distribution neutral. To the extent that distribution neutrality has some tendency over time to prevail in fact, then hypothetical distribution-neutral analysis undertaken for conceptual clarity would also tend to have direct practical applicability.

A similar conclusion emerges even when a political equilibrium regarding redistribution shifts. Thus, if a new election results in a realignment of power that favors somewhat more redistribution of income, that extent of redistribution is likely to come about one way or another, whether through purely redistributive tax reform, other programs, or some combination of the two. Taking that new, higher extent of redistribution as the new equilibrium, the foregoing analysis again applies. For example, in the 1993 U.S. tax reform, various components (not all of which were understood to be redistributive) were combined to produce an increase in redistribution along the lines of the perceived mandate from the 1992 election.

The preceding points about political practicalities are admittedly crude. Each of the claims will at best be true only approximately. Nevertheless, the distribution-neutral analytical approach that is advanced here on conceptual grounds is hardly irrelevant to understanding the actual world of policy-making.[25]

In concluding this chapter, it is helpful to sketch how these ideas will be employed later in the book. After assessing the pure question of redistribution in chapters 4 and 5, chapter 6 will present formally the first fully developed application of the distribution-neutral approach, for the case of differential commodity taxation. At that point, account will be taken of the distortionary effect of labor income taxation and how it may in turn be affected by differential commodity taxation. That discussion will strengthen the argument for distribution-neutral analysis because it will be seen to offer both great simplification and illumination regarding tax distortions.

This approach will again be applied in detail in chapter 8, in the case of government expenditures on goods and services. In this instance, of course, overall budget balance requires not tax revenue neutrality but a tax increase just sufficient to finance the government expenditures. Nevertheless, essentially the same distribution-neutral scheme, with the same two-step decomposition, proves useful, and for precisely the

---

[25] In addition to the reservations identified in note 19, the present discussion by implication casts further doubt on the practical reality of the other income tax adjustments typically postulated in various literatures precisely because they are not generally distribution neutral.

same reasons. Then, in chapters 9–12, distribution-neutral analysis will be deployed (at this point, more quickly and with less attention to methodological subtleties) across a range of subjects: taxation of capital, estate and gift taxation, the social security system, and the problem of how taxes should be adjusted in light of different family configurations. In some instances, the approach will reinforce existing understandings; in others, it will reveal them to be misunderstandings and will open the way to new insights.

What may seem most surprising about the method presented in this section is that a wide range of policies that are viewed substantially, sometimes primarily, in distributive terms are suggested to be analyzed in a distribution-neutral fashion. This feature may seem all the more unexpected in a book substantially concerned with the subject of redistribution. What should be kept in mind, however, is that the two-step decomposition does not disregard distributive effects but instead isolates them from other effects so that each may be brought into sharper focus.

It is helpful to distinguish the question of *how much* to redistribute from that of *how best*—that is, most efficiently—to go about the task. If one can answer the latter question, one can accomplish more redistribution at a given cost, or alternatively reduce the cost of achieving a given level of redistribution. All income classes stand to gain. To achieve this goal, it is necessary to understand all the tools that are available and to determine which tools are most suitable for which tasks. This can be accomplished by making apples-to-apples comparisons using the technique of distribution-neutral income tax adjustments. Such analysis will reveal that, when it comes to redistribution, the income tax and transfer system is indeed a distinctive tool. Other policy instruments should often play different, more specialized roles (ones that may be qualitatively different from what would otherwise be expected), and in those instances in which other tools may usefully aid the income tax in performing its redistributive function, distribution-neutral analysis will significantly clarify how they should optimally be used in their supporting role.

3

The Social Objective

Optimal income tax analysis employs the standard welfare economic approach to policy assessment. Because much analysis of tax policy and related subjects in public economics does not employ this method, this chapter begins by explaining the need for explicit attention to the social objective function. Many of the policies to be examined pose tradeoffs, not only in choosing the overall extent of redistribution but also in making many specific design decisions, and coherent formulation of these tradeoffs is often impossible without direct reference to the social objective. Such explicitness is also helpful in articulating research agendas because it is necessary to identify which factors and effects need to be analyzed in the first place, and for many tax policies the pertinent list is difficult to discern unless the social objective is specified.

This chapter then elaborates the welfare economic framework in the form ordinarily used in optimal income tax analysis. In so doing, attention is given to the difference between a social preference for equality due to the formulation of the social welfare function (SWF) and a preference for equality arising from the concavity of individuals' utility functions. Comments are offered on the relationship between a variety of theories of distributive justice and particular SWFs and on the redistributiveness of some standard SWFs. Finally, the chapter explains the impact, or lack thereof, of the particular choice of SWF (from within a standard class) on the analysis in the rest of the book.

A. Motivation

This section begins by offering a variety of examples that illustrate the range of demands regarding social evaluation of tax policy. Then it draws out their implications.

1. Examples

Most obviously, it is necessary to be able to measure the benefit of greater equality quantitatively in such a manner that one can answer questions like whether a given increase in equality is worth a specified reduction in average income.[1] One also needs to be able to assess reforms whose effects on inequality are more complex. For example, replacing a graduated income tax with a flat tax—one that raises the same revenue and has a moderately higher exemption—may well improve the lot of both the near-poor and the rich at the expense of the middle class.[2] Whether such a redistribution raises or lowers social welfare is not immediately obvious.

Tax design routinely raises even more subtle distributive questions, such as those involving whether to substitute administratively simpler but less accurate forms of presumptive taxation, how much to spend on reducing assessment errors, and the optimal degree of randomization in enforcement. In each case, cheaper solutions may result in some individuals paying more and others less tax than would be ideal, thus posing another sort of tradeoff between efficiency and distribution.

Additionally, there are important elements of heterogeneity in the population that raise distributive issues. For example, it is generally supposed that unhealthy or disabled individuals should pay less (or receive more), ceteris paribus, but it is not obvious to what extent this should be done or how significant the welfare loss would be if it were not. Even greater systematic heterogeneity involves differences in family units, concerning both the number of and relationship among adults in the same household and the number and ages of children or other dependents. It is necessary to determine the appropriate relative tax burdens (or subsidy entitlements) across family types, a matter of substantial dispute that has been resolved differently over time and across jurisdictions.

Other specific tax policy problems involve further complications. For example, in assessing estate and gift taxation, it is insufficient merely

---

[1] This familiar requirement has important although often unrecognized implications for the measurement of inequality, poverty, progressivity, and redistribution, as discussed in section 15.A.

[2] For further details, see note 9 in chapter 2.

to consider such matters as a possible distortion of savings. Transfers affect the utility of both donors and donees—thus involving an externality of sorts—and transfer taxation will likewise affect both groups. Relatedly, such private transfers involve voluntary redistribution.

Even if one has all of the pertinent facts, there still exists a need to make a balancing judgment in each of these instances. Knowing certain elasticities will help, but it is not immediately obvious, especially in the latter sets of examples, which elasticities are most relevant, what other information is required, and how all the inputs should be combined to form a social decision. As a corollary, setting research agendas in many of these areas is hardly straightforward.

2. Implications

The welfare economic approach to social assessment is designed to address the issues raised by the examples in subsection 1. This method of evaluation has two aspects: specification of a common denominator and adoption of a method of aggregation. First, one determines the effects of any policy under consideration on each individual's utility—also referred to as an individual's well-being or welfare. Thus, whether considering matters involving accuracy or assessment errors, treatment of different family units, or estate and gift taxation, the necessary (and sufficient) positive analysis entails identifying policies' consequences for each individual. Second, to form a social assessment, the information on everyone's utility is aggregated using an SWF, in particular an individualistic SWF, indicating that social welfare is a function (only) of individuals' utilities. The chosen functional form implicitly indicates the weight given to equality, whether, for example, the benefits to the near-poor and rich under the postulated flat tax reform outweigh the added burdens on the middle class, and how one should evaluate the effects of estate and gift taxation on donors, donees, and other individuals.

Although this method of social assessment, which is elaborated in section B, is widely accepted by economists in principle (though less so by others), it is not usually employed explicitly in studying many features of tax policy. Often analysts, following a range of prominent public finance economists from Musgrave and Musgrave (1973) to Stiglitz (2000, pp. 456–481), refer to the multiple objectives of tax policy, offering lists that typically include efficiency, fairness or equity (itself usually stated to be multidimensional, including horizontal and vertical equity, among other principles), revenue adequacy, simplicity, and administrability. Such formulations obviously suffer from a lack of a common denominator and of a principle of aggregation. Many of the objectives (for example, simplicity and administrability) relate to efficiency even though they are separately listed, and they may also involve distributive concerns and thus be related to fairness or equity.

As will be explored further in chapter 15, these fairness or equity notions are particularly problematic. Many, such as the familiar "ability to pay" principle, are highly indeterminate. Additionally, there exist multiple, often conflicting, notions of tax equity that seem to be invoked selectively, in an ad hoc manner, guided largely by intuition. Some of these concepts are incomplete or even incoherent. For example, the insistence that taxes used to finance public goods adhere to one of the so-called sacrifice theories or the benefit principle is meaningful only if there is no other taxation: If redistributive taxation is also present—and by definition it need not adhere to such principles (how can redistributive taxes and transfers involve equal sacrifice under any of the sacrifice theories?)—there is no real constraint on the tax system as a whole. Moreover, some of these principles are arbitrary even when considering public goods in isolation. Notably, under the sacrifice theories, it is not true in general that tax burdens equal benefits from public goods, so redistribution is involved, and the magnitude of this redistribution is determined by the amount of public goods provided. Thus, the technological happenstance of which goods are "public" and which of those happen to be efficient to provide determines the extent of taxation and, accordingly, the extent of redistribution that results.

Both the lists of general criteria and particular notions of fairness and equity can best be understood as loose, intuitive proxies for social welfare, or at least for aspects thereof.[3] Generally, simplicity is a virtue (ceteris paribus, that is); likewise for administrability. Greater efficiency is better (again, ceteris paribus). And some notions of equity are related, even if indirectly, to a coherent notion of social welfare.

---

[3] See subsection 13.A.3.c and chapter 15.

This loose and incomplete relationship between many asserted objectives of tax policy and social welfare is not, however, sufficient in many settings. Ultimately, it is necessary to state with some precision one's actual objective function. Without doing so, many of the examples in subsection 1 cannot be analyzed meaningfully. For instance, without a specified SWF, how is one to trade off the greater simplicity and administrability of coarser rules against the resultant reduction in equity? Furthermore, partial analyses are sometimes taken (perhaps by policymakers unaware of their proxy character) as complete, which can be affirmatively misleading.

Regarding the latter concern, a problem of great relevance to the subject of this book involves analyses that examine only inefficiency, often captured by measures of deadweight loss. This approach is legitimate when there are no distributive effects. Thus many studies of inter-asset or inter-sector distortions in the taxation of capital may provide a reasonably complete indication of overall effects on social welfare because of the similar pattern of ownership of different physical and financial assets. Moreover, as suggested in chapter 2, it is often best—precisely because of the normative relevance of distributive effects—to undertake distribution-neutral policy comparisons, in which case only efficiency is at stake.

However, distribution-neutral analysis is not the norm in many areas of inquiry, yet sometimes distribution is nevertheless ignored.[4] The use of representative-agent models—wherein everyone is assumed to be identical, in which case there are no distributive effects—does not legitimize application of the results to the actual world of heterogeneous individuals. The problem is especially acute when the tax instruments under analysis, notably the income tax, are employed precisely on account of distributive concerns. For example, many analyses of environmental policies—comparisons of regulations, taxes, permit systems, and the like—report deadweight loss estimates as the measure of social welfare even though the deadweight loss arises significantly (sometimes predominantly) on account of differences in the redistributiveness of the policies

---

[4] This point is developed further in subsection 8.C.3 with regard to government expenditures on goods and services, and it is applied to regulation in section 8.G.

under consideration. Two policies may have similar effects on the environment, but one may involve greater use of redistributive income taxation. The more redistributive policy will cause greater distortion and accordingly be deemed inferior, but the greater distortion is due precisely to the fact that the policy increases redistribution. The presumed benefit of such greater redistribution, however, is ignored in the welfare assessment. To avoid such problems, even policies like certain environmental interventions that may appear to be unrelated to distributive issues must be analyzed explicitly in terms of a well-specified SWF—or, alternatively, one must in fact hold distribution constant or employ some other suitable technique if one is to justify analysis in terms of partial or proxy criteria.

As suggested by the examples in subsection 1, ignoring distribution when it may be relevant is but a part of the overall problem. In some settings, such as in deciding how to trade off inequality and efficiency or in assessing replacement of a graduated income tax with a flat tax, distributive concerns are at the fore. And in many other contexts, such as those involving accuracy and error, taxation of the family, and estate and gift taxation, the challenge concerning more subtle distributive effects may not be one of avoiding their accidental omission but rather one of determining how to incorporate them.

Explicit attention to the social objective offers the solution to these problems. In the study of tax policy, this is currently done mainly in the field of optimal income taxation. Indeed, one of the important (although underemphasized) contributions of Mirrlees (1971) was precisely his synthesis of positive and normative analysis. However, much work on taxation and other subjects in public economics is not seen primarily as posing the tradeoff between redistribution and efficiency, and it is not generally conducted using this inclusive framework. There is tremendous variation in the extent to which existing work is deficient because of the failure to undertake explicit social welfare analysis. As will be seen in later chapters, careful attention to the social objective will in many instances affirm the validity of existing understandings. In other settings, prevailing results will need to be modified. And sometimes it will be necessary to reorient thinking substantially. Furthermore, many issues—like taxation of the family—have proved largely intractable, yet significant progress is possible when analysis is related directly to an SWF. Proceeding in the spirit of Mirrlees, rather than invoking familiar lists of tax policy criteria and various notions of fairness and equity, has the potential to illuminate and guide analysis of a wide array of subjects in taxation and other areas of public economics. Important prior work demonstrates the value of such an approach, and this book seeks to apply it in additional settings.

B. Exposition

This section begins by presenting the standard welfare economic approach as it is applied in the assessment of income redistribution. Next, a range of possible SWFs is discussed. Finally, remarks are offered concerning the relevance of the choice of a particular SWF to the analysis in the rest of this book.

The task here is purely expositional. Matters of normative justification are deferred to chapters 13 and 14 because most economists and other policy analysts are at least roughly comfortable with the welfare economic approach and because a number of the most controversial philosophical issues do not in any event relate very directly to most of the analysis in intervening chapters.

1. Social Welfare Functions

A social welfare function $SW(x)$ indicates how any regime or social state x (taken as a complete description thereof) is evaluated. Here we are concerned with individualistic SWFs, wherein social welfare depends only on individuals' utility or well-being. The normative premise, referred to by Sen (1977, 1979) as "welfarism," is that the only relevant aspect of a regime is the manner in which it affects each individual's well-being. An implication is that notions of fairness or equity have no role unless they are concerned with the distribution of utility or they are in some respect a proxy for effects on utility. (For further elaboration, see section 13.A.)

In assessing redistributive taxation, it is common to use an additive social welfare function that assumes a continuous population.

$$SW(x) = \int W(u_i(x))f(i)\,di, \tag{3.1}$$

where u is a utility function, subscripts index individuals' types, and $f(i)$ is the density of type i individuals in the population.[5] Because welfare is taken to be the integral of some transformation W of individuals' utilities, this functional form for the SWF is not necessarily utilitarian; the functional form of W on the right side of (3.1) incorporates a view of distributive justice. This can be seen from the following formulation used, for example, in Stern (1976).

$$\begin{aligned} SW(x) &= \int \frac{u_i(x)^{1-e}}{1-e}f(i)\,di, \text{ for } e \neq 1 \\ &= \int \ln u_i(x)f(i)\,di, \text{ for } e = 1, \end{aligned} \tag{3.2}$$

where $e \geq 0$ indicates the degree of aversion to inequality in the distribution of utility levels.[6] Thus, $e = 0$ indicates that social welfare is the sum of utilities—utilitarianism—and taking the limit as e approaches infinity yields the maximin formulation associated with Rawls (1971), under which all weight is placed on the utility of the least-well-off individual.[7]

It is useful to distinguish two different factors in expression (3.2) that may favor a more egalitarian distribution of disposable income. The magnitude of e has already been identified as one factor: The greater is e, the greater the increase in social welfare due to a given redistribution from an individual with a higher utility to one with lower utility, ceteris paribus. The second factor is the concavity of u itself, that is, the rate

---

[5] For a finite population of n individuals,

$$SW(x) = \sum W(u_i(x)),$$

where the summation is over i from 1 to n.

[6] To explain the latter version in (3.2), for the case in which $e = 1$, the numerator in the former may alternatively be written as $u_i(x)^{1-e} - 1$ (subtracting the constant having no effect on the ordering of social states). Then, taking the limit as e approaches 1 (using l'Hôpital's rule) yields the latter expression.

[7] For more on Rawls and maximin, see subsections 13.B.4 and 14.A.1.a.

at which individuals' marginal utility of consumption falls as consumption rises—equivalently, individuals' degree of risk aversion. To elaborate, consider the oft-used constant-relative-risk-aversion utility function,

$$u(c) = \frac{c^{1-\rho}}{1-\rho}, \text{ for } \rho \neq 1$$

$$= \ln c, \text{ for } \rho = 1, \tag{3.3}$$

where c denotes consumption (typically, income after taxes and transfers) and ρ is individuals' coefficient of relative risk aversion.[8] The case in which $\rho = 0$ is one of risk neutrality; higher levels of ρ indicate greater risk aversion, which likewise indicates a greater rate at which the marginal utility of consumption falls as consumption rises. Hence, ceteris paribus, a higher ρ also favors greater equality in the distribution of consumption. (Note that, for ease of exposition in this section, the formulation in expression (3.3) abstracts from the effect of labor effort on utility, which obviously will be important in the subsequent analysis of optimal income taxation in chapter 4.)

In some of the literature, including work on optimal income taxation and inequality measurement (see Atkinson 1970, 1973), analysis employs a reduced-form SWF (which, again, abstracts from the effect of labor effort on utility),

$$SW(x) = \int \frac{c_i^{1-\gamma}}{1-\gamma} f(i)di, \text{ for } \gamma \neq 1$$

$$= \int \ln c_i f(i)di, \text{ for } \gamma = 1, \tag{3.4}$$

where γ indicates the degree of aversion to inequality in the distribution of consumption. That is, in formal analysis and simulations, analysts may consider the overall social aversion to inequality in consumption, without regard to how much of that aversion is attributable to individuals' decreasing marginal utility of consumption (ρ in expression (3.3))

---

[8] Regarding the case in which $\rho = 1$, see note 6.

and how much is attributable to the concavity of the SWF in utility levels (e in expression (3.2)).

It is important to distinguish these two components because the former is a matter of empirical fact about individuals whereas the latter involves a normative judgment, external to the individuals in question, that must be grounded in a theory of distributive justice.[9] It is worth observing, moreover, that the more concave are individuals' utility functions (the greater is ρ in (3.3)), the less relevant will be the degree of concavity in social welfare as a function of individuals' utility levels (3.2). The reason for this tendency is that when utility is more concave, there may be little relative difference in utility levels even when there are significant relative differences in individuals' marginal utilities of consumption.[10] (A further technical complication that will not be explored here is that, despite appearances, there are difficulties in interpreting the function in expression (3.4) as a simple composite of those in expressions (3.2) and (3.3).[11])

2. Comments on a Range of Social Welfare Functions

Although, as the next subsection explains, the overall redistributiveness of the SWF (which may be captured in the formulation of expression (3.4) by the composite parameter γ) does not qualitatively affect most of the analysis in this book, it provides a useful orientation to consider a

---

[9] Subsequent authors interpreted the parameter in Mirrlees (1971) corresponding to e as entailing a normative judgment about the SWF, whereas Mirrlees (1982, p. 77 n. 21) indicates that he adheres to a utilitarian norm, with the parameter e indicating possible degrees of concavity of individuals' utility functions.

[10] See Kaplow (2003a). As explained there, this result is more pronounced as consumption rises. Therefore, concavity in the welfare function is likely to matter most at the bottom end of the income distribution (for example, to the design of transfer programs that differ in their treatment of the near-poor and very poor) and less so at the top (for example, to choices of tax rate graduation that affect the distribution between upper-middle-income individuals and the rich).

[11] If one directly combines (3.2) and (3.3), one would need to multiply by the constant $(1-\rho)^e$ on the right side of (3.4), which itself would not affect the optimization, and one would have $\gamma = 1-(1-\rho)(1-e)$. However, if one considers the case in which $\rho > 1$ or $e > 1$, this formulation is problematic. For further exploration, see Kaplow (2003a).

variety of possible SWFs and the degree of redistributiveness that they entail. It is helpful to situate such a discussion by considering a spectrum of distributive theories, which might crudely be presented as follows:

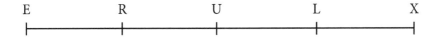

E   R   U   L   X

At the left end is pure egalitarianism, E, favoring complete equality at all costs. Next is a Rawlsian view, R, indicating that one should continue redistribution toward the least-well-off individual until the point at which further redistribution actually worsens that individual's situation. (Note that this is the most egalitarian view that is not obviously inconsistent with the Pareto principle.) Utilitarianism, U, favors the degree of redistribution that maximizes the sum of individuals' utilities. Libertarianism, L, opposes all redistribution. At the right end of the spectrum, denoted by X, one might consider a view under which as much wealth as is feasible should be concentrated in the hands of one or a select few (perhaps a governing elite that deems itself so entitled).

The formulation in subsection 1, entailed by the SWF in expression (3.2), encompasses the range from R to U and thus is restrictive. Positions to the left of R might be ruled out by invoking the Pareto principle. (Indeed, even position R is understood to be quite extreme, for it would favor a regime that reduces everyone to complete misery as long as it promotes the well-being of the most miserable individual by even an infinitesimal amount.[12]) If one adopts position L, no redistribution is warranted, rendering rather uninteresting the inquiry into how best to redistribute income. (Of course, this still leaves potentially relevant territory between U and L uncovered.) And position X, although it unfortunately seems to approximately describe many actual regimes in history, commands little normative support.

Much argument about the proper SWF proceeds by simple intuition. At one time, utilitarianism was seen as quite radical. Today, however,

---

[12] See, for example, Arrow (1973, p. 251) and also the further discussion in subsection 14.A.1.a.

many progressively minded economists and philosophers view utilitarianism as insufficiently concerned with equality. Such expressions are more aesthetic hunches than arguments, as explored in section 14.A. Moreover, they suffer from a number of specific drawbacks: Such views often fail to appreciate how much redistribution is implied by various SWFs; intuitions may well be based on equality of income (which is directly observable and thus more tangible) rather than on that of utility; and the optimal degree of redistribution entailed by any given SWF is itself a subtle matter that depends on a range of parameters concerning individuals' utility functions (the concavity parameter ρ and also parameters relating to the elasticity of substitution between consumption and leisure), the shape of the distribution of ability, the available technology of taxation, and a variety of other potentially important factors. Accordingly, any view about how much redistribution is appropriate that eschews normative argument and technical analysis is difficult to maintain.

Another form of argument about the choice of an SWF proceeds from the concept of equality, but equality has diverse and conflicting meanings. In a formal sense, the SWF described in expressions (3.2) and (3.4) is egalitarian in that each individual's utility is treated symmetrically and thus given equal weight. A libertarian view that opposes any redistribution also entails a formal sense of equality. Some favor equality of opportunity, but that too can be interpreted to favor just about anything from a libertarian view to a purely egalitarian one. If one looks at the specific method of aggregation, a utilitarian view gives equal weight to contributions to each individual's utility—that is, each individual's *marginal* utility is treated identically. More egalitarian SWFs place greater weight on equality of utility *levels,* but in the process do not treat contributions to each individual's utility equally. Thus, a belief in equality in the abstract is hardly a sufficient basis for choosing an SWF, even if one posits that equality per se should be the sole criterion for decision.

Finally, consider briefly the degree of redistribution implied by various SWFs. Attention here will be confined to a utilitarian SWF, but as the discussion in the preceding subsection suggests, one can to some extent translate these results to more concave SWFs by reinterpretation of the various parameters—specifically, by considering a value of γ in expression (3.4) that exceeds ρ in (3.3). Initially, suppose that there are no incentive effects associated with redistribution. Then, in the simple case in which all individuals have the same utility function and there is some degree of diminishing marginal utility of consumption ($\rho > 0$ in expression (3.3)), a utilitarian SWF favors perfect equality, as suggested by Edgeworth (1897). (Lerner (1944) extends this result to the case in which individuals' utility functions may differ and the government cannot observe utility functions.) Of course, the result would be the same if the SWF were more concave.[13]

Consider instead the case in which redistribution distorts labor effort. This considerably more complex problem is the focus of chapter 4 and much that follows. But insight can quickly be gleaned by undertaking partial analysis for some simple cases.[14] Suppose first that individuals' utility functions are given by ln c, that is, $\rho = 1$ in expression (3.3). Marginal utility equals $1/c$. For instance, the marginal utility of a poor person with consumption of $10,000 is ten times that of an upper-middle-class individual with consumption of $100,000 and is one hundred times that of a rich individual with consumption of $1,000,000. Thus, even if distortion was so great that for every $10 taken from the upper-middle-class person (or every $100 from the millionaire) only $1.01 reached the poor person, a utilitarian SWF would favor the redistribution. If one instead takes the case of $\rho = 2$, marginal utility is inversely proportional to the square of consumption, so the factors of ten and one hundred in the foregoing example would become one hundred and ten thousand. Accordingly, the extent of deadweight loss from redistribution that is tolerated by a utilitarian SWF is extremely high.[15] Furthermore, it

---

[13] Sen (1973b) in turn extends Lerner's result to any concave SWF. An interesting feature noted by Mirrlees (1971, p. 201) is that, if labor effort were involved but incentive problems could be avoided, utilitarian redistribution would overshoot the point of equal utility because highly able individuals would optimally work very hard—due to their higher productivity—and on account of the disutility of labor would be worse off than the less able. Thus, a utilitarian SWF would in a sense be more redistributive than more concave SWFs.

[14] The illustrations continue to abstract from the effect of labor effort on utility. Alternatively, one could allow labor to affect utility in an additively separable manner.

[15] These illustrations offer a perspective on studies reporting high efficiency costs of redistribution. For example, Feldstein and Feenberg (1996) find that the 1993 tax rate increase

should be noted that utility function concavity parameters in the range of 1 to 2 are widely considered plausible, and some estimates (notably, from the finance literature) are substantially higher.[16] Hence, SWFs in the range from U to R, which are commonly examined in the optimal income tax literature, entail substantially redistributive social preferences.

3. Relevance of the Choice of a Particular Social Welfare Function

As it turns out, the degree of overall weight on equality in the SWF—the level of γ in (3.4), whether attributable to concavity in u, as indicated by ρ, or concavity in W, as indicated by e—often has little or no effect on the qualitative nature of many results in this book. One reason for this is that, as section 2.C indicates, much of the analysis will be undertaken using distribution-neutral comparisons, in which case the social weight on equality does not matter at all. Just as cost-effectiveness analysis is useful in determining, for example, how to save the most lives for a given expenditure on safety—without having to specify a value of life—so too the determination of how best to achieve a given degree of redistribution is essentially independent of how much social value is placed on that redistribution.

Some analysis, particularly that in the next chapter on the optimal extent of redistribution, will depend on the SWF. One can, however, explore results for a range of parameters concerning the overall preference for equality (γ), allowing such results to be interpreted for various

---

in the United States, which was concentrated on high-income individuals, involved so much distortion that for each dollar raised, high-income taxpayers were worse off by two dollars. Clearly, the marginal social value of a dollar to those who benefited could well have been greater, especially given that some of the revenue was used to fund an increase in the Earned Income Tax Credit. See also Browning and Johnson (1984) (finding in their benchmark case that the income-equivalent loss to individuals in the top three quintiles is $3.49 per dollar of income-equivalent gain to those in the lowest quintile) and Browning (1993) (finding that the marginal efficiency loss, taking into account the value of additional leisure, is $3.23 from a supplemental proportional tax that finances an equal grant to all households).

[16] See, for example, Barsky et al. (1997), Campbell (1996), Choi and Menezes (1992), and Kocherlakota (1996).

combinations of empirical estimates of the concavity of utility functions (ρ) and views of the appropriate concavity of the SWF (e). Typically, the effect will be one of degree: The greater the social preference for equality, the more redistribution will be optimal.

Some problems, however, involve greater subtlety, notably, when a higher marginal utility of consumption is associated with a higher rather than a lower level of total utility. This conjunction does not ordinarily arise when examining income redistribution because, as one increases an individual's income, marginal utility falls as utility rises, and conversely when income is reduced. Accordingly, the posited situation of both utility levels and marginal utility being higher (or both being lower) is generally due to factors other than differences in consumption levels, such as when individuals have different constitutions (for example, disabilities), are in different family units (for example, when children are present), or are beneficiaries of amenities, public goods, or in-kind transfers that influence the marginal utility of consumption differently from how it is affected by changes in consumption levels.

In such cases, the functional form of W matters qualitatively. With a purely utilitarian SWF (that is, W is linear; equivalently, $e = 0$ in (3.2)), only individuals' marginal utilities matter for redistributive purposes; ceteris paribus, redistribution toward higher-marginal-utility individuals is always favored. But if W is strictly concave (equivalently, $e > 0$ in (3.2)), then redistribution toward lower-utility-level individuals is also favored. The more concave the SWF, as a function of utilities, the more utility levels matter and the less individuals' marginal utilities matter. In the limit, as e approaches infinity (maximin), only the utility level of the least-well-off individual counts, regardless of how low that person's marginal utility is or how high the marginal utilities of others are. Thus, the direction of optimal redistribution can in some settings depend on the shape of the SWF.

Foreshadowing chapter 12, an important illustration of this phenomenon arises in connection with issues concerning the proper unit of taxation. For example, adults who voluntarily choose to have children and succeed in having healthy children will presumably achieve a higher level of utility as a consequence (as implied by their choice to conceive children). They may also, however, have a higher marginal utility of consumption because their available resources now must be shared among a greater number of individuals. If the SWF is utilitarian or slightly concave, redistribution toward families with children will tend to be optimal, whereas if the SWF is strongly concave in utilities, redistribution would optimally be away from families with children. In such instances, the approach taken in this book will be to present the possibilities, explaining how the nature of the SWF may affect the character of optimal treatment.

The relevance of the choice of SWF to optimal tax policy varies greatly: often with no effect, sometimes a difference in magnitude, and occasionally a difference in direction. Nevertheless, it is usually the case that analysis can proceed without a commitment to a particular SWF. Accordingly, further exploration of the choice of an SWF will be deferred to part V. Likewise deferred are a range of other normative issues, such as the merits of welfarism, the nature of well-being, the possibility of interpersonal utility comparisons, and the question of whose utility should be included in the SWF.

PART II: OPTIMAL TAXATION

Optimal Income Taxation

This chapter begins with a description of the optimal income taxation problem as generally formulated in the literature and then presents the main results and simulations both for the special cases of a linear income tax and a two-bracket income tax and for the general case of a nonlinear income tax. As is conventional, the model considered will involve a one-period setting in which individuals' only choice variable is their degree of labor effort, there is a single composite consumption good, and government expenditures on public goods are taken as given. Much of the remainder of this book considers how the analysis changes when a variety of extensions are made. Although the presentation in this chapter is largely standard, some of the elements examined, especially regarding certain qualifications, have not often been addressed and may not be widely appreciated.

A. Statement of the Problem

An individual's utility is given by $u(c, l)$, where c denotes consumption, l denotes labor effort, $u_c > 0$, and $u_l < 0$, where subscripts denote derivatives with respect to the identified argument.[1] An individual's consumption is given by

---

[1] Much literature on optimal labor income taxation expresses utility as a function of leisure, or $1-l$, where "1" denotes a normalized amount of time available to each individual. Additionally, it is common to use indirect utility functions, perhaps expressed as a function of lump-sum or virtual income and of a net-of-tax wage rate. Though these devices offer advantages, for purposes of the present inquiry the use of direct utility expressed as a function of consumption and labor minimizes notation and is more transparent.

$$c = wl - T(wl), \tag{4.1}$$

where w is the individual's wage rate and T is the tax-transfer function (usually referred to simply as a tax function or schedule). Each of these components deserves further elaboration.

The motivation for redistributive taxation is that individuals differ, in particular in their wages, that is, their earning abilities. The distribution of abilities is denoted $F(w)$, with density $f(w)$, the population being normalized to have a total mass of one. In standard formulations of the optimal income tax problem, individuals' abilities are indicated by their given wage rate, taken to be exogenous. Their pre-tax earnings are the product of their wage and level of labor effort. More broadly, one can interpret effort as including not only hours of work but also intensity, and not only productive effort but also investments in human capital.

Taxes and transfers, $T(wl)$, at any income level may be positive or negative, as depicted in figure 4.1. The term g refers to the grant received by an individual earning no income, that is, $-T(0)$, reflecting that the tax schedule T is taken to represent the entire tax-transfer system. Taxes may include sales taxes or VAT payments in addition to income taxes.[2] Transfers include those through the tax system (such as the Earned Income Tax Credit in the United States), welfare programs (see chapter 7), and, under some interpretations, public goods (see chapter 8).[3]

---

[2] Many would include payroll taxes as well; whether this is proper depends on whether the social security system is better viewed as an additional component of the redistributive apparatus or as a compulsory insurance/retirement scheme. Similar reasoning applies to social security benefits and to public unemployment and disability systems (see chapter 11).

[3] The inclusion of transfers is extremely important both practically, since they are in fact significant, and conceptually, since otherwise redistribution would be limited to reallocations between the rich and the middle class, once the poor were exempted from the tax system. The role of transfers will be central in many subsequent discussions, for example, in the analysis in chapter 6 of whether it makes sense to tax necessities at differentially low rates when the option of direct transfers is available. As a corollary, analyses of taxation, expenditures, and regulation may reach quite different and misleading conclusions if they implicitly assume that transfers are unavailable or cannot be adjusted. See also the discussion in section 6.D of Ramsey taxation.

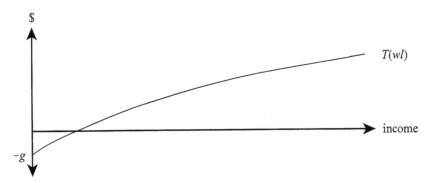

Figure 4.1. Nonlinear Income Tax and Transfer Schedule

Taxes and transfers are taken to be a function of individuals' incomes, assumed to be observable, and it is this dependence of taxes on income that is the source of distortion. If taxes could instead depend directly on individuals' abilities, w, individualized lump-sum taxes would be feasible and redistribution could be accomplished without distorting labor supply. Ability, however, is assumed to be unobservable. (For further discussion, see subsection 5.C.1.)

Individuals choose the level of labor effort l that maximizes $u(c,l)$ subject to their budget constraint, expression (4.1). An individual's first-order condition is

$$w(1-T'(wl))u_c + u_l = 0, \tag{4.2}$$

where a prime denotes the derivative with respect to a function's only argument—in this case $T'(wl)$ indicating the marginal tax rate of an individual earning income of wl.

The government's problem is taken to be the choice of a tax-transfer schedule $T(wl)$ to maximize social welfare, which (appropriately modifying expression (3.1)) can be stated as

$$\int W\big(u(c(w),l(w))\big)f(w)dw, \tag{4.3}$$

where c and l are each expressed as functions of w to refer to the level of consumption achieved and labor effort chosen by an individual of type (ability) *w*. This maximization is subject to a revenue constraint and to constraints regarding individuals' behavior. The former is

$$\int T(wl(w))f(w)dw = R, \qquad\qquad (4.4)$$

where R is an exogenously given revenue requirement.[4] Here, revenue is to be interpreted as expenditures on public goods that should be understood as implicit in individuals' utility functions; because these expenditures are taken to be fixed, they need not be modeled explicitly. (Public goods will be considered in chapter 8.)

Regarding the latter constraints, individuals are assumed to respond to the given tax schedule optimally, as described by their first-order conditions (4.2). Specifically, the first-order conditions are differentiated with respect to some marginal adjustment of the tax schedule to determine how labor effort will respond. Because individuals are at an optimum before the adjustment, their labor effort response has no first-order effect on their utility. Hence, the welfare implications of a tax adjustment will depend on its direct effect on utility (for example, paying a higher tax will reduce utility to an extent indicated by an individual's marginal utility of consumption) and on its revenue effects, which themselves are both direct (for example, a higher tax rate applied to existing income will yield more revenue) and indirect (notably, individuals' adjustments of their labor effort will affect revenue). Individuals' behavioral responses are therefore relevant only to this final effect regarding revenue.[5]

---

[4] Some of the literature expresses this constraint in terms of aggregate resource balance, which requires that the sum of resources devoted to private and public goods equal the amount produced by all individuals' labor efforts. In whichever form, this constraint is sometimes expressed as a weak inequality, but this distinction is immaterial because the constraint is always binding in problems of interest.

[5] This intuition can alternatively be expressed in terms of a tax revenue externality: In adjusting their labor supply, individuals take into account effects on their own utility—through the changes in consumption (equal to after-tax income) and effort, which are offsetting at the margin at the utility-maximizing optimum—but ignore the effect on tax revenue, which is the difference between what their labor produces and the portion that they are able to consume, after tax.

It is known to be problematic to assume that behavior is accurately described by individuals' first-order conditions because of multiple optima, which in turn can produce discontinuities in behavior.[6] Although this problem is discussed in some of the more technical literature on optimal income taxation, it is usually ignored in practice. As will be seen, however, this simplification can be problematic when examining how individuals adjust labor supply because nonconvex tax-transfer schedules that can give rise to multiple optima are of interest. For example, it is important to determine whether marginal rates on lower-income individuals should fall after income guarantees are quickly phased out (that is, at high marginal rates) or whether marginal rates should be falling for very high-income individuals, which some analyses and simulations suggest may be optimal. Discontinuities can also arise with regard to the decision whether to supply any labor at all (the participation decision, or extensive margin), such as in the presence of fixed costs of working.[7]

B. Results

Despite Mirrlees's (1971) elegant formulation and analysis and subsequent work on the subject, the optimal income taxation problem remains formidable.[8] Accordingly, no attempt is made here to replicate existing formal derivations or to extend them. Instead, attention is focused on articulating the main results and the intuition behind them—which will be sufficient to appreciate most of what follows in later chapters—and presenting some simulations from the literature. This section begins with the simpler cases of a linear income tax and a two-bracket tax and then considers the more general case of a nonlinear income tax.

---

[6] See, for example, Grossman and Hart (1983) and Ebert (1992).

[7] For models of the participation decision, see, for example, Diamond (1980) and Saez (2002b).

[8] For surveys, see Atkinson and Stiglitz (1980), Stiglitz (1987), Tuomala (1990), and Salanié (2003).

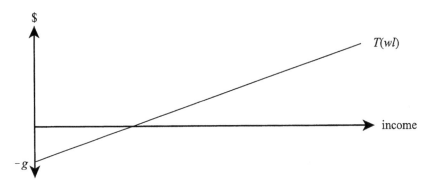

Figure 4.2. Linear Income Tax Schedule

1. Linear Income Tax

A linear income tax is defined by

$$T(wl) = twl - g, \tag{4.5}$$

where t is the (constant, income-independent) marginal tax rate and g is the uniform per capita grant, as described in chapter 2's discussion of a flat tax. See figure 4.2.

The government's welfare maximization problem can be written in Lagrangian form as choosing t and g to maximize

$$\int \left[W\big(u\big((1-t)wl(w)+g, l(w)\big)\big) + \lambda\big(twl(w) - g - R\big)\right] f(w)dw, \tag{4.6}$$

where λ is the shadow price of revenue, referring to the constraint (4.4), and (4.5) is substituted into (4.1) so that consumption is expressed in terms of the specific linear tax system under consideration.

The first-order condition for the optimal tax rate can usefully be expressed as

$$\frac{t}{1-t} = -\frac{\mathrm{cov}\big(\alpha(w), y(w)\big)}{\int y(w)\varepsilon(w)f(w)dw}, \tag{4.7}$$

where $y(w) = wl(w)$, income earned by individuals of ability w; $\varepsilon(w)$ is the compensated elasticity of labor effort of individuals of ability w; and

$\alpha(w)$ is the net social marginal valuation of income, evaluated in dollars, of individuals of ability w.[9] The latter valuation is given by

$$\alpha(w) = \frac{W'u_c(w)}{\lambda} + tw\left(\frac{\partial l(w)}{\partial g}\right). \tag{4.8}$$

The numerator of the first term on the right side of (4.8) indicates how much additional (lump-sum) income to an individual of ability w contributes to social welfare—u_c indicates how much utility rises per dollar of consumption and W' indicates the extent to which social welfare increases per unit of utility—and this is converted to a dollar value by dividing by the shadow price of government revenue. The second term takes into account the income effect, namely that giving additional lump-sum income to an individual of ability w will reduce labor effort ($\partial l(w)/\partial g < 0$), which in turn reduces government tax collections by tw per unit reduction in $l(w)$.

Expression (4.7) indicates how various factors affect the optimal level of a linear income tax. Beginning with the numerator, a higher (in magnitude) covariance between α and y favors a higher tax rate. The net marginal social valuation of income, $\alpha(w)$, will be falling with income (under assumptions ordinarily postulated).[10] Note that in the present

---

[9] There are many derivations of this condition, and it is expressed in a variety of equivalent ways. The present notation and manner of expression is close to that in Stiglitz (1987, p. 1016, expression (29)), and his derivation appears in his note 31. See also Atkinson and Stiglitz (1980, pp. 407–408). For a more extensive analysis, see Stiglitz (1976). These derivations, it should be noted, typically do not take into account that some individuals (those of low ability) will choose not to work, in which case (4.2) no longer characterizes their behavior (because they are at a corner solution). This problem is more often addressed in analyses of the optimal nonlinear income tax and in simulations.

[10] Note that when $t = 0$, $\alpha(w)$ is unambiguously falling with income. As t is raised further, the second term of expression (4.8) becomes more important, but the implication for the correlation of $\alpha(w)$ with $y(w)$ is unclear. (The term is negative; in addition to t, its magnitude depends on w, which is rising with income, and on $\partial l/\partial g$, which may plausibly fall with income, depending on the utility function.) Furthermore, if there is any inequality, a positive (but nonconfiscatory) tax rate will be optimal, so at the optimum we know that the left side of (4.7) must be positive, although this argument does not guarantee that $\alpha(w)$ is falling with income everywhere.

setting, a large covariance does not refer to a close (negative) correlation, which is always assumed to be present, but rather to a high dispersion (standard deviation) of α and of y. The dispersion of α will tend to be greater the more concave (egalitarian) is the welfare function W and the more concave is utility as a function of consumption (that is, the greater the rate at which marginal utility falls with income).[11] Income, y, will have a higher dispersion (again, under standard assumptions) when the distribution of underlying abilities is more unequal. In sum, more egalitarian social preferences, greater individual aversion to risk, and higher underlying inequality will all contribute to a higher optimal tax rate.

The denominator on the right side of (4.7) indicates that a higher compensated labor supply elasticity favors a lower tax rate. It will be noted that the other terms in the integrand mean that, ceteris paribus, the labor supply elasticity matters more with regard to high-income individuals and at ability levels where there are more individuals (typically the middle of the income distribution), because of the greater sacrifice in revenue. Note further that, if this compensated elasticity is taken to be constant, the denominator is simply the elasticity weighted by average income.

Although the foregoing discussion addresses each of the terms in (4.7), it is incomplete. First, it is worth emphasizing that income effects (and thus deviations between compensated and uncompensated elasticities of labor supply) are indirectly relevant, as they influence the value of α through the second term in (4.8) (and also through the

---

[11] The shadow price of government revenue, λ, appears in the denominator of the first term of (4.8). An interpretation of this factor is that it represents a sort of average social marginal valuation since in the present setting additional government revenue would be used to raise g, the per capita grant. Thus, the first term of (4.8) will contribute to a larger covariance the greater is the relative dispersion in the population of marginal social welfare and marginal utility. This can be confirmed by solving for λ using the first-order condition for the optimal g (Stiglitz 1987, p. 1016 n. 31, expression (31)) and substituting into (4.8) (but using w^* to refer to the wage in (4.8) since w is now used as a variable of integration on the right side) to yield

$$\alpha(w^*) = \frac{W'u_c(w^*)}{\int W'u_c(w)f(w)dw}\left(1 - \int tw\frac{\partial l(w)}{\partial g}f(w)dw\right) + tw^*\left(\frac{\partial l(w^*)}{\partial g}\right).$$

shadow price λ; see note 11). Whether this effect increases or reduces the covariance term in (4.7) is not a priori obvious, and existing simulations do not explore this directly. Second, the values on the right side of (4.7)—including those present via (4.8)—are endogenous. Thus, if one performs the optimization with, say, a different labor supply elasticity— implicitly, a different utility function—essentially everything except $f(w)$ changes, including the shadow price of the government revenue constraint. Accordingly, it is treacherous to make confident statements regarding the effect of changing one or another parameter without more elaborate analysis or simulations. The literature has largely taken the latter path.

The most reported optimal linear income taxation simulations are those of Stern (1976). For his preferred case—an elasticity of substitution of 0.4,[12] a government revenue requirement of 20% of national income, and a social marginal valuation of income that decreases roughly with the square of income[13]—he finds that the optimal tax rate is 54% and that individuals' lump-sum grant equals 34% of average income. (These estimates refer to the combination of all taxes; all government expenditures and all redistribution are financed by this single tax.) To illustrate the benefits of redistribution, a scheme that uses a lower tax rate, just high enough to finance government expenditures on goods and services (that is, with a grant of zero), produces a level of social

---

[12] In many simulations, including this one by Stern (1976, pp. 151–152), investigators calibrate labor supply responsiveness by the elasticity of substitution between consumption and leisure in a CES (constant elasticity of substitution) utility function. Such elasticities do not directly translate into a compensated or uncompensated elasticity of labor supply. In fact, Stern's 0.4 elasticity of substitution corresponds to a case in which the uncompensated labor supply elasticity is negative.

[13] Stern (1976) does not include the word "roughly," but his preferred case uses a social welfare function in the form of expression (3.2) with an equality parameter of 2, which indicates that the social marginal valuation of *utility* decreases with the square of *utility*. His CES utility function, however, is not linear in income due to the presence of a term involving leisure; given the levels of consumption that seem implicit in his simulations, his utility function exhibits modest concavity, which augments the redistributive preference entailed in the social welfare function itself. See generally subsection 3.B.1, and for further pertinent detail on Stern, see Kaplow (2003a).

welfare that is lower by an amount equivalent to approximately 5% of national income.[14]

An important benefit of Stern's calculations is that they indicate the sensitivity of the optimal linear income tax rate to key assumptions. First, the optimal tax rate depends on the welfare benefit associated with equality. As noted, his central estimate assumes that the social marginal valuation of income decreases roughly with the square of income. As explained in subsection 3.B.1, such an assumption might be rationalized by evidence that individuals' marginal utility of income diminishes at this rate, or by an assumption that marginal utility diminishes more slowly but that society should place additional weight on equality (that is, more weight than implied by a utilitarian formulation). To suggest the sensitivity to this assumption, he calculates that if there is virtually no weight on equality,[15] the optimal tax rate is only 25%, and that if there is extreme weight on equality, specifically, the maximin case, the optimal tax rate is 87%.

Second, Stern explores sensitivity to labor supply assumptions. In his central case, an extremely low elasticity implies an optimal tax rate of 79%, and an elasticity as high as had been used in some earlier literature implies an optimal tax rate of 35%.[16]

Third, Stern's central estimate assumes that (nonredistributive) government expenditures are approximately 20% of national income. In the absence of the need to finance such expenditures, the optimal tax

---

[14] Stiglitz (1976) derives a formula to approximate the welfare gains from optimal redistributive taxation. For the case he considers, they are 2.5% of national income. Had he assumed instead, for example, that marginal utility was inversely proportional to the square of income (closer to Stern's social valuation) rather than to income (Stiglitz's base case), the approximated welfare gain would have been 10% of national income.

[15] Stern (1976, p. 153) describes this case as having no special "preference for equality," but in light of the comment in note 13, one should bear in mind that this translates into a utilitarian social welfare function applied to utility functions that do exhibit some concavity so that redistribution does make some contribution to social welfare in this case.

[16] The central case elasticity is 0.4. As indicated in note 12, this refers to the elasticity of substitution between consumption and leisure, not the elasticity of labor supply. The low elasticity of substitution estimate referred to in the text is 0.1 and the high estimate is 1.0 (which Stern approximates using a figure of 0.99).

rate is 48%, and if expenditures are twice as high, the optimal tax rate is 60%. The intuition is that, for a given tax rate, a greater revenue requirement implies a smaller grant g; hence, at that tax rate, there will be more variation in the marginal social valuation (4.8), which favors a higher tax rate according to (4.7).[17]

2. Two-Bracket Income Tax

The two-bracket income tax has received some attention because actual income tax systems tend not to be linear but they also do not have smoothly varying rates or an exceedingly large number of tax brackets. Additionally, a two-bracket income tax is easier to analyze than a non-linear tax, yet it also provides some insight into whether optimal marginal tax rates are likely to be rising or falling with income.

A two-bracket income tax applies a constant rate t_1 to all income up to some specified level y° and another constant rate t_2 to all income over the specified level y°. The tax schedule, an example (matching the simulations, below) of which is depicted in figure 4.3, therefore is

$$T(wl) = \begin{cases} t_1 wl - g, & wl \le y^\circ, \\ t_1 y^\circ + t_2(wl - y^\circ) - g, & wl > y^\circ. \end{cases} \tag{4.9}$$

Here, the government chooses t_1, t_2, y°, and g to maximize social welfare.

This problem is explored by Slemrod, Yitzhaki, Mayshar, and Lundholm (1994).[18] They report simulations for an optimal two-bracket income tax using functional forms and parameters similar to those

---

[17] Stern also considered differences in the skill distribution in the population. Generally, a greater dispersion, which entails greater inequality, will make a higher tax rate optimal.

[18] Sheshinski (1989) had argued that, under certain assumptions, an optimal system necessarily had $t_1 \le t_2$. However, Slemrod et al. (1994) show that his demonstration was in error because it implicitly ignored the possibility of "jumpers" (individuals who under a nonconvex tax schedule might discontinuously increase their labor supply in response to a reduction in t_2). And indeed, their simulations reported in the text to follow (see also figures 6 and 7 in Slemrod et al. 1994, pp. 282–283) confirm that this possibility should not be ignored in practice, as will be discussed further in subsection 3.b.

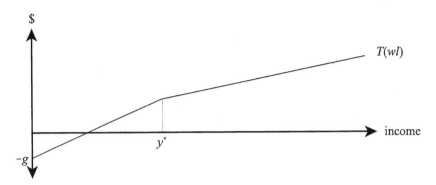

Figure 4.3. Two-Bracket Income Tax Schedule

employed by Stern (1976) and others.[19] In all of the cases they consider, the optimal upper-bracket marginal tax rate is less than the optimal lower-bracket rate. Nevertheless, in all simulations in which the optimal transfer, g, is positive, the overall income tax schedule is progressive, defined as exhibiting rising average tax rates. In the simulation closest to Stern's central case, the optimal linear income tax has a rate of 58%, whereas the optimal two-bracket tax has a marginal rate of 60% on low incomes and 52% on high incomes.

The intuition behind their results is that the lower rate on high-income individuals induces greater labor effort and thus raises more revenue without having to sacrifice revenue on income subject to the lower-bracket rate. This allows a larger grant g to be financed. Put another way, raising the bottom rate, while keeping the top rate fixed, is inframarginal regarding upper-bracket individuals; it collects $\Delta t_1 y^\circ$ from them without distorting their labor supply. Indeed, there is also an income effect on upper-bracket individuals that further increases their labor supply and thus revenue.

---

[19] Specifically, they use CES utility with elasticities of substitution of 0.2, 0.4, and 1.0, revenue requirements (as a fraction of national income) of 0, 0.05, and 0.10, and equality parameters in the social welfare function of 1 (utilitarian) and -2 (the latter implying that the marginal contribution to social welfare falls with the cube of utility). They approximate (using 1000 types) a lognormal wage distribution with parameters $\mu = -1$ and $\sigma = 0.39$.

Interestingly, as the social preference for equality increases, not only do the tax rates and level of grant increase, but also the absolute size of the gap between the two tax rates widens. That is, a greater preference for equality makes it optimal for the marginal tax rate on low-income individuals to be further above the marginal rate on high-income individuals. The intuition is essentially that just noted: Allowing the first rate to be higher enables additional revenue to be raised from high-income individuals to fund a higher transfer g, and this increase in g is relatively more valuable the greater is the social benefit from redistribution.

Slemrod et al. (1994) also explore the effect on social welfare of being able to use a two-bracket tax rather than being confined to a linear tax. In their simulations, the greatest benefit is equivalent to 0.2% of national income, while the lowest value is only 0.0002% of national income. Against this benefit, one would compare the administrative costs involved in using a two-bracket rather than a single-bracket system, which they suggest would be smaller than their highest estimate of benefits but would exceed their lowest estimate of benefits.

3. Nonlinear Income Tax

a. Analysis. Returning to the more general formulation of the optimal income taxation problem described in section A (see figure 4.1), the government chooses a tax schedule $T(wl)$ to maximize the social welfare function (4.3) subject to a revenue constraint (4.4) and constraints requiring that individuals of all ability levels be maximizing their utility (4.2), taking the tax schedule as given.

Mirrlees (1971) and many subsequent investigators employ control-theoretic techniques to address this problem. In this formulation, the government might be posited to choose labor effort and utility (or perhaps income and consumption) for each ability type w, which entails the choice of a tax function. (For a given ability w, a specified labor effort $l(w)$ will yield income of $wl(w)$, and one can then use the utility function to identify what tax or transfer is necessary from that income level to produce the specified level of utility to be achieved by an individual of ability w.) In this maximization, the constraints regarding individuals' maximizing behavior are that no individual of any type w will prefer the choice specified for any other type $w°$.[20] This also can be translated into the version of the problem described in section A. When an individual of ability w chooses $l(w)$ to maximize utility, which depends on the given tax schedule, we can see that the individual is not choosing some other level of labor effort and thus achieving some other level of income, such other levels being optimal for other types of individuals (for instance, a somewhat lower-ability individual would tend to end up at a somewhat lower level of income).

This analysis can be summarized in a first-order condition for the optimal marginal income tax rate at any income level y^*, where w^* and l^* correspond to the ability level and degree of labor effort supplied by the type of individual who would earn y^*. Following presentations elsewhere, make the simplifying assumption that utility is separable between consumption and labor effort and add the further assumption (relaxed below) that marginal utility u_c is constant, in which case the condition can be expressed as[21]

---

[20] This approach is related to the now more familiar revelation principle. Similarly, following Stiglitz (1982a), many have advanced intuition and derived results by considering models with a finite number of types of individuals, often two. (This analysis parallels models on adverse selection in insurance and on nonlinear pricing.) Corresponding incentive-compatibility constraints require that individuals will not wish to mimic other types, the problem in the case of redistributive taxation usually being that high-ability types may wish to mimic low-ability types in order to pay lower taxes.

[21] For example, the relationship between Atkinson and Stiglitz's (1980) expression (13-54) on page 417 and that in the text here is entirely straightforward, requiring only that one conform notation and engage in some rearrangement of terms. The most notable difference is that their term ξ^* appears in the numerator rather than in the denominator due to a difference in how ξ^* is defined (the definition here is the reciprocal of theirs); the reason for the deviation is that it is more useful to follow convention and employ an ξ^* that corresponds more directly (and in particular is positively related) to the elasticity of labor supply. (Additionally, the assumption that u_c is constant, relaxed below, allows some further simplification at this point.) Expression (4.10) and Atkinson and Stiglitz (1980) are essentially identical to Stiglitz (1987) (expression (25) on page 1007 and the expression in note 17 on page 1008), Diamond (1998) (expression (10) on page 86, which is already stated without income effects), Dahan and Strawczynski (2000) (expression (2) on page 682), and Auerbach and Hines (2002) (expressions (4.12) and (4.15) on pages 1381–1382). It is also similar to the two formulations in Saez (2001, p. 215); an important difference involves the attention he devotes to translating the results from ones in terms of the distribution of abilities (which is unobservable) to ones

$$\frac{T'(w^* l^*)}{1-T'(w^* l^*)} = \frac{1-F(w^*)}{\xi^* w^* f(w^*)} \cdot \frac{\int_{w^*}^{\infty}\left(1-\frac{W'(u(w))u_c}{\lambda}\right)f(w)dw}{1-F(w^*)}, \qquad (4.10)$$

where $\xi^* = 1/(1 + l^* u_{ll}/u_l)$—which, when utility is quasi-linear as assumed here, equals $\varepsilon/(1+\varepsilon)$, where ε is the elasticity of labor supply. (This ε is often stated to be the compensated elasticity, but with quasi-linear preferences there is no income effect, so the compensated and uncompensated elasticities are identical.) Note that this formulation includes $1-F(w^*)$ in both the numerator and the denominator on the right side. The motivation is that, in the first term, $(1-F(w^*))/f(w^*)$ is purely a property of the distribution of w, and, in the second term, because the numerator is an integral from w^* to ∞, the term as a whole gives an average value for the expression in brackets in the integrand. Both aspects facilitate interpretation, as will be seen in the discussion to follow.

For aid in understanding expression (4.10), it is helpful to have in mind the simple perturbation of the income tax schedule that underlies this first-order condition. If one begins with some tax schedule $T(wl)$, assumed to be optimal, it must be that no slight adjustment to the schedule will change the level of social welfare. Specifically, expression (4.10) is based on an adjustment that slightly raises the marginal tax rate at the income level y^* (say, in a small interval from y^* to $y^*+\delta$), leaving all other marginal tax rates unaltered. There are two effects of such a change. First, individuals at that income level face a higher marginal rate, which will distort their labor effort, a cost. Second, all individuals above income level $y^*+\delta$ will pay more tax, but these individuals face no marginal distortion. That is, the higher marginal rate at y^* is inframarginal for them. Since those giving up income are an above-average slice of the population (it is the part of the population with income above $y^*+\delta$), there tends to be a redistributive gain.

---

in terms of the distribution of income (taking into account that the tax rules and other parameters will determine the relationship between the underlying ability distribution and the resulting income distribution).

Expression (4.10) can readily be interpreted in terms of this per-turbation.[22] Begin with the first term. Revenue is collected from all individuals with incomes above y^*, which is to say all ability types above w^*; hence the $1 - F(w^*)$ in the numerator. One distorts only the behavior of the marginal type, which explains the $f(w^*)$ in the denominator. The larger the fraction of the population paying more tax and the smaller the group being distorted—or put more compactly, the greater the ratio of the former to the latter—the higher is the optimal tax rate. The denominator also contains weights of ξ^*, indicating the extent of the labor supply response, and w^*, indicating how much production and thus revenue is lost per unit of reduction in labor effort.

The second term applies a social weighting to the revenue that is collected. The expression in brackets in the integrand in the numerator is the difference between the marginal dollar that is raised and the dollar equivalent of the loss in welfare that occurs on account of individuals above w^* paying more tax. As in the interpretation of (4.8), u_c is the marginal utility of consumption to such individuals, W' indicates the impact of changes in utility on social welfare, and division by λ, the shadow price on the revenue constraint, converts this welfare measure into dollars. This integral, as previously noted, is divided by $1 - F(w^*)$ to convert it to an average for the affected population.

Much attention has been devoted to considering how these factors bear not just on the overall level of tax rates but on the shape of the tax schedule, namely, whether optimal marginal tax rates rise or fall with income in different ranges of the income distribution. The latter term in expression (4.10) tends to favor rising rates. The greater is w, the lower is W' (unless the welfare function is utilitarian, in which case this is

---

[22] The reader will also note that this expression resembles (4.7), the first-order condition for the linear income tax. If one cancels the $1 - F$ in the numerator of the first term and denominator of the second term, it is clear that the denominators in (4.7) and (4.10) are similar (the main difference being that in (4.7) for the linear tax, one is averaging over the population rather than focusing on the marginal type) and the numerators have some correspondence (the difference being that in the linear case one looks throughout the income distribution at the relationship between the social weight and income, whereas in the present case with the perturbation in question, one is implicitly comparing the upper group, the only ones who pay the tax increase, to the whole population).

constant) and, if we had not for the moment assumed quasi-linear preferences, the lower would be the marginal utility of consumption u_c; hence at higher w^*, the average value of the term subtracted in the integrand is smaller, making the entire term larger. Note further that if social welfare (or utility) is reasonably concave, $W'u_c$ will approach zero at high levels of income, at which point this term will be nearly constant in w^*.[23] That is, the term favors rising marginal tax rates when income is low or moderate, but it has little effect on the pattern of marginal tax rates near the top of the income distribution.[24]

The first term has more complicated effects. The numerator falls with income, which favors decreasing marginal tax rates: Because there are fewer individuals who face the inframarginal tax and provide revenue to redistribute as one moves up in the income distribution, this core benefit of higher marginal tax rates is falling. In the extreme, if there is a known highest type in the income distribution, the optimal marginal rate on the highest-earning individual would be zero because $1-F$ would be zero: A higher rate collects no revenue but distorts the behavior of the top individual.[25] However, when there is no highest type, known with certainty in advance, this result is inapplicable. Furthermore, even

---

[23] In the maximin case noted in chapter 3, this term literally equals zero once one passes the lowest type, so the term has no impact on the pattern of optimal marginal tax rates.

[24] Brito and Oakland (1977) and Seade (1977) showed that the optimal marginal tax rate at the bottom of the distribution is zero, a phenomenon that can be understood by reference to this term: If the higher marginal rate applies to literally everyone, so they all pay the same increment in tax, then there is no redistribution, but there still is distortion of the lowest type, who is subject to a positive marginal rate. However, since it is typical that the optimum has all individuals below some low ability level not working, it is not in fact the case that there is no redistribution from applying a positive marginal rate to the lowest type who chooses to work, and Ebert (1992) shows that a positive marginal tax rate at the bottom is indeed optimal in this case. Hence, the result of an optimal zero rate at the bottom of the tax schedule is inapplicable in practice; furthermore, simulations suggest that the optimal tax rate at the bottom is quite high.

[25] This result first appears in Phelps (1973) and Sadka (1976) and is explored in some detail by Seade (1977). In (4.10), $1-F$ also appears in the denominator of the second term; however, the integral in the numerator of the second term also equals zero. As w^* approaches its maximum, the second term as a whole approaches one minus the welfare weight on the top individual, whereas the first term approaches zero.

with a known highest type, simulations suggest that zero is not a good approximation of the optimal marginal tax rate even quite close to the top of the income distribution, so the zero-rate-at-the-top result is of little practical consequence.

In the denominator, the elasticity-related term, ξ^*, is usually taken to be constant. However, empirical evidence (see subsection 5.A.2) suggests that the pertinent behavior of high-income individuals may be substantially more elastic, which would favor falling marginal tax rates. The w^* component of the denominator definitely favors falling rates; the reason is that the change in the marginal type's behavior and thus the tax revenue loss is more important the higher is that type's productivity. Finally, the $f(w^*)$ component has varying effects. It indicates that the extent of the distortion is proportional to the number of individuals who face the higher rate at the margin. For ordinarily posited distributions of skills, f will be rising at low income levels and falling at higher income levels. The former adds yet another reason for marginal rates to be falling at low income levels, but the latter provides a reason for marginal rates to be rising after the mode of the income distribution. Whether the first term as a whole favors rising or falling rates at the top has been a subject of dispute, as will be explored later in reporting the results of simulations.

b. Qualifications. There are a number of caveats concerning the interpretation of the first-order condition (4.10). Initially, consider the expression's reliance on the oft-used assumption of quasi-linear preferences, under which u_c is constant. The primary motivation for this assumption is that the optimal nonlinear income tax problem is more analytically tractable when income effects are thus eliminated. Some offer the further justification that empirical evidence suggests that income effects on labor supply are small. Nevertheless, excessive focus on quasi-linear preferences is problematic. Empirical work does not clearly rule out the significance of income effects. Additionally, some smaller estimates are accompanied by similarly small estimates for the compensated elasticity of labor supply; since the latter is necessarily important in optimal income tax analysis, income effects cannot be assumed to have only second-order importance. Indeed, some believe that income effects exceed substitution effects, in which case ignoring the former while attributing significance to the latter could be quite misleading.[26] Furthermore, it should be emphasized that utility being nonlinear in consumption is not only important on account of income effects but also for measuring the social welfare impact of redistribution, as is apparent from the u_c term in expressions (4.10) and (4.8). As chapter 3 discusses, concavity of utility is plausibly an important source of redistributive preference, so ignoring it in optimal redistribution analysis is problematic. This is especially so in settings in which a utilitarian (linear) social welfare function is under examination.

Accordingly, following Atkinson and Stiglitz (1980) and some others, we can consider a version of the first-order condition that does not assume u_c to be constant:[27]

$$\frac{T'(w*l*)}{1-T'(w*l*)} = \frac{1-F(w*)}{\xi*w*f(w*)} \frac{\int_{w*}^{\infty} \frac{u_c(w*)}{u_c(w)}\left(1-\frac{W'(u(w))u_c(w)}{\lambda}\right)f(w)dw}{1-F(w*)}.$$

(4.11)

As written, the only differences between expressions (4.11) and (4.10) concern the integrand in the second term. (Additionally, it is no longer true that $\xi*$ simply equals $\varepsilon/(1+\varepsilon)$.) In the latter term, in large parentheses, we can now see that diminishing marginal utility to consumption indeed reduces the social weight on higher-ability types who pay the tax increase, which tends to favor higher marginal tax rates. Furthermore, the entire parenthetical expression in the integrand is weighted by $u_c(w*)/u_c(w)$, the ratio of the marginal utility of the type facing the hypothesized marginal rate increase to the marginal utility of the higher types for whom the increase is inframarginal. This ratio is rising in w, so even greater weight in the integral is placed on the higher types, for whom the term in large parentheses is the largest, also suggesting the optimality of higher marginal rates, ceteris paribus. Note, however, that the impact of this ratio tends to be relatively great for low $w*$ and

---

[26] Some of the pertinent empirical evidence is surveyed in section 5.A.
[27] Regarding the derivation, see note 21.

relatively slight for high w^*. When w^* is low, $u_c(w^*)$ is large and $u_c(w)$ for much higher w will be substantially less. (Higher-ability types consume more and thus have a lower marginal utility of consumption.) However, when w^* is high, $u_c(w^*)$ is low and marginal utility is much flatter, so even at rather high levels of w, this ratio will be comparatively smaller.[28] It would appear, therefore, that taking declining marginal utility of consumption into account introduces a factor that favors falling marginal tax rates. However, the complexity of the interaction of effects in the integrand combined with the fact that ξ^* has a different interpretation when income effects are allowed renders any such speculation problematic and may also help to explain why most of the literature does not examine this important case in any depth.[29]

Another important reservation regarding the interpretation of the first-order conditions (4.10) and (4.11) is that, as with (4.7) for the linear income tax, most of the components on the right side are endogenous; here, the problem is even more complex because the right side implicitly depends on marginal tax rates other than at y^*, notably, through the term $W'u_c/\lambda$. Thus, when one contemplates the effect on the optimum of, say, changing the elasticity of labor supply, one implicitly is changing other terms both directly (because one needs a different utility function to generate a different elasticity, and a different utility function will have other effects) and indirectly (because a different elasticity will affect other optimal marginal tax rates and the realized levels of consumption and of the shadow price, which in turn will affect the optimal marginal tax rate in question).

---

[28] Decreasing absolute risk aversion implies that the ratio of marginal utilities (lower consumption to higher consumption) falls as consumption rises proportionately. Here, a higher w^* does not push up consumption of higher types but instead cuts off the bottom of the distribution, which makes the phenomenon described in the text even more significant.

[29] Interestingly, of those cited in note 21 who present first-order conditions that do incorporate income effects, the $u_c(w^*)$ component is generally omitted from the interpretative discussion. This component—along with ξ^*—has its origin in individuals' incentive compatibility constraints (first-order conditions for labor effort). As the control problem is typically formulated, the constraints concern the rate at which utility changes with ability level (here, the wage); the greater is $u_c(w^*)$, the greater is this derivative and, of particular relevance, the more it changes as labor effort l is increased (where $l(w)$ is the control variable).

Compounding these difficulties, those performing simulations sometimes make additional adjustments, for example by changing additional terms in the utility function so that the output of the simulation in terms of average labor effort or the distribution of income closely matches a target drawn from data on the existing system.[30] Hence, when a particular consequence is shown to follow from a given parameter change, the stated change taken in isolation (ceteris paribus) may have the identified effect, a larger or smaller effect, or even the opposite effect—the difference being explained by the other adjustments that have been made. Thus, even the modest understanding that has been achieved through the examination of first-order conditions and sensitivity analysis in simulations is a qualified and incomplete one.

Other simplifications made for analytical convenience may also have important implications. One particular concern in this regard involves ignoring the possibility of "jumpers," individuals who, in response to the previously described sort of perturbation of the tax schedule, might discontinuously reduce their labor supply—a possibility noted at the end of section A. The tax increase at income y^* was asserted to be inframarginal for those earning above y^*, but such individuals would be able to avoid the tax increase if they reduced their earnings more than marginally, to some level below y^*. This phenomenon can arise when the tax schedule is nonconvex, which occurs when marginal rates are falling, a case that is of interest given the foregoing analysis and the results of simulations reported later.[31] In that event, there may well be some individuals

---

[30] An additional difficulty arises in analyses that impose some reduced-form net social valuation, say $\phi(w)$, on consumption to individuals of type w. The difficulty is that stipulating such a weighting scheme is not tantamount to choosing a social welfare function. As is clear from the analysis in the text, the actual weighting will depend on the choice of welfare function, the form of individuals' utility functions, and the level of labor effort chosen and consumption achieved by individuals of type w, the latter being endogenous. Hence, it is unclear what it means to specify the ultimate weights a priori. Specifically, it is not obvious that there will exist a plausible social welfare function that simultaneously rationalizes a set of weights and is itself optimized when the reduced form using the stipulated weights is optimized. And, even if such a function were to exist, it is implausible that it would continue to rationalize yet another optimum when, say, one considered a different distribution of underlying abilities.

[31] As noted previously, the participation decision may also involve discontinuous labor supply behavior.

who are indifferent between earning an income above y^* and an income below y^*.[32] When this is true, there is an additional factor in the optimization, clearly favoring a lower marginal rate: Individuals who jump downward in response to a marginal rate increase at y^* cause a discrete fall in revenue with no offsetting social welfare gain on account of higher utility (these individuals are indifferent, the loss in utility from reduced after-tax consumption just offsetting the utility gain from reduced labor effort).

This possibility is usually ignored for convenience, sometimes motivated by the notion that the number of jumpers is likely to be small. But, a priori, it would appear that jumpers may be significant. In terms of revenue raised, there is, as noted, a discrete revenue loss for each jumper, whereas the revenue gain from those who do not jump is a marginal one for each individual. Indeed, in Slemrod et al.'s (1994) examination of jumpers in the two-bracket income tax, their formal analysis indicates that jumpers may well be important, and their simulations confirm this (see note 18).

c. Simulations. The foregoing discussion of the first-order condition (4.10) and of further complications makes clear that it is difficult to have strong a priori views as to the likely contours of the optimal nonlinear income tax. Beginning with Mirrlees (1971), analysts have used simulations to help join the theoretical analysis with empirical estimates of labor supply elasticities and of distributions of skills or income in order to provide additional illumination. Of course, any results are qualified not only by the limits of existing knowledge of the world but also by the already-noted limitations of the models employed.

---

[32] The possibility of multiple tangencies between an individual's indifference curve and the opportunity set due to the assumed nonconvexity of the tax schedule is discussed, for example, in Mirrlees (1971) and Stiglitz (1987). Taking the simplest case of the two-bracket income tax of subsection 2, if the upper-bracket rate is less than the lower-bracket rate, there will necessarily be some type (assuming a continuum of types) who will be in this situation (see Slemrod et al. 1994). Further note that in this setting as well as in the more general one in the text, when there is jumping there will be gaps in the income distribution; in addition, in the case in the text, the gap will include the income level at which the perturbation is being performed, in which case distortion of the marginal type that is the normal focus of analysis would be moot.

The discussion here will emphasize how the shape of the optimal nonlinear income tax varies from linearity because subsection 1 on the optimal linear income tax already reports how the overall level of taxation is affected by various parameters of the problem. Tuomala (1990) offers a useful survey and set of calculations. Perhaps his most notable conclusion is that, in all the cases he reports, "the marginal tax rate falls as income increases except at income levels within the bottom decile of the distribution" (p. 95). Mirrlees's (1971) original calculations displayed a similar tendency, but later investigators questioned the extent to which the result may have depended on the social preferences he stipulated or the arguably high labor supply response he assumed. Subsequent work, however, suggests that a greater social preference for equality or a lower labor supply response tends to increase the optimal level of marginal tax rates but does not generally result in a substantially different shape for the tax schedule. In particular, neither strong egalitarian preferences nor a very low labor supply response (nor both in combination) produces increasing marginal rates at high income levels. For example, in one case of interest, Tuomala reports that a lower labor response leads to higher optimal marginal tax rates, but it increases the optimal marginal tax rate more for lower- and middle-income individuals than for high-income individuals. This result is mirrored in Slemrod et al.'s (1994) findings, reported earlier, for the optimal two-bracket income tax. Tuomala also considers the strength of the tendency of the optimal marginal tax rate to approach zero at the top end of the income distribution. He finds that, although marginal tax rates are generally falling at the high end, they do not rapidly approach zero, not even at the 99.9 percentile of the distribution.

Work by Kanbur and Tuomala (1994) offers what may be an important qualification to these results about decreasing marginal tax rates. Their calculations suggest that when inequality in the distribution of individuals' abilities (wages) is significantly greater than previously assumed (but in ranges they suggest are empirically plausible), optimal marginal tax rates do increase with income over a substantial range, although for upper-income individuals optimal marginal rates still fall with income.

Further attention has been devoted to exploring the effect of the shape of the distribution of individuals' abilities on the shape of the optimal tax schedule. Diamond's (1998) analysis examines a Pareto distribution of skills (instead of the commonly used lognormal distribution), under which the $(1-F)/f$ component of (4.10) rises more rapidly at the upper end of the distribution, and finds that optimal marginal tax rates are rising at the top. However, Dahan and Strawczynski's (2000) simulations indicate that Diamond's result was driven in large part by his additional assumption that preferences were quasi-linear, thus removing income effects. Nevertheless, their diagrams do suggest, consistent with Diamond's claim, that moving from a lognormal to a Pareto distribution favors higher rates—still falling, but notably less rapidly—at the top of the income distribution. Saez (2001), using income distribution data in the United States from 1992 and 1993, finds that the shape of the distribution of $(1-F)/wf$ is such that optimal rates should fall substantially, well into the middle of the income distribution, to an income of approximately $75,000, rise until approximately $200,000, and then be essentially flat thereafter.[33] For example, in his simulation with a utilitarian welfare function, a compensated elasticity of labor supply of 0.5, and a functional form for utility that has income effects, his optimal schedule has a marginal rate near 80% at the bottom of the income distribution that falls to approximately 40% at $75,000, and then rises to about 65% at the upper end, where it roughly levels off. However, his functional form for utility has income effects that rise with income to an extent that the uncompensated elasticity approaches zero as w increases, which favors higher marginal rates at the top than otherwise. In sum, income effects, and in particular their magnitude near the top of the income distribution, may well be important in determining optimal marginal tax rates, but explorations to date are insufficient to provide great clarity regarding the phenomenon (for further examination, see Dahan and Strawczynski 2004).

Another important conclusion in Mirrlees's (1971) original work is that the optimal nonlinear income tax is approximately linear. If this is true, it may be that there is little loss in social welfare if only a linear

---

[33] As footnote 21 implies, Saez (2001) does not directly consider $(1-F)/wf$, which is unobservable, but instead uses the observed distribution of income and takes into account how it will differ from the underlying distribution of abilities.

income tax (which may have administrative advantages) is used. As noted, subsequent investigators report a range of cases in which the optimal nonlinear income tax departs more substantially from a linear tax, but they do not generally report how much welfare loss is involved in using only a linear scheme. Recall that Slemrod et al.'s (1994) simulations indicate only modest welfare gains in moving from a linear tax to a two-bracket tax (with falling rates).

An additional result from the simulations is that, at the optimum, a nontrivial fraction of the population does not work, and this fraction is larger when social preferences favor greater redistribution and when the labor supply elasticity is higher. This outcome should hardly be surprising because, as the analysis of (4.10) and the simulations suggest, high marginal rates tend to be optimal at the bottom of the income distribution, along with a sizable grant. Relatedly, little productivity and thus little tax revenue is sacrificed when those with very low abilities are induced not to work, whereas substantial revenue is raised from the rest of the population, for whom marginal tax rates on their first dollars of income are inframarginal.

4. Discussion

Both the analysis and the simulation results make clear that simplistic a priori views about the shape of an optimal income tax schedule, and of how that shape depends on the extent to which social preferences are egalitarian, cannot be sustained. Both subtleties in the analysis and empirical contingencies—concerning not only labor supply elasticities but also other aspects of individuals' utility functions and the shape of the distribution of underlying abilities—make it difficult to offer confident statements even after engaging in the relevant inquiry. A few broad conclusions, however, do seem possible.

First and foremost, lower labor supply elasticities, greater underlying inequality, and a greater social preference for equalizing income all unsurprisingly favor higher marginal tax rates, which allow a larger transfer to be funded. However, although each of these factors favors higher overall tax rates, none has an unambiguous effect on the shape of the optimal income tax schedule. This point is well illustrated by Slemrod et al.'s (1994) two-bracket income tax simulations and is reinforced by the analysis and simulations for the more general nonlinear income tax. As one may recall from chapter 2, if one abstracts from incentive considerations, both a nonredistributive tax and the most redistributive tax are linear (at a 0% and a 100% rate); hence it is not obvious why one should have expected clear, particular deviations from linearity for intermediate degrees of redistribution.

Furthermore, whatever deviations from linearity prove to be optimal, it is not certain how important they are for social welfare. Stern's (1976) simulations suggest that the welfare benefits from redistribution under an optimal linear income tax may be on the order of 5% of national income; Slemrod et al.'s (1994) simulations found much smaller incremental gains from adding an additional bracket; and work on optimal nonlinear income taxation has not offered substantial information on the benefits from further refinements. If it were in fact true that a linear tax achieved most of the attainable benefits, this conclusion would be significant in light of the advantages in terms of administration and limiting tax avoidance of certain linear schemes, such as sales or value-added taxes and withholding on wages at constant rates.

Finally, it is interesting to consider the relationship between the optimal income tax and transfer scheme and those actually employed in developed countries.[34] Optimal levels of tax rates are quite high in many of the simulations, higher than is observed in many such countries. (The gap is less than it may first appear since the tax and transfer systems in the analysis here are taken to include all forms of taxation, not just those nominally described as income taxes.) Of course, existing systems are not the product of maximizing an analyst's preferred social welfare function; instead, observed schemes reflect political economy considerations beyond the scope of the present investigation.[35]

Regarding the shape of tax and transfer schemes, the simulations rather uniformly support fairly high marginal rates at the lower end of the income distribution. This is certainly in accord with practice when

---

[34] In less developed economies, it is more difficult to implement income tax and transfer schemes, so a close correspondence between their tax systems and the optimal schedules examined here should not be expected.

[35] For a survey, see Persson and Tabellini (2002).

one takes into account the rapid phase-outs in transfer programs (indeed, as will be seen, they can produce aggregate marginal tax rates in excess of 100%, well above what is optimal). Such high marginal rates are thought to result in a significant number of low-ability individuals not working at all, and this feature is confirmed in many of the simulations. Nontrivial work disincentives are optimal because little revenue is lost whereas the higher marginal rates are inframarginal for all individuals with higher incomes. (For further elaboration, see chapter 7.)

Although many simulations suggest that optimal rates are falling at the top, rising marginal rates (or, more recently, flat marginal rates beyond upper-middle levels of income) are ordinarily employed. Thus, often-proposed and sometimes enacted middle-income tax cuts may be contrary to the optimal prescription. Slemrod et al. (1994) emphasize that the optimal use of nonlinearity in their two-bracket income tax results in middle-income taxpayers paying more (relative to a linear scheme), to the benefit of both the poor and the rich. Politics may offer an explanation for this divergence between the optimum and practice, notably, if tax rates are heavily influenced by the preferences of median voters. On the other hand, if one accepts some of the subsequent analyses of Diamond (1998) and Saez (2001), the optimal shape may more closely match what is typically observed.

Any such comparison of the optimal to the actual is subject to all the foregoing caveats concerning what is in fact ideal, in addition to political economy considerations. Furthermore, many factors identified in the next chapter and in some others that follow may call for significant revision and thus will bear on the extent to which existing tax and transfer systems can properly be thought of as optimal and on how far from the ideal they actually may be.

5

Elaboration and Extensions

The classical analysis of the optimal labor income taxation problem presented in chapter 4 suggests the importance of further exploring the elasticity of labor supply. Additionally, that analysis is subject to numerous qualifications regarding matters of administration, the relationship between income and underlying earning ability, the nature of individuals' preferences, various market imperfections, general equilibrium considerations, and other factors. This chapter briefly considers these issues. Many of the questions addressed here have received limited attention despite their potential significance, and some topics that have benefited from greater scrutiny nevertheless remain unresolved.

A. Behavioral Response to Labor Income Taxation

Empirical work on the incentive effects of labor income taxation has gone through many generations. This section begins with studies of the elasticity of labor supply, then examines more recent literature on the elasticity of taxable income, which includes a broader range of behavioral responses, and finally considers the long-run effects of taxation, which may be poorly illuminated by existing evidence.

1. Labor Supply Elasticity

Initially, most empirical work assumed that changing an individual's marginal tax rate has essentially the same effect as does changing the before-tax wage. This view follows from the individual's first-order condition for labor effort (4.2), indicating that behavior depends on the after-tax wage, $w(1 - T')$. Furthermore, much of this literature viewed labor effort in terms of hours and focused on the labor supply of working-age males. This research generally identified quite low labor supply elasticities. Compensated elasticities were often found to be near 0.1 or 0.2, which implies an elasticity of substitution between leisure and consumption of near 0.5 (in the particular CES utility functions often used in the optimal income tax simulations reported in chapter 4; see note 12 there).[1]

An important early refinement accounts for the existence of rate graduation in existing income tax systems in light of the fact that a taxpayer's behavior will reflect not only the pertinent marginal tax rate but also income effects due to marginal rates at lower levels of income. Work by Hausman (1981) designed to address this issue (and others) implies a compensated labor supply elasticity significantly higher than that found in previous work. Subsequent research, however, particularly by MaCurdy, Green, and Paarsch (1990), suggests that such results are products of restrictions imposed by the estimation technique. Their reanalysis produces results closer to those obtained in earlier, less sophisticated analyses.[2]

Another extension attends to workers' labor force participation decision, as emphasized in Heckman's (1993) survey. If there are fixed costs of entering the labor market, individuals face an effective choice between working zero hours and a significant number of hours. Furthermore, if a tax rate increase induces even a few percent of workers to quit, the lost tax revenue could be as large as if the entire work force reduced its hours by a few percent. The participation decision may

---

[1] See, for example, the literature reviews by Killingsworth (1983) and Pencavel (1986). More recent surveys include Blundell and MaCurdy (1999) and Russek (1996). In a survey of economists' opinions by Fuchs, Krueger, and Poterba (1998), the mean estimate of the compensated labor supply elasticity for men was 0.22 among labor economists and 0.26 among public finance economists; labor economists' mean estimate for women was 0.59 (public finance economists were not asked to estimate this).

[2] See also Triest (1990). An additional problem is that many leading data sources provide poor measures of individuals' actual hours of work, which some suggest involve biases that may be responsible for underestimates of labor supply responses (see Juster and Stafford 1991 and Bound et al. 1989, discussed in Heckman 1993).

be particularly important for married women, many of whom have a realistic option not to work and face high marginal rates even on modest earnings.[3]

The emergent consensus was that indeed the elasticity of married women's labor supply was substantially greater than that of men (or single women) (see the survey by Killingsworth and Heckman 1986). Reanalysis by Mroz (1987), however, indicates that many of the results were an artifact of poorly specified empirical models, and he concludes that married women's hours are fairly inelastic. Nevertheless, subsequent work suggests that married women's labor supply (notably, their participation decision) is fairly responsive to taxation.[4] In light of these results, some have proposed changes in the manner of taxing two-earner families, a subject considered further in subsection 12.B.1.b. More recently, Blau and Kahn (2007) find that married women's labor supply elasticities fell by just over 50% from 1980 to 2000, so that in this respect as in others (participation rates, responses to spousal earnings) married women's labor supply behavior is converging toward that of married men.

2. Taxable Income Elasticity

It has long been understood that behavioral responses to taxation are not confined to participation and hours (see, for example, Rosen 1980). To address this point empirically, Lindsey (1987), Feldstein (1995), and others propose that one examine the response of taxable income to changes in tax rates (for a survey, see Giertz 2004). Taxable income is

---

[3] Contributing to this phenomenon are the failure to tax imputed income and the impact of the social security system (see Feldstein and Samwick 1992), as well as the use of joint filing combined with graduated rates, such as in the United States, under which a second earner from the outset faces the primary earner's high marginal income tax rate.

[4] See, for example, the studies surveyed in Blundell and MaCurdy (1999). Much recent work has examined the effects of changes in the Earned Income Tax Credit on the labor supply of single women and married women with children. See Eissa and Liebman (1996), Eissa and Hoynes (2006a, 2006b), Ellwood (2000), Meyer and Rosenbaum (2001), and the survey in Hotz and Scholz (2003), as well as the discussion of some of this work in Blundell and MaCurdy (1999). For contrary evidence, see Cancian and Levinson (2006).

determined not only by participation and hours but also by intensity of effort, job choice, the fraction of compensation received as tax-preferred fringe benefits, other avoidance activity, and evasion.

In theory, this approach is appealing because taxable income is, by definition, what is subject to tax and thus what individuals have an incentive to reduce in any way possible when tax rates increase. Accordingly, one should expect individuals' responses to tax changes to be qualitatively more varied and, because there are more margins of response, overall more substantial than their responses to a change in their before-tax wage.[5] Moreover, as Feldstein (1999) emphasizes, many of these responses involve distortions like those due to simple labor supply responses, so the welfare implications are similar. If individuals are optimizing, all marginal responses to changes in taxation should produce the same incremental deadweight loss, equal to the marginal tax rate, whether they involve, say, the substitution of leisure for work or the substitution of fringe benefits for cash. Exceptions are tax-preferred activities that confer positive externalities (such as charitable contributions) or that augment receipts from other taxes (for example, shifts from the personal to the corporate income tax base).

Feldstein's (1995) study of the effects of the 1986 Tax Reform Act finds a taxable income elasticity greater than or equal to 1.0, a figure that is substantially higher than previously measured labor supply

---

[5] Slemrod (2001) provides a useful model. Because of avoidance opportunities, the pure labor supply effect is diminished: Some earnings are sheltered, and having a higher income plausibly makes it easier to shelter a given amount. It follows that estimates of labor supply elasticity should be lower in studies that examine variation in the after-tax wage due to tax rate differences than in those in which variation is due to real wage differences. Furthermore, because the traditional labor supply response is moderated by avoidance opportunities, the overall taxable elasticity could in theory be lower on account of avoidance, although when the labor supply elasticity is fairly low to begin with, the net effect of avoidance is a larger overall response of taxable income to changes in tax rates. Another important caveat, emphasized by Slemrod and Kopczuk (2002) (discussed further in section B), is that the elasticity of taxable income is not purely a property of individuals' preferences but rather depends substantially on the definition of the tax base and tax enforcement policy. One implication is that the elasticity of taxable income is not a constant but instead should vary as the tax system changes. For example, it is likely to be lower after the base-broadening of the 1986 tax reform, on which see Kopczuk (2005).

elasticities.[6] Similar findings were reported by Auten and Carroll (1995) using a larger Treasury Department database and by Moffitt and Wilhelm (2000) using a panel spanning six years.[7] Goolsbee (2000a), by contrast, finds that the 1986 reform is associated with an elasticity of just over one-third when one accounts for income growth unrelated to the tax change. Gruber and Saez (2002) examine all tax reforms in the 1980s and find an elasticity of 0.4, and Saez (2004c) finds that from 1960 through 2000 reported income was unresponsive to tax rate changes except for a modest reaction by those with incomes in the top 1%. Goolsbee (1999) determines the taxable income elasticities associated with tax reforms between 1920 and 1975 and finds substantially lower values than those reported in studies of more recent reforms, suggesting that the higher estimates may arise from various uncontrolled biases. Feldstein and Feenberg (1996) estimate the effects of the 1993 tax reform and find an elasticity of 0.74. Sillamaa and Veall (2001) study the 1988 tax reform in Canada and find an elasticity of only 0.25.[8]

It should also be emphasized that the elasticity of taxable income appears to differ greatly among taxpayers, being far higher for high-income individuals and those in occupations that provide greater opportunities for manipulating taxable income.[9] For example, Gruber and

---

[6] Caution must be employed in comparing estimates from different literatures because labor supply elasticities are often defined with respect to changes in the marginal tax rate whereas taxable income elasticities are commonly defined with respect to changes in the net-of-tax rate (one minus the tax rate), in which case signs differ and given magnitudes have different meanings.

[7] Feenberg and Poterba's (1993) examination of tax return data on reported incomes of very-high-income taxpayers finds the sharpest rise in 1987 and 1988, suggesting that the 1986 reform may have been partly responsible. See also Lindsey (1987), who in a study of tax rate cuts earlier in the 1980s found an even greater elasticity.

[8] Surprisingly, Aarbu and Thoresen (2001) find an elasticity of taxable income between -0.6 and 0.2 for the 1992 Norwegian tax reform. Caution should be employed in comparing estimates for the elasticity of taxable income across jurisdictions or significantly different periods of time because, as will be discussed in section B, this elasticity depends on the tax system (for example, the breadth of the tax base), which may well not be constant in such comparisons.

[9] By contrast, Juhn, Murphy, and Topel (1991) find that uncompensated labor supply elasticities (for men) fall with income, from about 0.3 at the bottom of the wage distribution to less than 0.1 at the top.

Saez's (2002) estimate of 0.4 is driven primarily by a 0.57 elasticity for those with incomes over $100,000 (and even higher for the subset who itemize deductions); the elasticity is less than a third as high for lower-income individuals. Moffitt and Wilhelm (2000) find that the very rich contribute greatly to their high elasticity estimate, and Alm and Wallace (2000) report similar results, attributing the difference to the very rich having greater control over financial matters, especially their form of compensation (see also Giertz 2006). Auten and Carroll's (1999) estimate for "investors" is 2.37, for farmers and the self-employed, 1.12, and for executives and managers, 1.09, compared to an overall average of 0.57. Sillamma and Veall (2001) report similar results for the 1988 tax reform in Canada. The finding of significantly higher taxable income elasticities for high-income individuals is particularly important for the analysis in chapter 4 of the level and shape of the optimal income tax schedule, especially given the vastly disproportionate share of income and income tax payments contributed by these individuals (see Slemrod 2000).

Empirical studies of the taxable income elasticity, however, may overstate the pertinent elasticity. First, some of the reduction in tax payments due to a tax increase may involve shifts of taxable income to future years, such as when individuals add to their retirement accounts. Second, as noted earlier, there may be shifts among taxable entities. Slemrod (1996a) indicates that a substantial source of the increase in personal taxable income among the highest-income taxpayers after the 1986 act probably involved changing C corporations (taxable under the corporate income tax) to S corporations and partnerships (the income of which appears on individuals' personal tax returns). See also Gordon and Slemrod (2000), who find a more moderate shift. Third, problems regarding endogenous sample selection and nontax sources of income variation may lead to overestimation; correcting for these factors, Auten and Carroll (1999) find an elasticity of 0.54 rather than 1.10 for the 1986 tax reform.[10] Additional difficulties are controlling for exogenous but irregular income trends and mean reversion in individuals' incomes (see Giertz 2006).

---

[10] Auten and Carroll (1999) examine a variety of additional factors and find that the elasticity remains in the neighborhood of 0.6.

Studies based on tax reforms, including many of those measuring the taxable income elasticity, risk misestimation if they compare behavior shortly before and after a reform.[11] Many individuals may not have realized that a change has occurred, and those who are aware may not yet have been able to respond fully. For those who are more savvy and nimble, anticipatory behavior may mask or exaggerate the effects of reform. For example, Sammartino and Weiner (1997) suggest that high-income individuals anticipated the 1993 tax rate increases and thus shifted income from 1993 to 1992, making it appear that the rate increases caused a substantial reduction in taxable income when this was not in fact the case. Similarly, Goolsbee (2000a) finds for the rich a short-run (one-year) elasticity of 3.6 but a long-run (three-year) elasticity of 0.4, a significant factor being that executives' taxable income from the exercise of options temporarily spiked in 1992. See also Goolsbee's (2000b) finding that top corporate executives' responses, constituting 20% of the short-term decline in adjusted gross income among rich taxpayers following the 1993 tax increase, are almost entirely due to income shifting.[12] In part to avoid these difficulties, a number of studies use a wider window, with three years being common.[13] The tradeoff is that comparisons across longer periods of time greatly increase the likelihood that factors other than the tax rate changes in question will be responsible for identified effects or will mask real responses so as to make them undetectable, which is a major reason that short time frames are so often employed.

In sum, the elasticity of taxable income is not yet known with confidence. Nevertheless, it appears that this elasticity is significantly

---

[11] Additional problems with such studies, often relying on difference-in-difference methods, have been noted, for example, by Blundell and MaCurdy (1999) and Heckman (1996).

[12] As suggested, it is also possible that anticipation could mask real effects. For example, if some individuals who anticipate higher future tax rates switch to less demanding jobs before a reform takes effect—perhaps because some convenient opportunities to change arise immediately—this behavioral response will diminish the measured effect by making pre-reform taxable income appear lower rather than augmenting the measured effect as in principle it should.

[13] In addition to those just mentioned, see, for example, Feldstein (1995), Gruber and Saez (2002), and Sillamaa and Veall (2001).

larger than the elasticity of labor supply with regard to hours and participation alone.[14]

3. Long-Run Elasticity

Probably the greatest uncertainty concerning estimated behavioral responses to labor income taxation is due to the fact that long-run reactions, which cannot readily be measured, may well be much greater than short-run responses. More gradual or delayed but ultimately substantial behavioral changes include individuals' investments in human capital (notably, higher education, including specialized professional and vocational training), locational decisions (whether to obtain more remunerative employment in another region), occupational choices, entrepreneurial undertakings, and moves into and out of the labor force during one's career or upon retirement.[15] These responses may have much more substantial effects on participation, hours, and earnings than do short-run adjustments to changes in tax rates. Likewise, the length of the work day and the structure of production (such as the ability to work flexible hours or at home) may be relatively fixed in the short run but might vary substantially over the course of decades.[16] The same is also true of responses in the area of fringe benefits and some other forms of tax avoidance (for example, the decision to work in sectors where tax reduction opportunities are more plentiful). Furthermore, labor supply and related phenomena are plausibly influenced a good

---

[14] Studies of taxable income elasticity that also report hours find that hours respond little, if at all, even when taxable income changes significantly.

[15] Although some decisions, like retirement, can be made quickly by some workers, planning (for example, prior savings behavior) may be important even for many who in principle could quit immediately.

[16] Most obviously, employers' organization of production will adjust more, given additional time. One should also consider the evolution of other organizations (for example, the availability of child care and the structure of school schedules) and of technologies (for example, facilitating market employment at home and improving durables that substitute for labor in household production). As an indication that flexibility in production may be important, Showalter and Thurston (1997) find that self-employed physicians have much higher labor supply elasticities than those who are employees.

deal by social norms (say, concerning what constitutes laziness) and personal habits, and these too might shift over the long run if there are sufficient economic pressures. Hence, it may be that raising taxes from 30% to 50% would moderately reduce taxable income in the next few years but produce very large reductions over the course of a generation. See, for example, Lindbeck's (1993) interpretation of long-term labor trends.[17]

For long-run responses to be significantly greater than short-term reactions, it seems that uncompensated elasticities would have to be nontrivial. If, instead, long-term uncompensated elasticities were near zero, little long-term adjustment would be necessary, so institutional factors that might otherwise limit the magnitude of short-term adjustments would be relatively unimportant constraints. Furthermore, note that in a redistributive tax system, in which substitution effects are always negative (assuming that aggregate marginal tax rates are positive), income effects vary with income: They further discourage labor effort for low-income individuals, who receive net transfers, but encourage labor effort for high-income individuals, who pay net taxes. Hence, even if some part of the income distribution has an uncompensated long-run responsiveness to redistribution that is near zero, so behavioral adjustments are not required, individuals at other levels of income should be expected to have nonzero uncompensated long-run elasticities, and, accordingly, the extent of their response should be increasing over time.

Unfortunately, there is limited empirical evidence that illuminates this important issue. As mentioned in the preceding subsection, some estimates of the taxable income elasticity do span a three-year window, which may be sufficiently wide to introduce significant confounding factors yet still not wide enough to capture many of the pertinent responses. International comparisons could also be fruitful because there are significant differences in countries' levels of taxation over substantial

---

[17] Additionally, Alesina, Glaeser, and Sacerdote (2006) argue that there is a social multiplier effect, a form of network externality, wherein some individuals' increase in leisure raises the value of others increasing their own leisure (a phenomenon suggested by the tendency to have common nonwork days despite contrary economies in the utilization of capital and also by regularities in employment by age and gender).

periods of time, and typical work habits (such as length of work week and vacations) vary as well. However, due to the even greater range of potentially confounding factors (for example, differences in technology, factor availability, unionization, culture), it is unclear whether such analysis would yield clear results. Prescott (2004) indicates that differences between hours worked in the United States and Europe are due to differences in marginal tax rates, whereas Alesina, Glaeser, and Sacerdote (2006) offer evidence that instead attributes the differences largely to unionization and regulation, with reinforcement of differences resulting from social network effects. Long-term trends of shorter work days and work weeks and longer vacations as economic development advances suggest that the uncompensated elasticity is negative—although again inferences are difficult because so many other conditions have also changed significantly over time. Greenwood and Vandenbroucke (2008) conclude that higher wages have in fact led to decreased hours over the past century, although part of the decline may be attributed to technological changes that have increased the value of leisure (although technology that reduces the need for household labor has contributed to an increase in female labor force participation).[18]

In commenting on work on the elasticity of taxable income, Slemrod (1990a) emphasizes that there is a hierarchy of responses: Timing shifts (such as capital gains realizations) are most readily made, accounting changes and adjustments of organizational form are next, and real responses are last. To the extent that this is the case, the short time frame of much empirical work is problematic. Realizing a capital gain takes a phone call or a few clicks at a website; reeducating oneself for a new line of work and moving one's family to another region can take years to accomplish. It should also be kept in mind that many of the quicker reactions that may explain an important fraction of existing empirical estimates have a one-shot character. Realizing capital gains before the effective date of a permanent rate increase can be done only once; over the long run under a new regime, such transitional effects are of lesser

---

[18] A complication is that, more recently, high-salaried workers' hours are increasing, which Kuhn and Lozano (2005) attribute to such workers receiving higher wage rates for working longer hours.

consequence (although the different regime may imply different behavior regarding patterns of realizations and so forth).

B. Problems of Implementation

1. Administration and Enforcement

The analysis of optimal income taxation in chapter 4 does not account for public administrative and private compliance costs or problems of tax avoidance and evasion.[19] However, views about these considerations underlie the framing of the optimal income tax problem. Notably, it is ordinarily assumed that income taxation, including a nonlinear scheme under which it is necessary to attribute income to particular taxpayers, is feasible, whereas a (nondistortionary) tax based on individuals' earning abilities is not. Even if such assumptions are useful for analysis, they are far from the truth. For example, in the United States, public and private collection costs for the income tax are approximately 10% of revenues, and it is estimated that over 15% of tax liability is unpaid.[20] As emphasized by Mirrlees (1971), Atkinson and Stiglitz (1980), Slemrod (1990b), and others, analysts of optimal tax policy need to take a broad view that addresses the choice among tax systems, the manner in which practical considerations influence how each component should be implemented, and enforcement policy—and also the interactions among these dimensions of the problem. The present section is limited to considering some of the principal ways that administration and enforcement bear on the foregoing discussion of optimal income taxation and accordingly on applications throughout this book.

Most directly, the possibility of tax avoidance and evasion suggests that higher tax rates will not collect as much revenue and, given the amount of revenue they do collect, will tend to involve more distortion

---

[19] For surveys, see Andreoni, Erard, and Feinstein (1998), Cowell (1990), Roth, Scholz, and Witte (1989), and Slemrod and Yitzhaki (2002).

[20] See, for example, Guyton et al. (2003), Internal Revenue Service (1996, 2005), and Slemrod (1996b).

than otherwise.[21] Indeed, as described in section A, this recognition provides much of the motivation for the move from narrow measures of labor supply response to the concept of the elasticity of taxable income, which incorporates avoidance and evasion. As the analysis and simulations presented in chapter 4 indicate, a greater elasticity tends to favor lower tax rates. Furthermore, the empirical work surveyed in subsection A.2 suggests that this elasticity is particularly great for very-high-income individuals. This tendency favors lower rates both in a linear income tax and at the top end for a nonlinear tax.[22] Interestingly, this differential responsiveness is probably not a consequence of evasion, which appears to decline with income in percentage terms, the explanation being that compliance is particularly low in the cash economy, consisting in significant part of small businesses and lower-income individuals who work in the informal sector.[23] Instead, the greater taxable income elasticity for high-income taxpayers is probably due to such individuals being in occupations with greater avoidance opportunities.

---

[21] The earliest models of tax evasion did not uniformly produce such conclusions because they considered taxpayers' risk aversion regarding penalties to be the only limit to evasion. When avoidance and evasion are assumed to entail direct costs in adjusting behavior or hiding income, higher rates are likely to increase noncompliance due to the added incentive to escape taxation. Additional factors, such as that many taxpayers have some preference to be honest that is more likely to be overcome as the inducement increases (see Gordon 1989), reinforce this conclusion. See the surveys cited in note 19.

[22] Regarding the linear income tax, recall from the first-order condition (4.7) that individuals' elasticities are weighted by earnings. Because the highest-income individuals earn a substantially disproportionate share of total taxable income, their having a high elasticity is important in moderating the optimal linear income tax rate despite their constituting only a small fraction of the population. There is, however, a distinction between lower effective rates and lower stated rates; it is possible for optimal stated rates to be higher while the optimal effective rate is lower than it would be in a world with no avoidance or evasion. See, for example, Cremer and Gahvari (1994) and the discussion in subsection 2 of the effect of a non-comprehensive tax base on optimal tax rates.

[23] Christian (1994) reports on data from the 1988 Taxpayer Compliance Measurement Program showing that nonbusiness taxpayers with incomes over $100,000 reported 96.6% of tax liability on average, whereas the figure is 85.9% for those with incomes below $25,000; the difference was greater for tax returns reporting business income. Lemieux, Fortin, and Fréchette (1994) present evidence that welfare recipients (who face very high aggregate marginal tax rates; see subsection 7.B.1) are most likely to shift work to the informal sector.

Slemrod and Kopczuk (2002) emphasize that the elasticity of taxable income, particularly as it relates to tax avoidance and evasion, is not exogenous but rather is itself a product of government policy. Although greater problems of avoidance and evasion tend to favor lower tax rates, it is also true that higher tax rates warrant greater expenditures to reduce avoidance and evasion. To the extent that the latter is accomplished, the resulting elasticity of taxable income will be lower, which itself will justify even higher rates.

More broadly, administrative and enforcement concerns should not be understood as part of some list of tax policy objectives, along with efficiency, equity, and so forth (see subsection 3.A.2 in this regard). Instead, as more recent analysts have indicated, these factors need to be integrated into an optimal taxation framework with an explicit SWF.[24] In other words, as stated at the outset, the problem really is one of joint optimization. The discussion of tax base broadening in subsection 2 will make this interaction more concrete.

Administrative and enforcement considerations are specifically relevant to the choice between a linear and a nonlinear income tax. A linear tax has the significant advantage that it is irrelevant to the fisc which taxpayer earns a given amount of income. Collection (at a constant rate) at the source thus becomes a fully effective substitute for individual payments. Moreover, there is no need to worry about schemes to shift income among taxpayers—from high-bracket to low-bracket individuals—which partly undermine nominally nonlinear rate structures and waste social resources in the process.[25] Against these benefits of linear income taxation must be weighed the costs of a less fine-tuned redistributive system, which were measured in some of the simulations reported in chapter 4.[26]

---

[24] See, for example, Kaplow (1990, 1996a, 1998a), Mayshar (1991b), Slemrod (2001), and Slemrod and Yitzhaki (1987).

[25] Realistically, under a linear system there may continue to be tax-exempt entities such as domestic nonprofit organizations and certain foreign taxpayers.

[26] As another example, considered in subsection 9.B.1, many analysts favor a cash-flow consumption tax over an income tax primarily on account of administrative and enforcement concerns, which are viewed to be more important than what may be fairly modest real differences between (pure) consumption and income taxes.

Another issue posed by problems of administration and enforcement concerns the role of commodity taxes, such as a sales tax or VAT, as a substitute for or a supplement to an income tax. As chapter 6 explores, as a first approximation commodities should be taxed uniformly; moreover, a uniform commodity tax is equivalent to a linear labor income tax, or a uniform adjustment to a nonlinear income tax. Hence, on grounds of administrative convenience, it would seem best to dispense with commodity taxation altogether.[27] Difficulties in income tax enforcement, however, may lead to different conclusions. As noted in subsection 6.C.5, in the case in which income taxation is largely infeasible, such as may be true in developing economies, one must rely entirely on commodity taxes (and other forms of taxation), in which event the analysis of optimal taxation is qualitatively different.[28] More broadly, theoretically equivalent taxes—notably, a proportional wage tax and uniform sales taxes or VATs—may not be equivalent to administer and enforce because of the types of entities involved in compliance. Kopczuk and Slemrod (2006) show how some tax bases may be preferable because of their greater reliance on remittances by firms that engage more in arm's-length transactions that are more difficult to hide from tax authorities.

It has been further suggested that commodity taxes may be an important supplement to income taxes when there is substantial evasion in some sectors, notably the cash economy (likely to include many self-employed, providers of small-scale services, and those engaged in illegal activity). The intuition is that individuals who evade the income tax would still pay taxes on their consumption (in most sectors). Yet Kesselman (1993) shows that, when general equilibrium effects on prices and wages are taken into account, this idea is incorrect in the case in which commodity taxes are fully evaded in the same sectors as those in which the income tax is evaded—a plausible scenario since commodity tax

---

[27] Or, if a linear income tax were best, all things considered, one would choose between a linear income tax and a uniform commodity tax system based on which was cheapest in terms of administrative and compliance costs rather than relying on some mix of the two.

[28] For an explanation of how evasion through operation in cash influences tax structures in developing countries, see Gordon and Li (2005).

evasion typically will be both possible in such cases and also necessary to avoid detection of the income tax evasion. The reason is that the ultimate incidence is the same regardless of whether a tax is levied on a producer's inputs (in particular, labor) or on sales. Switching from labor income taxes to commodity taxes therefore fails to reduce the ultimate burden borne by suppliers in the taxed sector; all that matters is the sum of the taxes on income and on consumption, contradicting the notion that multiple taxes at lower rates have an inherent advantage over a single tax at a high rate. Kesselman does find some benefit to shifting toward commodity taxation when evasion of it (unlike evasion of the income tax) is incomplete, but he argues that this benefit is small for plausible parameter values.[29]

2. Lack of Comprehensive Tax Base

The income taxes considered thus far are presumed to tax all income, whereas actual income tax systems contain myriad deductions, exemptions, credits, and so forth. Many deviations reflect administrative considerations: Taxing imputed income may be thought impractical; certain fringe benefits (aspects of working conditions that have elements of consumption) may not be expressly exempt but may effectively go untaxed; and, when capital income is also taxed, measurement involves simplifications through standard depreciation schedules and deductibility of intangibles (notably, R&D and marketing) and through the realization requirement for gains and losses.[30] Other departures reflect distinct policy considerations: Deductions for charitable contributions or conservation expenditures and special treatment of R&D might be seen as corrective taxes. In addition, tax preferences may lack normative justification but exist due to the efforts of organized interest groups.

Many of these deviations from a comprehensive tax base are akin to differential commodity taxation, the subject of chapter 6. The analysis

---

[29] Boadway, Marchand, and Pestieau (1994) find supplementation with commodity taxation to be desirable in a model in which commodity taxation, unlike income taxation, is not subject to evasion.

[30] Whether capital income should be taxed at all is another question, considered in chapter 9.

there will suggest that most departures from uniformity are likely to be suboptimal. For those resulting from administrative convenience, direct cost savings should be traded off against the cost of distortions. Even if that is done properly, however, some differentiation will remain, in addition to that which may be inevitable due to political forces. Taking this state of affairs as given, we can ask how optimal income taxation is affected.

The analysis is similar to that in the case of avoidance and evasion and, as noted in subsection 1, is related as well to the broader focus on the elasticity of taxable income.[31] A higher stated tax rate on a less-than-comprehensive base will be associated with a lower effective rate on total income. Because that effective rate is associated with more distortion than if it were the result of a lower nominal rate on a more comprehensive tax base, less redistribution will tend to be optimal. Nevertheless, the effect on the level of nominal tax rates is formally ambiguous, for a given nominal rate now bears less harshly on the labor-leisure choice and results in less redistribution (leaving a wider dispersion among individuals in the marginal social value of disposable income).[32]

As in the case of tax avoidance and evasion, the optimal tax policy involves setting both tax rates and other dimensions of government policy so that each is optimal in light of the others. Slemrod and Kopczuk (2002) examine this problem for the case of the breadth of the tax base in a model in which only administrative cost considerations interfere with comprehensive income taxation.[33] Their main conclusions are

---

[31] See, for example, Kaplow (1990, 1996a), Kopczuk (2005), Mayshar (1991b), Slemrod (2001), Slemrod and Kopczuk (2002), and Yitzhaki (1979).

[32] The relevant phenomena can be seen from examining the various first-order conditions in chapter 4, taking into account that the elasticity now has a different interpretation, that pertinent shadow prices are affected, and that the other values on the right side of these conditions are endogenous. To illustrate the possibility of higher stated tax rates being optimal, suppose that there is little substitution between expenditures producing deductions or exclusions and those fully taxed. Then a given stated rate on the narrow base would have consequences similar to those of a lower stated rate on a comprehensive base. Accordingly, a higher stated rate would be optimal on the narrower base than on the comprehensive base.

[33] Arguably, similar logic is pertinent to political forces: The greater the cost of special interest tax provisions, the more one might expect them to be resisted. Indeed, sometimes

that a social desire for a more redistributive tax system should be accompanied by greater administrative expenditures to broaden the base; similarly, the more costly it is to expand the base, the less redistribution is optimal.[34]

C. Income and Ability

1. Taxation of Earning Ability

The second theorem of welfare economics holds that any Pareto optimum—corresponding to any desired distribution of welfare—is obtainable if individualized lump-sum taxes are available. The assumed infeasibility of such nondistortionary individualized taxes is the reason that society must use a distortionary income tax to achieve distributive objectives. Nevertheless, following Mirrlees's (1971) suggestion, it is worth exploring idealized taxes because it may be possible to identify partial measures that improve the distribution–distortion tradeoff even if they cannot eliminate it.

The individualized lump-sum taxes of the second welfare theorem are, in the present setting, ability taxes, for it is the ability to earn income that is assumed to vary among individuals. A first-best tax would be entirely a function of ability. Relative to any scheme that involves distortionary income taxation, ability taxation could be used to achieve a Pareto improvement. For individuals of any ability level (type), substitute a lump-sum tax (or transfer) equal to the amount that the corresponding type of individual pays (or receives) under the existing tax-transfer scheme. This alternative scheme raises the same net revenue. Furthermore, individuals are all better off: If behavior (labor effort) is held constant, utility is unaffected; but since the marginal return to work is no

---

pressure for more tax revenue is met by closing loopholes. On the other hand, the higher are marginal tax rates, the more special interest groups gain from deductions and exemptions. This latter view is consistent with the simultaneous reduction of rates and broadening of the tax base in the United States and some other countries in recent decades, although other explanations obviously exist.

[34] Kopczuk (2005) analyzes the base broadening of the 1986 Tax Reform Act in this light.

longer taxed, individuals will all choose to work more, which they only opt to do because their utility is thereby increased.[35] Note that even if the initial income tax scheme achieves a second-best optimum, this new nondistortionary scheme generally would not be optimal. Further redistribution could be accomplished distortion free, and under standard SWFs it would be optimal to do so until—actually past (see chapter 3, note 13)—the point of equality.[36]

With regard to the practical limitations on the observability of ability, it is worth keeping in mind, as subsection B.1 indicates, that serious difficulties in measuring income have hardly led to the abandonment of income taxation.[37] Accordingly, consider three sorts of approaches to measuring ability.[38] First, for those with market earnings, ability could be inferred from income if labor effort, perhaps reflected by working hours, could be observed—a possibility considered further in subsection 7.D.2 on work inducements in transfer programs. After all, income

---

[35] In substituting the lump-sum tax for the income tax, there is no income effect, only a substitution effect. A qualification to the statement in the text is that very-low-ability individuals who do not work at all may still not work because they remain at a corner solution.

[36] Helpman and Sadka (1978) consider whether the optimal ability tax is progressive with respect to a base of full income. Allingham (1975) explores ability taxation in a setting in which individuals' preferences between consumption and leisure are heterogeneous (a problem considered independently of ability taxation in subsection 2).

[37] Another approach, not well developed in the literature, involves the use of menus to induce individuals to reveal more information about their abilities (other than by the level of income they earn). Individuals could be offered (ex ante) choices of tax schedules; schedules with lower marginal tax rates would have higher lump-sum taxes (or lower lump-sum transfers). Higher-ability types would select schemes with lower marginal rates—which would benefit them more given their higher productivity—and higher lump-sum payments, whereas lower-ability types would avoid high lump-sum payments and thus choose schemes with higher marginal rates. In general, incentive schemes of this sort are more efficient than schemes that constrain the principal (here, the government) to offer a single schedule to everyone. See Alesina and Weil (1992).

[38] This list is not exhaustive. To note one other possibility, ability might be inferred from *past* earnings, which would permit nondistortionary taxation in the future, although such a scheme presumes that, in the prior periods, individuals did not anticipate the subsequent regime. See subsection 9.C.2 on the relationship between this sort of scheme and a capital levy.

is simply the product of the wage or ability level and effort.[39] But hours are very difficult to observe in many sectors, including those for the self-employed and self-directed (many professionals and traveling sales-people, for example). Furthermore, even if hours could be measured crudely, true effort would still be difficult to assess. Work intensity varies greatly. Moreover, a tax that inferred ability from hours would lead to distortionary avoidance whereby individuals would inflate apparent hours and effort to lower the implied level of ability and therefore their tax burdens, by extending the work day, deeming commuting time and time on the telephone or Internet to be work, and so forth. As fewer jobs involve physical labor in readily observed routine tasks and as more production moves out of the formal workplace, such problems may well increase (although the feasibility of electronic monitoring may grow as well). Despite these substantial problems, however, it appears that coarse measurements should be possible. Given that underlying wages in the United States vary from $200 per week at the bottom to $2,000, $20,000, or more at the top, even hours or effort estimates with substantial errors may be highly probative.[40]

A second strategy would be to attempt to directly measure components of ability. Tests of general intelligence or other attributes believed to contribute to productivity could be employed, or one could look to other indicators of ability such as educational attainment. Unfortunately, as is well known from empirical work predicting income, such

---

[39] A related possibility is that wages may be directly observable, as suggested by Blomquist (1984). Basing taxes on observed wage levels would raise issues of manipulation similar to those arising when taxes are based on inferred wage levels and would also present the possibility explored later that basing taxes on wages would distort investments in human capital. In either case—whether wages are directly observed or inferred—as an alternative to ability taxation one could accomplish an equivalent result by taxing full income, including so-called imputed income from household production and leisure, thereby eliminating the disincentive to supplying market labor.

[40] The major source of error would likely be with regard to high-ability individuals who work part-time with flexible, self-directed schedules; they may successfully masquerade as individuals of lower ability. Additionally, talented individuals may choose jobs with lower effort requirements or higher nonpecuniary returns in other dimensions. As noted later, however, errors involving underestimation of ability at the high end of the distribution are less problematic than ones involving overestimation of ability at the low end.

measures explain only a modest portion of the variance. In part this limitation is due to the difficulty of estimating many important dimensions of skill, such as organization, perseverance, personality, and creativity, and in part this reflects large elements of luck. In addition, if such measures determined tax liability, measurement itself might be manipulated (individuals might attempt to perform poorly on a pertinent test), and all attempts to measure ability, directly or indirectly, including the income tax itself, would likely influence important elements of labor effort involving the accumulation of human capital. There are some limits to this problem because high-ability individuals probably derive greater utility (or suffer less disutility) from such investments, but if these activities were taxed more directly, greater distortion of them may be expected to occur.[41]

A third method would be to look to readily observable attributes to infer ability. Most notably, one might infer low earning ability from physical disabilities, as is done under both social and private insurance arrangements. Other aspects of health status, gender, age, race, geography (location), occupation, and additional factors might also correlate with earning ability (although some, such as occupation, are endogenous, as is income).

In all, many potential means of identifying ability exist, most of which are undoubtedly highly imperfect and are accompanied by incentive and other costs or limitations. However, because the alternative is to rely on income as the sole proxy for ability, which itself is imperfectly measured and the taxation of which involves significant distortion, some use of other measures would probably improve welfare. Unfortunately, this problem has received only limited attention.

Stern (1982) offers the most direct analysis of the problem. He compares an ability tax—supplemented by a purely proportional income

---

[41] Blumkin and Sadka (2005) show that, if education is a signal of ability, then, abstracting from other factors (for example, liquidity constraints), some tax on education is optimal if the benefits are sufficiently large (larger benefits arise when the welfare gain from redistribution is large, the labor supply elasticity is high, and the distortion of the educational decision is low). A (perhaps small) positive tax is not always desirable even when education signals ability, because there is a preexisting distortion of the educational decision due to the income tax, which implies the desirability of a subsidy if the ability-signaling effect is not sufficiently large.

tax—with an optimal nonlinear income tax.[42] He assumes that classification according to ability (but not income) is subject to some level of error and considers how large the errors have to be under the ability tax to make a pure nonlinear income tax preferable. Unfortunately, this is not a clean comparison, both because income is assumed to be perfectly observable and because he links the ability tax to a different income tax (a linear one) than in his pure (nonlinear) income tax regime.[43]

Stern's principal qualitative finding is that, the greater is the preference for equality, the less attractive is an ability-tax scheme. The reason is that mistakes in which low-ability individuals are misclassified as high-ability types (requiring them to pay high taxes despite their limited ability to pay) are more costly as greater weight is placed on the well-being of low-ability individuals. (For similar reasons, Mirrlees (1990) finds that large errors in income measurement under an income tax may favor a lower marginal income tax rate, and that the extent to which this is so may be greater the stronger is the social preference for redistribution.) Stern suggests that the most likely errors might involve the opposite sort of misclassification because low-ability individuals would never attempt to masquerade as high-ability types. If few errors involve low types being misclassified as high types, reliance on an ability tax is attractive even when the error rate is rather high. Nevertheless, because high-ability individuals have an incentive to mimic low-ability types, a tax authority will find itself primarily concerned with classifying as high ability some of those individuals who represent themselves as having low ability, which may include individuals who actually are of low ability. In that case, as noted, ability taxation is less attractive. In any event, Stern's analysis implicitly suggests that the level of resources devoted to classification and the choice of proof burdens are important features of any attempt to base taxation on indicators of ability (or, for that matter, on income).[44]

---

[42] See also the simulations in Carruth (1982), which further explore Stern's model in light of the general equilibrium effects on wages examined by Allen (1982), the subject of subsection E.3.

[43] Furthermore, a nonlinear income tax can often perform quite well, without supplementation, in the sort of two-type model that he analyzes.

[44] For example, if a system embodied a strong presumption of low ability in the absence of clear evidence to the contrary, the pattern of error would fit Stern's latter case, whereas if

As noted, the model analyzed by Stern is special in a number of respects. To analyze the case of imperfect observation of ability more generally, it is helpful to think of the government as being able to set a separate income tax and transfer schedule for each group that can be separately identified according to some signal(s).[45] Let θ (possibly a vector) denote the observed parameter(s), (each of) which can be interpreted as an index of discrete classifications or as a continuous variable. The first-order condition (4.10) for the optimal nonlinear income tax (the case without income effects) becomes

$$\frac{T'(w^* l^*, \theta)}{1 - T'(w^* l^*, \theta)} = \frac{1 - F(w^*, \theta)}{\xi^* w^* f(w^*, \theta)} \frac{\int_{w^*}^{\infty} \left(1 - \frac{W'(u(w))u_c}{\lambda}\right) f(w, \theta) dw}{1 - F(w^*, \theta)}.$$

(5.1)

The only difference between expressions (5.1) and (4.10) is that the tax function, T, in (5.1) is allowed to depend on θ and the density and distribution functions, f and F, depend on θ.[46] The optimizations for each value of θ are linked by the common shadow price on revenue, λ.[47]

---

one insisted on the best guess as to ability level—adjusting the inference to take account of high-ability individuals' incentive to pass themselves off as low-ability types—the pattern of errors would be more symmetric. On burdens of proof in disability classification, see Diamond and Sheshinski (1995), and on accuracy and the income tax in general, see Kaplow (1998a).

[45] Akerlof (1978), noted later, and Bennett (1987) consider models with only lump-sum transfers, which can be varied by observed type. Similarly, Parsons (1996) extends Akerlof (1978) to consider two-sided errors (some disabled individuals classified as able and some able classified as disabled), but there are only two types of individuals and two levels of effort (work and no work), so many features of an optimal income tax schedule cannot be explored.

[46] Additional possibilities are raised if individuals' utility functions are allowed to differ across groups and thus depend on θ, as is portrayed in expression (12.9), which is introduced in chapter 12 for purposes of examining the taxation of different family groupings. Roberts (1984) finds it useful for an optimal income tax to depend on observable indexes that are correlated with individuals' marginal utilities of income, although the optimal extent of such adjustments is limited by the extent to which individuals are induced to manipulate the indexes.

[47] One can think of the marginal dollar being distributed pro rata across the entire population or being concentrated on certain groups; which assumption is made does not

In general, the optimal income tax schedule will depend nontrivially on any variable that is correlated with ability. Suppose, for example, that there are two identifiable groups that have different distributions of ability. (The groups could overlap; indeed, they may be only modestly different. Put another way, the signal θ could be noisy to any degree.) Starting from identical schedules, it would tend to be optimal to increase the lump-sum grant to the group with lower ability and reduce the grant to the group with higher ability.[48] The optimal adjustment of the schedule of marginal tax rates is more subtle because it depends importantly on the degree of dispersion within the group. Taking the limiting case in which one of the groups is homogeneous (all of one type), it is clear that the optimum would involve a zero marginal tax rate, with all redistribution to or from that group being implemented through a lump-sum transfer or tax. This is essentially the structure of Akerlof's (1978) model, in which it is assumed that a subset of the lowest-ability group can be identified ("tagged"). Kremer (2001) considers the possibility that income tax schedules might depend explicitly on age and finds in a static setting (ignoring the interdependence of earnings and consumption decisions across time) that it may be optimal to tax the young at lower marginal rates because of the difference in their distribution of skills—$(1-F)/f$ may be substantially lower—and their possibly higher labor supply elasticity. (Kremer offers similar observations regarding older workers, women, and some racial minorities.) A more general discussion of the problem for the case in which ability is observed imperfectly, which focuses on marginal tax rates as well as the level of the grant, appears in section 7.C on categorical assistance (such as in transfer systems that provide more generous treatment to individuals who have children or are disabled). See also subsection 12.B.1.b on the possibility of taxing spouses under different schedules.

---

matter because, at the optimum, the marginal social value of increasing the transfer will be the same for all groups.

    [48] In the optimal nonlinear income tax problem, there is no explicit grant g, but as chapter 4 notes, for purposes of interpretation g is taken to equal $-T(0)$. The statement in the text is crude because the mean ability level is not the only relevant factor; however, except by coincidence, a standard SWF will not lead to the same grant being optimal for two different distributions of ability.

Ability-based taxation also suffers from limited empirical and applied analysis. There is little evidence regarding how good of a measure of ability is feasible. Similarly, there has been little attention to the likely magnitude of the error costs and secondary distortions that would result from the use of various proxies for ability. Yet, as previously noted, ability-based features characterize many existing programs. Some depend on the observation of individuals' disabilities. Other proxies figure into eligibility requirements for various welfare and job training programs. Perhaps most notable are work requirements for welfare eligibility (which are relaxed for those having young children or demonstrated disabilities). Furthermore, one way to view work requirements is by reference to the observability of hours, discussed earlier, which is a task that these programs implicitly assume to be feasible, at least roughly, for lower-income individuals.[49] (Additional discussion of work inducements in transfer programs appears in section 7.D.)

Although ability-based taxation is no panacea for ameliorating the labor-leisure distortion, it may have important unrealized potential that deserves further exploration, and its current uses should be thoroughly assessed. As mentioned, the potential importance of ability-related taxation is reinforced by the fact that measurement problems also impede our capacity to use income taxation to accomplish redistribution.

2. Income as an Indicator of Ability versus Preferences

In standard formulations of the optimal income taxation problem, earning ability is the only source of heterogeneity, and income is an unambiguous signal of ability. If individuals vary, however, in how their consumption is transformed into utility or their labor effort into disutility, then what income signals is ambiguous, which makes the problem more complex.[50] This difficulty is not merely technical; many have

---

[49] The aforementioned circumvention wherein individuals work more hours at a lower wage may be limited by the presence of a binding minimum wage. Alternatively, a program could specify a target minimum wage for purposes of assessing compliance with work requirements.

[50] Income may be a noisy signal of ability for reasons other than heterogeneity in individuals' preferences. When nonpecuniary aspects of jobs vary, compensating wage differentials

suspected that the nature of the optimum may change in important ways. Perhaps high income is a signal of a high value of consumption, which may appear to favor taxation that is less redistributive. Or high income might signal a low disutility of labor, seemingly justifying more redistributive taxation. Although such conjectures have been informally expressed, the issue has received little sustained attention.[51] It turns out that this problem is rather subtle and that common intuitions are potentially misleading because they do not take into account either adjustments in labor effort or all relevant effects on marginal and total utility. The analysis to follow attempts to provide a fuller understanding of the subject, although it is heuristic and incomplete.[52]

Suppose that individuals' utility takes the form $u(\gamma c, \delta l)$, where γ and δ are positive constants that vary among individuals and are unobservable to the government. A higher level of γ indicates that an individual is more efficient in converting tangible consumption into utility from consumption. (Possible reasons include different skill in home production and different tastes.[53]) A higher level of δ means that an individual suffers more disutility from a given level of labor effort. (Reasons may concern labor effort per se and tastes for leisure time.)

---

arise, in which case income signals a mix of ability and working conditions. If occupation and thus the likely extent of compensating differentials are observable, it would tend to be optimal to adjust income tax liability.

[51] Ebert (1988) and Tarkiainen and Tuomala (1999) examine largely technical issues presented by adding another unobservable trait. Tarkiainen and Tuomala (1999) do offer some simulations, but given the special features of their example and that the mean of the parameters in their two-dimensional case differs, often significantly, from values in the one-dimensional case, it is hard to interpret their claim that optimal redistribution is greater in the two-dimensional case. Sandmo (1993) examines the case in which tastes vary but earning abilities do not. See also Boadway et al. (2002), focusing on which self-selection constraints are binding in a model in which preferences are of two types; note 63, discussing an example in Stiglitz (1987); and Strnad (2004).

[52] For further exploration that emphasizes how heterogeneity in preferences affects the relationship between optimal income taxation, on one hand, and optimal commodity taxation, public goods provision, and Pigouvian taxation, on the other hand, see Kaplow (2007e).

[53] Apps and Rees (1999) consider a version of the former case.

In examining this model, attention will be confined to the linear income tax. The first-order condition for individuals' choice of labor effort can be expressed as

$$u_1 = -\frac{\delta}{\gamma w(1-t)} u_2,$$ (5.2)

where u_i denotes the derivative of utility with respect to its ith argument. The two expressions embodying the first-order condition for the optimal linear income tax, (4.7) and (4.8), reproduced here for convenience, are

$$\frac{t}{1-t} = -\frac{\text{cov}(\alpha(w), y(w))}{\int y(w)\varepsilon(w)f(w)dw},$$ (5.3)

$$\alpha(w) = \frac{W'u_c(w)}{\lambda} + tw\left(\frac{\partial l(w)}{\partial g}\right).$$ (5.4)

(As noted in chapter 4, any interpretation is complicated by income effects and the fact that values are endogenous, matters that will not be considered further here.) To determine how the first-order condition of the optimal linear income tax problem is influenced, let us begin with a generic effect involving the relationship between ability and income. For any initial distribution of w, introducing heterogeneity with respect to γ or δ will tend to produce more variation in the resulting distribution of y. (Whether and when this occurs is discussed later.) Ceteris paribus, a greater variation in y tends to favor a higher t, that is, a more redistributive income tax, as can be seen from condition (5.3).[54]

There are three qualifications to this basic claim about the effect on the optimal level of redistribution of adding heterogeneity to the model. First, most simulations use data on the distribution of y rather than of w; hence, to the extent that a given distribution of w implies a wider distribution of y on account of other sources of heterogeneity, this effect would already be reflected in the assessment. Indeed, for a given, observed distribution of y, greater heterogeneity with respect to γ or δ will tend to be associated with less variation in the underlying distribution

---

[54] This suggestion is reinforced by Kanbur and Tuomala's (1994) simulations for the nonlinear case (reported in subsection 4.B.3.c) that consider different distributions of ability.

of w, which tends to favor a less redistributive income tax. Second, this tendency assumes that the distributions of γ and δ are independent of the distribution of w. Positive or negative correlations could augment or offset this tendency. Finally, which combination of γ, δ, and w produces a given level of y may have other effects, notably on α, the net social marginal valuation of income; see expression (5.4).[55] Indeed, such effects are the source of existing conjectures about the problem; to their analysis we now turn.

First, hold γ constant and consider differences in the disutility of labor effort, δ. Individuals' first-order condition (5.2) indicates that those with higher levels of δ will choose lower levels of l, yielding lower levels of y (making the standard assumptions that u_1 rises as consumption falls, the magnitude of u_2 falls as labor effort falls, and cross-effects are not too large). Therefore, when the government observes two individuals with the same level of y, if one of them has (unobservably) bad luck regarding δ—an above-average disutility of labor effort—it must be that the individual also has (unobservably) good fortune regarding w. (Recall that we are holding γ constant.) Indeed, these effects must be perfectly offsetting in all relevant respects. Specifically, if y is the same, it must be that δ and w are higher by the same proportion, which is to say that δ/w is the same. This is most easily seen if, in $u(\gamma c, \delta l)$, one substitutes y/w for l, giving $u(\gamma c, (\delta/w)y)$. Examining this formulation and the first-order condition (5.2) makes it apparent that the ratio δ/w determines income (again, making the standard assumptions about u).[56]

Hence, individuals with different levels of δ who nevertheless have the same y have the same marginal utility of consumption (which is γu_1 in this case) and also the same total utility, implying that W' is also the same. Accordingly, the first term of (5.4), the direct indication of the

---

[55] It may also influence the elasticity, ε.

[56] Suppose that (holding γ constant) two individuals with the same y had different ratios, δ/w. Intuitively, the individual with the higher ratio would also have a higher magnitude of u_2, as is apparent from the reformulated utility function, whereas the level of u_1 is the same (ignoring cross-effects). The first-order condition (5.2) could not hold for both individuals (if cross-effects are not too large). Formally, one can differentiate the first-order condition, with δ and w changing in the same proportion, to show that l adjusts so as to keep income y constant.

marginal social value of income, is the same for both individuals. (Furthermore, it can be shown that, if both δ and w are changed by the same proportion, the income effect term in (5.4) is unchanged as well.) In sum, for any observed level of y, heterogeneity with regard to δ has no effect on the optimization problem once one takes into account how behavior adjusts, as well as the implications of different levels of δ for the level of w that must exist to produce a given level of income. Nevertheless, it remains true that heterogeneity in δ, for a given distribution of w, will tend to produce greater dispersion in y, which as noted tends to favor a more redistributive linear income tax. Before leaving the subject of differences in δ, however, it should be emphasized that the foregoing demonstration pertains to one particular formulation of the utility function; others could readily yield different, more complex results.[57]

Second, hold δ constant and consider differences in the efficiency of converting consumption into utility, γ. From the first-order condition (5.2), it is not obvious how differences in the level of γ will influence individuals' choices of labor effort. Although a higher level of γ reduces the value of the right side, ceteris paribus, it also reduces the value of the left side because u_1 is lower when γc is higher. The intuition is that a higher level of γ encourages labor effort because such effort is ultimately more productive in a sense, but it also reduces the marginal utility of returns from labor effort because it implies a higher preexisting level of effective consumption.

To make this idea concrete, consider an additively separable utility function wherein the first component is logarithmic in effective consumption (that is, there is constant relative risk aversion of one; see

---

[57] Consider, for example, the simple variation in which utility takes the form $u(\gamma c, \delta(1 - l))$, so now the second argument of the utility function depends on leisure rather than labor and the interpretation is that a high δ indicates a high utility of leisure rather than a high disutility of labor. Under this formulation, raising δ and w has the additional effect (supposing for the moment that l falls so as to keep income constant) of raising effective leisure, which is ordinarily taken to be subject to diminishing marginal utility. Accordingly, l will not fall sufficiently to keep income constant (and in principle l could even rise), presenting a qualitatively different and more complicated case than that in the text. This contrast further suggests that the cardinalization of utility functions—a more pressing issue when tastes are heterogeneous—may affect the nature of the optimum (see also Boadway et al. 2002 and Sandmo 1993).

expression (3.3)): $u(\gamma c, \delta l) = \ln(\gamma c) - z(\delta l)$. The first-order condition (5.2) for this utility function is

$$\frac{1}{\gamma c} = \frac{\delta}{\gamma w(1-t)} z'. \tag{5.5}$$

The effect of γ on each side is precisely offsetting, so individuals' choices of l and their levels of y are unaffected. Accordingly, the notion that an additional dimension of unobservable heterogeneity tends to imply a greater dispersion in the distribution of y (for a given distribution of w) is false in this particular case. Furthermore, the marginal utility of consumption is unaffected (it is $(1/\gamma c)\gamma = 1/c$), so one channel of effect on the first term of (5.4) is removed. It is true, however, that, for a given level of income, total utility is higher when γ is higher, so if the welfare function W is strictly concave in individuals' utilities, the first term of (5.4) does vary with the unobservable parameter γ.[58] The effect of this additional source of dispersion in α for any given y on the optimal level of redistributive taxation is rather subtle and ambiguous.[59]

The foregoing illustration shows that the standard intuition that individuals who are more efficient in converting consumption to utility will have a higher marginal utility of consumption is not generally correct.[60] For other utility functions, specifically, those for which the coefficient of relative risk aversion is less (greater) than one, individuals with a higher γ will have a higher (lower) marginal utility of consumption because the diminishing-marginal-utility effect is less (greater) than the efficiency effect.[61] In such cases, a given distribution of w will

---

[58] For this particular utility function, it can be shown that the income effect term in (5.4) is unchanged for a given y as γ varies.

[59] Although greater dispersion in α raises the magnitude of the covariance in (5.3), the increase in noise in the relationship between α and y reduces the magnitude of the correlation between the variables, which reduces the magnitude of the covariance. Which effect is larger would depend, among other things, on the distribution of γ, on how that distribution varies with w, and on the concavity of W at different levels of utility.

[60] Sandmo (1993) obtains the same result in a model in which individuals differ only in their preferences and not in their earning abilities.

[61] Suppose that utility from consumption takes the constant-relative-risk-aversion form in expression (3.3), where ρ is the risk-aversion coefficient. Then we have $u(\gamma c, \delta l) =$

be associated with a more dispersed distribution of y, tending to favor more redistribution, ceteris paribus. But this is not the only effect. If relative risk aversion is less than one, higher income tends to signal a higher γ, which in turn indicates a higher marginal utility of consumption, and if this effect more than offsets any contrary effect when W is strictly concave, then the magnitude of the covariance between α and y is reduced, favoring less redistribution on this account (and conversely if the effect from the concavity of W is dominant).[62] If instead relative risk aversion exceeds one, a higher γ is associated with a lower marginal utility of consumption, so individuals of a given w work less; hence, higher income tends to signal a lower γ, and in this case a lower γ indicates a higher marginal utility of consumption, favoring less redistribution, an effect that is accentuated to the extent that W is strictly concave. In sum, the relationship between differences in the efficiency of converting consumption to utility, γ, and the optimal level of a linear income tax is hardly straightforward, and it is dependent on the assumed functional form.[63]

$(\gamma c)^{1-\rho}/(1-\rho) - z(\delta l)$. The marginal utility of consumption is $\gamma^{1-\rho} c^{-\rho}$, which is rising (falling) in γ if ρ is less (greater) than one.

[62] The concavity of W is relevant because, in this instance, a higher γ implies a higher utility level and thus a lower level of W'. In the case that follows in the text, the lower level of γ that is signaled implies a lower utility level and thus a higher level of W'.

[63] This sensitivity to functional form includes more than the coefficient of relative risk aversion. Suppose, for example, that the first component of separable utility was $\ln(c^\gamma)$ rather than $\ln(c\gamma)$. Then, consistent with the familiar intuition, a higher level of γ would lead an individual to choose a higher level of l, and the marginal utility of consumption for a given y would be higher. Stiglitz (1987, pp. 1018–1019) offers an entirely different example in which the utility from both consumption and leisure—really, utility as a whole—is multiplied by a common factor. He observes that—when that factor has a sufficiently strong positive correlation with w and, moreover, marginal utility declines very gradually (much more so than ordinarily supposed)—it is possible for a utilitarian welfare function to favor redistribution toward the rich. (A more concave SWF may favor greater redistribution toward the poor if higher-earning-ability individuals also had higher levels of utility for a given level of earnings.) In any event, it is hardly obvious that, if ability to generate utility varies, those who are most productive in the labor force will tend to be much more effective at enjoying both consumption and leisure.

D. Interdependent Preferences

Most analysis of optimal income taxation assumes that well-being depends only on each individual's own consumption and level of labor effort, not also on those of others. If individuals also care about others or if others' situations otherwise bear on an individual's own utility, the optimal extent of redistribution may differ.[64]

Initially, consider a sort of generalized altruism, in which individuals care to some extent about overall social welfare.[65] As a first approximation, such preferences would not directly affect the analysis but rather would indicate that maximization of social welfare is all the more valuable.[66]

If individuals' altruism is more focused, in particular if there is a greater concern for the poor, then more redistribution than otherwise would tend to be optimal. The analysis would be similar to that under an SWF that places additional weight at the bottom of the income distribution. For example, Hochman and Rodgers (1969) suggest that some degree of redistribution (although plausibly much less than indicated by a standard SWF) may even be Pareto optimal, assuming that literally all who are more well off have the stipulated preferences.

---

[64] For discussion of whether such other-regarding preferences should be credited in normative assessment, see subsection 13.B.3.

[65] Individuals having a preference regarding the level of social welfare should be distinguished from their having an opinion about social welfare.

[66] Formally, if individuals' utility is additively separable with respect to the preference for social welfare and if the SWF is utilitarian, then the maximization problem would be fully equivalent. In other instances, there may be subtle effects, for example, if the level of social welfare affects individuals' marginal utility of consumption or if the SWF is strictly concave so that individuals' utility levels (now presumed to depend on the level of social welfare) matter. In such cases, the objective would remain the maximization of the stipulated SWF, although the precise solution could differ. In the latter example, for instance, if raising social welfare increased all individuals' utility by the same amount, the higher utility level at the bottom would reduce the optimal extent of redistribution. The foregoing assumes that individuals' preferences are for social welfare as defined by the SWF; if individuals' preferences instead relate to a different notion of welfare, then the optimum according to the given SWF would, to an extent, move toward the optimum under individuals' preferred SWF(s).

Observe that this consideration is premised not only on altruism toward the poor but also on a lack of altruism toward others more broadly; as previously indicated, a generalized (unweighted) altruism has no particular effect on the optimal extent of redistribution. Motivations for more focused concern include tangible externalities—for example, if the poor commit more crime in the absence of additional redistribution—as well as psychological externalities, which might be triggered by direct contact with homeless people. In these cases, redistribution may, following Pauly (1973), be more of a local public good, helping to explain local jurisdictions' motivation for engaging in redistribution. It is sometimes suggested that, in light of these sorts of considerations, a poverty measure (or an inequality index) should be deemed a component of a broader SWF.[67] This conclusion does not follow, however, because the basis for additional redistribution depends on what individuals' preferences happen to be, which in turn may depend on how redistribution affects crime and so forth. Various poverty measures may or may not be well correlated with such factors and in any event should be viewed as providing proxies for elements of social welfare rather than being constituents of social welfare (see section 15.A).

Aside from altruism, generalized or otherwise, individuals may be influenced by the effect of redistribution on others as a whole, particularly with regard to the overall level of consumption. To the extent that greater redistribution tends to reduce average consumption due to incentive effects, there could be negative externalities if aggregate production involves positive spillovers (for example, through learning effects or innovation) or if there are network externalities.[68] Negative effects of total consumption are also possible, which would favor greater redistribution. Tangible externalities, such as from pollution and congestion, may be reduced as labor supply and production fall. (Subsection E.4

---

[67] Wane (2001) offers an analysis of the optimal income tax problem when a poverty index is taken to be a component of welfare.

[68] In light of income effects, redistribution could increase average consumption, reversing the arguments in the text. A more particular qualification is that redistribution itself could enhance favorable network externalities. For example, the density of Internet usage may rise with equality even if total income is reduced.

considers this and other nontax distortions.) Adverse psychological effects of higher consumption by others, however, have probably received the greatest attention over the ages.

Veblen (1899), Duesenberry (1949), and a number of more recent analysts such as Frank (1984a, 1984b, 1985, 1999) have identified individuals' concern for status and their related envy about others' consumption as important issues, with some suggestion that greater redistribution would provide a corrective.[69] Put another way, even if everyone were identical in ability, a no-tax equilibrium may be distorted as individuals engage in excessive work to support extravagant lifestyles that are personally rewarding but reduce others' well-being.[70] However, redistribution, through reduced overall consumption, serves as a corrective only under certain assumptions. First, individuals must care about the level of others' consumption and not just relative position or ranking, the latter being largely unaffected by redistribution.[71] Second, it must be that individuals are envious of others' consumption rather than of their well-being—for if preferences depend on the latter, there would tend not to be a direct effect on the social welfare optimum, just as in the previously noted opposite case of generalized altruism.[72] Specifically, the posited additional benefit of redistribution is that consumption and thus labor effort are too high, but if individuals seek to raise leisure (taken to be the only

---

[69] See also, for example, Hirsch (1976), Scitovsky (1976), McAdams (1992), and Ireland (1998, 2001).

[70] In this regard, Dupor and Liu (2003) usefully distinguish jealousy—individuals' utility is reduced by others' higher consumption—from "keeping up with the Joneses"—wherein individuals' marginal utility of their own consumption is raised by others' higher consumption. It is the former phenomenon that involves a negative externality, although the extent of the distortion may be enhanced when the latter is also present.

[71] The argument also assumes that after-tax income rather than before-tax income is the relevant magnitude for determining status or envy, but some have suggested otherwise (see Atkinson 1983).

[72] For example, Boskin and Sheshinski's (1978) demonstration that individuals' concern for relative status warrants greater redistribution assumes that relative income or consumption, not utility, is what is envied. The authors caution that the evidence for an extremely strong concern for relative consumption is "virtually nonexistent, let alone convincing" (1978, p. 599). For similar analyses, see Brennan (1973), Layard (1980), Oswald (1983), and also Tuomala (1990) for a survey and extensions.

other component of utility) as well as consumption, there may be no net distortion due to this phenomenon. Others' consumption may be more relevant if consumption is observable whereas leisure is not, but this hypothesis seems overly simple. Long vacations, frequent visits to second homes, spouses not in the labor force who engage in visible activities, appearances at country clubs rather than mere membership, time spent exercising in order to look physically fit, and various other leisure pursuits are noticed by others. In addition, many aspects of consumption are not.

It is sometimes suggested that the problem of conspicuous consumption may involve particular goods, justifying selective luxury taxation (which would otherwise tend to be inefficient; see chapter 6). If the relevant consumption activities cannot readily be identified or if they change too rapidly (such as with fashion), it may be that, again, a generalized tax on consumption—more redistributive taxation—would be desirable, in which case the already-noted qualifications are applicable. Note, however, that similar logic would also favor taxation of leisure endeavors thought to be undertaken to excess. Moreover, if these could not be identified, taxing all leisure—which effectively entails reducing the generalized tax on consumption—would be in order.

Finally, consider the possibility that individuals' long-run preferences tend to be relative, having a zero-sum character in society as a whole. The notion is that, in a given society at a particular moment in time, utility depends on relative position, but higher average consumption does not imply greater well-being either across societies or over time. Results from surveys of "happiness" from different countries are often offered in support of this proposition (see, for example, Easterlin 1973, 1974).[73] More localized evidence includes Frank (1984a, 1984b,

---

[73] For contrary evidence, see Gallup (1976). Some of the more recent work, surveyed by Easterlin (2001) and Frey and Stutzer (2002), focuses more heavily on longitudinal studies; see also Blanchflower and Oswald (2004). Easterlin (2001) notes important evidence against his thesis, namely that respondents at any point in time describe themselves as happier than in the past and less happy than they expect to be in the future. He rationalizes this finding with the argument that individuals are oblivious to their own shifts in aspirations. He does not, however, offer evidence rejecting the simpler explanation that happiness in fact rises

1985), indicating that highly talented individuals are willing to accept lower wages and less talented individuals require higher wages to work in the same firm, which suggests that the former must gain utility from being linked to others who rank lower and the latter must lose utility from their association with individuals whose position is superior. See also Luttmer (2005), offering evidence that individuals feel worse off when their neighbors earn more.

There is some basis for this utility-is-relative view in evolutionary psychology; specifically, preferences tend to be adaptive, as success is maximized by seeking improvements and avoiding being outdone by others. The extent to which the zero-sum postulate actually holds, however, is uncertain. Most happiness surveys employ a measurement instrument—namely, asking individuals how happy they are—that has built-in relativity (for the term in any society is of little use in communication unless it conveys different points along the spectrum that is relevant for that society).[74] Other shortcomings with the pertinent studies have also been identified, and contrary findings also appear in the literature.[75] In addition, certain behavior seems inconsistent with such a view, notably the affirmative wish of individuals with above-mean income in poor countries to emigrate to wealthy countries or regions and

---

with income over time while language usage at any time and place is relative, as noted in the text to follow.

[74] For comparison, as Easterlin (1974) acknowledges, words like "tall" are undoubtedly used comparatively; in a society in which individuals are tall by global or historical standards, if everyone was referred to as tall, even the relatively short, then no useful information would be conveyed (see Silver 1980). Luttmer (2005) is among the few to address this concern directly. Although he claims that his result is not driven by changes in people's definition of happiness, based on a consideration of other outcome measures, the two (of three) measures he considers that are most objective, depression and health status, do not support this conclusion. (There is some support from the depression measure, but he finds his result only for the lowest measured level, which is where the measure—like the happiness measure itself—is most subjective and thus most susceptible to the problem of definitional relativity that he is trying to dismiss.) See also Wierzbicka (2004), a linguist, who objects that the term "happiness" does not always translate well, there being significant, systematic differences across societies both in its meaning and in individuals' willingness to use such language in describing themselves.

[75] See, for example, Veenhoven (1991) and Hagerty and Veenhoven (2003).

the lack of desire of below-average-income individuals in rich countries to move to poorer countries.[76] Nevertheless, general understandings of human nature and the existing evidence provide some basis for expecting that utility levels are, to an extent, relative in the long run, with a sort of built-in mean reversion for society as a whole.[77]

Assuming that some relativistic tendency exists, what is the implication for the optimal degree of redistribution? To the extent that preferences are more relative than absolute, lower-income individuals should gain more from redistribution than otherwise, but higher-income individuals should lose more as well, so the net effect on the optimum is unclear. Also, the relevant comparison group is uncertain. Frank's (1984a, 1984b, 1985) investigations suggest that it is the workplace, but most redistribution is across workplaces.[78] Perhaps the long-run tendency of preferences to adjust suggests that the marginal utility of consumption rises more slowly with income than is generally believed. However, what matters for redistributive purposes is the relative marginal utility of the rich and the poor, determined by the curvature of the utility schedule (see subsection 3.B.2). For example, under a utilitarian SWF, if one multiplied everyone's utility by a common factor less than one and then added a common constant—indicating the same average utility but a flatter schedule—the maximization would be entirely

---

[76] It might be suggested that individuals willingly move to wealthier countries where they will occupy lower relative positions because of a sort of myopia under which they act on the short-term absolute gain, failing to appreciate the consequent relative loss. Under that view, however, one might also expect even successful individuals to return once they appreciate that their relative position is lower.

[77] It is generally believed that this tendency is more important for developed countries, it being more readily accepted that there are long-run differences in average utility between, say, a wealthy country and a country where most individuals live on the brink of starvation.

[78] Despite Frank's evidence, it is unclear that his interpretation is very plausible. Much comparison among individuals involves others in one's community (the focus of Luttmer 2005), former classmates, friends and relatives, and fellow religious congregants, not just peers at work. If spouses' preferences matter, this point is even more likely to be important. Additionally, individuals often change jobs, but any consumer durables obtained from prior earnings—automobiles, homes—do not automatically adjust. Finally, many individuals in the firms studied are likely not to know each other or even be much aware of each other's existence.

unaffected. For a strictly concave welfare function, the same transformation would reduce the optimal extent of redistribution because the modification would decrease the difference in utility levels between the rich and the poor. These prescriptions run counter to conventional wisdom on the subject.

E. Additional Considerations

1. Liquidity Constraints

The optimal level of redistribution may be greater than otherwise if redistribution enhances efficiency with respect to individuals who are liquidity constrained. One benefit concerns investment: Individuals with positive future prospects may be unable to raise funds to invest in their own human capital or entrepreneurship on account of asymmetric information or an inability to repay in certain states of the world. Redistribution can increase the initial availability of capital—since younger individuals may earn significantly less income than they do later in life—and can raise individuals' capacity to make payments when their realized income is below expectations.[79] In addition, liquidity constraints combined with a rising or hump-shaped earnings profile suggest that redistribution may efficiently facilitate consumption smoothing.[80]

The significance of liquidity constraints is disputed. Some research infers the existence of significant liquidity constraints from certain failures of the life-cycle hypothesis, although others suggest alternative explanations.[81] Additional evidence about the extent to which liquidity

---

[79] See Hoff and Lyon (1995), who further show that, among those who are able to obtain funds to invest in their human capital, some (the higher-risk individuals in that pool) will overinvest because they do not bear the full downside risk, whereas they would bear more of it under a redistributive scheme.

[80] See Polinsky (1974). Hubbard and Judd (1986) present simulations indicating that this benefit may be significant, favoring both more redistributive taxation and taxation of capital income (because it favors consumption in earlier years), although their commentators (Hall 1986 and Summers 1986) are more skeptical about the nature and magnitude of the problem.

[81] See, for example, note 80 and Meghir and Weber (1996), Runkle (1991), and Zeldes (1989).

constraints affect individuals is derived from using the behavior of un-constrained households to estimate desired debt by constrained house-holds, from inter vivos giving behavior, and from the reactions of po-tential or existing entrepreneurs to the receipt of inheritances.[82] Whatever is the extent to which individuals are liquidity constrained, however, it is not obvious that adjusting redistributive taxation is the most direct so-lution; for example, social security taxes might be reduced for the young and increased for the middle-aged. Nevertheless, to the extent that oth-erwise unalleviated liquidity constraints exist, the optimal degree of re-distribution may be greater. This possibility is one of many reasons that it is important to consider an intertemporal setting, explored further in chapters 9 and 11.[83]

2. Uncertain Labor Income

Another efficiency justification for some redistributive income taxation is that it serves as insurance against uncertain labor income.[84] Because of the concavity of utility in consumption—risk aversion—all individ-uals would, in the presence of uncertainty, prefer to have income transferred from high- to low-earning states, which a redistributive

---

[82] See, respectively, Cox and Jappelli (1993), Cox (1990), and Holtz-Eakin, Joulfaian, and Rosen (1994a, 1994b). See also Cameron and Taber (2004), who find an absence of evidence that borrowing constraints limit educational attainment, although their findings pertain to a regime in which various subsidies and loan programs are available, and Hurst and Lusardi (2004), who examine a range of evidence suggesting that liquidity constraints do not affect entrepreneurship, although they note that some of their findings may reflect the existence of government institutions that aid small businesses.

[83] Subsection 11.B.3 explicitly considers the relevance of liquidity constraints in analyzing forced savings under social security.

[84] See, for example, Eaton and Rosen (1980a, 1980b, 1980c), Tuomala (1990), Varian (1980), and the additional literature briefly surveyed in Kaplow (1994a). Subsequent work includes Strawczynski (1998), Low and Maldoom (2004), and Nishiyama and Smetters (2005). Unfortunately, although most of the literature frames the taxation and uncertainty problem as one that is equivalent to a standard insurance or principal-agent problem, little use is made of the analysis in those literatures. Nor is there much work that integrates such analysis with the optimal redistributive income taxation problem, in which ex ante heteroge-neity plays a central role.

income tax does.[85] Given that existing income taxes and optimal schemes examined in the literature often involve high marginal tax rates even without uncertainty, the optimal adjustment for uncertainty may not be that large, both because the preexisting distortion is significant and because quite substantial implicit insurance would already be provided.

The general problem of optimal income taxation in the presence of uncertainty has not been the subject of extensive study. Mirrlees's (1990) preliminary analysis (examining a linear income tax where the degree of variation in skill and the extent of uncertainty are assumed to be small) suggests that, taking as given the total variation in observed income, greater income uncertainty most plausibly favors a lower tax rate. For a given degree of aggregate variation, higher income uncertainty implies less variation in skill, and it turns out that skill variation is more powerful than income uncertainty in leading to a higher optimal tax rate.[86] (Uncertainty in future labor income also may have implications for capital taxation, as discussed in subsection 9.A.2.)

There are two caveats regarding the use of the income tax as insurance against uncertain labor income. First, to the extent that income uncertainty involves systematic risk, which to an extent it does, the government is not able to solve the problem: Its resulting budget uncertainty must be addressed, for example, by raising taxes or reducing spending if the resolution of uncertainty is adverse.[87] Second, the standard

---

[85] Varian's (1980) simulations suggest that, in light of moral hazard (that is, the labor-leisure distortion), the optimal level of insurance may be only a few percent, whereas Strawczynski's (1998) and Low and Maldoom's (2004) simulations suggest that high marginal tax rates may be optimal, and Nishiyama and Smetters's (2005) simulations indicate that a graduated income tax may be preferable to flat consumption tax proposals in the presence of significant uninsurable wage shocks.

[86] Tuomala (1990, section 9.3) offers a different analysis for a nonlinear income tax. He finds that uncertainty in wages at the time effort is chosen (capturing such decisions as investment in human capital and occupational choice) favors rising marginal tax rates, the intuition being that high realizations are substantially attributable to luck, so the disincentive effect of taxing them more heavily is modest. His results, however, are surprising in that the extent to which this is true increases as uncertainty falls, which seems to contradict both the given intuition and the results of his simulations elsewhere in the book that generally display falling marginal rates when there is no uncertainty.

[87] See, for example, Bulow and Summers (1984) and Gordon (1985).

analysis ignores private insurance, the possibility of which renders government insurance through taxation not only unnecessary but also inefficient. Specifically, if the main inhibitor of private income insurance is moral hazard, as much of the literature asserts, the government cannot combat it either; indeed, that is why there is a labor-leisure distortion from income taxation.[88] However, if adverse selection or other imperfections impede private insurance, then government insurance such as through taxation may be optimal. It should be kept in mind, however, that private and government insurance does exist for some important sources of uncertainty in labor income, notably for disability and temporary unemployment, and various other means allow individuals to mitigate income uncertainty to some extent.[89]

3. General Equilibrium Effects

Most work on optimal income taxation implicitly assumes that the tax system does not affect the distribution of pre-tax wages. Specifically, in the standard analysis all labor effort is of the same general type, so that ability differences consist entirely of different output rates per unit of effort. That is, a worker with twice the median ability performs the same work in half the time and thus receives twice the wage per hour. Because productivity is given, relative wages are fixed.

Some investigations instead consider a model in which there are two types of workers, skilled and unskilled, whose labor is qualitatively different.[90] For example, a doctor and a nurse supply related services, but

---

[88] See Kaplow (1994a), who explains that even if government insurance is not excessive, its presence will lead individuals to choose levels of private insurance that, combined with government insurance, are excessive. The reason is that a portion of the moral-hazard cost of private insurance is borne by the government. A further implication of this distortion is that, taking as given that there is significant income taxation (this sort of externality is present regardless of whether its level is augmented on account of uncertainty), it may be optimal to tax or otherwise restrict private insurance against income risk.

[89] See Cochrane (1991) and Mace (1991) for empirical evidence suggesting that, in the aggregate, individuals are substantially insured against income risks through private and public insurance and informal arrangements.

[90] See Feldstein (1973) for an initial exploration, followed by the work of Allen (1982), Carruth (1982), and Stiglitz (1982a).

the doctor's higher wage does not arise from doing exactly the same work, only more quickly. In this setting, income taxation can have conflicting effects. In addition to its standard, direct redistributive effect, reducing the labor effort of the skilled tends to raise their wages and reduce the wages of the unskilled, which increases inequality. On this account, it may be optimal for high-income individuals to face lower marginal tax rates than otherwise and for low-income individuals to face higher rates.[91] On the other hand, redistribution's tendency to reduce the labor supply of the least skilled (through both income and substitution effects) may increase their wages and thus further reduce inequality. This subject, unfortunately, has received little attention in recent decades, and existing results and empirical evidence do not confidently indicate the likely importance of this phenomenon.[92]

4. Nontax Distortions

The optimal extent of redistributive labor income taxation will depend on other distortions that affect individuals' choices between labor and leisure.[93] For example, if monopoly pricing is widespread in the economy, there is a wedge between individuals' marginal productivity and what they are able to buy. That is, there already is a distortion against market labor, and a labor income tax would exacerbate the preexisting distortion.[94] Because the marginal cost of distortion rises with the magnitude of distortion, this consideration favors lower income tax rates.

Other distortions, however, may make it efficient to increase leisure above no-tax levels. For example, much market production causes

---

[91] This implies that, in models in which the optimal tax rate on the highest-income individual would otherwise be zero, the optimal rate in this setting is negative.

[92] Feldstein's (1973) simulations identify subtle countervailing effects and furthermore suggest that only modest error in calculating optimal tax rates may result from failing to take into account the effect of income taxation on wages. By contrast, Allen (1982) emphasizes the possibility that the offset due to general equilibrium effects could be so large that an antiredistributive tax might be optimal.

[93] See Browning (1994) and Kaplow (1998b).

[94] This analysis is incomplete because it does not address who ultimately benefits from the monopoly profits, which is in part determined by the nature of capital taxation.

negative externalities, such as pollution and congestion, that are not taxed and thus not reflected in product prices.[95] (Consider also the consumption externalities addressed in section D.) In such instances, the amount of market labor is too high in the absence of income taxation, so some degree of redistributive labor income taxation would be a corrective and additional labor income taxation would be less distortionary on this account. Unfortunately, existing work does not provide a strong basis for predicting either the direction or the magnitude of any appropriate adjustment to what otherwise would be the optimal income tax.[96]

[95] Even if pollution regulation optimally controls the amount of pollution produced by a given production process, the resulting level of pollution would usually be positive, in which case it is optimal for prices to reflect the residual pollution (see Kaplow 1998b).

[96] Browning (1994) suggests that a substantial correction is required in the direction of less redistributive taxation; however, Kaplow (1998b) indicates that many of the components Browning identifies are mischaracterized and other countervailing factors are omitted.

6

Income and Commodity Taxation

🌱

Much government activity, even aside from pure labor income taxation and income transfer programs, is motivated by or has the effect of redistributing income. This obviously includes other forms of taxation—such as the taxation of various commodities and exemptions from broad consumption taxes (like a VAT) for food or other necessities, corporate and other capital taxation, wealth and transfer (estate-gift) taxation, and the social security tax and transfer system. Redistribution also occurs as a consequence of expenditures on public goods and all manner of regulation, whether of externalities, workplace safety, or international trade.

This chapter will focus on one specific means of indirect redistribution, so-called commodity taxation ("commodity" being a misnomer because all forms of consumption are understood to be included), also known as indirect taxation.[1] Commodity taxes are chosen for study

---

[1] The language of direct versus indirect taxation used to be more common, the former usually referring to income taxes and the latter to other taxes, especially taxes on goods and services. The standard interpretation is that direct taxes can plausibly be tailored to individuals' circumstances, allowing notably for uniform per capita taxes or transfers and for nonlinear taxation. By contrast, indirect taxes, such as commodity taxes, are impersonal; they do not allow a uniform levy because individuals cannot (at least for purposes of indirect taxes) be identified. Relatedly, nonlinear indirect taxation is presumed to be impossible because of the infeasibility of charging different rates that depend on the amount an individual consumes, which would require identification of who purchases commodities and also that resale (arbitrage between individuals whose different consumption choices lead them to face different marginal tax rates) be preventable.

because they are the most basic form of indirect redistribution, have been analyzed extensively, and provide a useful model that may readily be extended to other settings, as will be done in several chapters that follow.

The analysis in this chapter formalizes the suggestion in chapter 2 that, as a first approximation and as a useful benchmark for analysis, redistribution should be confined to the income tax and direct transfer programs whereas other government policies should be assessed solely on efficiency grounds. Regarding commodity taxation in particular, this idea was developed by Atkinson and Stiglitz (1976) under the assumption that income taxes are set optimally, and it was generalized in Kaplow (2006c) using a more direct and intuitive approach (originally employed to analyze the provision of public goods) that will be followed here.[2]

It is useful to begin by considering the basic reason why commodity taxes are not fundamentally a sensible way to redistribute income when an income tax is available. Consider a tax on yachts, designed to further redistributive objectives. Such a tax will distort consumption expenditures of the rich; they will spend less on yachts and more on mansions, air travel, and other diversions. Furthermore, luxury taxes will distort labor supply in a manner similar to that caused by income taxation. To illustrate this point, suppose that, on account of taxes on yachts and the like, disposable income effectively buys 2% less than it otherwise would. This reduction in purchasing power will reduce the utility benefit of incremental earnings just as would a higher marginal income tax rate that directly reduced disposable income by the same amount. As a result, using commodity taxes to redistribute income imposes the same sort of cost in terms of labor supply distortion as the income tax does and also imposes additional costs through the distortion of consumption choices. Thus, although second-best reasoning indicates that it is not generally true that a greater number of distortions implies more

---

[2] The technique was first used by Hylland and Zeckhauser (1979) in arguing that distributive concerns should play no role in cost-benefit analysis and was developed further in Kaplow (1996d, 2004) (see section 8.C). Other analyses of commodity taxation in the presence of nonlinear income taxation that may not be optimal include Konishi (1995) and Laroque (2005). Additionally, Atkinson and Stiglitz (1976) and Deaton (1979) characterize the restrictions on utility functions necessary for no differentiation to be optimal when the optimal income tax is restricted to be linear.

distortion overall, in the present setting this is so because adding distortions across commodities does not in the basic case reduce the distortion of labor effort due to redistributive income taxation.[3]

The particular method of analysis employed here to make the argument rigorous follows that sketched in chapter 2. At its core is a construction in which any reform of commodity taxation is joined with an adjustment to the income tax (and transfer) schedule that, taken together, leaves the distribution of utility constant. It can be demonstrated in a basic case that, when such a combined reform is implemented, labor supply is unaffected as well. As a consequence, the only effect of the composite policy—the commodity tax reform and the corresponding income tax adjustment—will be on the efficiency of individuals' consumption decisions. Accordingly, uniform commodity taxation—equivalent to no commodity taxation—is most efficient because it avoids any distortion of consumption choices.

The conclusion that the availability of income taxation undermines the redistributive role of commodity taxation reinforces the book's overall theme that an integrated view of government activity is necessary to properly assess any particular policy. The argument presented in deriving this result also supports the more specific idea that distribution-neutral policy analysis has important virtues even when considering policies that are generally understood to have important distributive implications.

After establishing these claims and applying them to all manner of commodity tax reforms, a variety of qualifications will be discussed. An important lesson is that these qualifications are largely orthogonal to the idea that commodity taxation should be assessed directly in redistributive terms, so the central conclusion from the basic case indeed provides the appropriate benchmark for policy analysis. A final section addresses the relationship between the present analysis and the substantial body of literature on Ramsey taxation.

---

[3] A related intuition—that having additional instruments to address a problem tends to be beneficial—is likewise inapplicable in the basic case: The proposition is only weakly true, and in this instance it is optimal to set the additional instruments to zero. This point, as well as that in the text about the number of distortions, is, not surprisingly, subject to qualifications, as elaborated in section C.

A. Statement of the Problem

The model employed in chapter 4 for studying income taxation can be modified to incorporate commodity taxation as well. Instead of a single, composite consumption good c, it is now supposed that individuals may spend their after-tax-and-transfer income, $wl - T(wl)$, on any of n commodities, $x_1, \ldots, x_n$. Commodity prices (which equal constant unit production costs measured in units of income and thus may be thought of as prices paid to competitive producers) for goods x_i are p_i and commodity taxes are τ_i (which may be subsidies, in which case they are negative). The vector of commodity taxes is denoted $\boldsymbol{\tau}$. Individuals as consumers thus face net prices of $p_i + \tau_i$, assumed to be positive.

An individual's budget constraint, instead of that given in expression (4.1), is now

$$\sum (p_i + \tau_i) x_i(wl) = wl - T(wl), \tag{6.1}$$

where summations throughout are from i equals 1 to n and the notation $x_i(wl)$ denotes the level of x_i chosen by an individual of earning ability w and l likewise implicitly refers to the labor effort of an individual of type w. The government's budget constraint, instead of (4.4), becomes

$$\int \left[T(wl) + \sum \tau_i x_i(wl) \right] f(w) dw = R. \tag{6.2}$$

The only difference here is that the government, in addition to collecting income tax from or paying transfers to each type of individual, also collects taxes and pays subsidies on various commodities.

Before undertaking the analysis, it is useful to discuss the relationship between the average overall level of commodity taxation and of income taxation, along with related matters of normalization. Initially, observe that there are infinitely many equivalent ways to describe and implement any commodity tax system. To see this, consider uniform commodity taxes, that is, commodity tax schemes for which $\tau_i = \alpha p_i$, for all i. Compared to a baseline with no commodity taxation, if $\alpha > 0$ everyone pays proportionally more for any bundle of commodities. The introduction of such a commodity tax system could be combined with an adjustment to the previously existing income tax schedule such that everyone's after-income-tax income is greater by the same proportion α. If this is done, individuals can afford precisely the same bundles of commodities as they could without the commodity taxes. Moreover, since relative commodity prices are unchanged, they will make the same consumption choices as before. Furthermore, this composite adjustment to the commodity tax–income tax system is revenue neutral; the additional commodity tax revenue just offsets the reduction in income tax revenue. In sum, for any α, positive or negative (but above -1), the adjusted scheme is fully equivalent to a scheme in which $\alpha = 0$.

An immediate implication of the foregoing analysis is that undifferentiated commodity taxation is equivalent to linear income taxation—or, with a nonlinear income tax, a supplemental component to the tax. To see this, consider the budget constraint (6.1) for the case with purely proportional commodity taxation, $\tau_i = \alpha p_i$, for all i, and no income tax at the outset:

$$\sum (p_i + \alpha p_i) x_i (wl) = wl. \tag{6.3}$$

Factoring $1 + \alpha$ outside the summation on the left, dividing both sides by $1 + \alpha$, and letting $t = \alpha/(1 + \alpha)$, yields

$$\sum p_i x_i (wl) = \frac{1}{1 + \alpha} wl = (1 - t) wl. \tag{6.4}$$

The left side of expression (6.4) is the cost of consumption in a world with no commodity taxes, and the right side is disposable income for the case of a linear income tax (with no grant). Introducing uniform commodity taxation is indeed equivalent to a uniform shift in the level of income taxation.[4]

---

[4] It is sometimes believed, therefore, that a model with commodity taxation and no income taxation is equivalent to one that also allows linear income taxation. This belief, however, is incorrect because an important feature of a linear income tax (see subsection 4.B.1) is that it permits a uniform lump-sum grant (or tax) g, which a system of pure (anonymous) commodity taxation does not allow (see note 1). As explained in section D, this essential difference—between models that allow some form of income taxation and those based on Ramsey (1927) that do not—is a central reason that the results in these two types of models are qualitatively different.

It should be apparent that analogous reasoning is applicable to non-uniform commodity tax schemes. For example, one could adjust preexisting commodity taxes τ_i so as to proportionally increase or decrease consumers' net prices of $p_i + \tau_i$ and simultaneously make an offsetting adjustment to the income tax, producing an entirely equivalent system. For this reason, analysts have not focused on the questions of whether there should be commodity taxation or what its average overall level should be—in this simple setting, such questions are meaningless—but rather on whether and how commodity taxes should be differentiated. This focus will be employed in the present chapter and throughout the book when considering related issues. (Specifically, it is sometimes helpful to consider a particular normalization of a commodity tax scheme, namely, one in which no net revenue is generated through commodity taxes. For differentiated schemes, this obviously involves a mixture of taxes and subsidies. Examination of such a normalized scheme makes even more clear that the analysis is not about revenue but concerns only which forms of consumption are to be relatively discouraged or encouraged.[5])

B. Optimal Commodity Taxation

It will be assumed that individuals' utility functions are weakly separable between labor (leisure) and all other commodities, taken together. That is, their utility functions can be expressed as $u(v(x_1, \ldots, x_n), l)$, where v is a subutility function. This formulation implies that, for a given level of after-income-tax income, individuals will allocate their disposable income among commodities in the same manner regardless of the level of labor effort required to generate that level of income. Put another way, the ratio of the marginal utility of consumption for any two commodities, at given levels of consumption of those commodities and of all other commodities, is independent of the level of labor effort. (For

---

[5] Other normalizations are also useful. For example, in considering externalities and the device of corrective, Pigouvian taxation, it is natural to think in terms of taxing negative externalities and subsidizing positive externalities, where commodities producing no net externalities are neither taxed nor subsidized (for them, $\tau_i = 0$).

commodities i and j, this ratio is simply $u_v v_i / u_v v_j = v_i / v_j$.) As will be seen, this property further implies that changes in the allocation of after-tax income among commodities that are caused by commodity tax reforms—if income is adjusted in a compensating fashion, in the sense that utility is held constant—will not affect the choice of labor effort. This separability assumption will be discussed further in subsection C.2.

Using this framework, it will now be explained why any system of differential commodity taxation is inferior to uniform taxation. Specifically, it will be shown how one can eliminate differential commodity taxation and adjust the income tax schedule in a manner that generates a Pareto improvement.

As noted previously, the analysis follows Kaplow (2006c). Begin by defining a differentiated tax system $\{\tau_1, \ldots, \tau_n\}$, $T(wl)$ as one for which there exists i, j such that $(p_i + \tau_i)/(p_j + \tau_j) \neq p_i/p_j$. In other words, the ratio of net prices of at least one pair of goods does not equal its production cost ratio. We will now consider a commodity tax reform that eliminates all differentiation in the commodity tax regime, specifically, by moving to a regime in which $\tau_i^* = 0$, for all i.

1. Distribution-Neutral Income Tax Adjustment and Labor Effort

Moving to this new commodity tax vector will tend to change individuals' utility because they no longer pay commodity taxes (or receive subsidies) and because, with a new relative price vector, they will change their consumption vectors. Whatever is the net effect on utility for any ability level w and given labor effort $l(w)$, we can now define an intermediate income tax schedule $T^\circ(wl)$ at each income level so as to offset the net effect on utility.[6] This is the distribution-neutral, or offsetting, income tax

---

[6] Concretely, if at some income level commodity tax payments were initially 10% of disposable income, the income tax schedule at that level of income would be raised so as to leave a level of disposable income that was 10% lower. In addition, because such individuals will adjust consumption allocations, utility will also be higher, say by an amount equivalent to 2% of disposable income, so the level of the income tax would have to be raised additionally on this account. Of course, as the income tax is raised further, individuals may choose

adjustment introduced in chapter 2. Specifically, we will examine an income tax schedule $T°(wl)$ that has the property that, if all individuals (of every type w) continue to choose the same level of labor effort $l(w)$ as under the initial tax system, then their utility will be unchanged.[7]

To define the schedule $T°(wl)$ formally, it is helpful to introduce notation for the indirect subutility function. Define $V(\tau, T, wl)$ as the value of $v(x_1, \ldots, x_n)$ maximized over the x_i's when the stated tax regime and level of before-tax income are taken as given. That is, V is the maximized value of v subject to the budget constraint (6.1). Because v depends only on the x_i's and the constraint (6.1) depends only on the x_i's, τ, T, and wl—but not on w or l independently—the indirect utility function V is the same for all individuals, regardless of their type w.[8] Using this fact, we can now define $T°(wl)$ as the income tax schedule that satisfies $V(\tau, T, wl) = V(\tau^*, T°, wl)$ for all wl. (To construct the schedule $T°(wl)$, for each value of wl one raises or lowers the original tax schedule $T(wl)$ to the point that the original level of subutility is restored.)

Next we consider how this combination of eliminating commodity taxes and adjusting the income tax schedule will influence labor effort. As will now be explained, there will be no effect. This result holds because the income tax adjustment guarantees that every level of (before-tax) income generates the same level of utility as it did under the initial regime, so no individual will find it optimal to earn more or less income than was previously optimal. Specifically, utility in the initial regime can be written as $u(V(\tau, T, wl), l)$, and utility in the intermediate regime as

---

to consume different mixes of commodities and the extent of the utility gain may change somewhat. For the construction, however, all that is necessary is to adjust the level of the income tax continuously at each level of income until individuals at that income level are just indifferent compared to their utility level in the initial regime.

[7] It is familiar to refer to this experiment as involving a (utility) compensated change, so at each level of income, wl, $T(wl) - T°(wl)$ is the (Hicksian) compensating variation associated with the change in relative prices due to the commodity tax reform. (A difference is that, in the present formulation, labor supply is held constant, although it will be demonstrated that this is indeed the case in any event.)

[8] As will be apparent in the argument to follow, it is sufficient for present purposes that individuals' subutility functions, v, are identical (which implies that their V functions are identical as well). The assumption that utility functions, u, are also identical is only for expositional convenience.

utility

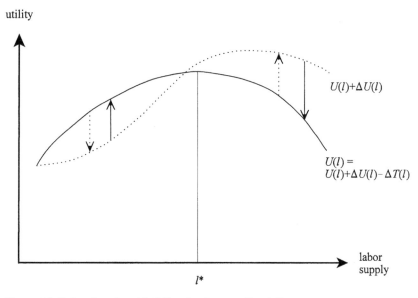

Figure 6.1. Labor Supply with Offsetting Income Tax Adjustment

$u(V(\tau^*, T^\circ, wl), l)$, and the foregoing construction of $T^\circ(wl)$ guarantees that, for each type w, these expressions are equal for any choice of l. In other words, $U(l(w)) = U^\circ(l(w))$ for all $l(w)$, where the reduced form $U(l(w))$ refers to the level of utility achieved for any choice of l by the given type w. Since utility as a function of labor effort is precisely the same under the new, intermediate regime as it is under the initial regime, it follows that whatever level of labor effort $l(w)$ maximizes $U(l(w))$ will also maximize $U^\circ(l(w))$. Accordingly, individuals will indeed choose the same level of labor effort under the newly constructed intermediate regime.

The foregoing argument is illustrated in figure 6.1. The solid curve in this figure represents $U(l)$ for a given individual of some type w (where the w is suppressed for convenience) in the initial regime.[9] In

---

[9] These functions, because denominated in utility, will differ among individuals with different earning abilities. With homogeneous preferences (it is sufficient that subutility functions v be identical) and weak leisure separability, as assumed here, the same tax adjustment (denominated in dollars) will work for all individuals, so for individuals of any given earning ability, a diagram corresponding to figure 6.1 can be constructed.

the absence of the commodity tax reform and accompanying income tax adjustment, the individual will choose the level of labor supply l^* that maximizes $U(l)$. Suppose now that the commodity tax reform is implemented, but for the moment we will imagine that no income tax adjustment is required. It is supposed that the reform by itself generates effects on utility of $\Delta U(l)$. For example, if the original commodity tax scheme subsidized necessities (such as food) and taxed luxuries, then a reform that eliminated commodity taxation might be expected to reduce utility for low-earning individuals and raise utility for middle- and high-earning individuals. Then the individual's utility as a function of labor effort will shift as indicated by the dotted arrows to the dotted curve, which is $U(l)+\Delta U(l)$. Because $\Delta U(l)$ in the illustration is taken to be negative for low-earning individuals and positive for others, the dotted curve falls below $U(l)$ for low-earning individuals and above it for everyone else. Finally, introduce the offsetting income tax adjustment, here denoted $\Delta T(l)$ (equal simply to the difference between $T^\circ(wl)$ and $T(wl)$ for the given type w, but denominated in utils so as to be comparable with $U(l)$ and $\Delta U(l)$), which by construction is set precisely equal to $\Delta U(l)$. When this offsetting income tax adjustment is taken into account, this dotted curve shifts, as the solid arrows indicate, back to the original solid curve, which now may be denoted as $U(l)+\Delta U(l)-\Delta T(l)$. Since $\Delta T(l)$ was chosen to be identical to $\Delta U(l)$, we can be certain that we indeed are back to precisely the original curve, $U(l)$. Now, when we ask what labor supply the individual will choose if the commodity tax reform combined with the offsetting income tax adjustment is enacted, it must be the same level of labor supply as chosen previously, l^*.

It is worth reflecting on the properties of this offsetting adjustment to the income tax schedule and what they depend upon. Obviously, the construction produces a reform package—here, a commodity tax reform and an income tax adjustment—that is distribution neutral. Indeed, the result is somewhat stronger than this, for everyone's utility is precisely the same as it was initially. In addition, as just explained, there is no effect on labor supply (which, as elaborated in subsection C.2, is a product of the weak separability assumption). In other words, this method of income tax adjustment allows one to begin with any income tax system and any initial commodity tax regime and construct a commodity tax – income tax reform combination that holds utility, distribution, and labor supply constant. Moreover, nothing in the analysis depended on the fact that it was a commodity tax reform under consideration rather than, say, a change in expenditures on public goods or modification of an environmental regulation. Thus, the approach employed here may be applied generically in examining reforms of government policy, and accordingly this framework will be utilized repeatedly throughout the rest of this book.

2. Elimination of Differential Commodity Taxation

To complete the demonstration that the elimination of differential commodity taxation can produce a Pareto improvement, we need to show that this reform, in combination with the distribution-neutral tax adjustment involving the intermediate income tax schedule $T°(wl)$, generates surplus revenue. The formal demonstration in Kaplow (2006c) can be understood intuitively through the following heuristic construction.

Suppose that the income tax schedule adjustment is performed in three stages: First, the schedule is preliminarily adjusted to offset the effect of the commodity tax reform on utility under the hypothetical assumption that individuals' consumption does not change. Second, the schedule is further adjusted to offset the effect of consumption adjustments on utility, ignoring any effects of such adjustments on commodity tax revenues. Third and finally, account is taken of any effect of the stage-two consumption adjustments on commodity tax revenues (and any feedbacks therefrom).

Beginning with the first stage, as noted, the reform changes individuals' commodity tax payments (even assuming that they do not change their consumption decisions), and the first step of the income tax adjustment offsets this effect. Clearly, this combination will be revenue neutral as a whole because each type of individual's income tax payments rise or fall by just the amount that the type's commodity tax payments fall or rise. (The income tax adjustment is calibrated to hold utility constant at each stage; since consumption decisions are held constant in the first stage, the income tax adjustment serves merely to ensure that individuals can still afford their original consumption bundle, no more and no less.)

In the second stage, due to the changes in relative prices, individuals will be induced to change their consumption of various commodities.

This change can only increase utility (for otherwise individuals would not choose to adjust their consumption choices), and because relative prices are changing, individuals' utility will in fact be strictly greater on this account. Hence, the second-stage income tax schedule adjustment required to offset this effect on utility will result in additional revenue being raised, generating a surplus.

The third stage, designed to account for effects of stage-two consumption adjustments on commodity tax revenues, is a nullity for the reform under consideration. Recall that this reform sets $\tau_i^* = 0$, for all i. Hence, consumption adjustments will have no effect on commodity tax revenues, which are zero regardless. (This stage is nevertheless included because other reforms—including a reform in the reverse direction from that contemplated and the reforms considered in subsection 3—generally will have stage-three effects, which can prove decisive.)

In sum, the first and third stages have no effect on revenue, and the second stage produces a surplus. To complete the argument, one can further adjust the income tax schedule to rebate this surplus, say in equal amounts to every individual.[10] Because everyone's pre-rebate utility is the same under the intermediate regime and the initial regime, it must be that, with the rebate, everyone's utility is greater in the final resulting regime that eliminates differential commodity taxation than it is in the initial regime.

3. Other Reforms of Commodity Taxation

The complete elimination of differential commodity taxation is not the only reform that generates a Pareto improvement when accompanied by a distribution-neutral adjustment to the income tax schedule. Any proportional reduction in differential commodity taxation also can generate a Pareto improvement (though obviously involving a lesser utility gain). The argument, however, is not entirely straightforward: When individuals adjust their consumption choices, there will not only

---

[10] More precisely, as the surplus is rebated, there will tend to be income effects, which in turn reduce income tax revenue. Accordingly, the level of the rebate will tend to be smaller than the per capita surplus generated by the hypothetical, intermediate tax regime $T^\circ(wl)$.

be an increase in utility but also an effect on commodity tax revenue (because, unlike in stage three of the previous case, the reform contemplated here does not eliminate commodity taxation). Nevertheless, it can be demonstrated that this incidental effect also contributes to a revenue surplus in the case of a proportional reduction in differential commodity taxation. The basic reason is that consumption changes will tend to involve shifts from commodities that were subsidized (but now are subsidized less) to commodities that were taxed (but now are taxed less), and from lower-taxed to higher-taxed commodities (because the tax differential is now less), and from highly subsidized to less highly subsidized commodities (because the subsidy differential is now less). All such shifts raise additional revenue. Because of complementarities in consumption, not all shifts are necessarily of this nature, but in aggregate the net effect is to increase revenue.[11]

What about other commodity tax reforms that do not proportionally reduce or totally eliminate differential taxation?[12] Looking only at changes in commodity tax rates, no simple conclusions are possible. For example, if there were three commodities, two taxed at 10% and the third untaxed, it is not clear whether lowering one of the 10% rates to 8% would be a reduction in differentiation. Distortion would be reduced between the commodity for which the tax rate is lowered and the untaxed commodity, but distortion would be introduced between the two taxed commodities. One cannot say a priori whether overall distortion would rise or fall. It turns out, however, that whether a Pareto improvement is possible depends entirely on whether a commodity tax reform reduces consumption distortion in a simple, traditional sense.

More precisely, a Pareto improvement is possible when

$$\sum p_i \int x_i^o(wl) f(w) dw < \sum p_i \int x_i(wl) f(w) dw. \tag{6.5}$$

The right side of expression (6.5) is the total value of real resources consumed under some initially given regime. The left side is the total

---

[11] Again, the formal analysis appears in Kaplow (2006c).

[12] Dixit (1975) and others characterize efficient partial commodity tax reforms, although in a Ramsey model in which there is no concern for distribution and no income tax (see section D).

required under a regime with reformed commodity taxes and an inter-mediate income tax $T°(wl)$ that produces a distribution-neutral com-bined reform. Because, by construction, everyone's utility is the same in the initial regime and in the intermediate, hypothetical reform regime, when expression (6.5) holds, it must be that fewer resources are required to bring individuals to the same level of utility, which is a natural defini-tion of increased efficiency. Observe that if fewer resources are expended on the commodities themselves and everyone's income is the same as it was previously, it must be that total tax payments are greater under the reform with the offsetting income tax adjustment.[13] Hence, as in the preceding demonstration, there will exist a surplus, and a Pareto im-provement will be possible.

This final result reinforces the basic theme of chapter 2 and this chapter that distribution-neutral analysis of government policies is useful and may be conducted without regard to distributive concerns and labor supply distortion caused by redistributive income taxation. The distribution-neutral (offsetting) income tax adjustment essentially creates a hypothetical world in which labor supply is fixed. It is as if in-dividuals' incomes were simply the result of some initial endowment that they did nothing to create. Furthermore, any distributive effects of the commodity tax reform itself are fully offset. In this simplified world, it is not surprising that standard efficiency conditions indicate which reforms are desirable and, in particular, when a Pareto improvement is possible. The distribution-neutral tax adjustment allows us to treat a second-best world as if it were a simpler, first-best world because it holds constant the pertinent second-best considerations.

C. Qualifications

As suggested previously, the conclusion that redistributive consider-ations should be confined to the income tax and transfer system whereas

---

[13] This method of argument is equivalent to that used earlier for the case of elimination of differential taxation. Demonstrating that total tax revenue is greater under the intermedi-ate regime and demonstrating that fewer productive resources are utilized amount to the same thing in the present setting.

other policies, here commodity taxation, should be assessed on narrow efficiency grounds (ignoring both redistribution and labor supply distortion caused by redistributive income taxation) is offered as a benchmark for analysis. The practical applicability of this benchmark was addressed in subsection 2.C.3 with particular attention to reforms not implemented in the hypothesized distribution-neutral fashion. It was emphasized that, in such cases, it is conceptually useful to employ a two-step decomposition: First, the contemplated reform is assumed to be implemented with a distribution-neutral income tax adjustment, and, second, a further, purely redistributive tax adjustment is made to reflect that actual, non-distribution-neutral proposal. The foregoing analysis governs the first component, and the second is subject to the analysis in chapter 4 on optimal income taxation. Distinguishing these two steps enhances clarity and facilitates specialization. Additional issues, including matters of political feasibility, were also explored.

The present section will examine qualifications that are pertinent even in a distribution-neutral framework.[14] Such consideration is necessary to appreciate the limitations of the proposed benchmark and also reinforces one's understanding of the main results. It should be noted at the outset that most of the qualifications, although they may require important adjustments in particular settings, are orthogonal to the core redistributive question in the following sense: They generally do not systematically favor moving away from uniformity in a simply redistributive direction, such as by subsidizing necessities and taxing luxuries. Instead, the optimal adjustments tend to be more subtle and context specific. They can readily be in either direction—it may be optimal to tax some necessities and subsidize some luxuries— and the adjustments may well involve commodities with no distinct income-related pattern of consumption.

---

[14] Although a number of qualifications are explored here, the list is not exhaustive. For others, see, for example, Cremer, Pestieau, and Rochet (2001), who find a role for commodity taxation when individuals have unobservable endowments; Naito (1999), who shows how differential factor taxes may redistribute indirectly by affecting relative wages when workers of different abilities supply different types of labor (assuming that the different types of labor cannot themselves be differentially taxed); Saez (2004a), who demonstrates that Naito's result does not hold in the long run when occupational choice is endogenous; and Naito (2004), who obtains his prior results when individuals have differential abilities to accumulate human capital.

1. Externalities

It is optimal, ceteris paribus, to tax activities that impose negative externalities and subsidize those that generate positive externalities. The assumption that individuals' utilities depended only on their own consumption and level of labor effort ruled out externalities. Introducing them would reinstate the usual prescriptions. Furthermore, as section 8.G will explain, these prescriptions are (roughly) restored in their simple, first-best form. Concerns explored in recent literatures about the possibility of a "double dividend" or exacerbation of the labor-leisure distortion caused by the income tax are largely misplaced for reasons analogous to those presented in the foregoing analysis.

2. Preferences Nonseparable in Labor

The assumption that individuals' utility is weakly separable in labor (leisure) was used in arguing that commodity tax reforms combined with offsetting income tax adjustments have no effect on labor effort. Without separability, this will not generally be the case. For example, taxing movie tickets or swimsuits (relative to other goods) may make leisure relatively less attractive. Given the distortion in favor of leisure caused by the income tax, this effect would be beneficial. Eliminating such commodity taxation combined with an offsetting income tax adjustment would not leave labor effort unaffected. Instead, labor effort would tend to fall, which would reduce income tax revenues and thereby provide an offset to the increased revenue attributable to the reform's efficiency with regard to consumption choices. Hence, at least some degree of differential commodity taxation would be efficient: Introducing differentiation initially imposes no first-order cost, whereas the improvement in labor supply is first-order. Because of the second-best setting that exists due to the assumed impracticality of taxing leisure directly, it is optimal to distort other activities if (but only if) the preexisting distortion (here, of the labor-leisure choice) is thereby mitigated.[15]

---

[15] The now-familiar point that it tends to be advantageous to tax leisure complements and to subsidize substitutes was first introduced by Corlett and Hague (1953), although in a Ramsey tax setting (on which, see section D). This standard intuition is, however, somewhat

The practical significance of this nonseparability qualification has received relatively little attention. Barnett (1979) finds that consumers substitute durable goods for leisure, implying that, relative to other consumer goods, they should be subsidized. Another interesting case involves meals. Iorwerth and Whalley (2002) assess the common practice of exempting food from sales taxes and VATs. They explain that food is an input in household production of meals, a process that requires significant leisure time. By contrast, restaurant meals, which generally are not tax exempt, involve others providing the labor effort, saving time for the consumer. As a consequence, it may well be optimal to reverse the common practice by taxing food (perhaps at above-normal rates) and exempting (or at least favoring) purchases of restaurant meals.[16] Iorwerth and Whalley present evidence suggesting that there may be significant efficiency gains from such a reform. The standard motivation for exempting food from taxation while taxing restaurant meals is, of course, redistributive, but if income taxes are adjusted to offset distributive effects, this consideration is moot and efficiency concerns are decisive. See also Blundell and Walker (1982) and Browning and Meghir (1991), who present evidence of nonseparability in considering spouses' labor supply decisions.

Although nonseparability is a qualification to the result that all differentiation is inefficient, the analysis of nonseparability reinforces the notion that redistributive concerns are not directly relevant to the

---

treacherous because the terms "complement" and "substitute" have different meanings. Christiansen (1984) discusses different usages in some detail and relates them to the Atkinson-Stiglitz (1976) uniformity result. For present purposes, the argument in the text indicates the relevant relationship: What matters is the direction of the labor supply effect when the contemplated commodity tax reform is coupled with a distribution-neutral (offsetting) income tax adjustment.

[16] One might have supposed that it would be optimal to tax all readily identifiable leisure activities, from yachting to ski trips to sporting events. However, as this example in the text highlights, most leisure activities tend to require both time and commodity inputs, for it typically takes time to engage in consumption (see Christiansen 1984 and Kleven 2004). What matters is which commodities are *relatively* more complementary to leisure. Hence, just as it may be optimal to tax groceries and subsidize restaurant meals, it also may be optimal to tax purchases of baseballs and other sporting goods but to subsidize attendance at expensive sporting events because the former involve a relatively high ratio of time to expenditure compared to the latter.

assessment of differential commodity taxation. It might be tempting to go further and state that redistributive concerns are not at all relevant. Yet this is not accurate because such concerns are indirectly relevant in the following sense: Adjustments that are optimal with nonseparability are beneficial because they indirectly reduce the labor-leisure distortion, and that distortion is itself a product of redistributive taxation. Put another way, if one can thereby reduce the marginal distortion caused by redistributive taxation, then for a given SWF it will tend to be optimal to increase the extent of redistribution. This point makes the foregoing example involving food and restaurant meals seem even more paradoxical because the imposition of appropriately higher taxes on a necessity and lower taxes (or subsidies) on a luxury, on their face regressive reforms, nevertheless results in greater redistribution when the overall system, specifically, the income tax, is adjusted optimally.

3. Preferences Dependent on Earning Ability

As explored in subsection 5.C.1, it is assumed that ability cannot readily be taxed directly. Mirrlees (1976) explains that this limitation may make commodity tax differentiation optimal to the extent that preferences for some commodities depend directly on individuals' abilities (rather than on their incomes, which reflect their abilities). Specifically, it tends to be optimal to impose a heavier burden on commodities preferred by the more able and a lighter burden on those preferred by the less able.

To illustrate, society might consider taxing expenditures related to fine art (acquisitions of art, attendance at museums and the opera, and purchases of high-brow literature) and subsidizing simpler pleasures (bowling, attendance at professional wrestling, and purchases of tickets to trashy movies).[17] Notice, however, that this argument does not imply

---

[17] As obnoxious as this policy may seem to some readers, high ability is largely responsible for making the former expenditures more congenial to some individuals than to others. Note that those who have significant influence on or direct control over such matters as government expenditures on the arts are disproportionately high-ability individuals who benefit from a suboptimal policy. Likewise, writers over the ages, such as Mill (1861), and many contemporary philosophers, who argue that high-brow activities are somehow intrinsically

that one should tax luxuries in general; as explained throughout, luxuries are purchased with earnings, so taxing luxuries does distort the labor-leisure decision. The present consideration is distinctive because it depends on preferences that vary with ability per se. The relevant question is whether, assuming two individuals were to earn the same income, the higher-ability person would, relative to the other, prefer a different mix of commodities. If so, by taxing what higher-ability individuals prefer relative to what low-ability individuals prefer, one can accomplish additional redistribution without causing as much distortion of labor supply. There are, however, limits on the extent to which such differential taxation is optimal because it does result in distortion of consumption choices.

4. Preference Heterogeneity

When individuals' preferences vary (other than purely as a function of ability or income), it may no longer be possible to implement an efficient commodity tax reform in a manner that produces a Pareto improvement.[18] Specifically, a reform that, say, eliminates differentiation will redistribute—within income groups—away from those with atypically strong tastes for those commodities that were initially treated relatively favorably. If the losses to these individuals exceed their pro rata share of the efficiency gains, then they will be net losers from the reform. A Pareto improvement would still be possible if preference differences were wholly related to observable characteristics, such

---

superior, are likewise high-ability individuals themselves. The purpose of the sort of differential taxation described in the text is not, of course, to encourage or discourage any of these activities; indeed, any such effects are counted as costs in the analysis. Rather, the motivation is to attempt to adjust tax burdens indirectly based on underlying ability when doing so directly is infeasible.

[18] More precisely, as indicated in note 8, only heterogeneity regarding the subutility function v matters for the present analysis. Preference heterogeneity has been addressed previously in the context of public goods by Boadway and Keen (1993), Hellwig (2004), Hylland and Zeckhauser (1979), Kaplow (1996d, 2006e), and Ng (1984b). Subsection 5.C.2 analyzes heterogeneity in preferences for consumption as a whole and for labor; that discussion, however, is relevant to determination of the optimal income tax schedule but does not directly pertain to differential commodity taxation (because consumption is treated as a single good).

as age, geographic location, or family composition, because an income tax adjustment could in principle take such distinctions into account. However, some preference differences will be more idiosyncratic, rendering compensatory income tax adjustments impossible.

The implications of uncompensated heterogeneity for differential commodity taxation are not entirely straightforward because individuals with idiosyncratic tastes for one or another commodity may have higher or lower levels of utility or marginal utility. If these relationships could be ascertained—perhaps individuals who are worse off due to unobservable aspects of their physical constitution have different consumption patterns—then some differential commodity taxation could be identified that would increase overall social welfare.[19]

It is important to observe that such adjustments, although their motivation is redistributive in a sense, are not conventionally redistributive, that is, from the rich to the poor, because income-based differences are taken to be observable and thus are already addressed directly through the income tax itself. Here, average utility in all income groups is held constant by the posited income tax adjustment, and any change in the overall income distribution that was optimal could be accomplished directly through the income tax and transfer system. Thus, the relevant question regarding heterogeneity is whether, among individuals of the same income (and ability), there would be a social gain from indirectly redistributing across individuals with unobservably different preferences. As in previously explored instances, differential commodity taxation distorts consumption choices, so this cost would have to be traded off against the benefits of intra-income-group redistribution.

---

[19] The implications of heterogeneous preferences for commodity taxation are analyzed in Kaplow (2007e). Prior work includes Saez (2002a), who considers imperfect correlation between commodity demands and ability or the disutility of labor (the subjects of subsections 2 and 3); Marchand, Pestieau, and Racionero (2003), who examine differences in the source of disutility of labor across individuals (which are stipulated to be relevant to social welfare) that are related to preferences for different commodities; and, less directly, the references cited in subsection 5.C.2. Welfare analysis of heterogeneity is in some cases analogous to the assessment of the social welfare loss associated with horizontal inequity when that loss is determined by reference to a standard SWF. See Kaplow (1989) and section 15.B.

5. *Administration and Enforcement*

Perhaps the most important qualification is not conceptual but practical. As discussed in subsection 5.B.1, all tax systems are costly to administer, and tax avoidance and evasion present serious challenges. In some respects, these considerations reinforce the argument for uniform commodity taxation: Differentiation adds to administrative costs and presents opportunities for avoidance because the categorization of expenditures and receipts becomes important.[20] Furthermore, if a commodity tax system is to be uniform, it can be eliminated entirely, avoiding the administrative costs of a supplementary tax system.

Such analysis, however, is incomplete. Suppose, for example, that those who evade income taxation disproportionately consume particular commodities. Perhaps this is true of certain luxuries that are commonly purchased by those with high illegal incomes. But, as noted in subsection 5.B.1, the greatest evasion problems are not primarily among the rich, but rather involve the cash economy, particularly small businesses and individuals working in the informal sector. Thus, it is hardly obvious what sort of differentials in commodity taxation are justified on account of difficulties with income tax enforcement. The primary exception to this conclusion concerns developing economies, where income taxation may largely be infeasible. Then it may be necessary to rely almost entirely on commodity taxation, in which case the prescriptions are quite different from what is suggested above (on which, see section D).

Another subtlety is that the present analysis, following that of the nonlinear income tax in chapter 4, assumes that any particular shape of the income tax schedule is feasible. Typical income taxes, however, do not have very many tax brackets. If the optimal income tax schedule is more complex—suppose that in some region it features smoothly rising marginal rates rather than a lower bracket followed by a higher bracket, or in the limiting case a single bracket, as with a linear tax system—then differential commodity taxation might allow some improvement.

---

[20] On the other hand, some activities (perhaps financial services) might be costly to tax on a par with most others.

The adjustments, however, would be rather different from typically imagined commodity tax proposals. For example, if individuals in the upper range of an income tax bracket that ends at $50,000 should ideally be paying somewhat more tax, it would be optimal to impose a relatively greater burden on commodities preferred disproportionately more by those who earn, say, $48,000 to $50,000 compared to those who earn significantly more or significantly less. It seems implausible, however, that such commodities could often be readily identified or that much differentiation would be optimal. Moreover, it seems easier and would be less distortionary to make income tax brackets smoother instead.[21]

6. Taxpayer Illusion

The analysis in this chapter (and throughout the book) implicitly assumes that taxpayers' behavior reflects the actual operation of the system. For example, in section A it was stated to be irrelevant whether individuals pay, say, an additional 10% tax on all commodities or instead have their disposable income equivalently reduced by the income tax. Although perceptions do not always reflect reality, in the present setting it may seem unlikely that significant tax illusion would exist. Even if commodity taxes

---

[21] In fact, the direct administrative costs of adding income tax brackets, or even providing a smooth schedule, are negligible, especially when taxes are computed electronically. The major cost involves bracket arbitrage, but this problem depends on the magnitude of the differences between marginal rates, not on the number of brackets. (Smoothing large jumps may even reduce somewhat the extent of shifting across brackets.) An important exception is that there are substantial potential savings in having a purely flat income tax because, as discussed in subsection 5.B.1, income sources and taxpayers would not need to be distinguished. Then it is possible that differentiated commodity taxes would have some role. For example, if the optimal income tax resembled the two-bracket tax simulated by Slemrod et al. (1994), discussed in subsection 4.B.2, but a linear tax was to be employed, then optimal differential commodity taxation would involve a relative preference for goods consumed disproportionately by the rich or by the poor, with heaviest taxes falling on goods consumed disproportionately by those in the middle. The literature on optimal commodity taxation when the income tax is constrained to be linear is concerned essentially with such adjustments. In that case, Atkinson and Stiglitz (1976) and Deaton (1979) show that no differentiation is nevertheless optimal if individuals' Engel curves are linear with identical slopes, because then relative consumption allocations would not vary with income.

are hidden (say, they are paid by producers and not stated separately in prices offered to consumers), individuals' behavior will plausibly be the same, for their budget constraint (6.1) does not require that they know how the net price they face, $p_i+\tau_i$, breaks down between production costs and commodity taxes. Likewise, if a linear income tax is imposed as a payroll tax on employers, behavior is unaffected since the analysis assumes only that individuals know their net, effective wage, not its origins. Especially in the long run, it seems plausible that individuals would come to associate certain levels of earnings or after-tax income with a given standard of living, so significant earned-income illusion seems unlikely. Nevertheless, behavioral anomalies have been documented, and some may be relevant to taxpayer behavior.[22]

7. Political Economy

Related to taxpayer illusion is the question whether systems that are equivalent economically will be treated identically by the political system. One consideration is that misperceptions may present a more significant problem. If government representatives' constituents do not understand that two systems are really the same, one may be politically preferred to another.[23] Or if distributive effects of some policies are hidden from many voters (even if fully perceived by certain affected parties and their expert lobbyists), inefficient means of redistribution may be implemented. Indirect means of subsidizing agriculture are often offered as an example. Another factor is that different policies may be under the jurisdiction of different legislative committees or executive bureaus, and coordination may be imperfect. Hence, especially when political forces have varying effectiveness in different settings, some policies may be implemented even when they are equivalent or inferior to others. Such possibilities may be relevant to understanding observed

[22] For preliminary explorations, see Bernheim and Rangel (2007), Krishna and Slemrod (2003), and McCaffery and Slemrod (2006). Myopia in particular is addressed further in subsection 9.A.2 on capital taxation and in subsection 11.B.1 on the forced-savings aspect of social security.

[23] See, for example, Krishna and Slemrod (2003) and Baron and McCaffery (2006).

policy choices and ultimately to giving more politically savvy advice, but they are not dealt with in this book.

Regarding commodity taxation and income tax adjustments in particular, Atkinson and Stiglitz's (1976) original demonstration of the inefficiency of differential commodity taxation, recall, involves the case in which the income tax is set optimally. When that is true, no income tax adjustments are required in small (local) reforms because any welfare effects of changes in distribution will—because the system is at the social welfare optimum—just offset welfare effects of changes in the labor-leisure distortion. Furthermore, if not at the optimum, it remains true that there will be partial offsets. For example, if a commodity tax reform increases redistribution and this increase is desirable because the system is short of the optimum, it is nevertheless true that the reform will also increase labor supply distortion, even though the welfare cost of the distortion is by assumption less than the welfare benefit of the improvement in distribution.

In any event, the primary lesson of this chapter is conceptual, emphasizing that even if the extent of redistribution is not optimal, commodity tax reforms that improve efficiency in the narrow, traditional sense—such as by reducing or eliminating differential taxation in standard cases—are desirable and, indeed, Pareto improving if the income tax is adjusted in a distribution-neutral manner. In addition, even if political considerations prevent enactment of optimally redistributive policies, it is not implausible as a crude approximation that they may still allow reforms that preserve the political equilibrium regarding distribution and also tend to raise everyone's welfare, as suggested in subsection 2.B.3.

D. Ramsey Taxation

This chapter's analysis of optimal commodity taxation, which suggests that uniformity is optimal in the basic case, stands in sharp contrast to familiar principles of Ramsey taxation and calls into question the results in a number of literatures that build on the Ramsey model. It is useful to set forth this conflict and to explain why the use of Ramsey principles is inappropriate when there is an income tax.

Ramsey's (1927) seminal paper on optimal taxation addressed the question of how to raise a given amount of revenue through commodity taxation when distributive considerations are ignored and an income tax is assumed to be unavailable.[24] The familiar prescription is that, in the simplest case (which among other things assumes independent compensated demand schedules, that is, zero cross-elasticities), taxes should be inversely proportional to the elasticity of demand because distortion is less when the elasticity is lower. The major qualification involves distribution, which favors higher taxes on goods consumed disproportionately by higher-income individuals (see, for example, Atkinson and Stiglitz 1972, 1976; Feldstein 1972; and Diamond 1975). These competing considerations pose a tradeoff, especially because it is often supposed that necessities, consumed disproportionately by the poor, have relatively inelastic demands, and conversely for luxuries.

Ramsey tax principles are widely taught, featured in nearly all texts and surveys, and have provided the basis for extensive literatures on particular subjects, such as the taxation of capital, taxation and imperfect competition, and public sector pricing.[25] However, the foregoing analysis of optimal commodity taxation—which suggests that uniformity is optimal in the basic case without regard to demand elasticities or to whether goods are disproportionately consumed by the rich or the poor—stands in sharp contrast to the leading principles of Ramsey taxation.[26] It is useful to elaborate this tension and explain why reliance on Ramsey principles is misplaced in the presence of an income tax.

Begin with the original Ramsey analysis in which individuals are assumed to be identical and the government's sole objective is to raise revenue with minimal distortion. When one allows for an income tax (linear or nonlinear)—one feature of which is the possibility of a uniform lump-sum tax or subsidy (which, unlike individualized lump-sum

---

[24] For surveys of subsequent literature, see Atkinson and Stiglitz (1980), Auerbach (1985), Auerbach and Hines (2002), and Sandmo (1976).

[25] Regarding the latter, setting public sector prices above or below marginal cost corresponds to taxing or subsidizing private goods. For a survey, see Bös (1985).

[26] Not all Ramsey principles differ. Notably, Corlett and Hague's (1953) argument (elaborated in subsection C.2) that leisure complements (substitutes) should be taxed (subsidized) relative to other commodities is still relevant (see note 15).

taxation, is feasible)—there is no need to rely on distortionary com-modity taxation.[27] This result obviously does not depend on any special assumptions about the form of the utility function.

A central reason that raising all revenue by uniform per capita taxes is problematic has to do with income distribution: In a world in which individuals' abilities vary, the poor are hit hard by such a tax, whereas social welfare may be maximized when they receive net transfers. (Like-wise, as noted, the simple Ramsey prescription arising from models that assume identical individuals favors commodity taxes that may fall most heavily on necessities.) When distributive concerns are incorporated, however, the analysis in section B, extending the seminal contribution of Atkinson and Stiglitz (1976), shows that differential commodity taxes still have no role in an overall optimal scheme (under simplifying as-sumptions examined in section C). Although Ramsey rules modified for distributive considerations differ from the simpler prescriptions derived when individuals are assumed to be identical, they still generally involve adjustments that deviate, perhaps substantially, from uniformity—even when weak separability of labor is assumed so that no differentiation is optimal in the presence of an income tax. For example, under Ramsey rules, commodities consumed primarily by the rich (poor) should typi-cally be taxed (subsidized) if inequality is sufficiently great and if dis-tributive concerns are sufficiently important. But this result does not hold when an income tax is available.

As explained earlier, any desired result from the use of commodity taxation regarding revenue and income distribution can better be achieved directly, through the income tax, which undertakes redistribu-tion in an across-the-board fashion. Interestingly, the grant component of the income tax involves a uniform tax when only distortion is a concern, rendering commodity taxes unnecessary, whereas the grant is positive—a subsidy—in most simulations of an optimally redistributive income tax, under which commodity taxes are also unnecessary in the basic case.

---

[27] See also the discussion in note 4 regarding the confusion about whether commodity taxes alone can mimic a linear income tax, ignoring the essential role of the grant component of an income tax.

In sum, whether or not distribution is a concern, results derived in the original Ramsey framework, in which no income tax is available, fail to provide proper guidance in a world with an income tax. Accordingly, this book, which assumes the availability of an income tax, will follow the prescriptions initially laid out by Atkinson and Stiglitz (1976, 1980) and subsequently reinforced by Stiglitz (1987).[28] In many settings this approach leads to qualitatively different results from those in standard literatures, the latter results often having been derived in a Ramsey-like setting.

As Stiglitz (1987) further suggests (and as was alluded to in subsection C.5), in developing countries in which the feasibility of income taxation is greatly limited, the lessons of the substantial literature that follows Ramsey (1927)—including that which extends the model to incorporate distributive concerns—do have relevance, although other modifications may be necessary given the differing nature of such economies. But when income taxation is possible, results based on commodity tax models like that used by Ramsey are often highly misleading, as the present exploration of commodity taxation clearly indicates and the analysis in subsequent chapters will reaffirm.

---

[28] See also Mirrlees (1994, p. 223), who takes a similar view regarding the inappropriateness of the Ramsey set-up in the analysis of public goods provision.

PART III: GOVERNMENT EXPENDITURES

7

Transfer Payments

The optimal income tax problem examined in chapter 4 involves selecting a tax and transfer schedule, $T(wl)$, to maximize social welfare. This chapter considers important features of many transfer programs. However, since transfers are already part of the schedule $T(wl)$ and since the domain of the schedule covers all income levels, including the lowest, one might wonder why additional attention is required. The main justifications are the existence of programs targeted at the poor, the possibility that special characteristics of the low-income population may require a qualitatively different approach, and the fact that under various social welfare functions and plausible utility functions the marginal welfare weight (per dollar) is far higher at the bottom of the income distribution. Nevertheless, in focusing on lower-income individuals and transfer programs designed for their benefit, analysis should be related to the overall optimal income tax framework, as Mirrlees (1971) emphasized.[1]

Section A draws directly on chapter 4 to elaborate an integrated view of the tax and transfer system. Section B applies this analysis to certain aspects of the existing regime in the United States, highlighting how the approach taken here differs from common views. Subsequent sections explore how the framework can be used to illuminate categorical assistance, work inducements, and in-kind transfers. Much of the analysis follows Kaplow (2007d).[2]

---

[1] There exists a substantial literature on transfer programs, although most work does not make this connection. See, for example, the collections and surveys in Garfinkel (1982), Meyer and Holtz-Eakin (2001), and Moffitt (2002, 2003).

[2] Kaplow (2007d) also explores some of the subjects in further depth, especially work inducements, and provides additional references to the literature.

A. Integrated View

1. Characterization

As noted, the tax schedules $T(wl)$ examined in chapter 4 are integrated tax and transfer schemes. Specifically, the schedules include a uniform per capita grant g along with marginal tax rates $T'(wl)$. When examining actual systems of transfer programs, one can interpret g as the sum of all forms of assistance available to those earning no income, and the marginal tax rate $T'(wl)$ can be taken as the sum of the explicit marginal tax rates of the income tax and other pertinent taxes and of the phaseout rates of various transfer programs. In other words, each tax and each transfer program can be represented by its own schedule $T^i(wl)$, and we can let $T(wl) = \Sigma T^i(wl)$.[3]

Recall the integrated tax and transfer schedule from figure 4.1, reproduced here as figure 7.1. This schedule can be described in the following equivalent ways (among others): (1) A standard income tax that exempts income below $y°$ combined with a separate transfer scheme that provides g, which is fully phased out when income reaches $y°$. Income level $y°$ may (but need not) be thought of as a poverty line. (2) An income tax that has an exemption level that is less than $y°$ (including one with no exemption) combined with a transfer scheme that provides g, which is not fully phased out until an income level above $y°$. (3) A single, integrated tax and transfer scheme such as the nonlinear income tax described in chapter 4; $y°$ denotes the income level that just happens to be the point at which net tax payments equal zero.[4]

---

[3] A complication is that some transfer programs have a so-called cliff or notch effect: When income reaches a certain point, certain benefits are lost altogether. Thus, some $T^i(wl)$ may be discontinuous, so $T'(wl)$ may not be defined at particular points. (There also may be kinks in the tax schedule, but these are less troublesome for analysis.) For the most part, these complications will be ignored here. The empirical studies reported in subsection B.1 address this problem by constructing an average marginal tax rate over intervals that may contain cliffs.

[4] Writing on the so-called negative income tax was among the first to emphasize this integrated view. See, for example, Green (1967) and also Diamond's (1968) review that foreshadows the optimal income taxation literature.

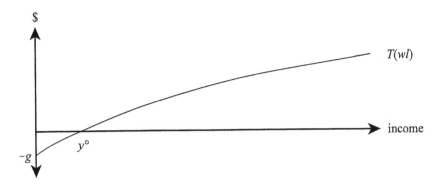

Figure 7.1. Integrated Tax and Transfer Schedule

A virtue of an integrated view that combines all taxes and transfer programs into a single function or diagram is that equivalences among systems are readily visible; relatedly, true differences are readily identified. To briefly illustrate these benefits, consider some common arguments. One concerns whether the income tax should exempt all income below some poverty line. Aside from the arbitrariness of such a threshold, there is little meaning to this question as long as transfer programs also exist: It simply does not matter if the income tax makes poor individuals pay some tax as long as the generosity of transfer payments makes up the difference.[5] Likewise, even in the absence of income tax obligations, the poor may be left in misery if transfers are insufficiently generous. Another debate is over whether transfer payments should be "means tested," that is, limited to individuals with low incomes.[6] But whether one limits g to low-income individuals, phasing it out as income rises,

---

[5] On poverty measures, see section 15.A. Another arbitrary concern is whether those with incomes modestly below the poverty line pay a few hundred dollars in income tax versus none, ignoring that the same individuals are subject to far heavier levies under payroll and other taxes that provide no exemption.

[6] See, for example, Garfinkel (1982). An additional focus of some analyses is on whether the marginal phase-out rate of transfer programs, at incomes just below y°, should be greater (perhaps substantially greater) than the marginal income tax rate on incomes just above y°. Levels of optimal tax rates (inclusive of phase-outs) on low incomes will be addressed in the next subsection and in sections C and D. None of the analysis will suggest that a sharp kink is likely to be optimal at y° or, for that matter, anywhere in the tax and transfer schedule (although kinks may sometimes be justified on administrative grounds).

or instead makes *g* universal, but applies a correspondingly higher marginal income tax rate at low income levels, is a difference in form, not substance. An additional area of frequent confusion involves provisions such as the Earned Income Tax Credit (EITC) in the United States, which will be discussed in subsection B.2.

2. Analysis

The discussion in subsection 1 makes clear that conceptually there is little point in examining in a vacuum questions like the optimal phase-out rate of this or that transfer program, the optimal design of the EITC, or the optimal level of the standard income tax for low-income individuals. Rather, the central issue concerns the optimal level of *g* and of the overall tax schedule $T(wl)$, here with special reference to the portion of the schedule that is applicable to low-income individuals (although, as will be reviewed in a moment, a central determinant of optimal marginal tax rates at low levels of income is their impact on the tax obligations of higher-income individuals).

Simulation results for optimal income tax schedules were presented in chapter 4. For the linear income tax, Stern's (1976) central case has a tax rate somewhat over 50% and a uniform grant equal to approximately one-third of average income. Slemrod, Yitzhaki, Mayshar, and Lundholm's (1994) corresponding results for the optimal two-bracket scheme has a similar grant and a somewhat higher marginal rate at the low end (approximately 60%) than at the high end. Standard simulations for the general, nonlinear case tend to have their highest marginal rates at the low end, often beginning to fall near the top. And other formulations that feature rising rates near the top still have quite high rates at the bottom—notably Saez (2001), with marginal rates at the bottom in the 70%–80% range in many cases. Furthermore, marginal rates tend to fall slightly or modestly, not precipitously, as income exceeds the poverty level and average tax rates become positive. Another important feature is that the optimum is typically characterized by a nontrivial fraction of individuals (often 5%–10%), those with the lowest abilities, not working at all, which is unsurprising given the generosity of optimal grants and high marginal tax rates at the bottom.

It is useful to recall the rationale for taxing low levels of income at high marginal tax rates, making use of the previously stated first-order condition (4.10) for the nonlinear tax (the case without income effects):

$$\frac{T'(w^* l^*)}{1 - T'(w^* l^*)} = \frac{1 - F(w^*)}{\xi^* w^* f(w^*)} \frac{\displaystyle\int_{w^*}^{\infty} \left(1 - \frac{W'(u(w))u_c}{\lambda}\right) f(w) dw}{1 - F(w^*)}. \tag{7.1}$$

Focusing on the first term on the right, we can see that three factors contribute to this result.[7] First, the numerator, $1 - F(w^*)$, is large: Raising marginal rates on very low incomes raises substantial revenue (allowing for a higher g) because most of the population has incomes higher than this level. Moreover, high rates at the bottom are inframarginal for this large group of individuals.[8] Second, in the denominator, $f(w^*)$ is not very high, indicating that only a moderate portion of the population has its labor supply distorted by high marginal rates in this income range. Third, w^* is low, so there is little lost productivity and thus little forgone revenue when such individuals reduce their labor supply.

On the other hand, the second term, reflecting the difference between the per capita revenue raised and the average welfare weight for individuals with abilities above w^*, provides some offset to the argument for high marginal rates at the bottom. Those who are inframarginal include some fairly low-income individuals, and their welfare weight is relatively high. It should be noted, however, that as long as a significant number of individuals do not work, the average welfare weight on beneficiaries of the redistribution resulting from higher marginal rates (even at very low levels of income) will be significantly greater than that on those paying higher taxes.[9] In sum, a plausible feature of

---

[7] In addition, although the elasticity component, ξ^*, in the first term is often taken to be constant, there is some evidence indicating that this elasticity is lower for low-income individuals, which would also contribute to a higher optimal marginal tax rate for them (see subsection 5.A.2).

[8] Additionally, in the more general formulation (expression 4.11), the resulting income effect induces greater labor supply, which further increases revenue.

[9] As noted in chapter 4, note 24, the result in the optimal nonlinear income tax literature that there should be a zero marginal tax at the bottom holds only in the case in which everyone works.

the optimum is that low levels of income will, in aggregate (combining explicit tax rates and phase-out rates), be subject to rather high marginal rates, consistent with the simulation results.

B. Existing System

1. Aggregate Marginal Tax Rates

To appreciate the effects of the tax and transfer system as a whole, or of any of its particular components, and to assess the desirability of proposed reforms, it is necessary to understand what exists in the aggregate. In the United States, for example, in the 1990s there was substantial welfare reform, expansion of the EITC, and proposals for comprehensive health care that contained significant implicit taxes. Yet it is not apparent whether those contemplating these policies had a clear picture of the overall situation of lower-income individuals before or after such reforms.[10]

Describing the shape of the actual schedule $T(wl)$ depicted in figure 7.1 is particularly complex at lower levels of income because of the number of transfer programs, their complexity, interactions (benefits under one program may affect those under others), and variations across jurisdictions and programs with regard to eligibility rules, income definitions, phase-out rates, availability, participation, and other factors. To address these problems, some authors employ microsimulations that consider effects averaged across populations of individuals, whereas others consider certain family configurations (say, a single parent with two children) in a particular jurisdiction or averaged across jurisdictions.

The findings of Giannarelli and Steuerle's (1995, p. 14) microsimulation, which predates the 1990s welfare reform, are indicative. In summary, they state:

Tax rates on incremental or additional earnings—even without regard to work expenses—average 3/4 of income or more across

---

[10] This problem is emphasized by Giannarelli and Steuerle (1995) and Wilson and Cline (1994).

most income ranges affecting low-income persons who decide to work any more than 1/4 time. When work expenses are added, the rates would be higher still. A significant portion of the population faces tax rates of 100 percent or more for work at a full-time minimum wage job or for increasing their work effort beyond some minimal level.

Other studies of that time period obtained similar results.[11] More recently, Sammartino, Toder, and Maag (2002) analyze tax and transfer law as of 1998 (after welfare reform) and find that a single parent with two dependents faces average (phase-out-inclusive) marginal tax rates of roughly 60%–70% when increasing earnings from half the poverty line to 125% thereof, of over 100% when moving to 150% of the poverty line, and of just over 30% beyond that point.[12]

Such high aggregate marginal tax/phase-out rates are generally decried. It should be kept in mind, however, that optimal marginal rates for lower-income individuals are likely to be high—not near or over 100%, but quite high nevertheless. That high marginal rates produce work disincentives, leading very-low-ability individuals not to work at all, is optimal, as previously noted. Even so, in some income ranges it

---

[11] Keane and Moffitt (1998) use a microsimulation approach to examine effects on typical families, and Wilson and Cline (1994) examine combined tax-transfer rates in Minnesota; both find high aggregate tax rates similar to those in Giannarelli and Steuerle (1995). Dickert, Houser, and Scholz (1994) reach somewhat less harsh conclusions, which Giannarelli and Steuerle attribute to not considering as full a range of programs and features and not making as broad a range of relevant comparisons. For previous analysis of transfer programs in the United Kingdom, see Atkinson (1983).

[12] Their analysis ignores the phase-out of Medicaid benefits and excludes work-related expenses (for example, ignoring child care costs but including benefits of child care credits). Additional studies after the mid-1990s welfare reforms reach roughly similar conclusions. See Acs et al. (1998), Gokhale, Kotlikoff, and Sluchynsky (2002) (presenting lifetime marginal tax rates in Massachusetts for two-parent couples with children), Hepner and Reed (2004) (providing a detailed examination of federal and state programs in Oklahoma, along with child care costs), and Shaviro (1999). Examination of the studies both before and after the welfare reforms reveals that the levels of benefits and thus aggregate marginal tax rates (consisting largely of benefit phase-outs) vary substantially across states due to state implementation of state-federal programs as well as unique state programs; the pattern of marginal rates as income rises also varies significantly from the norm in some states.

seems that existing aggregate marginal rates may be too high. Setting aside administrative considerations, one might equivalently address this problem through reduced phase-out rates in one or another program, greater income tax relief, or other measures.[13] On the other hand, after phase-outs are completed, existing marginal rates tend to be low, which also is unlikely to be optimal.

2. Application: Earned Income Tax Credit

Some tax and transfer systems offer earnings subsidies to low-income workers. For example, the EITC in the United States currently provides to single parents with two or more children a 40% earnings subsidy on earnings up to approximately $12,000, a benefit that is then (starting at about $16,000) phased out at a rate of just over 20%.[14] Considered in a vacuum, such a scheme may seem odd. Among other things, it seems unlikely that a 60% difference in marginal tax rates would be optimal on incomes only a few thousand dollars apart.

As the preceding discussion indicates, however, the EITC does not exist in a vacuum, but rather in a system with other taxes and transfer programs. Other transfers in the aggregate are phased out at extremely rapid rates (in certain ranges for some individuals, at rates over 100%). A subsidy like the EITC is, for many, equivalent to making the phase-out of other transfers more gradual.[15] For low levels of earnings, the phase-out may be reduced, say, from a rate of 100% to 60%. Then, as more benefits still remain, an additional phase-out is provided, in this case adding about 20% at somewhat higher earnings levels until no EITC benefits remain. (A possible explanation for the expansion of the

---

[13] Numerous specific features of the system probably warrant reform. Notably, the independent design of various components produces marginal rates well in excess of 100% in narrow income bands or cliff effects (see note 3), with far lower marginal rates in adjacent bands, features that are unlikely to be optimal (see also subsection 3).

[14] Benefits are less for only one qualifying child and quite low for earners with none.

[15] Because of differences in definitions of income or earnings, eligibility rules, and so forth, the effect varies greatly across individuals, but for many the situation is similar to that depicted in the text. In particular, those who receive the greatest EITC payments, single parents with children, also tend to receive the greatest welfare benefits under (and be in the phase-out ranges of) Temporary Assistance for Needy Families (TANF) and food stamps.

EITC—now the largest source of cash assistance to low-income individuals—in lieu of directly providing more generous welfare phase-outs is political: Reducing phase-out rates makes welfare more expensive and increases the number on the dole, whereas expanding the EITC is a tax cut to individuals who work, a seemingly substantial yet purely semantic difference.)

Because the EITC does not exist in a vacuum and changes in the EITC are largely fungible with other reforms, it is difficult to assess most arguments about its merits. Suppose, for example, that the tax-transfer schedule in figure 7.1 described an existing system and was optimal. If that existing system already includes something like the EITC—reducing otherwise excessive aggregate marginal rates on very low incomes and augmenting otherwise insufficient marginal rates on somewhat higher incomes—then the EITC would make sense (though one could readily substitute alternatives as well). Conversely, if the existing system had the appropriate shape without an EITC, then enacting one (and making no offsetting adjustments) would be undesirable. The information on the existing system in subsection 1, which incorporates both welfare programs and the EITC, suggests a mixed assessment. On one hand, marginal rates are quite high in the phase-in range of the EITC, suggesting that for many the aggregate marginal tax rate would be well over 100% in its absence. On the other hand, above the poverty line, aggregate marginal rates are now over 100% for many, in part due to the EITC phase-out. This situation may have arisen because neither EITC expansion nor reforms of various welfare programs are systematically considered in an integrated framework in which the true impact of policies can be properly appreciated.

The general difficulty of assessing the merits of the EITC per se carries over to particular arguments. The EITC is favored as a work incentive (itself a questionable characterization since it has this feature in the phase-in range but the opposite result in the phase-out range, the latter being applicable to more individuals).[16] However, as noted, adjustments in welfare phase-outs would have the same consequences; what matters

---

[16] In addition, because the EITC depends on family income, it tends to discourage work by second earners (the earnings of the primary earner placing many families in the phase-out range), as documented by Eissa and Hoynes (2006b).

with regard to labor supply is the aggregate system. Moreover, because it may well be a feature of an optimal system that the least able do not work, it is hardly obvious that the system should be engineered to provide a significant work incentive at the low end. Recall the foregoing review of the arguments favoring high marginal rates at the bottom and keep in mind that the optimal income tax framework already incorporates the effects of work on both individuals' utility and tax revenue. These points are explored further in section D on work inducements. There it is also noted that the analysis would need to be modified if there were externalities associated with work by the poor, problems of myopia, or certain other imperfections; even then, it is hardly obvious whether it is more important to move some individuals from no work to a low level of work or to avoid discouraging those at a low level of work from further increasing their efforts or skills.

The EITC also is promoted as a means of redistribution to the poor. However, one must again consider the system as a whole. And one must ask, compared to what? If revenues were instead spent on an across-the-board tax cut, the result would be less redistributive, but if they were spent raising grants to those with no earnings, the benefits would be more concentrated on the poorest of the poor.[17] The optimal income tax design problem addresses both work incentives and distribution and considers the entire income range in a comprehensive manner. As noted, it is not generally meaningful to assess whether a single piece of the system, such as the EITC, is ideal in totality or with respect to particular effects that it, in isolation, may have.

3. Administration, Eligibility, and Measurement of Need

Most transfer programs (the notable exception in the United States being the EITC) are administered through a bureaucracy independent

---

[17] The relationship between the distributive and incentive features of the EITC is often obscured. The EITC tends to favor work most clearly in comparison to expending the same revenue to increase grants to those with no earnings, which is a more redistributive scheme. The EITC is more redistributive than an across-the-board tax cut but has less desirable incentive properties than does this alternative (notably, under the EITC, all those above the EITC benefit range fail to receive a rate reduction).

from the tax authority. Typically, administrative costs for transfers are substantially higher than for taxes, a difference that in part reflects disparate and complex determinations of eligibility and the level of need under various transfer programs. Family unit and dependency definitions are more elaborate, income definitions also differ from those under the income tax, asset tests are often employed, and assistance may be provided in response to immediate changes in need.[18]

A possible rationale for devoting greater administrative resources to transfer programs is that accuracy of needs assessment is more important for low-income individuals.[19] (Additional justifications are addressed in sections C through E.) Abstracting from incentive effects, random errors in taxes and transfers reduce individuals' utilities by an amount that reflects their risk premiums, the magnitude of which is determined by individuals' degree of absolute risk aversion. If individuals have roughly constant relative risk aversion (see expression (3.3)), as commonly supposed, then absolute risk aversion falls (significantly) with income. (For example, if $u(c) = \ln c$, there is constant relative risk aversion of one, but absolute risk aversion is given by $1/c$, so individuals with a tenth as much consumption have ten times as high a level of absolute risk aversion.) Accordingly, the social welfare cost of a given absolute error is far greater for the poor. Two additional considerations are relevant. First, errors in measuring, say, income, matter in proportion to marginal tax rates, and, as noted previously, both optimal and actual marginal tax rates on the poor are quite high. Second, the magnitude of

---

[18] Transfer programs may determine eligibility and assistance levels monthly rather than yearly, presumably reflecting the view that when need is very great, it is costly to wait until the end of the year to determine what transfer an individual should previously have received. See, for example, Weisbach and Nussim (2004). Some of these traits of transfer programs also characterize the EITC, with a significant fraction of the resulting costs incurred by recipients, who often rely on paid tax preparers.

[19] See Kaplow (1998a). Of course, the large costs associated with disparities among programs in eligibility, income definitions, and so forth are difficult to justify, entail forfeiting substantial scale economies in public administration and private compliance, and produce incoherent overlaps and gaps in coverage. Nor does it appear to be the case that the public welfare bureaucracy is able to detect unreported income, which may be common among welfare recipients (see Jencks and Edin 1990).

measurement errors may tend to be proportional to income rather than constant, which would offset the tendency for errors regarding the poor to be more important.

In any event, many of the deviations between transfer programs and the income tax with respect to the measurement of need do not reflect pure matters of income measurement. One of the greatest differences between the tax system and various transfer programs involves the way family units are defined, including rules about who counts as dependents. Additionally, adjustments for family size under the income tax diminish in significance at high income levels, both because most adjustments (such as exemptions) are measured absolutely and thus decrease in relative magnitude and because many are phased out at high levels of income. As discussed in subsection 12.A.5, it is hardly clear that this relationship between adjustments and income is optimal. Moreover, even if optimal family unit adjustments should depend on income, it seems unlikely that they should change greatly just as transfers are phased out (although there may be some administrative convenience in terminating complex adjustments when they cease to be very important).

Another important difference is that many transfer programs use asset tests, for example, requiring that one's assets be fully depleted before one becomes eligible for transfers. Although the proper taxation of returns to capital is best deferred to chapter 9, it seems quite unlikely that what is essentially a 100% tax on the *principal* of one's savings makes sense from an ex ante point of view.[20] Especially for lower-income individuals (say, those with incomes modestly above the phase-out point),

---

[20] Even ignoring savings incentives, the implicit view of need that apparently underlies the propriety of asset tests seems confused. Recall the analysis in subsection A.1 (and figure 7.1) of the arbitrariness of distinguishing transfers from a single, integrated view of the tax and transfer system. Consider, for example, a scheme that is equivalent to a grant of g and a constant (linear) tax t on all income. Every individual (even the richest) receives g (that is, receives a credit of g when tax liability is positive). Fluctuating income has no effect per se on lifetime tax obligations, for as long as average income is the same, total tax payments (and total credits of g) are the same. When the optimal scheme is nonlinear, the analysis is more subtle, but it seems difficult to argue that one with fluctuating income should pay significantly more tax over time as a consequence of losing eligibility for g in low-earning years (especially since those with high incomes, fluctuating or not, never forfeit g).

any serious prospect of fluctuating income (or fluctuating eligibility, such as the possibility of having a child) will make it optimal to save little. Hence, the primary effect of asset tests may not be to reduce the cost of transfers but rather to curtail savings and related activity (such as obtaining health and disability insurance) of lower-income individuals.[21] Some empirical evidence suggests that such effects do arise.[22] Nevertheless,

---

[21] To illustrate the disincentive, consider the following simple case (for a similar discussion, see Diamond 1968). An individual has fluctuating income: In high-earning years he earns YH and in low-earning years YL. (1) Suppose that there is a 100% asset test that is effectively enforced in low-earning years. This individual would not save in high-earning years to assist in low-earning years because any such savings would be taxed in full: Consumption in high-earning years would be sacrificed, while yielding nothing in return. Hence, in high-earning years consumption will be YH and in low-earning years $YL + TP$, where TP is the transfer payment. (To simplify, other taxes are ignored—YH and YL can be thought of as after-tax income—and it will be assumed that the years alternate between YH and YL.) (2) Suppose that there is no asset test. Then the individual will wish to save S in high-earning years to help out in low-earning years (because of the declining marginal utility of income, this reallocation will increase his expected utility). His consumption will then be $YH - S$ in good years and $YL + TP + S$ in bad years. (Ideally, S would be set to equalize these amounts.) In this example, moving from a 100% asset test to no asset test raises welfare: The government is no worse off and the individual is better off, in essence because of self-insurance (he redistributes from himself when he is relatively rich to himself when he is relatively poor). More realistically, individuals would often evade an asset test (by transferring assets to relatives, converting assets to forms that are exempt, and hiding assets), in which case the total distortion would be less, but it would remain true that the government would gain little revenue.

[22] See Gruber and Yelowitz (1999) (finding both that Medicaid eligibility significantly reduces savings and that asset tests more than double the magnitude of this effect), Hubbard, Skinner, and Zeldes (1995) (demonstrating through simulations that limited savings by low-income households can be explained by asset tests), and Powers (1998) (showing that lower AFDC asset limits significantly reduce savings); but see Hurst and Ziliak (2006) (finding no statistically significant increase in assets, except possibly for vehicle ownership, as a consequence of states' increases in asset limits). As the text suggests, the provision of public insurance to the poor also reduces the value of private insurance to lower-income individuals, who in adverse circumstances may well qualify for the free public insurance. For empirical evidence, see Brown and Finkelstein (2004) (showing that Medicaid's partial, asset-tested coverage drives out more comprehensive private insurance for long-term care), Cutler and Gruber (1996) (indicating that expansion of Medicaid eligibility reduces private insurance coverage), and Sloan and Norton (1997) (finding that Medicaid long-term care insurance reduces private long-term care insurance).

there may be settings in which asset tests would have some value as screening devices.[23]

C. Categorical Assistance

Many transfer programs are more generous toward or are entirely limited to certain categories of individuals, such as families with children, single-parent families, the disabled, or the elderly. In addition, work inducements, the subject of section D, are often closely related, for they can be viewed as offering a different formula for assistance to those who are thought able to work, typically those not in some of the categories just mentioned. To examine categorical assistance, the approach here is to build on the analysis of ability-based taxation in subsection 5.C.1 to explore in greater depth how the tax and transfer system should optimally be employed when different types of individuals can be identified.[24] Existing programs are then examined in light of the resulting lessons.

1. Optimal Categorical Assistance

As a point of reference, recall the modification of the first-order condition for the optimal nonlinear income tax problem (5.1) introduced in subsection 5.C.1 on ability taxation:

$$\frac{T'(w^*l^*,\theta)}{1-T'(w^*l^*,\theta)} = \frac{1-F(w^*,\theta)}{\xi^* w^* f(w^*,\theta)} \cdot \frac{\int_{w^*}^{\infty}\left(1-\frac{W'(u(w))u_c}{\lambda}\right)f(w,\theta)dw}{1-F(w^*,\theta)}. \qquad (7.2)$$

---

[23] Asset tests serve this function in Golosov and Tsyvinski (2006), in which individuals might become permanently disabled and thus qualify for continuing disability insurance, but where disability itself is unobservable. See also the discussion in subsection 9.A.2 of the related argument favoring some taxation of capital income. Whether much use of an asset test would be optimal with an imperfect but moderately accurate direct test for disability, and in a world in which savings have other benefits, is not explored.

[24] In addition to the literature cited there, see Immonen et al. (1998).

This modification allows the distribution and density functions, F and f, to vary across groups, indexed by the variable θ.[25] Designing categorical assistance amounts to choosing the optimal tax and transfer schedule for each value of θ.

Beginning with a simple, special case, suppose that it is possible to observe perfectly which individuals have abilities below some low level, w°. Then that group can be given a high transfer g, which would not be very costly to finance because g could be fairly low for everyone else without fear that such individuals would be destitute since, by assumption, they all can earn at least a minimal income. Relatedly, it would be optimal not to tax initial earnings in the group for whom $w \geq w^\circ$ because such abstention would avoid any labor supply distortion at the bottom of the group. (The usual argument for high marginal rates near the bottom of the income distribution, reviewed in subsection A.2, is inapplicable when all earn above some minimum level because then it is more efficient to reduce the grant g than to apply a positive marginal tax at the bottom.[26])

More realistically, signals about ability will be noisy. Even though some features, such as age or certain disabilities, can be observed nearly perfectly at low cost, there will usually be differences in ability associated with these characteristics. And other traits, including some disabilities, cannot be observed perfectly. Accordingly, suppose that a low-cost signal makes it possible to divide the population into two groups (that is, θ can take two values): Group L consists mostly of individuals with very low ability, and group H contains few such individuals. That is, by reference to the population density function $f(w)$, the density $f(w,L)$ is heavily concentrated at low levels of w and the density $f(w,H)$ is very

---

[25] As noted previously and explored further in chapter 12 on the taxation of different family groupings, one could also allow individuals' utility functions to differ across groups and thus depend on θ. Although not the focus in the present chapter, this further extension is pertinent to categorical transfer programs because some of the categories receiving different treatment are different family units (for example, single-parent households) and other groupings are based on factors (for example, physical disability) that may well affect utility functions.

[26] The optimality of a zero marginal rate at the bottom in this situation is one of the results in the optimal nonlinear income tax literature (see chapter 4, note 24).

thin at the bottom. For concreteness, it may be useful to think about the case in which group L consists of individuals with physical disabilities and group H consists of everyone else. Group L would then have the stated features and, once group L is removed from the rest of the population, those who remain, group H, would necessarily have a thinner density at the bottom.

The analysis of the optimal nonlinear income tax in chapter 4 provides the basis for making conjectures about the optimal tax and transfer schedule for each group. Initially, it seems plausible that $g^L > g > g^H$. Because transfers to the lower group are limited to a subset of the population and, moreover, these individuals are disproportionately the neediest, their optimal grant will be high, both by comparison to the optimal grant under a single schedule (g) and, even more so, by comparison to the optimal grant for the group consisting mostly of more able individuals.

To determine the shape of the optimal tax schedule for each group, consider the first-order condition (7.2).[27] Begin with the more able group and focus initially on low levels of income. The first term will be notably higher than in the single-group version of the problem. The $1-F$ component in the numerator will be somewhat greater because almost everyone in the group will have higher incomes. More significantly, the f component in the denominator will be smaller, indeed, very small if the categorization is even moderately accurate. This suggests that the optimal marginal tax rate at low levels of income should be substantially higher than in the standard problem. Some offset will be provided through the second term because the fact that $g^H < g$ and the existence of higher marginal tax rates at low income levels both imply that individuals at higher income levels, associated with abilities $w > w^*$, will have lower levels of consumption and thus somewhat higher welfare weights. (This offset is likely to be most significant at the very

---

[27] As discussed in subsection 4.B.3.b, interpretations based solely on the first-order condition are inevitably speculative. Ultimately, the problem may best be illuminated through simulations of actual programs, wherein the greatest challenge will be ascertaining with reasonable accuracy each group's underlying density function, which drives the analysis in important respects.

bottom of the income scale, but only if g^H is significantly less than g, which may not be optimal.[28]) At higher levels of income, there may be less deviation between the optimal tax schedule for high-ability individuals and the optimal common tax schedule for the standard problem. At any given income (wl), $1 - F$ will be larger, favoring higher rates; f will also be larger, favoring lower rates; and the second term will continue to favor somewhat lower marginal rates. The significance of each of these factors will diminish as income increases.

For the less-able group, the results reverse. The $1 - F$ component will, after extremely low levels of income, be substantially smaller than in the combined problem, and f will be much larger, favoring low marginal rates in this income range. Some offset will be provided by the second term: Because of the more generous grant and lower initial marginal rates, the welfare cost of higher payments by those with greater income will be less than otherwise.[29] At higher levels of income, $1 - F$ and f will each be much lower, which has no clear effect on the optimal level of marginal tax rates, and the reduced second term will differ from that in the common problem to a lesser degree as income increases.

2. Application to Existing Programs

As a very crude first approximation, the system in the United States can be described as having the following elements: greater levels of g to

---

[28] Even there, the offset is unlikely to be very large because the second term is the difference between the per capita revenue gain and an average weight for the entirety of group H who have incomes above that under consideration, which includes virtually all middle- and upper-income individuals, whose social welfare weights are comparatively low. Note also that the problem of misidentifying very-low-ability individuals as having higher ability might be mitigated, even with a fairly low g^H, by making available public service employment, which could be designed as a screening device that would tend to be attractive only to individuals truly of low ability, who were not eligible for g^L because of misclassification. See the discussion of Brett (1998) and Drèze and Sen (1989) in note 38, and compare note 49 on in-kind assistance.

[29] However, by analogy to the first point in the preceding footnote, since group L includes few middle- and upper-income individuals, the average welfare weight on inframarginal individuals within this group is unlikely to be very low, so the second term as a whole is unlikely to be very high.

individuals or families deemed to have little ability to work, marginal tax rates on very low incomes that substantially consist of phase-outs of grants and hence are much higher for those receiving significantly more generous grants, and a common income tax schedule on incomes beyond the phase-out ranges. That lower-ability groups receive more assistance is optimal. Furthermore, the foregoing analysis had no clear implications for how the tax schedules for low- or high-ability groups should deviate from the optimal common schedule once income passes the lower end of the distribution, so the failure of the existing income tax to make significant distinctions is not obviously problematic.

Existing phase-outs, however, do not seem to reflect the basic features of optimality. Subsection 1 suggests that optimal marginal tax rates on fairly low incomes may be rather high for the high-ability group and low for the low-ability group. But welfare phase-outs tend to have the opposite character: When benefits are high, as they are for low-ability groups, aggregate phase-out rates are correspondingly high because there are more benefits being phased out, as documented in subsection B.1. Yet it was just suggested that optimal aggregate (phase-out inclusive) marginal tax rates for such individuals may be low, even if this means that the substantial grant is not fully phased out until income reaches higher levels. For high-ability groups, benefits are low so that there is little to phase out, and phase-out rates are correspondingly low, but the foregoing analysis explains that high marginal tax rates may nevertheless be optimal. To be sure, work will be discouraged, but by assumption there are few whose abilities would put their incomes in this range and the high marginal rates are inframarginal for everyone else.

This apparent deviation from optimality seems to be a product of unintegrated thinking. It tends to be assumed that when transfers are granted, they must be phased out, and that the phase-out must be complete at reasonably modest levels of income, lest welfare become too expensive and available to non-needy individuals.[30] And when there is little welfare to be phased out, there is thought to be, correspondingly,

---

[30] This assumption about transfers and phase-outs often characterizes formal analyses, not just political debate, as reflected, for example, in Moffitt's (2002) survey.

no need for high marginal tax rates. As section A explains, it is artificial and misleading to view components of the system in a vacuum. It is also inappropriate to allow arbitrary properties, such as phase-out targets, to guide analysis. As noted, for example, the point $y°$ in figure 7.1, the income level at which taxes and transfers net to zero, is a byproduct of optimization, not a policy target determined exogenously. (Aspects of the existing system that seem suboptimal might, however, be rationalized by externalities to work, considered in subsection D.3, or other factors such as those examined in section E on rationales for in-kind assistance.)

3. Endogenous Categorization

Categorical systems offer a more generous tax and transfer schedule to some groups than to others. Such favoritism, however, creates incentives to change one's category. If transfers are more generous when children (or a greater number of children) are present or if there is a single head of household, incentives to procreate and to marry will be affected. Likewise, preferential treatment of individuals who are disabled or otherwise unhealthy will produce moral hazard. This consideration may favor reducing the degree of differentiation to an extent that depends on the elasticity of the pertinent behavior.[31]

If categorization is employed, it is also necessary to design the classification system itself. There are issues of the burden of proof (the optimal tradeoff of type one and type two errors), optimal investments in accuracy, and the development of methods (such as application fees or waiting times) to induce individuals to self-select at the application stage.[32] Optimal classification and optimal treatment of those receiving a given classification are obviously interrelated problems, ones that require linking all the analysis—including that of administrative issues—explicitly to the social objective.

---

[31] For further discussion with regard to the family unit, see subsection 12.B.2.

[32] Various facets of these and related issues have been explored, largely in somewhat different contexts, by Diamond and Sheshinski (1995), Kaplow (1998a), and Parsons (1991, 1996).

D. Work Inducements

1. Rewarding Earnings

At various times and places—including, for example, the present in Canada, the United Kingdom, and the United States—there has been an emphasis on getting welfare recipients to work. In the foregoing analysis, however, no significance was attributed to work per se. Inefficient work disincentives are a byproduct of positive marginal tax rates, and their cost is factored into the analysis. Additionally, it was noted that a feature of the optimum in a unified system is that the lowest-ability individuals end up not working at all. In a perfect categorical system, this would continue to be true of those with the least ability, for it would be optimal to give them a generous grant despite its work disincentive effect. If those of at least a minimum ability can perfectly be identified, they will, as noted, be induced to work because their grant, g^H, will be set at a low level. When categorization is imprecise, these results will be approximated imperfectly.

Although the analysis thus appears to be complete, it is interesting to examine schemes that might induce additional work effort. One might reduce transfers by the extent to which earnings are less than some target level, perhaps the income earned in a full-time minimum-wage job. Then, the marginal return to work in the relevant range, for one who could earn only the minimum wage, would be double the wage (the earnings directly, plus a one-for-one reduction in the shortfall penalty) minus taxes and benefit phase-outs. Supposing that the latter aggregated to under 100%, the effective marginal tax rate would be negative, a net subsidy to earnings.

If everyone subject to such a regime has the requisite ability such that in an optimal scheme they all would earn at least the target level, then this policy is unproblematic. As discussed in subsection C.1, with perfect classification there should be no marginal tax on the bottom (among able) individuals, and this regime produces an outcome close to that result. However, if there are classification errors—notably, if some who are subject to the work inducement have a lower ability—then the foregoing analysis suggests that this scheme is not optimal. The possibly extremely low implicit grant level may well be too low, and marginal rates should be high, possibly quite high, rather than negative near the target. Also, it is quite unlikely to be optimal for the marginal tax rate to jump on the order of 100 percentage points at the target income level.

A more extreme version of this sort of scheme would be closer to an actual work requirement. One could take away all welfare benefits (or a significant portion of them) if an individual earned even slightly below the target earnings level.[33] Once again, if classification were perfect, and in the optimal scheme everyone would meet the target in any event, this sort of approach would be benign. However, with classification errors, this extreme approach would be worse than the previously mentioned gradual penalty, a result implied by the analysis in subsection C.1.[34] Forcing individuals to increase earnings with very heavy marginal rewards tends not to be optimal despite the problem of labor supply distortion.

2. Rewarding Hours

As explored in subsection 5.C.1, it is possible to improve on the result of the optimal income tax problem if more information can be obtained, in particular, about individuals' earning abilities. Moreover, it was explained that abilities—here, wages—can be inferred if, in addition to earnings, hours can be observed. Since some work inducement schemes assume the observability of hours, it is useful to examine this possibility further.

---

[33] In considering this scheme, it is useful to note that due to phase-outs (or, under an integrated scheme, positive and possibly high marginal tax rates), the remaining benefit at the target level of work would be modest.

[34] Consider further a scheme that, say, makes a grant (or a significant increment to a meager base-level grant) available only if one reaches a target income and that applies a zero marginal tax rate on incomes up to that level. Suppose that one reduced this work-reward grant and increased the grant available at zero income. If done in a revenue-neutral manner, one could not raise the base grant in full because additional individuals, those with such low ability that they do not reach the target, would now be eligible. The redistributive effect (holding labor supply fixed) would obviously be positive. Furthermore, some individuals would now work less—both very low-ability individuals who did not previously reach the target and moderate-ability individuals who were at the target—but these adjustments raise their utility and have no effect on revenue. Finally, the negative income effect (due to the lower combined grant) on those who previously earned above the target results in greater labor supply, increasing their utility and also raising additional revenue.

As previously noted, if ability is fully observable, the first best can be achieved, using individualized (ability-based) lump-sum taxes and transfers and subjecting all individuals to a 0% marginal tax rate. One could impose work requirements in such a regime, but there would be no point since labor is undistorted; forcing individuals to work more than they would choose is feasible but suboptimal.

Another case of interest is a sort of conditional observability of ability: If ability is inferred from the (presumed perfect) observability of earnings and hours, then ability is observed for all except those who do not work at all. This qualification prevents achievement of the first best because individuals who at the optimum would work (but who would not reap the rewards because of the differential lump-sum taxes) would mimic those who, at the first-best optimum, do not. In the resulting second-best optimum, the grant to non-workers would have to be smaller and the extraction from higher-ability types less severe, although zero marginal tax rates on the earnings of those who do work would remain optimal (see Dasgupta and Hammond 1980).[35]

This optimal design contrasts sharply with existing and proposed work inducement schemes premised on the observability of hours. For example, there are schemes that reduce benefits by an hours shortfall multiplied by a target wage rate, such as the minimum wage (rather than by an earnings shortfall, as in the example in subsection 1).[36] There are also stronger versions, for example, that make a work-reward grant

---

[35] See also related models by, for example, Diamond (1980) and Saez (2002b) that focus on the participation decision and find, with certain further assumptions, that subsidizing work of the lowest types may be optimal because the alternative of raising the uniform grant causes some higher types to forgo work altogether. (The high types are assumed to be unable to mimic the lowest working types by earning a modest income with little effort.)

[36] See, for example, Mead (2004), describing such a program in Wisconsin. Stated more precisely, let $w°$ and $l°$ denote the target wage and required labor supply and t the (flat) pre-existing aggregate (inclusive of phase-outs) marginal tax rate below the target income level. Then, for $l < l°$, disposable income available for consumption, c, is

$$c = g + wl(1-t) - w°(l° - l), \text{ or}$$
$$= [g - w°l°] + wl(1 - \tau),$$

where $\tau = t - w°/w$. Also observe that wage subsidies are similar.

contingent on reaching a target denominated in hours (rather than income, as in subsection 1).[37] Neither of these schemes closely resembles the optimum just described.[38]

In addition, as subsection 5.C.1 further notes, hours are likely to be highly manipulable. Employers may conspire with employees to overstate or inflate hours (and understate the wage), and outside the formal sector's large employers, potential circumvention could be far worse, for no one except the worker regularly observes the worker's total hours.[39] Accordingly, the preceding analysis of categorization based on a noisy signal, where within each category only income is observed, becomes fully applicable, and we have already seen that the optimal regime for those classified as able differs markedly from work inducement arrangements.

3. Other Reasons to Encourage or Discourage Work

Perhaps special attention to work incentives beyond that already incorporated in the optimal income tax framework can be justified on other

---

[37] See, for example, Blundell and Walker's (2002) examination of the Working Families' Tax Credit in the United Kingdom and Michalopoulos, Robins, and Card's (2005) study of an experimental program in Canada.

[38] Fortin, Truchon, and Beauséjour (1993) find that introduction of a strong work requirement may be welfare improving by reference to their benchmark of a negative income tax with a 100% grant phase-out rate, but they find other, less extreme negative income tax proposals with no work requirement to be even better. Besley and Coate (1995) reach a contrary result in a model in which the objective is not welfare maximization but rather minimization of the cost of bringing all individuals up to a target level of consumption without regard to the utility they thereby achieve. They find that a form of workfare, under which the poorest perform unproductive public service jobs with high disutility, is optimal. (In essence, individuals are subject to a nonmonetary penalty if they wish to receive cash assistance rather than work in the private sector.) When Besley and Coate instead consider a goal of providing a minimum target level of utility rather than of consumption, such workfare is no longer optimal. With a standard objective function, Brett (1998) finds that tying benefits to public sector work may be optimal if such work is sufficiently productive, because limiting benefits in this fashion is selectively advantageous to low-ability individuals, who forgo less market income than do high-ability types when they engage in public rather than market employment. In a similar spirit, Drèze and Sen (1989) discuss the self-selection benefits of public employment in disbursing famine relief in developing countries.

[39] Moffitt (2002) suggests that the manipulability of wages and hours explains why earnings rather than wage subsidies are more common.

grounds. Work by the poor might augment their human capital, leading to increases in effective earning ability in the future. If individuals are not myopic, however, they should already be taking this benefit into account. (To be sure, the benefits are discounted in light of positive marginal tax rates, but this distortion is similar to the basic distortion in labor supply already considered.) Nevertheless, myopia might be a real concern; indeed, more myopic individuals who accordingly make insufficient investments in their own human capital may for that very reason be disproportionately concentrated at the lower end of the income distribution.[40]

Externalities may also be present. It is often suggested, for example, that parents serve as role models for their children, so the failure to work perpetuates poverty, harming both the children (and future generations) and others, such as by increasing crime. Additionally, individuals who work, having less free time, may themselves be less likely to engage in criminal activity. Also, there may be a psychological externality to other citizens who derive utility (or avoid negative utility) from the fact that lower-income transfer recipients work. On the other hand, if parents, especially single parents, are encouraged or forced to leave the home for a greater period of time, child care and supervision may suffer. The significance of these concerns and how they vary by family configuration, age of children, and income level are empirical questions about which little is known with confidence.[41] It might be supposed that, as

---

[40] Lawrance's (1991) evidence that low-income, less-educated individuals appear to have a greater subjective discount rate may reflect a higher susceptibility to myopia rather than different underlying preferences.

[41] Grogger and Karoly (2005) find that welfare reforms tended to raise children's well-being only when the reforms raised family incomes (through generous work incentives), while reforms that were more likely to reduce welfare dependency were more likely to be associated with negative effects on children. Levine and Zimmerman (2005) explore whether welfare spells adversely affect children and find that, with proper controls, there is no significant detrimental effect. Antel (1992), however, finds that a mother's welfare participation increases the likelihood of her daughter's subsequent participation. Duncan, Hill, and Hoffman (1988) survey earlier literature that provides mixed evidence, some of which suggests a degree of transmission of dependency, although determining causation is difficult.

with returns to investment in human capital, these effects are largely internal to the family (though effects on crime obviously are not). However, as will be explored in section 12.A on the taxation of different family units, this is not the case: Parents consider only the benefit to themselves (even if it is a highly altruistic benefit) and not the additional benefit to the children. Accordingly, if there are significant effects on children, one way or the other, they may justify departures from what the basic analysis would otherwise indicate to be optimal.

E. Cash versus In-Kind Transfers

The standard presumption is that transfers should be made in cash because preferences vary and individuals tend to have better information about their own situations than does the government. Nevertheless, a substantial portion of transfers are given in kind, through food stamps, medical care, and housing, and there is universal provision of free public education. In some instances, in-kind provision makes little difference, such as with food stamps if there is little restriction on the use of the vouchers and the amount does not exceed what recipients would otherwise have spent on food (or if black market trade is possible).[42] But voucher amounts may exceed intended expenditures and less cash-like provision may vary from what individuals would otherwise have chosen in quality and quantity.

A number of considerations may nevertheless support in-kind provision.[43] Most broadly, poor individuals may be thought to lack the skills to make good decisions or may suffer from myopia and thus underspend in certain important categories.[44] As noted, such infirmities might

---

[42] For empirical evidence that food stamps do not affect consumption allocations, see Moffitt (1989).

[43] Many of the arguments are noted by Nichols and Zeckhauser (1982).

[44] See, for example, Lawrance (1991), in note 40, on myopia, and Shore (1997), who suggests that personality disorders are prevalent among the poor, which may favor offering some assistance in-kind in the form of treatment.

be especially prevalent among the poor because these shortcomings may be important causes of individuals' low earning ability.

In addition, a range of externalities may be present: Better housing may reduce crime, immunizations may prevent the spread of communicable disease, and education may produce myriad benefits. Such externalities may apply to the population at large; indeed, free education is not limited to the poor, compulsory education requirements exist, and many immunizations are effectively mandatory. In some instances, however, externalities may be especially pronounced at very low levels of consumption that may be likely only for the poor. There may also be psychic externalities, notably if taxpayers feel better about transfers knowing that most will be spent on food, shelter, medical care, or education.[45] Additionally, taxpayers may be subject to the Samaritan's dilemma, concerned about strategic imprudence by potential beneficiaries who anticipate being bailed out after the fact by concerned donors, public or private; hence, compulsory health and other social insurance programs may be particularly appealing.[46]

Another type of externality is that parents who control household resources may give insufficient weight to the well-being of their children, as mentioned in subsection D.3. Much in-kind provision does force an allocation of benefits to children: Medical care may be freely available to children but not amenable to being cashed out by parents, school breakfast and lunch programs ensure that some food is consumed by children, and free education combined with compulsory attendance laws obviously prevents parents from benefiting at their children's

---

[45] See, for example, Garfinkel (1973). Taxpayers may have such feelings on account of the aforementioned considerations; for instance, they may believe that the poor are myopic. Or certain sorts of suffering—homelessness being a notable example—may be particularly visible. There is also the somewhat elusive category of merit goods or wants. See, for example, Musgrave (1959). Most goods or services so classified seem to be public goods, goods producing externalities (including psychic benefits to taxpayers), or goods where paternalism based on information infirmities may be warranted—that is, those for which the other justifications noted in the text are applicable. To the extent that merit goods are not of these types, the rationale for their subsidization or in-kind provision is unclear.

[46] See, for example, Bruce and Waldman (1991) and Coate (1995).

expense.[47] As with some other externalities, it may be believed that serious deficits of a sort that can be remedied through in-kind provision are most likely to occur only at very low incomes; otherwise, general subsidies or universal requirements may be more appropriate.

Of special relevance to the present inquiry are possible justifications for in-kind provision that relate more directly to the work disincentives attributable to redistribution. As discussed in section 6.C on qualifications to the conclusion that commodities should be taxed uniformly, it may be optimal to favor expenditures on goods and services complementary to labor (perhaps child care) and on commodities that tend to be more attractive to low-ability (as distinguished from low-income) individuals.[48] In-kind provision can play a similar role, although these rationales apply to everyone, not just to individuals below some income threshold. There are also other subtle reasons that in-kind provision may help mitigate labor supply distortion.[49]

---

[47] Currie (1994) offers evidence that in-kind programs do channel greater benefits to children.

[48] Not only may low-ability individuals have different preferences, but high-need individuals may as well. For example, otherwise identical individuals may have different health needs that are not observable. To channel assistance to unhealthy individuals without making the more generous allotment attractive to healthy mimickers, the aid may be in the form of subsidies to medical expenditures or in-kind provision of medical services. See, for example, Blackorby and Donaldson (1988).

[49] It is sometimes suggested that giving low-quality in-kind goods (such as mediocre housing) may be advantageous because it would discourage high-ability individuals from mimicking low-ability individuals. However, when high-ability individuals mimic, they do so by actually earning less. Given their resulting low disposable income, it is not obvious that they would have preferences for goods of higher quality than those preferred by low-ability individuals earning the same income. Essentially forcing low-income individuals to consume less-preferred consumption bundles does discourage mimicking; however, it could be discouraged more efficiently by providing cash assistance of equal value to the degraded good but, by assumption, of lesser cost (compare Munro 1989). Employing value-reducing in-kind provision is pointless unless it somehow discriminates by ability rather than by income level. (Similar analysis applies to reduction in the attractiveness of transfer payments through stigmatization. Compare the discussion of workfare in note 38.) The situation would be different if the high-ability mimickers in fact earned more but were able to evade taxes, in which case their income reports would match those of low-income individuals but their true income and thus preferences for goods would not.

In all, many factors may support in-kind provision or differential taxation (subsidization) of particular goods and services. Although the conventional forms of in-kind benefits track many of these justifications, it is an empirical question whether and to what extent existing departures from cash assistance make sense.[50]

---

[50] In-kind medical care, which when measured by its cost constitutes a significant fraction of assistance to the poor, is subject to question. It is not obvious that some of these resources would not be better allocated to food, shelter, or other items. Moreover, some evidence suggests that other (wisely chosen) expenditures may contribute more to health than some categories of expenditures on medical care itself.

8

Goods and Services

🦎

Government expenditures on goods and services constitute a substantial fraction of GDP in most countries.[1] Accordingly, their distributive incidence is presumptively important, especially since it cannot be assumed that the benefits of such government provision are distributed proportionately to private goods consumption. In particular, publically provided goods and services may contribute heavily to the standard of living of the poor, especially in countries with a large public sector. Thus, there is reason to believe that the omission of goods and services from analysis pertaining to redistribution would provide an incomplete and potentially misleading understanding of the subject.

More specifically, as chapter 2 emphasizes, one cannot assess the redistributiveness of taxation without regard to how the proceeds are spent. It was further suggested (for example, in section 2.A's discussion of flat tax proposals) that the level of taxation may be more important than the shape of the tax schedule in assessing the extent of redistribution precisely because of how the additional funds are expended. The initial formulation of the problem assumed that all revenue was spent on a uniform transfer, g. Chapter 7 explicitly examined transfer programs, which may be more focused on the poor. This chapter completes the picture by considering revenue that is spent on goods and services rather than on transfers.[2]

---

[1] This chapter considers government expenditures on all goods and services, regardless of the extent to which they are public goods in the technical sense. Nevertheless, the term "public goods" will often be employed for convenience and also because optimal government provision will tend to be concerned primarily with true public goods.

[2] The subjects obviously blur, such as in the case of in-kind transfers. The distinction is, however, conventional, often fairly clear, and useful in exposition, although nothing in principle turns on the classification.

The simplest approach is to treat direct expenditures in the same manner as transfers. The uniform transfer g might be interpreted as the sum of a uniform cash transfer and per capita expenditures on goods and services. Or, if some public expenditures are concentrated, say, on the poor, one could reflect this, just as with direct transfers, as part of a single, integrated schedule, following the approach in chapter 7. The unified tax-transfer system would now be understood as a tax-transfer-expenditure system. The choice between transfers and direct expenditures would be made on ordinary efficiency grounds associated with the determination of the optimal provision of public goods—that is, the Samuelson (1954) rule, under which the sum of individuals' marginal benefits is equated to the marginal cost of provision.

Two caveats are standard. First, one cannot just stipulate some simple distributive incidence for public expenditures. If the actual incidence in fact involves a uniform dollar benefit to all, then reflecting this as a higher g would be appropriate. However, because the distributive incidence of public goods varies, many suggest that distributive weights be incorporated in cost-benefit analysis.[3] But whether and how one should account for distributive effects in a framework like that here, in which the income tax and transfer system is taken to be an integral part of the analysis, needs further exploration.

Second, because redistributive income taxation is distortionary, it has long been suggested that the distortionary costs of finance must also be accounted for in considering the optimal level of government provision of public goods and services.[4] Moreover, the provision of goods and services itself may affect labor supply and hence the extent of distortion. For example, if a public good is more valuable the greater is one's income (suppose that the value of police protection of private property is proportional to the value of the property that is thereby protected), then greater provision may encourage labor supply. Likewise, provision

---

[3] See, for example, Weisbrod (1968), Feldstein (1974), and Drèze and Stern (1987).

[4] The concern was first introduced by Pigou (1928); subsequently explored by Diamond and Mirrlees (1971), Stiglitz and Dasgupta (1971), and Atkinson and Stern (1974) in models of optimal taxation; and further developed in additional work, much of which is surveyed in Mayshar (1991a), Fullerton (1991), and Ballard and Fullerton (1992).

of public goods that are particularly valuable to the poor (who perhaps cannot afford superior private substitutes) may discourage work. These considerations pertaining to labor supply distortion thus appear to require adjustments to simple cost-benefit analysis.[5]

The relevance of the distributive incidence of public expenditures and the distortionary cost of finance is not limited to the determination of the optimal provision of public goods and services. The optimal extent and nature of redistributive taxation, one would suppose, is influenced by both of these considerations. After all, the distributive incidence of public goods affects the extent of inequality, which is a central determinant of the optimal income tax schedule. In addition, the level of taxation necessary to finance public goods might affect the marginal distortionary cost of redistribution.

To address these and related issues, the distribution-neutral approach outlined in chapter 2 and formalized for the case of differential commodity taxes in chapter 6 can be extended to incorporate government expenditures on goods and services. This method is illustrated in section A. Section B analyzes the case in which government expenditures on goods and services are a perfect substitute for consumption of private goods. In this instance, modeling government expenditures as a simple increase in g is correct, and it can be shown that optimal government provision is determined by the ordinary cost-benefit test (with no adjustments for distribution or labor supply distortion) and that the determination of the optimal extent of redistribution is essentially unaffected. Sections C and D analyze more general cases and determine the implications for optimal public good provision and optimal redistribution, respectively. The ideas developed in these sections

---

[5] Effects on labor supply can be related to the idea that government expenditures may be modeled as a simple increase in g. If this formulation were correct, there would be income effects that are relevant in a second-best setting. Actual public goods, however, may not have income effects, notably, when public goods are additively separable in individuals' utility functions. (In this case, as discussed later, utility rather than dollar benefits would be constant as a function of income, which implies that benefits measured in dollars would rise with income due to the diminishing marginal utility of consumption.) Furthermore, a range of substitution effects is possible, depending on how government expenditures enter into individuals' utility functions.

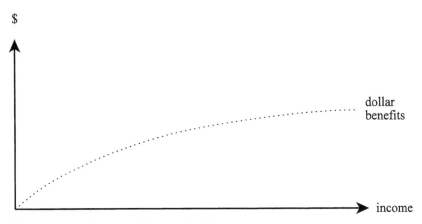

Figure 8.1. Distributive Incidence of Public Good

are also employed in section E to illuminate familiar problems involved in the measurement of the distributive incidence of government expenditures and in section F to clarify disputes about the appropriate concept of benefit taxation. Finally, section G extends the analysis of government expenditures to another important sphere of government activity, namely, regulation, where concerns about distributive incidence are often raised and interactions with labor supply distortion attributable to redistributive income taxation have become an important subject of research.

A. Distribution-Neutral Income Tax Adjustments

To begin, in considering whether to undertake some project (say, the provision of a public good, like a park), one would examine its distributive incidence, as portrayed in figure 8.1 (which abstracts from the preexisting system of taxes, transfers, and other expenditures). In this example, the benefits (measured in dollars) are assumed to rise with income, but at a less-than-proportional rate.

The next step is to choose an adjustment to the income tax and transfer system to finance this public good. As emphasized in chapter 2, the adjustment chosen is an essential determinant of the overall distributive incidence. Three examples are considered.[6]

---

[6] In each case, the tax adjustment may have a feedback effect on the valuation of the

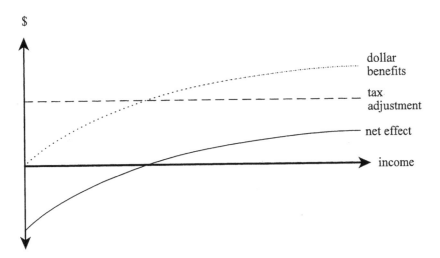

Figure 8.2A. Public Good Financed by Uniform Tax Adjustment

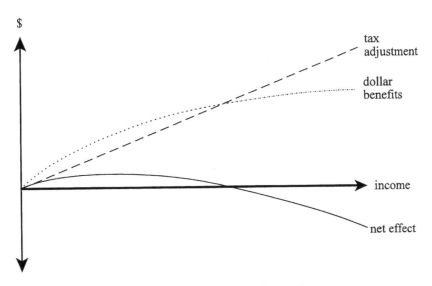

Figure 8.2B. Public Good Financed by Proportional Tax Adjustment

Figure 8.2A depicts a uniform tax adjustment: Every individual's taxes are raised (or transfers reduced) by a dollar amount equal to the average benefits of the public good. The net effect (the dollar

public good at different levels of income; however, if one considers a marginal change in the level of the public good, this effect will be negligible.

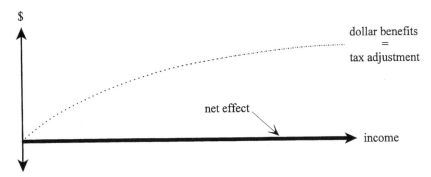

Figure 8.2C. Public Good Financed by Distribution-Neutral (Offsetting) Tax
       Adjustment

benefits minus the tax adjustment) is to redistribute from the poor to
the rich.

In figure 8.2B, the tax adjustment is proportional—that is, the same
amount is added to everyone's marginal income tax rate—and the revenue is again just sufficient to equal the total dollar amount of individuals'
benefits. Here, the net effect is to redistribute from the rich to the poor.
Just as chapter 2 emphasized that any particular tax could have a wide
range of distributive effects depending on the public expenditures it was
assumed to finance, these figures illustrate the converse: that, for any
given public good, the net effect regarding redistribution depends on
how it is financed.

Furthermore, chapter 2 suggested that it is useful when assessing
policies to consider distribution-neutral finance, that is, an adjustment
to the income tax and transfer system that just offsets the distributive
incidence of the project in question. As figure 8.2C indicates, it is
straightforward to determine the distribution-neutral (offsetting) tax
adjustment for any public good. One simply sets the tax adjustment
equal to the dollar benefits of the public good at every level of income.
(This is identical to the approach used in chapter 6 for income tax
adjustments to accompany commodity tax reforms.) By contrast to the
preceding two examples, the result is that there is no redistributive effect
whatsoever.

These examples reinforce the claim that it may be misleading (or,
arguably, meaningless) to contemplate the distributive incidence of

government expenditures on goods and services in isolation from how they are to be financed. In addition, it is suggested that distribution-neutral (offsetting) finance is the most useful means to consider. When that is done, the distributive incidence of government expenditures would seem to be irrelevant for the simple reason that the net incidence is zero. Likewise, figure 8.2C suggests that labor supply effects also will not exist, for the net effect of the project and finance is nil—and, moreover, is unaffected by how much income one chooses to earn.

Finally, examination of figures 8.2A and 8.2B provides support for a closely related idea: In this setting, redistribution and labor supply distortion are opposite sides of the same coin. With the proportional tax (figure 8.2B), there is a net redistributive effect; as the figure reveals, earning higher income is less attractive (and earning lower income more attractive) than without the reform package. With the uniform tax (figure 8.2A), there is a net reduction in redistribution; earning higher income is more attractive (and earning lower income less attractive) than otherwise. The seemingly neutral result for the distribution-neutral (offsetting) tax adjustment (figure 8.2C) lies at the balancing point between these other two cases. It is characterized by no change in distribution and no direct change in labor supply incentives.

In all, these illustrations suggest that although the distributive incidence of government expenditures is presumptively important, it may not have the effects on the analysis of optimal government provision of goods and services or of optimal redistributive taxation that one might have initially supposed. These notions—and their limitations—are made more precise in the sections that follow.

B. Special Case: Government Provision
Perfect Substitute for Consumption

The approach here parallels that used in chapter 6 to analyze commodity taxation. Throughout this chapter, individuals' utility functions are assumed to be of the form $u(v(c,G),l)$, where c is consumption, G is expenditures on public goods and services, l is labor supply, and v is a subutility function. As before, this formulation embodies weak separability of labor, which means here that individuals' marginal rates of substitution between ordinary consumption c and public goods G do not depend on the level of labor effort l that was necessary to support a given level of consumption. Further assumptions and notation are the same as in prior chapters.[7]

In this section only, it will be further assumed that the subutility function v takes the following particular form:

$$v(c,G) = v(c+b(G)), \qquad\qquad\qquad\qquad (8.1)$$

where $b(G)$ indicates how government expenditures translate into consumption-equivalent (dollar) benefits. That is, government expenditures are taken to be a perfect substitute for consumption, the only question being the efficiency of the substitute.[8]

Constructing the distribution-neutral (offsetting) income tax adjustment is straightforward. First, recall that, beginning with the income tax and transfer schedule $T(wl)$, we seek the tax schedule $T°(wl)$ with the property that, if all individuals (of every type w) continue to choose the same level of labor effort $l(w)$ as under the initial tax system, then their utility will be unchanged. For a marginal change in G, the tax adjustment is given by individuals' marginal rate of substitution, $v_G/v_c = b'/1 = b'$. (As before, subscripts denote derivatives with respect to the identified argument and primes denote derivatives with respect to a function's only argument.) For a discrete change, say from G^0 to G^1, the tax adjustment is $b(G^1) - b(G^0)$. Observe that this tax adjustment is independent of income because the government expenditures are equivalent (in utility) to cash, to an equal degree for everyone.[9]

---

[7] Both c and G can be interpreted as vectors, but the scalar representation will be used to simplify exposition. Most of the qualifications discussed in section 6.C are pertinent here but will not be repeated.

[8] For empirical evidence on the plausibility of this case, see Ahmed and Croushore (1996) and Aschauer (1985).

[9] These concepts are separate. For example, if the subutility function were instead $v(c(1+b(G)))$, government expenditures would be like cash, but in an amount that was proportional to expenditures on ordinary consumption. (This formulation corresponds to the police protection example in which the service has a value proportional to consumption because consumption is assumed to be what is protected from theft.)

A number of implications are immediate. First, any individual (regardless of earning ability w) will choose the same level of labor effort l in the initial regime and in that with a different level of G financed by this distribution-neutral tax adjustment. The reason is that, due to the offsetting tax adjustment, both subutility, v, and utility, u, are the same for any choice of l in both regimes, so whatever l maximizes utility initially will also do so with the reform.

Second, this result entails that everyone's utility is the same as in the initial regime, which implies that the distribution of utility is also the same. In sum, neither labor supply effects nor concerns about the distributive incidence of public provision are relevant.

Third, whether more or less of such a public good should be provided depends entirely on its efficiency, namely, on whether $b' > 1$. If this condition holds, then raising G, financed by the stipulated tax adjustment, generates a surplus, which can be rebated (say, pro rata) making every individual better off. If $b' < 1$, then a reduction in G would generate a surplus, again with a pro rata rebate making everyone better off. (This part of the argument also follows that in chapter 6.)

Fourth, in this case the level of public provision has essentially no effect on the optimal extent of redistribution. The government expenditure on the good or service can be treated as tantamount to the use of government revenue to finance the uniform grant g. Considering the case in which $b' = 1$, changes in the level of public provision, financed by the offsetting tax adjustment, leave the problem of optimal redistribution totally unaffected. If instead it were possible to expend revenue on a program for which $b' > 1$, the only difference would be that, for a given initial income tax and transfer schedule, it would now be possible to finance (in a sense, for free) a somewhat higher grant g. If that were done, the resulting reduction in inequality would make redistribution somewhat less desirable, so the optimal level of marginal tax rates would fall. (This follows from the first-order conditions for both the optimal linear and nonlinear income tax problems, as discussed in chapter 4.) That is, efficient expenditures on public goods of this sort would, at the resulting redistributive optimum, involve somewhat less inequality and somewhat less distortion than otherwise (and conversely if inefficient expenditures on such public goods were made). Formally, changes in such expenditures have the same effect on the optimum as an exogenous change in the revenue requirement in standard optimal income tax analyses.[10]

Although the present case is, on reflection, trivial, it is nevertheless illuminating. It shows that there exists a special case (indeed, one examined in some of the pertinent literature, as noted later) in which two simple, important results hold: Optimal provision is determined by the simple cost-benefit test, and the optimal income redistribution problem is essentially unaffected. These results are important because, regardless of the empirical plausibility of the case in question, they show that a number of standard views about policy analysis of government provision are not correct as a general matter. Furthermore, when one considers a broader range of cases, it is hardly clear whether and in which direction the various conclusions will change. As will be seen, some parts of the problem are simpler and others subtler than has been appreciated.

C. General Case: Distributive Incidence and Optimal Provision

1. Analysis

Return to the more general formulation of the utility function $u(v(c,G), l)$, which still maintains the assumption of weak separability of labor. Again, the approach will be to identify the distribution-neutral (offsetting) adjustment to the income tax and transfer system, show that it does not affect labor supply, and determine whether it generates a budget surplus or deficit.

The offsetting tax adjustment for a marginal change in G is given by the marginal rate of substitution, v_G/v_c. To verify this, we need to consider whether this shift in the schedule T will be such that $\partial u/\partial G = 0$ for all types w and at every level of l that each type might supply. (This is a partial derivative because labor supply is being held constant; in the

---

[10] The analysis in this paragraph is presented more fully and rigorously in Kaplow (2006e).

next step, it is shown that individuals indeed do not change labor effort when this tax adjustment is employed.) Thus, we consider

$$\frac{\partial u}{\partial G} = \frac{\partial u}{\partial v}(v_c c_G + v_G), \tag{8.2}$$

where c_G denotes the (here partial) derivative of c with respect to G. From the budget constraint (4.1),

$$c_G = -\frac{\partial T(wl, G)}{\partial G}, \tag{8.3}$$

where the notation $T(wl, G)$ is used to indicate how the tax schedule will be adjusted as G is changed. If the tax adjustment is set equal to v_G/v_c, as suggested, then $c_G = -v_G/v_c$. Thus, substituting (8.3) into (8.2) yields the result that $\partial u/\partial G = 0$ for any given w and l.

Consider next whether individuals in fact would change their labor supply in response to a change in G financed by the specified adjustment to the tax schedule T. Just as in the prior case in which it was assumed that public goods were a perfect substitute for cash, it should be apparent that individuals of all types w would not in fact change their labor supply. The reason is that expression (8.2) equals zero for any given l and hence for all l. Therefore (for each type w), if l^* was superior to all $l \neq l^*$ before G was changed, this will remain true afterward because the utility at each and every l is unaltered by the change in G, when combined with the offsetting adjustment to T. The analysis is the same as that in chapter 6 on commodity taxation, although the particular tax adjustment necessary to offset the contemplated reform differs. (Figure 6.1, which displays this result in terms of the reduced-form utility function $U(l)$, is directly applicable; one can simply interpret the depicted reform as involving a change in the level of a public good rather than a change in commodity taxation.)[11] Also recall that the intuition behind

---

[11] For a more formal derivation along these lines as well as one that differentiates the first-order condition for l with respect to G and uses the result to demonstrate that $dl/dG = 0$, see Kaplow (1996d, 2006e) and also Auerbach and Hines (2002).

this result is suggested by figure 8.2C, which shows a public good financed by an offsetting tax adjustment: Because the net effect is nil at every level of income, one would not expect anyone's incentive to earn income to be affected by such a reform package.

Hence, government provision of a good or service when financed by a distribution-neutral (offsetting) tax adjustment keeps everyone's utility (and hence the distribution of utility) constant and everyone's labor supply unchanged. It remains to determine how the government's budget is affected. But this is straightforward because the tax adjustment equals (at the margin) individuals' marginal rates of substitution. Total revenue, therefore, is given by the integral of individuals' marginal rates of substitution, so there will be a surplus if the Samuelson rule is satisfied. As before, when the project passes the cost-benefit test, it is possible to rebate the surplus to make everyone better off. (When the project fails the test, there would be a deficit, which implies that a movement in the opposite direction will make possible a Pareto improvement.)

2. Examples

It is instructive to examine concrete examples. First, consider a government expenditure, say on parks improvement, that results in a uniform dollar benefit of $100 for everyone. (This would correspond to the case in section B in which the project is a perfect substitute for consumption and thus equally valuable, in dollars, to everyone.) The distribution-neutral (offsetting) tax adjustment would be $100, regardless of income level. This combination leaves everyone (regardless of income level) equally well off as before, and it is apparent that labor supply would be unaffected. Hence, there will be a surplus if and only if the project cost is less than $100 per capita, which is to say if and only if the standard cost-benefit test is satisfied. Note further that, although finance is stipulated to be provided by a uniform (lump-sum) adjustment to the tax system, the ordinary objections to lump-sum taxation are inapplicable. A uniform adjustment is feasible (by contrast to individualized lump-sum taxation that depends on unobservable traits like earning ability). Also, it is not distributively problematic because it is being used to finance a project with the same incidence, producing an equal dollar gain to every individual.

Second, consider the example of increased spending on police protection that reduces theft, the benefit of which is assumed to be proportional to consumption. In this case, the offsetting tax adjustment in the simple case of a linear tax with no grant would raise everyone's marginal income tax rate by the same amount, so as to reduce consumption by an amount just equal to the benefit. Again labor supply is unaffected: The reduction in the return to additional labor effort due to the higher marginal tax rate will—by construction—just equal the increase in the return to additional labor effort due to the fact that one loses less income to theft. Thieves take less at the margin and the government takes more, in offsetting amounts. Thus, a standard cost-benefit test is appropriate here as well.

More generally, government expenditures on goods and services may have any incidence whatsoever, as explored in subsection 1 and as depicted for an arbitrary case in figure 8.2C. But, as that figure illustrates, whatever is the distributive incidence of the program, one can define an offsetting tax adjustment that is identical in magnitude at each level of income, and the remainder of the analysis proceeds as before.

It is worth reflecting further on the source of the result that the combined package of a government expenditure and a distribution-neutral (offsetting) income tax adjustment has no effect on labor effort. It must be that, whatever would have been the labor supply effect of the tax adjustment considered in isolation, the government expenditure has precisely the opposite labor supply effect. This can be seen in each example. In the first, a uniform dollar increase in everyone's tax obligation involves a pure income effect that would raise everyone's labor supply. At the same time, the public good that is equivalent to cash for everyone has a pure income effect that is opposite in direction and identical in magnitude to that of the tax adjustment. In the second example, the increase in everyone's marginal tax rate would produce a substitution effect that reduces labor supply, but the public good itself, by making earnings more valuable, has an offsetting positive substitution effect.

More generally, it need not be true that any income or substitution effect of the tax adjustment be matched, respectively, by an offsetting income or substitution effect of the government project. All that is required is that the net effect on labor supply from the tax adjustment (combining the income and substitution effects) match the net effect on labor supply from the project. An example in the margin illustrates how this result can arise more subtly than in the two preceding examples.[12] All complications aside, the intuition from figure 8.2C (and also from figure 6.1) makes the bottom line clear: Because the tax adjustment is, by construction, offsetting, the utility associated with every level of income is the same as it was initially, so it must be that there is no net change in any individual's labor supply.[13]

3. Comments

The foregoing analysis suggests that in an important sense the question of optimal provision of government goods and services dissolves into a pure matter of their efficiency. Both the distributive incidence of a project and the distortionary cost of income taxation are irrelevant.

---

[12] It may not be obvious that this argument holds when the reason a public good or service is more valuable to the rich is not that it produces greater tangible benefits as income increases but instead that, due to the decreasing marginal utility of consumption, willingness to pay increases with income. A pure case would be when utility is additively separable in consumption, a public good, and labor (see Kaplow 1996d, p. 531). A public good then produces constant utility (rather than dollar) benefits for everyone and patently has no effect on labor supply. The public good will have a higher dollar value to the rich because the marginal rate of substitution has the marginal utility of consumption in the denominator, and this is falling with disposable income. However, the offsetting tax adjustment still results in labor supply being constant. In this case, to be sure, the offsetting tax adjustment will be rising as a function of income, reflecting precisely the extent to which the marginal rate of substitution is rising with income. This tax adjustment will produce a substitution effect that reduces labor effort and an income effect that increases labor effort. It necessarily follows that these two effects will be precisely offsetting. (The additional tax burden rises with income to an extent determined by the rate at which marginal utility falls, but that rate is also what determines the strength of the income effect. Differentiating the first-order condition for labor effort with respect to G and substituting for the offsetting tax adjustment determined by this utility function, one can verify that these effects are identical in magnitude—that is, $dl/dG = 0$—as indeed they must be in light of the more abstract, general argument given in subsection 1.)

[13] Only the rebate of any surplus (or additional tax to finance any deficit) will have an effect on labor supply. Specifically, a pro rata rebate produces an income effect that reduces labor supply and thus revenue; hence, the extent of the rebate that restores budget balance will be less than the original per capita surplus. Note that this rebate is not itself part of the definition of the distribution-neutral (offsetting) tax adjustment.

Although this conclusion is subject to numerous qualifications (pertaining to the assumed weak separability of labor effort, possible heterogeneity, and other factors examined in section 6.C), it provides a useful benchmark for understanding the problem.[14] Section A, through figures 8.2A, 8.2B, and 8.2C, suggests that when considering finance by adjustments to the income tax system, redistribution and distortion tend to move together: As one becomes more favorable (say, greater redistribution), the other becomes less so (more distortion). When one adopts a distribution-neutral approach, neither is affected.

This view of public provision, associated with an emerging body of work, contrasts sharply with that in the literatures noted in the introduction to this chapter. Hylland and Zeckhauser (1979) were the first to present a rigorous argument, using offsetting tax adjustments, that distributive incidence should be ignored.[15] Christiansen (1981) and Boadway and Keen (1993) show that the simple cost-benefit test for public goods provision is correct, although their demonstrations assume that the income tax is set optimally; they take advantage of the fact that, when at the optimum, the marginal benefit of additional redistribution equals the marginal cost of additional labor supply distortion, so that marginal adjustments to the tax system have no net effect on social welfare. Kaplow (1996d, 2004, 2006e) builds on Hylland and Zeckhauser's approach to advance the view that both distribution and labor supply distortion can be ignored with regard to a wide domain of government

---

[14] In particular, if weak separability is violated, then public provision is (dis)favored relative to the level implied by the standard cost-benefit test when it is complementary to labor (leisure). For example, improvements to central city amenities may encourage labor effort whereas improvements to the attractiveness of leisure destinations may discourage labor effort. Given the preexisting downward distortion of labor supply on account of redistributive income taxation, more of the former and less of the latter than otherwise would be optimal. However, the reasoning underlying this exception reinforces the intuition supporting the general conclusion in the basic case in which such interactions between public goods and the labor-leisure choice are lacking.

[15] Hylland and Zeckhauser (1979) formally analyze cases like that in section B in which the government project is a perfect substitute for private consumption, but as subsequent literature and the present discussion demonstrate, the argument generalizes to any utility function weakly separable in labor. See also Ng (1984b).

policy, notably including the provision of public goods.[16] As should be apparent from the analysis in subsection 1 (and the analogous argument in chapter 6 on commodity taxation), when a distribution-neutral (offsetting) tax adjustment is employed, features of the initial income tax and transfer system—notably, whether it is set optimally—are irrelevant. Because the adjustment produces a combined package of project and finance that holds both distribution and labor supply constant, the package may be evaluated without regard to distributive effects or concerns about labor supply distortion.

Given that the methods of demonstration regarding government provision of goods and services and commodity tax reforms are so similar, it is natural to consider whether the two sorts of policy change can be related at a more intuitive level. Indeed, this is possible.[17] As chapter 6 explains, it is optimal to tax or subsidize a private good (relative to a baseline of uniform treatment) only to the extent that it is, respectively, a complement of or substitute for leisure. That is, in the basic case, the simple rule that commodities should be taxed uniformly is correct, even in a setting in which distribution matters and income taxation distorts labor supply. Providing more of a public good than indicated by the Samuelson rule is analogous to subsidizing an ordinary private good (relative to other goods), and providing less of a public good is analogous to taxing a private good. The commodity tax result essentially indicates that first-best marginal conditions should determine the allocation of resources among goods and services. Whether those marginal conditions are satisfied through private goods trade in a perfectly competitive economy or hypothetical trade that includes public goods in a fictional economy with Lindahl (1919) pricing is irrelevant for these purposes.

The specific differences between the present view and that in much of the previous literature (mentioned in the introduction) can now be explained. Work advocating distributive weights in cost-benefit analysis does not for the most part explicitly consider how the public project will

---

[16] See also Ng (2000b).

[17] See Mirrlees (1976), Konishi (1995), and Kaplow (1996d, 2004).

be financed or how the distributive incidence of the project may affect labor supply. In that sense, the analysis is incomplete in the manner discussed in section 2.A. The literature on the distortionary cost of public goods provision, by contrast, typically does identify a method of finance, such as an increase in everyone's marginal tax rates, but the distributive effects of the tax adjustment and of the public good tend to be ignored. For example, the literature sometimes considers a public good that is a perfect substitute for cash (the case in section B), but assumes redistributive finance. Or other subtle combinations of assumptions may be employed that result in a combined package of public good and finance that increases redistribution, as in figure 8.2B.[18] The problem, however, is that this analysis is often presented in a representative-individual model in which the resulting redistributive benefit is artificially taken to be irrelevant.[19] In all, most work in both literatures fails to offer a complete,

---

[18] See Ballard and Fullerton's (1992) survey and interpretation of the literature. Regarding one case of interest, they explain that if a public good is independent of labor supply, the marginal cost of public funds will exceed 1.0 when the uncompensated labor supply curve is upward sloping, as is often assumed. To understand this case, it is useful to take the simplest version, with additive separability in utility of private consumption, the public good, and labor. In this instance, their condition for an adverse effect on labor supply is the same as the condition for an increase in redistribution. The reason is that the labor supply curve assumption requires that the income effect not be too large. This restriction in turn requires that the marginal utility of consumption does not fall very rapidly, which directly implies that the marginal value of the public good does not rise sharply as a function of income. To take another set of examples, Allgood and Snow (1998) show that a substantial portion of differences in leading empirical estimates of the marginal cost of funds and of redistribution can be attributed to subtle ways in which different authors' simulations implicitly change the level of effective lump-sum transfers and thus the extent of redistribution assumed to take place.

[19] If individuals actually were identical, then it is familiar that a uniform (lump-sum) tax would be feasible and optimal. The use of distortionary labor income taxation is motivated by concerns for distribution that arise when individuals vary—notably, in their earning abilities. Hence, when assessing policies that change the extent of reliance on distortionary labor income taxation instead of allowing uniform (lump-sum) shifts in the tax schedule—policies that change redistribution and make sense only if distribution is a concern—it is inappropriate to employ a framework in which distribution is ignored. Compare the discussion in section 6.D regarding the inappropriateness of Ramsey models of taxation when an income tax is available.

integrated view that assesses the results by reference to a social welfare function that takes into account both efficiency and distribution.[20]

This failure can produce systematically misleading policy analysis because, as noted, distribution and distortion tend to move in opposite directions in the present setting. Consider an analysis finding that a public project combined with its method of finance increases labor supply distortion. This result would ordinarily be understood to indicate that the project should be viewed less favorably: Benefits must be sufficiently in excess of costs in light of the marginal cost of funds. However, in this setting such a project tends to produce redistributive gains. If the system is at the redistributive optimum, these gains have an effect in terms of overall social welfare that fully offsets that of the labor supply distortion. If there were too little redistribution, these gains would exceed the distortionary cost; indeed, greater distortion would be a symptom of a social welfare improvement.

The use of distributive weights can similarly be problematic. Suppose that applying these weights makes a project look more favorable. The standard interpretation would be that, even if unweighted benefits are somewhat less than costs, the project may nevertheless be desirable. In this setting, however, such a project would tend to produce greater labor supply distortion due to the increase in redistribution, which would offset the social welfare gains from greater redistribution if the status quo was at the optimum and would exceed those social welfare gains if there was too much redistribution already.

These literatures on distributive weights and on the distortionary cost of financing government expenditures on goods and services do not adopt a distribution-neutral approach, which would (in basic cases) render moot both of the concerns in question. Under such an approach, the simple cost-benefit test indicates which projects would advance

---

[20] Unlike most of the literature, Slemrod and Yitzhaki (2001) present a test for the optimal provision of public goods that takes into account both the distributive and labor supply effects of both the public good and the method of finance. In the basic case, all of these adjustments cancel out if there is distribution-neutral finance; with non-distribution-neutral finance, the two-step decomposition (see subsection 2.C.3) suggests that all effects that do not cancel will be associated with a pure change in redistribution in the standard settings considered in the literature.

social welfare. As the earlier illustrations suggest—and as the discussion in subsection 2.C.3 elaborates—there are great conceptual and practical virtues in a distribution-neutral approach. Moreover, in cases in which one cannot assume that a project will be financed in a distribution-neutral manner, it was explained that one should employ a two-step decomposition, separating a package of project and finance into a distribution-neutral reform (as analyzed here) and a purely redistributive reform (the subject of chapter 4). Thus, in all cases, the distribution-neutral approach to policy analysis is useful.

D. General Case: Distributive Incidence and Optimal Redistribution

1. Introduction

The question under consideration in this section is how increasing government expenditures on some good or service affects the desirability of income redistribution and, in particular, how this effect depends on the distributive incidence of that good or service. Suppose that the income tax was set optimally and that it became efficient (perhaps due to technological change) to supply more of some public good. Once that was done, what if any adjustment to the extent of redistribution would be appropriate? Clearly, the answer to this question will depend on how the public good is financed in the first instance. For example, if it were financed by taxing the poor (rich), it is likely that more (less) redistribution would be in order, but that would tell us little about how changing the public good affected the desirability of redistribution. Accordingly, it is useful once again to contemplate finance of the public good by a distribution-neutral (offsetting) tax adjustment, so that the change in public good combined with its finance preserves the preexisting distribution. Under these circumstances, if additional redistribution then becomes desirable, it would be meaningful to say that changing the provision of a public good affects the desirability of redistribution.

To motivate the inquiry, suppose that there is in place an optimal income tax that includes a $5000 per capita grant and that the new public good costs $1000 per capita and produces benefits slightly in excess of that amount. Is the optimal per capita grant still the same? Slightly lower because redistribution has become less desirable on account of the need to raise taxes to finance the public good? Lower by approximately $1000 because the public good in a sense substitutes for the grant? Lower by less than $1000 because, as the grant is reduced, individuals' marginal utilities rise, most sharply for the poor? Furthermore, how do these answers depend on the distributive incidence of the public good and the tax adjustment used to finance it?

The answers do not appear to be self-evident. One might conjecture that with distribution-neutral finance there is no further need to adjust the extent of redistribution. Indeed, when a public good is a perfect substitute for cash, worth the same dollar amount to everyone, this conjecture is true, as shown in section B. More generally, however, redistribution may become more or less desirable, through two channels. First, the reform package may affect the relative marginal utilities of consumption of the rich and the poor. (With a strictly concave social welfare function, changing relative utility levels would also matter, but the distribution-neutral tax adjustment keeps these constant.) Second, the reform package may affect the revenue impact of adjustments to redistributive taxation. After the hypothesized reform, raising marginal tax rates, for instance, may have different labor supply effects and, for a given labor supply effect, it may have different effects on revenue than it did before. Analysis of each channel is somewhat subtle, so only brief sketches of the intuition are offered here. For a formal treatment, see Kaplow (2006e).

2. Analysis

Begin with the effects of a reform package on individuals' marginal utilities of consumption. For concreteness and simplicity, it is useful to examine the additively separable case, $v(c,G) = z(c) + b(G)$—where $z(c)$ is the subutility function for consumption—so that only the tax adjustment will affect individuals' marginal utilities of consumption. Because everyone's taxes increase, everyone's marginal utility will increase. But the desirability of redistribution depends on individuals' relative marginal utilities, so further analysis is required.

Note that a marginal change in G has the same subutility benefit for everyone, measured in (sub)utility rather than dollars. An offsetting (distribution-neutral) tax adjustment, therefore, will be rising with income because marginal utility is falling with income. For example, individuals with half the marginal utility will have their taxes go up twice as much. On one hand, it may seem that the marginal utility of the rich would fall more than that of the poor, since the rich face a greater reduction in consumption. On the other hand, because the rich are in a flatter region of their utility functions than are the poor, changes in consumption have less of an effect on marginal utility.

These effects just balance in the case of a subutility function for consumption that exhibits constant relative risk aversion (CRRA) of one: $z(c) = \ln c$ (see expression (3.3)). In this instance, it can be shown that the offsetting tax adjustment involves everyone's tax rate increasing by the same absolute amount and that everyone's marginal utility will change by the same relative amount. The latter implies that there will be no change in individuals' relative marginal utilities and thus no change in the desirability of redistribution on this account. For CRRA above one, the offsetting tax adjustment is progressive rather than proportional— the more rapidly falling marginal utility of consumption means that the marginal tax rate increment is higher on the rich than on the poor. In this case, the marginal utility of the rich rises relatively more than that of the poor. Accordingly, redistribution becomes somewhat less desirable due to this factor. Note, however, that this reduction is relative to a benchmark tax adjustment that is itself progressive. In sum, the optimal net tax adjustment would still involve a greater marginal rate increase for the rich, but less than that necessary to produce a distribution-neutral result. (The analysis for CRRA below one is analogous, with the direction of the effect reversed.)

The second set of channels concerns the revenue impact of redistribution. Increasing redistribution tends to reduce labor supply, which in turn reduces revenue. The question is how this effect may change when more of a public good is provided, financed by a distribution-neutral tax adjustment. There are two considerations. First, assuming that the labor supply effect of further redistribution is unchanged, a given reduction in labor supply will have a greater (lesser) adverse revenue effect if marginal tax rates are higher (lower) on account of the reform. In the previous examples for an additively separable utility function—and more generally for any public goods that are more valuable to those with higher income—the offsetting tax adjustment involves higher marginal rates, so redistribution will become less desirable. Note again, however, that this characterization is relative to the distribution-neutral tax adjustment, which in this case by assumption involves greater tax increases on the rich than on the poor. This revenue effect has a moderating influence, suggesting that the overall tax adjustment would involve the rich paying more than the poor, but not by as much as is required for a distribution-neutral outcome overall.

The second revenue consideration is that the labor supply response to further redistribution would itself be different. After all, individuals both face a different tax system and also have different levels of public goods and consumption—the latter being relevant to behavior even when public goods in isolation do not affect behavior (as in the additively separable case). Unfortunately, there are multiple competing effects, so without further specification of the functional form for utility and of various parameters, it is not possible to identify how this factor bears on the optimality of further redistribution.

In sum, when moving beyond the simple case in section B in which government expenditures on goods and services are a perfect substitute for cash, providing more public goods and services financed by a distribution-neutral (offsetting) income tax adjustment may affect the desirability of further redistribution. The effects are many and subtle; in special cases, some can be signed. Given the limited empirical knowledge of individuals' utility functions (see section E), it is quite difficult to say whether the level of government provision has a significant effect on the optimality of redistribution. It should be kept in mind that all of the analysis in this section is relative to a benchmark of distribution-neutral finance. Thus, say, for public goods that are worth much more to the rich, the uncertainty concerns how much one should deviate from a tax adjustment that already fully taxes the rich to an extent reflecting their additional benefits. In the special case considered in section B, the answer was: not at all.

3. Optimal Income Taxation and Revenue Requirements

The analysis in section C on optimal provision indicates that there is no necessary connection between the present analysis and the results on optimal income taxation because the analysis here does not depend on the initial tax system being optimal and the tax adjustment, at least preliminarily, is taken to be distribution neutral without regard to whether that would be optimal. Nevertheless, the present analysis illuminates the literature on optimal income taxation with regard to the familiar result in simulations that, the larger the revenue requirement, the less redistribution is optimal.[21] This result is normally obtained by varying the magnitude of an exogenous requirement, where the revenue in a sense vanishes from the model, which is to say that it does not finance public goods that enter individuals' utility functions.[22] If more revenue were in fact required for some exogenous reason (say, due to higher costs of collecting taxes per se) and the expenditure of this revenue did not independently affect utility, a greater revenue need would result in higher distortionary costs at the margin and thus less scope for redistribution (when the system is optimized).

Suppose instead that, consistent with the main motivation for imposing a revenue requirement, the revenue is used to finance government expenditures on goods and services. Suppose further that the income tax has been set optimally for a given initial level of the public good, G^0, and consider raising the level of the public good to G^1. To focus purely on any effects due to the required level of government expenditures, assume that the total dollar benefits of this increase in the public good precisely equal the costs of the increase. To determine the implication of this increase in the revenue requirement for the optimal extent of redistribution, suppose that the increase from G^0 to G^1 is financed by a distribution-neutral (offsetting) tax adjustment. When this is done, everyone's utility level remains exactly the same; hence, the distribution of well-being is unaffected. Furthermore, the revenue raised by this tax adjustment precisely equals the cost of the increase in the public good in the present case. Hence, the now-higher revenue requirement can be met while redistributing to the same extent as before

---

[21] See, for example, Mirrlees (1971) and Tuomala (1990).

[22] In interpreting the revenue requirement contained in expression (4.4), it was stated that the revenue should be understood as expenditures on public goods that may be viewed as implicit in individuals' utility functions, an approach that is unproblematic when such expenditures are taken to be fixed.

(taking into account the distributive incidence of the public good as well as the distributive effect of the income tax adjustment).

As discussed in subsection 2, this distribution-neutral income tax adjustment is not necessarily optimal. Nevertheless, it is clear that there is no necessary and straightforward connection between a higher revenue requirement and a lower optimal extent of redistribution. This conclusion is clearest in the case examined in section B in which the government expenditure is a perfect substitute for cash, for in that case no change in the extent of redistribution is optimal. That case also nicely illustrates how looking at the tax system alone can be misleading. The offsetting tax adjustment, recall, consists of lowering everyone's grant g. This grant reduction looks like a decrease in redistribution, consistent with the standard view in the optimal income tax literature on the implications of a heightened revenue requirement. Yet such a characterization neglects that the "effective" level of g is constant because the effect of the dollar reduction on utility is precisely offset by the effect of the increase in expenditures on the public good.

E. Measurement of Distributive Incidence

Measurement studies attempt to allocate government expenditures by income class. Such work generally distinguishes expenditures that can in some manner be allocated to particular individuals (education, to students or their families; roads, to owners of vehicles) from those that cannot (police; national defense). Both categories raise numerous challenges.

Problems with allocable expenditures can be seen in standard examples. A significant portion of the cost of building and maintaining roads is typically allocated pro rata to automobile owners. The implicit empirical assumption is that the dollar value of the benefit is equal to all. Even ignoring problems such as the inability to adjust for mileage, types of use, and so forth, this method is of doubtful plausibility because most benefits would seem to be increasing with income. Reduced congestion saves time, which tends to have a value closely related to the wage rate. Safety has a dollar value that rises with income. Even pothole repair, by reducing vehicle damage, may produce benefits proportional to the value of one's vehicle, which tends to rise with income.

Another major expenditure is on education, often allocated to students in the case of higher education and to students' families for primary and secondary education. The former allocation is misleading because it ignores life-cycle effects: Students, at the moment of receiving subsidized higher education, tend to be in the lowest income deciles, but the very fact that they are receiving higher education suggests that their lifetime incomes will be above average. For younger students, it is unclear that benefits should be allocated essentially to parents, although given the correlation between parents' and children's incomes, this method may not introduce a substantial bias. Valuation, taken to be equal for all, is more problematic. The poor's willingness to pay is probably less than the average value. Likewise, for the rich, many of whom may be on the brink of switching to superior but more expensive private schools, the value may be quite small. Spillover benefits, if any, are generally ignored.

The allocation of generalized expenditures is recognized to be difficult. Lacking contrary evidence, researchers usually assume that benefits are uniform.[23] Generally, this is interpreted as uniform utility rather than uniform dollar value. As suggested by the analysis in previous sections, much depends on the form of the utility function. Additive separability is sometimes assumed, in which case the incidence measured in dollars depends on the curvature of utility as a function of consumption. For example, Aaron and McGuire (1970) present results corresponding to CRRA of 1 (logarithmic utility) and CRRA of 2. In the former case, since marginal utility equals the inverse of consumption, dollar benefits are proportional to consumption (after-tax income). If such expenditures were financed by a proportional tax, there would accordingly be no distributive effect, in sharp contrast to the substantial redistribution from the rich to the poor that would exist if instead generalized benefits were assumed to have a uniform dollar value (as is done in some measurement studies). With CRRA of 2, individuals with twice the level of consumption have four times (rather than twice) the dollar valuation; hence, finance by a proportional tax would result in a substantial net

---

[23] Goldberg and Scott (1981), who analyze local fiscal incidence, suggest that some public services like police and fire protection favor the poor, who use them more intensively.

redistribution from the poor to the rich. Maital (1973), drawing on contemporary empirical literature, suggested a value of 1.5. A range of subsequent work in financial economics and other fields sometimes yields similar magnitudes but also produces some very high estimates (exceeding 10).[24]

In past decades, when more attention was given to the subject, a number of studies presented estimates of the distributive incidence of the public sector in the United States and elsewhere.[25] The results for the United States tend to find that there is nontrivial redistribution overall, especially at the lower end of the income distribution. Even though taxes are roughly proportional, benefits are more heavily concentrated among the poor and lower-income individuals.[26]

---

[24] See, for example, Barsky et al. (1997), Campbell (1996), Choi and Menezes (1992), and Kocherlakota (1996).

[25] For the United States, see Gillespie (1965), Menchik (1991), Musgrave, Case, and Leonard (1974), Page (1983), Reynolds and Smolensky (1977), Ruggles (1991), Ruggles and O'Higgins (1981), and Tax Foundation (1981), as well as Aaron and McGuire's (1970) and Maital's (1973, 1975) recompilations that use the approach described in the text for allocating general government benefits. See also Dodge (1975) for Canada; Gemmell (1985), O'Higgins and Ruggles (1981), and Mirrlees (1978) for the United Kingdom; Harding (1995) for Australia; and De Wulf (1975) surveying work on developing countries.

[26] Ruggles and O'Higgins (1981, p. 141) summarize their findings as follows:

[F]ederal taxes tend to be quite proportional to income, and local taxes tend to fall somewhat as a proportion of income as income rises. Expenditures, on the other hand, behave quite differently. Expenditure benefits are a much larger proportion of income for those at the lower end of the income scale than for those in the higher deciles, and in fact both local and federal expenditure benefits decline steadily as a proportion of income through the income range. In fact, over much of the income range, the mean dollar amounts received by households in different deciles are very similar. . . . As might, therefore, be expected, considerable redistribution between income classes appears to take place, on both the local and federal levels. Local net benefits are reasonably large and positive (i.e., benefits outweigh taxes) in the first seven deciles, and they become quite large and negative (i.e., taxes outweigh benefits) in the top two deciles. The same general pattern appears for federal net benefits, but these reach their peak in the third decile, and become negative in the sixth.

These results are potentially misleading for a number of reasons.[27] Many include direct transfers, so it is not clear that government expenditures on goods and services follow this redistributive pattern. As noted previously, the allocation of individual benefits is questionable, in some instances (for example, roads) being much less favorable to the bottom end of the income distribution than is ordinarily assumed. For general benefits, if one accepts Maital's (1973) or more recent, higher estimates of the curvature of utility functions, the incidence is substantially more favorable to the rich; however, if more government expenditures substituted for private consumption in a manner that provided more nearly uniform dollar benefits, the incidence would be much more favorable to the poor. The functional forms implicitly or explicitly underlying all these estimates are generally stipulated rather than based on empirical evidence.[28] Life-cycle problems are also serious. (Recall the higher education example; also, social security is treated as redistributive even regarding its reallocation of consumption from high-earning years to non-earning retirement years.)[29] Interestingly, many of these factors suggest that government expenditures on goods and services, combined with their method of finance, may be significantly less redistributive than the studies indicate (or even pro-rich). Finally, all such studies use program costs as a proxy for benefits, thereby ignoring surplus (hopefully, benefits often exceed costs, at least on average), scale economies, and waste.[30] Note that if there were more effort to measure the magnitude of benefits more directly, the process would likely reveal much about the benefits' actual incidence.[31]

---

[27] The list in the text is not exhaustive; additional discussions include Ruggles (1991). Studies of the distributive incidence of government operations also typically ignore the effects of government regulations.

[28] For a candid recognition of this shortcoming, see Aaron and McGuire (1970, pp. 910–911).

[29] Problems also arise in studies that allocate various benefits in accordance with wealth or capital; snapshot views (in contrast to a life-cycle approach) allocate such benefits more to the apparently wealthy than is appropriate.

[30] This issue is addressed in Piggott and Whalley (1987).

[31] For an attempt to measure net fiscal incidence at the local level, see Martinez-Vazquez (1982). Greater reliance could be placed on work such as that by urban economists, which may

There are additional limitations of existing work. Most of the data is outdated; for example, studies published in the 1970s may themselves draw on data that was decades old at the time. Furthermore, the nature of what is being measured is quite unclear. The current public sector is being compared to a world with no public sector, a state that is difficult to imagine and relative to which even minimal law and order would produce huge benefits that are not being credited. Finally, for local public goods that are arguably subject to interjurisdictional competition, such as in Tiebout's (1956) model (and even at the national level), some suggest that the allocation exercise is entirely unnecessary, for political economy models indicate that there will be limited redistribution, in which case benefits should be presumed to have the same distributive incidence as the taxes that fund them.[32] Of course, many political economy models suggest that redistribution will take place, especially at the national level, and if one wishes to test competing models, data on the distributive incidence of public expenditures would be pertinent.

As a guide to further inquiry, it is useful to reconsider the underlying motivation for empirical work on distributive incidence. An important conceptual difficulty with attempts to measure the distributive incidence of government expenditures on goods and services is the failure to identify the purpose for measurement.[33] The introduction to this chapter suggests the importance of the distributive incidence of governmentally provided goods and services given the magnitude of government provision and especially its importance in assessing the well-being of the poor. Individuals' utility levels (for strictly concave social welfare functions) and marginal utilities are relevant to the optimal redistribution problem, and these in turn may be significantly affected by government provision and its finance. Furthermore, the distributive incidence of government expenditures may be relevant to labor supply, as discussed in section C.

---

generate estimates of the value of education, roads, crime reduction, and other local public goods based on their impact on land values and wages. See, for example, Rosen (1979), Henderson (1982), Hoehn, Berger, and Blomquist (1987), and Blomquist, Berger, and Hoehn (1988).

[32] See Peacock (1974).

[33] Compare the discussion in section 15.A on difficulties due to the unclear purpose for measuring inequality and poverty.

Nevertheless, preexisting public goods and services can be taken as given for most purposes. Although it is necessary to ascertain individuals' utilities and marginal utilities, and how these are affected by various redistributive schemes, it is not necessary to identify the underlying source of those utilities. For example, it is important to know the well-being of an individual with $10,000 in consumption and how this changes if consumption is raised by $100, but there is no need to know how this would differ if, hypothetically, one were in a world with no governmentally provided goods and services.[34] Hence, many of the challenges of defining what such a world would be like and measuring how the status quo deviates from it need not be confronted.

Moreover, even if one determines that, say, an existing public good raises everyone's well-being to an extent equivalent to having an additional $1,000, it is not obvious that we should adjust our assessment of the aforementioned hypothetical individual's situation to an effective consumption level of $11,000 (and with a correspondingly reduced marginal utility of consumption from the imagined increment to consumption). This would involve a sort of double-counting to the extent that our assessment of the individual with $10,000 already presumes the existence of the public good in the background. If the public good, say interstate highways, mainly reduces the cost of freight transportation, allowing individuals to buy cheaper goods, this phenomenon probably is already reflected in the standard of living that we associate with a consumption level of $10,000. Likewise, if the public good is an existing system of parks, it too is probably part of what is taken as given in assessing the circumstances of an individual with $10,000. In other words, in thinking about the utility levels or marginal utility of consumption of individuals, we are imagining (or, if undertaking empirical work, measuring) these in the existing world, not in a fanciful world with no roads, no parks, and no state apparatus.

How then is the distributive incidence of government expenditures on goods and services likely to be relevant? First, when contemplating

---

[34] For critical comments on this hypothetical exercise, see, for example, Meerman (1978), Peacock (1974), and Reynolds and Smolensky (1977). See also Piggott and Whalley (1987), who emphasize that the distributive incidence of a marginal change in government activity may differ substantially from the average incidence.

changes in government provision, the focus of sections B through D, the construction of distribution-neutral (offsetting) taxes assumes knowledge of the distributive incidence of such changes. And if some other method of finance is employed (see subsection 2.C.3), determining the redistributive effect of the reform package of the public good and its finance mechanism requires knowledge of the distributive incidence of the change in government provision.

Second, if one wishes to compare well-being across jurisdictions, say for the purpose of setting foreign aid priorities, different levels of government provision of goods and services should be taken into account. Simply comparing disposable income, per capita GDP, or the percentage of individuals below a given poverty line would be misleading. This is especially true in light of the fact that the size of the public sector differs greatly across countries. Differences in natural amenities and other factors may also be relevant. Indeed, they may augment or offset government expenditures. For example, one country may spend more on malaria prevention, but this public good may be partially offsetting a natural bad of a higher incidence of malaria; hence, revising upward a measure of standard of living to account for higher per capita government expenditures on public health could produce a less accurate indicator of well-being, not a more accurate one. Ultimately, what we would like to know are actual well-being and the marginal effect of additional resources on well-being, taking as given differences in preexisting government expenditures and amenities. Whether measures of the distributive incidence of government expenditures would be particularly helpful in developing such a measure—rather than relying primarily on objective indicators such as longevity and literacy, or direct subjective indicators—is a pragmatic empirical question.

Third, political analysis may depend on the distributive incidence of government expenditures. Distributive incidence may be relevant in explaining existing government programs, and the incidence of reforms may be relevant in predicting the likelihood of enactment. (For example, does the median voter gain or lose from a proposed project, taking into account its distributive incidence and how it is likely to be financed?)

In sum, ascertaining the distributive incidence of the existing public sector as a whole seems unnecessary for most purposes and may also provide a misleading depiction of individuals' actual well-being. However,

measurement of the incidence of particular programs, especially those
that may be subject to reform, is relevant for both descriptive and normative purposes.

F. Benefit Taxation

This section considers the relationship between the distribution-neutral
(offsetting) income tax adjustment employed in the present analysis
and the long-discussed concept of benefit taxation (on which, see Musgrave 1959). The first observation is that this particular mode of tax
adjustment is indeed a sort of benefit taxation, as the magnitude of a
marginal adjustment equals marginal benefits. (Recall that, at each income level, the marginal tax adjustment equals individuals' marginal
rates of substitution.) For discrete changes, the offsetting tax adjustment
equals individuals' total benefits for the project. Surplus is included, as
the total tax adjustment at any level of income equals the area under the
implicit demand curve for the public good.

This tax adjustment, however, differs from prior understandings of
benefit taxation in important ways. First, as just explained, the posited
tax adjustment is equivalent to Lindahl (1919) pricing at the margin,
but it is not equivalent for a discrete change. Thus, if marginal benefits
are declining, the average rate of the offsetting tax adjustment would
exceed the Lindahl price, which equals the marginal benefit at the final
point of the increase in G. Second, the stated tax adjustment differs from
many notions of benefit taxation because it is based entirely on the benefits of a public project without regard to its cost. (To be sure, the offsetting tax adjustment must, in general, be further altered to produce budget balance, but how this is done is not part of the underlying concept.)
In a sense, it does seem natural for a benefit tax to be defined directly in
terms of benefits rather than cost, although such an approach is not
conventional.[35]

---

[35] One rationale for the conventional approach—see, for example, the Aaron-McGuire/
Brennan debate, discussed in note 37, and also Maital (1973)—is that a benefit tax is, in the
minds of many, supposed to allocate national income, and thus consumer surplus is irrelevant. Yet the reason for performing such an accounting allocation is unclear.

Various authors have proposed a number of candidates for benefit taxation, most of which differ from the present formulation in other ways as well.[36] Such work usually presents as its objective the derivation of a benefit measure that has certain properties in common with the market's pricing of private goods or that meets other a priori criteria, but the purpose motivating such measures is not explained.[37] By contrast, the distribution-neutral (offsetting) income tax adjustment is chosen because of its usefulness in policy analysis, and it also serves various positive purposes (for example, whether the median voter will favor a project depends on whether that voter's actual new tax obligation is less than the offsetting tax adjustment).

Another common feature of many prior analyses of benefit taxation is the interest in whether such taxation, once properly defined, would be progressive, regressive, or proportional.[38] But why this feature should be of interest is obscure. Indeed, as the preceding discussion suggests, it is misleading to consider the progressivity of the tax used to finance a government expenditure in isolation from the distributive incidence of

---

[36] See, for example, Hines's (2000) proposal and his review of Lindahl pricing and related alternatives, such as that advanced in Moulin (1987).

[37] The Lindahl approach to benefit taxation well illustrates the point that the appropriate definition depends on the purpose. Lindahl's solution answers a specific question, namely, what hypothetical pricing scheme for public goods could be joined with competitive market prices for private goods to support a decentralized equilibrium in a particular game that corresponds to the operation of a market economy in all goods. See, for example, Lindahl (1919) and Foley (1970). Aaron and McGuire (1970) endorse a benefit measure based on Lindahl pricing because multiplying an individual's marginal rate of substitution by the quantity of the public good is precisely analogous to how the income value of a private good is determined. Brennan (1976a) disagrees with this approach to allocating the benefits of public goods because he favors a different private goods benchmark. As is clear from Aaron and McGuire's (1976) reply and Brennan's (1976b) rejoinder, the dispute revolves entirely around which private good analogy is most apt in a context in which the goal is to find an appropriate measure of the overall distribution of income; however, the purpose for describing the distribution in one or another manner is not specified by either side in the debate. Hines's (2000) proposed variation, in turn, is motivated by the desire to better capture yet other aspects of private goods pricing, notably, the feature that every individual faces the same price.

[38] See, for example, Hines (2000) and Snow and Warren (1983).

the project it finances. Thus, as noted, the incidence of the distribution-neutral (offsetting) tax adjustment will be progressive (or otherwise) precisely to the extent that the incidence of the public project being financed disproportionally favors the rich (or otherwise), with the net incidence of the tax and the public project, taken together, being distribution neutral in all cases. It is unclear as a conceptual matter why one would favor a notion of benefit taxation that, when used to finance the public good whose benefit is being taxed, would result in an increase or decrease in the overall extent of redistribution.

Yet another reason for formulating a principle of benefit taxation (explored further in section 15.D) is to determine the proper manner of financing government expenditures on goods and services. Yet when there is also a system of redistributive taxation in place, which itself may freely be adjusted, the purpose of isolating the benefit tax component is not apparent. Moreover, when a public project does generate a surplus (or deficit), there is a priori no unambiguous way of determining how it should be distributed—which is why the question of how budget balance should be achieved if a change in public goods were financed as an initial matter by a distribution-neutral tax adjustment is left here as a separate question, one properly resolved using principles of optimal redistributive taxation rather than some stipulated principle of allocation.

However, from some normative perspectives, such as a libertarian one, benefit taxation may be required and any redistribution may be deemed impermissible. Such an approach does require selection of a particular definition, and it is also necessary to confront the difficult (some would say insurmountable) baseline question regarding the benchmark against which one measures the distributive incidence of the entire public sector.

G. Extension: Government Regulation

Although this part of this book is on government expenditures and the present chapter is on goods and services, it is useful to consider briefly government regulation because of its importance for the subject of redistribution and because the pertinent analysis closely tracks that for goods and services.[39] By some estimates, government regulation, such as of the environment and of workplace safety, involves costs of a similar order of magnitude to government expenditures on goods and services. A primary difference is that, under regulation, the costs are often borne in the first instance by private actors who respond to government incentives (such as from Pigouvian taxation) or comply with government edicts (such as command and control regulation). These costs as well as the resulting benefits (such as cleaner air, a public good) will have a distributive incidence, presenting many of the questions considered with respect to government expenditures. Some regulation (taxes and subsidies) also has its own more direct distributive incidence as well as a budgetary impact. And all such regulation, along with the tax adjustments that may be adopted in association with it, may affect labor supply. Accordingly, regulation (especially environmental regulation in recent times) has been a substantial subject of study regarding both distributive effects and labor supply distortion.[40] Regarding the latter, some have raised the possibility of a double dividend—a Pigouvian tax may both correct an externality and raise revenue without distortion, permitting reductions in distortionary income taxation—and a substantial literature has suggested instead that environmental policies may exacerbate the preexisting labor supply distortion due to income taxation.

As with government expenditures on goods and services, the commodity tax analysis in chapter 6 can be employed. Indeed, the connection is even more direct here because many forms of government regulation are quite similar in effect to differential commodity taxes, the pure case being Pigouvian taxes and subsidies. In a basic model, differential commodity taxation is inefficient, but that conclusion (as noted in subsection 6.C.1) abstracts from externalities. The underlying analysis demonstrates that consumer price ratios should reflect true social

---

[39] See Kaplow (1996d, 2004) and, for a formal analysis, Kaplow (2006d).

[40] That distributive effects might qualify the view that corrective taxes and subsidies should be set simply to internalize externalities was initially raised by Pigou (1928) himself and has subsequently been explored, for example, by Casler and Rafiqui (1993) and West (2004). For a survey and a collection of literature on distortion, see Bovenberg and Goulder (2002) and Goulder (2002), respectively.

costs, which in the present setting include both production costs and externalities. Hence, extending the commodity tax results, the conclusion is that Pigouvian taxes and subsidies are optimally set at first-best levels, equal to the marginal external social cost or benefit. That is, there need be no modifications on account of either the distributive incidence of the costs or benefits of the regulation or effects on labor supply in light of the preexisting distortion due to redistributive income taxation.[41] Setting a Pigouvian tax higher (lower) than this level is equivalent to raising (lowering) the relative tax on an ordinary private good from the point of neutrality, a deviation that we know to be inefficient in this basic setting.

A more complete demonstration would track the prior analyses of commodity taxes and of public goods. For concreteness, consider a proposal to increase the tax on gasoline, as a proxy Pigouvian tax to address externalities such as pollution, vehicle accidents, and congestion. See figure 8.3. The gasoline tax increase itself is assumed to be regressive, with an incidence that rises, although less than proportionately, with income. See the dotted curve, drawn here below the horizontal axis because tax payments constitute a loss to individuals.

The gasoline tax increase is also assumed to reduce gasoline consumption, which both entails financial costs and forgone utility to individuals and also produces benefits. See the dashed curve, "project benefits–nontax costs" (that is, ignoring the gasoline tax payments themselves), showing that the sum of these effects is assumed to be positive and rising with income at an increasing rate. The solid curve shows that the net impact of the project—consisting of the gasoline tax payments combined with these project benefits and nontax costs—is a moderate net loss to lower-income individuals and a rising net gain to higher-income individuals.

The distribution-neutral (offsetting) income tax adjustment is, of course, the same solid net impact curve. Accordingly, the overall net effect—just like in the case in figure 8.2C depicting a public good financed

---

[41] The irrelevance of distributive effects was first suggested by Zeckhauser (1981) in the context of regulation and by Shavell (1981) with regard to legal rules (see also Kaplow and Shavell 1994).

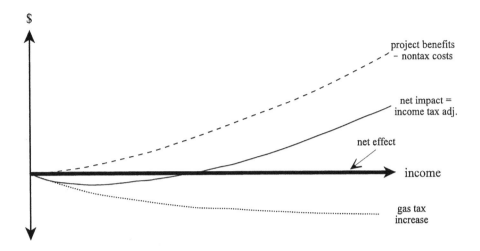

Figure 8.3. Gasoline Tax Increase and Distribution-Neutral (Offsetting) Tax Adjustment

by an offsetting tax adjustment—is nil at every level of income. Once again, we see that there is no distributive effect (by construction) and no effect on labor supply. The remaining question is whether there exists a surplus or deficit, and the answer again will depend on a simple cost-benefit test: Because the income tax adjustment absorbs all net benefits, net revenue is simply the sum of all costs and benefits. For a Pigouvian tax, therefore, if the movement is in the direction of internalizing an externality, there will tend to be a surplus, which can be rebated pro rata so as to make everyone better off.[42]

Accordingly, when accommodated by a distribution-neutral income tax adjustment, we see that first-best principles are correct (subject to the usual qualifications noted in section 6.C), just as with government expenditures on goods and services. Interestingly, it does not matter that the pertinent costs are incurred by private actors rather than the

---

[42] For more precise characterizations, see Kaplow (2006d). A different approach is taken by Pirttilä and Tuomala (1997) and Cremer, Gahvari, and Ladoux (1998), who present optimal commodity tax formulas (not permitting analysis of reforms away from the optimum) for the case in which the income tax is assumed to be optimal.

government; once the offsetting tax adjustment is taken into account, both distributive and labor supply effects come out the same, which is to say, they are not a factor.[43] Additionally, the foregoing analysis suggests that the literature concerning the double dividend—pro and con—is misleading for essentially the same reasons discussed in subsection C.3 with regard to the literature on public goods: The supposed tax adjustments typically involve changes in the extent of redistribution (increases, in the literature that typically finds additional distortion), whereas the social welfare benefits of redistribution are ignored, such as through the use of representative-agent models.[44]

As already suggested, this conclusion should not be surprising when one reflects on the analysis of commodity taxation in chapter 6. To further understand this point, recall that the overall level of commodity taxation (as distinguished from whether there are differential rates) is irrelevant because it simply reflects a different normalization with the labor income tax. (A proportional tax on all commodities is equivalent to a uniform reduction in after-tax income accomplished through an increment to the income tax.) In this setting, therefore, it cannot be true that a Pigouvian tax produces a double dividend whereas a Pigouvian subsidy involves an added distortionary cost, for these are identical: All that matters is the difference in the relative prices faced by consumers (say, for a clean and a dirty good, as in many models of environmental taxation). Likewise, Pigouvian taxes and subsidies cannot involve contrary distortionary costs through effects on labor supply. Differences in labor supply distortion can arise, however, if the environmental policies under consideration—combined with the income tax adjustments

---

[43] It should be apparent that the gasoline tax example is generic in this and other respects. Nothing turns on the shapes of any of the curves; all that matters is that, whatever their shape, the income tax adjustment is constructed to be offsetting. Many government regulations, notably command and control regulations, do not affect revenue directly (except to a modest extent through enforcement costs). Nevertheless, one can still consider (and a government can still choose to implement) a distribution-neutral income tax adjustment in order to isolate the efficiency effects intrinsic to the regulation in question, in accordance with the approach advanced in section 2.C and followed throughout this chapter.

[44] Some concrete examples of these features of the literature are noted in Kaplow (2006d). See also section 6.D on Ramsey taxation.

stipulated to accompany them—involve different degrees of redistribution, but in such cases the labor supply effect is best attributed to the change in redistribution, and the welfare effects of this change must be accounted for as well.

Analysis in the other sections of this chapter is similarly applicable to government regulation. Analogous issues arise, for example, in measuring distributive incidence. This is particularly true given that the more difficult valuation and allocation questions often concern the benefits, such as from pollution reductions, which have the character of public goods. In the gasoline tax example, the assumption that benefits rise disproportionately with income corresponds, for example, to the case in which the benefits of a public good enter utility in an additively separable manner and in which utility exhibits constant relative risk aversion in consumption with a risk-aversion coefficient exceeding one. Likewise, just as with public goods, one can ask whether changing the extent of regulation—when accompanied by a distribution-neutral (offsetting) adjustment to the income tax—makes redistribution more or less desirable than before. Consider, for example, the fact that as societies become wealthier, environmental regulation tends to become stricter, reflecting that valuations of environmental benefits are an increasing function of income. Note that if net environmental benefits (taking into account compliance costs) rise steeply with income, a distribution-neutral accommodation would involve what would otherwise appear to be a redistributive adjustment to the income tax system.[45] This situation presents another instance in which viewing the tax system in isolation can be misleading, for such a tax adjustment is necessary to avoid a change in the extent of redistribution in the hypothesized circumstances.

Government regulation should be construed broadly for purposes of this section. The category encompasses, for example, regulations (such as of health and safety) adopted primarily to address informational market failures rather than to internalize externalities. In that setting, incidence analysis would take into account likely wage or price

---

[45] It should also be kept in mind that, in the basic setting used here, this accommodation would, in combination with the change in regulation, have no effect on labor supply.

adjustments due to the regulatory costs and benefits that ensue, but, once that is done, the analysis can proceed as before.[46] Likewise, many incentive schemes are incorporated into the income tax itself (so-called tax expenditures, whether for energy conservation, low-income housing, or myriad other activities), and these too can be analyzed similarly.[47] In all, a broad range of governmental activity—that associated with the "allocative" function of government in Musgrave's (1959) taxonomy— can be assimilated into the present framework.

---

[46] Analogous complexities arise; for example, mandatory automobile safety regulation may produce benefits, valued in dollars, that are greater for higher-income individuals. In addition, if individuals are imperfectly informed, their behavior may diverge from that which truly maximizes their well-being.

[47] For example, Brannon (1980) and Griffith (1989) argue that the distributive incidence of tax expenditures should be deemed irrelevant because the tax rate structure can be adjusted to eliminate distributive effects. (Accordingly, whether subsidies should be provided as tax deductions rather than as credits, particularly refundable credits, depends on whether it makes sense for marginal subsidy rates to depend on individuals' marginal tax rates.)

PART IV: ADDITIONAL ASPECTS OF TAXATION

9

Taxation of Capital

The analysis of optimal income taxation in chapter 4, following convention, is conducted in a one-period setting in which individuals choose only labor effort; hence, the income tax under discussion is a labor income tax. The model in chapter 6 extends the analysis to consider the case in which individuals also allocate disposable income among different consumption goods. Following the approach of Atkinson and Stiglitz (1976, 1980) and others, this chapter adapts the same model to examine the taxation of capital income (the return to savings). This application is accomplished simply by viewing consumption in different time periods as an instance of consumption of different goods.[1] As will be discussed, the optimality of uniform commodity taxation in the basic case implies that, in an analogous setting, the optimal tax on capital income is zero.

This method, recall, explores reforms to differential commodity taxation under the assumption that the income tax is simultaneously adjusted so that the overall result is distribution neutral. Accordingly, the basic result and qualifications derive from efficiency concerns, even though the

---

[1] In this chapter, the taxation of capital income, of the return to savings, and of investment are not distinguished. In a closed economy, these are equivalent, whereas with capital flows they are not. The field of international taxation is significantly concerned with the taxation of capital, including the differences between taxing residents' savings and taxing local investment (see Dixit 1985, Gordon and Hines 2002, and Slemrod 1988). Furthermore, much analysis of capital taxation is concerned with interasset distortion due to differential taxation of different types of capital. This chapter focuses on capital taxation per se (one can think of a model with only one type of capital or in which all capital is taxed uniformly); corporation taxation, taken up in subsection B.3, is an exception.

subject of capital income taxation, like that of luxury taxation, is ordinarily thought to be importantly concerned with distributive issues.

After presenting the general analysis and qualifications, attention turns to a number of specific forms of taxation: the choice of an income tax (here, a full, standard income tax that includes in its base the return to savings as well as labor income) versus a consumption tax, wealth taxation, and corporate income taxation. (Transfer taxation is examined separately, in chapter 10.) Further extensions address uncertain capital income, transition issues and capital levies, and human capital.

A. Analysis

1. Taxation of Capital as Differential Commodity Taxation

Begin with the model in chapter 6 in which individuals may spend their after-tax-and-transfer income, $wl - T(wl)$, on any of n commodities, $x_1, \ldots, x_n$, commodity prices are p_i, and commodity taxes are τ_i. In that model, an individual's budget constraint is

$$\sum (p_i + \tau_i) x_i (wl) = wl - T(wl), \tag{9.1}$$

and the government's budget constraint is

$$\int \left[T(wl) + \sum \tau_i x_i (wl) \right] f(w) dw = R. \tag{9.2}$$

To introduce returns to capital and the possible taxation thereof, it is helpful to consider a two-period model wherein individuals work only in period 1 and consume in periods 1 and 2. (Period 1 can be thought of as an aggregate of an individual's working years and period 2 as retirement years; the extension to more periods or to a continuous-time model is straightforward.) Suppose further that there is only one type of commodity in each of the two periods, denoted c_1 and c_2. Thus, we are considering a two-good version of the commodity tax problem in which the first commodity is period 1 consumption and the second commodity is period 2 consumption. Individuals' utility is $u(c_1, c_2, l)$. Finally, normalize to one the price of each commodity in its own period, and let r be the return to capital (interest rate).

If there are no commodity taxes, the individual's budget constraint is

$$c_1 + \frac{c_2}{1+r} = wl - T(wl). \tag{9.3}$$

From a first-period perspective, the price of second-period consumption, c_2, is $1/(1+r)$, since that is how much first-period consumption, c_1, must be sacrificed to purchase a unit of c_2. (As is familiar, this implies that a higher r makes c_2 cheaper.) This price of c_2 is fully analogous to the price p_2 in the standard commodity tax model: There, it corresponds to the production cost, and here, likewise, $1/(1+r)$ can be considered to be a production cost because the interest rate being r (rather than, say, 0) can be understood as a consequence of the existence of production technology that allows one unit of c_2 to be produced at a sacrifice of $1/(1+r)$ units of c_1.

Next, introduce t_r, the tax rate applied to the return to capital, r, and the budget constraint becomes[2]

$$c_1 + \frac{c_2}{1+r(1-t_r)} = wl - T(wl), \tag{9.4}$$

which can also be written as

$$c_1 + \left[\frac{1}{1+r} + \frac{rt_r}{(1+r)(1+r(1-t_r))} \right] c_2 = wl - T(wl). \tag{9.5}$$

In terms of the original commodity tax model—compare budget constraint (9.1)—it is clear that taxing the return to capital, r, at the rate t_r is equivalent to imposing a commodity tax on c_2 of $\tau_2 = rt_r/(1+r)(1+r(1-t_r))$. Furthermore, since there is no tax imposed on c_1 ($\tau_1 = 0$), this levy constitutes a differential tax on c_2.

The analysis in section 6.B indicates that, when labor is weakly separable in the utility function, so we can write $u(v(c_1, c_2), l)$—and other

---

[2] One could also adjust the government's budget constraint, taking into account that the government may raise revenue in different periods and also undertake expenditures in different periods. The present setting implicitly assumes a fixed revenue requirement in each period (or, equivalently, a revenue requirement with a fixed present value) and that the government also can borrow and lend at the rate r. The analysis becomes more complex when income and thus government revenue are uncertain (see subsection C.1).

qualifications noted in section 6.C are inapplicable—no differential taxation is optimal. Because τ_2 optimally equals zero, t_r should equal zero (see Atkinson and Stiglitz 1976, 1980; and Stiglitz 1987).[3] For further exploration using an overlapping-generations model, see, for example, Atkinson and Stiglitz (1980), Ordover and Phelps (1979), and Stiglitz (1985).

The intuition for why income from capital should be neither taxed nor subsidized in this basic case is the same as that for the no-differentiation result in the more general version of the commodity tax problem. One can achieve any degree of redistribution (while meeting the revenue target) by adjusting the income tax schedule. Accordingly, differential taxation can be examined in the case in which the income tax is adjusted to hold distribution constant, in which event the only remaining question concerns efficiency.[4] In other words, the issue becomes whether individuals of a given earnings level should be taxed relatively more or less depending on whether they allocate more income to first-period or second-period consumption. Neutrality tends to be optimal because it avoids an additional distortion, here, of the intertemporal pattern of consumption.[5] Differentiation can be efficient only if it helps to offset the preexisting distortion of labor supply, but when weak separability is assumed, labor supply is unaffected. Hence, it is not optimal to tax or subsidize capital income.

The result that t_r optimally equals zero has also been obtained in other settings, but for qualitatively different reasons. Notably, the no-taxation

---

[3] Recall from chapter 6 that, although Atkinson and Stiglitz (1976) (and other work in similar spirit) examines only the case in which the income tax is set optimally, Kaplow (2006c) shows that their result generalizes if one employs a distribution-neutral income tax adjustment.

[4] For this reason, the notion that consumption taxes are less redistributive than standard income taxes because the rich have more savings and thus more capital income is not emphasized here; adjusting the tax schedule to allow a distribution-neutral comparison clarifies the analysis of intrinsic differences among different types of taxation. See also subsection B.1.

[5] As Feldstein (1978) emphasizes, the extent of distortion is not indicated by the change in savings but instead by the effect of differential taxation on consumption across periods. Note, for example, that even if savings were unaffected, it would still be true that c_2 falls relative to c_1 as t_r increases. The key distinction is that savings (adjusted for the net-of-tax interest rate) indicates expenditures on c_2, not the quantity c_2 itself. See also Buchanan (1959).

result arises in the long run in models with infinitely lived individuals (see Chamley 1986, Judd 1985, and the surveys in Auerbach and Hines 2002 and Bernheim 2002).[6] The significance of this and related findings, however, is limited for a number of reasons. Most important for present purposes, these results are derived in a Ramsey setting that assumes both identical individuals and the unavailability of an income tax (see Golosov, Tsyvinski, and Werning 2007). As noted in section 6.D, with identical individuals there is no redistribution problem and thus no need in principle to rely on distortionary taxation. But by stipulating the unavailability of an income tax (in particular, disallowing the possibility of a nonzero uniform component), only distortionary taxes are available in these models. In addition, many such results pertain to the steady state, not accounting for welfare in the transition, and implicitly involve an initial capital levy. As further noted in subsection C.2, capital taxation is beneficial in the short run—and initially is set at its maximally allowed level of 100%—because it acts as a lump-sum tax on old capital, the existence of which is exogenous. For further discussion of these models, see Stiglitz (1985, 1987).

2. Qualifications

This benchmark also clarifies the reasons for departing from the zero-tax result. The general qualifications to the suboptimality of differential commodity taxation introduced in section 6.C are, prima facie, applicable to capital taxation. However, because the taxation of capital is of special theoretical and practical interest and also raises some particular reasons for departure from the neutrality outcome, it is worth additional consideration.[7]

The most direct qualification involves nonseparability. One possibility is that higher consumption in period 1 enhances the value of leisure

---

[6] Many of the points to follow in the text are also applicable to overlapping-generations models of capital taxation, which are also surveyed by Auerbach and Hines (2002) and Bernheim (2002).

[7] As in section 6.C, no attempt is made to be comprehensive; likewise, the qualifications already raised in section 6.C will be revisited only selectively.

during that period because consumption can better be enjoyed if more time is available in which to consume; by contrast, additional consumption in period 2 has no effect at the margin because individuals are already retired. In this case, as noted by Ordover and Phelps (1979), it may be optimal to subsidize savings (second-period consumption) relative to first-period consumption: The reduction in first-period consumption makes first-period leisure less attractive, somewhat offsetting the labor-leisure distortion due to labor income taxation. A richer model, allowing for individuals to adjust the timing of retirement and to work part-time in later periods, would complicate this argument. On the other hand, there is some evidence that consumption declines when individuals reduce labor supply because of health problems or unemployment. To the extent that any such reductions do not reflect liquidity constraints or incomplete insurance, they indicate that leisure and consumption may be substitutes.[8] In that case, capital taxation rather than subsidization would be desirable.

The familiar implicit assumption that individuals are fully capable of maximizing their utility is subject to question in the intertemporal context. In particular, bounded rationality and limited self-control seem pertinent to savings decisions (see Bernheim 2002 and Bernheim and Rangel 2007). If individuals are sufficiently unsophisticated about savings and their decisions are heavily influenced by framing and other aspects of context (such as whether employment-based retirement savings depends on opting in versus opting out), the effects of capital taxation are less clear. At one extreme, naive individuals might simply ignore future taxes, in which case taxation of income from capital, which occurs after savings decisions are made, may not discourage savings and may not even be perceived as a burden on labor supply. In that case, consumption taxation (see subsection B.1) might be even more attractive, and schemes like Roth Individual Retirement Accounts (Roth IRAs)—which tax savings when earned but exempt subsequent capital income rather than deferring taxes from the point of earnings until the

---

[8] See Chetty (2006) discussing the evidence and also the literature cited in chapter 11, note 20, on falls in consumption upon retirement.

time of consumption, as under conventional IRAs and other retirement plans—would be unattractive.

In this context, myopia has received the most sustained attention. The tendency of myopia to produce undersavings would be exacerbated by capital taxation but might be offset by subsidization (see, for example, Laibson 1996).[9] In addition, when individuals are myopic, capital taxes or subsidies may have different effects on labor supply (see Kaplow 2006b and also subsection 11.B.1 on myopia, social security, and labor supply). Further complications arise if there is heterogeneity in individuals' susceptibility to myopia; capital subsidies that reduce undersaving by the myopic may lead to excessive saving by others.[10] Differentiated myopia also raises subtle distributive effects that may counteract or reinforce incentive considerations.[11]

Once it is acknowledged that individuals' behavior may not be rational, a broader array of corrective policies warrant consideration (see, for example, Bernheim 2002 and Laibson 1996). Possibilities in-

---

[9] See also O'Donoghue and Rabin (2006), who analyze and survey literature on the use of commodity taxes to address self-control problems involving overconsumption.

[10] Another consideration arises if the degree of myopia is negatively correlated to earning ability, suggested by the point that more myopic individuals may be less inclined to invest in their own human capital. In this case, savings decisions would be related to unobserved ability, which would favor subsidizing those who save less, such as through capital taxation. A similar implication arises if the true preferences of the less able lead to a lower savings rate or if those who save less are not myopic but rather rationally expect to spend a smaller portion of their life in retirement—perhaps due to a lower life expectancy (see Tuomala 1990)—and if this basis for low savings likewise signals low earning ability (see Saez 2002a).

[11] See Kaplow (2006b). Myopic individuals will, ceteris paribus, have lower utility (on an expected lifetime basis, as actually experienced). If the SWF is strictly concave in utility (not just in consumption), this factor favors redistributing toward the myopic, which would be an effect of raising more revenue through capital taxation. On the other hand, the effect of myopia on the marginal utility of consumption (which is all that is relevant under a utilitarian SWF and remains relevant under more concave SWFs short of maximin) is ambiguous: Myopic individuals, who misallocate consumption toward the present, will have a lower marginal utility for incremental consumption spent in the present but a higher marginal utility for consumption spent in the future; the latter effect is larger if individuals' utility functions are sufficiently concave. Compare subsection 12.A.1 on whether unequal sharing within the family favors more or less generous allocations. (On the role of marginal utility versus utility levels in redistribution generally, see subsection 3.B.3.)

clude forced saving, such as through social security systems (see section 11.B), penalties for early withdrawal of funds from retirement accounts, pro-savings defaults in retirement plans, and other devices that alter individuals' framing of their choices (as noted, immediate tax deductions may have a greater effect than deferred benefits of equal present value). Laibson's (1996) central simulation indicates that individuals with significant myopia and highly concave utility would value a successful corrective policy at nine-tenths of a year's worth of income.[12]

Another, rather different qualification is that individuals may save too much from a social perspective. When future labor income is uncertain, individuals rationally engage in precautionary savings, but the resulting higher net worth in future periods, after uncertainty is resolved, reduces labor supply at that time (through an income or wealth effect), which imposes a negative externality on the fisc.[13] See Diamond and Mirrlees (1978, 1986), addressing disability and retirement decisions; Golosov, Kocherlakota, and Tsyvinski (2003), examining stochastic abilities; Kocherlakota (2005), considering wealth taxes that depend on current and previous labor income; Albanesi and Sleet (2006), allowing taxes to depend on wealth and current labor income; Rogerson (1985), offering a general analysis of moral hazard in a repeated principal-agent relationship; and Golosov, Tsyvinski, and Werning (2007), providing a

---

[12] Running in the opposite direction, if individuals underconsume when young because of liquidity constraints, capital taxation—which shifts the lifetime tax burden toward later years—would be a corrective, as suggested by Hubbard and Judd (1986), although challenges are raised by Hall's (1986) and Summers's (1986) comments thereon, including the point that more direct means, such as reducing social security's forced savings, would tend to be more efficient. See also subsection 5.E.1. Another caveat is that if the government shares individuals' myopia when setting policy, the policies it chooses are less likely to improve welfare (see Krusell, Kuruşçu, and Smith 2000).

[13] Inducing individuals to save less reduces the marginal utility of first-period consumption and thus tends to depress first-period labor supply, also a cost to the fisc, although there is an offsetting effect from the resulting increase in the marginal utility of second-period consumption (which will be dominant if the curvature of utility as a function of each period's consumption is sufficiently large). Starting from the undistorted private savings optimum, however, the effect on the weighted-average marginal utility of consumption and thus on first-period labor supply is second order (see Kaplow 2006b). Therefore, introducing some wedge is optimal, abstracting from other considerations.

survey. On this account, some sort of taxation of capital income would be optimal, although the optimal form may have subtle features. For example, in Kocherlakota (2005), expected wealth taxes for each individual are zero, and no revenue is collected. The optimal wealth tax viewed in isolation (from the nonlinear labor income tax) is regressive—in the sense that it is positive (negative) for individuals whose realized skill is lower (higher) than expected—because this formulation best deters the sort of precautionary savings that would reduce work effort in subsequent periods and thus interfere with the insurance role of the labor income tax.

Additionally, in a general equilibrium setting in which wages are not fixed, capital taxes or subsidies may be optimal if they favorably influence the distribution of pre-tax income through the effects of changes in the capital stock on wage rates. See, for example, Stiglitz (1985, 1987), and compare the general equilibrium effects of labor income taxation noted in subsection 5.E.3. If capital tends to substitute for unskilled labor, as Krusell, Kuruşçu, and Smith (2000) suggest, some taxation of capital would be optimal, whereas if the relationship is complementary, a subsidy would raise social welfare. In this instance and more broadly, when the government cannot directly control the capital stock through debt or other policies, taxation or subsidization of capital can serve as a substitute instrument.

If the return to capital varies among individuals, another dimension of heterogeneity in ability, capital taxation may have a further distributive role.[14] If some individuals simply have a higher r, it may seem appealing to tax those individuals if differences in r are observable or, if not, to tax income from capital, although the overall distributive effects are subtle, as with myopia.[15] If individuals' levels of r are positively

---

[14] This aspect of the capital taxation problem has received little attention. An exception is Stiglitz (1985), who obtains a zero-rate-at-the-top result in a model in which individuals vary only in their ability to earn capital income.

[15] See note 11. Those with a higher r will, ceteris paribus, have a higher utility level, favoring heavier taxation if the welfare function is strictly concave in utility. Average marginal utility, however, need not be lower, because individuals with higher r's are more efficient at converting current labor income into future consumption; the more concave are individuals' utility functions, the lower will be the resulting average marginal utility as r rises.

correlated with w, their labor income earning ability, including the case in which labor effort is required to produce a higher level of r, then taxing capital income as a proxy for or aspect of taxing ordinary wage income will tend to be optimal. All of these results, however, tend not to hold if capital markets are efficient in the sense that individuals most productive at investment manage others' savings, a common but not universal phenomenon.

Other considerations are also pertinent to the optimal degree of taxation or subsidization of capital income. Many have suggested that administrative concerns favor a zero tax rate on capital income, as will be discussed in subsection B.1, which compares a traditional income tax to a cash-flow consumption tax. Intergenerational distribution may also be affected by capital taxation, although other instruments such as debt policy and social security schemes may be effective substitutes (see subsection 11.A.3 and Atkinson and Sandmo 1980). In any event, the zero-tax result of subsection 1 provides a useful benchmark for analysis. In particular, it serves as a reminder that, when an income tax (specifically, on labor income) is available, the simple notion that taxation of capital income aids redistribution because higher-ability individuals tend to have higher average savings is mistaken. Income tax adjustments can offset the straightforward distributive impact of capital taxation, so more subtle considerations, many related in some manner to the efficiency of labor income taxation, tend to be determinative.

B. Applications

1. Income versus Consumption Taxation

The superiority of income versus consumption (expenditure) taxation has long been debated. Although conventional income taxes have generally been employed in developed countries, writers from Mill and Marshall to Irving Fisher and Kaldor to the present have favored, at least in principle, some form of consumption taxation. Today, mixed systems, combining an income tax and a value-added tax (VAT), a form of flat tax on consumption, are most common. The foregoing analysis of labor income taxation supplemented by a possible tax on capital income helps to illuminate the issues.

It is useful to begin by revisiting a basic equivalence between two types of tax systems, which also allows pertinent differences to be highlighted. As explained in chapter 6, a purely proportional tax on all forms of consumption, $\tau_i = \alpha p_i$, for all i, with no labor income tax at the outset, is equivalent to a proportional labor income tax with no commodity taxation. Specifically, the budget constraint (9.1) for the uniform consumption tax is, as noted before,

$$\sum_i (p_i + \alpha p_i) x_i(wl) = wl. \tag{9.6}$$

As chapter 6 indicated, to show the equivalence, one can divide both sides by $1+\alpha$ and let $t = \alpha/(1+\alpha)$:

$$\sum_i p_i x_i(wl) = \frac{1}{1+\alpha} wl = (1-t)wl. \tag{9.7}$$

More broadly, any uniform component of consumption taxation could instead be implemented through a shift in the preexisting labor income tax schedule.

In the two-period, two-good model employed in subsection A.1, any system of uniform consumption taxation can therefore be represented as a pure labor income tax, as in the budget constraint (9.3). Furthermore, any nonuniform scheme can be represented as a labor income tax supplemented by a tax (or subsidy) t_r applied to the return to capital, r, as in the budget constraint (9.4). Against this background, a standard income tax, defined as a tax at equal rates on income from labor and capital, is seen to be a particular nonuniform tax in which t_r and $T(\cdot)$ are appropriately linked.[16] For the case of a linear labor income tax at rate t, one simply has $t_r = t$.[17]

---

[16] Because of the ubiquity of standard income tax systems, they are commonly used as a reference point for describing the pure labor income tax of the optimal income tax literature or a uniform consumption tax, each of which is accordingly characterized as equivalent to a standard income tax that exempts the return to capital. The point is patently obvious for the labor income tax, and it is straightforward for the consumption tax once the equivalence between it and the labor income tax is recognized.

[17] For the nonlinear case, t_r and $T(\cdot)$ each depend on both labor and capital income for a standard, comprehensive income tax, although under the so-called Scandinavian dual income tax, capital income is taxed separately at a flat rate.

A priori, there is little basis for supposing that a conventional income tax is even approximately optimal. In the simple case examined in subsection A.1, the optimal level of t_r is zero. The qualifications examined in subsection A.2 could, in aggregate, imply that the optimal t_r is positive or negative; however, even if it is positive, there is no particular reason to believe that the optimal level would (even roughly) equal t.

As the discussion in subsection A.1 indicates, there is no inherent distributive effect from taxing capital income—distribution can be held constant by adjusting the labor income tax schedule—which implies that distributive effects are not, in principle, central in the comparison of a traditional income tax and a consumption tax. Further note that employing nonlinear rates under a cash-flow consumption tax—should that be optimal—does not impose substantially different challenges from using nonlinear income tax rates; a cash-flow consumption tax would operate like a conventional personal income tax, except that it would allow a full and immediate deduction for all forms of savings and include in the tax base all dissavings.[18] Consumption taxes implemented as VATs or sales taxes do need to be linear as a practical matter. In fact, they are often employed in combination with nonlinear personal tax schedules. In this regard, it is interesting that the United States, which relies primarily on the income tax for redistribution, is generally viewed as engaging in less redistribution than many European countries, most of which rely heavily on a VAT.[19]

---

[18] As a definitional and accounting matter, note that a cash-flow consumption tax can be understood as a rearrangement of the familiar Haig-Simons definition: It holds that income is the sum of consumption and changes in wealth (net savings or dissavings); subtracting changes in wealth from both sides yields the base of the cash-flow consumption tax as described in the text. There is an important practical difference between the two taxes when they are nonlinear: If no averaging scheme is employed, individuals with fluctuating income or consumption are treated differently; however, consumption across accounting periods tends to be smoother than income as a consequence of individuals' borrowing and saving behavior. See Vickrey (1939), Liebman (2003), and subsection 11.A.2 on averaging, and Fullerton and Rogers (1993) on lifetime incidence more generally.

[19] The primary difference, however, may be due to European taxes being in aggregate at a higher level, with much of the additional revenue being spent in a fashion that, combined with the incidence of the taxes, produces greater redistribution (see section 2.A).

Administrative considerations offer an important distinction between income and consumption taxation. An argument favoring a conventional income tax is that it may be easier to tax labor and capital at the same rate since it is sometimes difficult to distinguish between them. Consider, notably, the income of entrepreneurs who own and operate their own businesses. Probably more attention, however, has been devoted to the administrative advantages of consumption taxation (see, for example, Andrews 1974, Bradford 1986, and Bradford and U.S. Treasury Tax Policy Staff 1984). Many of the difficulties in measuring income involve capital income—especially accruals and, relatedly, depreciation—but such measurement is unnecessary under a cash-flow tax: It is sufficient to monitor cash flows into and out of savings; the question of when gains and losses in various assets accrued is moot. Administrative ease also bears on choices between equivalent systems.[20] Under a pure labor income tax (a tax on wage income), it is, as noted, necessary to separate returns from labor and from capital, which may be difficult, whereas under a cash-flow consumption tax, all receipts regardless of source would be included.[21]

As a final, practical observation, it should be noted that existing income tax systems tend to be closer to pure consumption taxes than to pure income taxes.[22] Much retirement savings and imputed income

---

[20] The comparison to follow in the text considers ex ante (labor income) and ex post (consumption) forms of taxation that are equivalent. A conventional income tax reaches labor and capital income when earned, the latter being ex post relative to the moment of investment. It is possible in principle, however, to move readily between ex ante and ex post taxation of capital income, an implication of the observation in subsection 2, which follows, that an ex ante and an ex post wealth tax are each equivalent to a capital income tax. For the extension of the various equivalences to the case in which capital income is uncertain, see subsection C.1.

[21] A principal difficulty concerns savings in the case of consumer durables. For example, purchase of a residence is an investment that gives rise to a flow of consumption services over time. Of course, the problem of measuring imputed income from consumer durables also plagues standard income tax systems. Under a consumption tax, it is possible to use the tax prepayment method under which the purchase of a consumer durable is treated as an act of consumption (see Bradford and U.S. Treasury Tax Policy Staff 1984).

[22] Further mitigating the difference between income and consumption taxation is the point, developed in subsection C.1, that neither taxes the risky component of returns to capital.

from consumer durables, notably owner-occupied housing—which together constitute the bulk of financial and physical assets for most individuals—are exempt. Dividends and capital gains may benefit from preferential rates (including the exclusion of capital gains at death), depreciation is often accelerated, and the realization requirement provides substantial deferral on much remaining capital income.[23] In addition, as will be noted in subsection C.3, human capital, a large fraction of all wealth, is taxed substantially as it would be under a consumption tax.

Perhaps the most important countervailing factor is that typical income taxes significantly overtax capital income as a consequence of the failure to index for inflation.[24] Although tax brackets, personal exemptions, and the like are often indexed, the return to capital in most forms usually is not (at least in economies not subject to hyperinflation). To illustrate the impact of this phenomenon, suppose, for example, that the real interest rate is 2%, the nominal interest rate 10%, and the tax rate 50%. A fully indexed income tax would tax returns at one percentage point, reducing the real return from 2% to 1%. However, when the 50% tax is applied to a nominal return of 10%, the effective tax is five percentage points, reducing the real return from 2% to –3%; note that the effective tax rate on real returns in this example is 250%. In sum, existing income taxes may exempt or tax very lightly most capital but subject the rest to very high rates.[25] Whatever is the ultimate effect of all of these

---

[23] Examining the U.S. tax system in 1983, Gordon and Slemrod (1988) found that, in light of existing tax preferences and tax avoidance opportunities (including the deductibility of interest), essentially no net taxes on capital income were collected. For 1995, Gordon, Kalambokidis, and Slemrod (2004a) estimated that approximately $100 billion of revenue was derived from taxing capital income; the difference was attributed to less generous capital allowances and lower interest rates (reducing the benefits from the deductibility of interest payments). For 2004, Gordon, Kalambokidis, Rohaly, and Slemrod (2004) projected that revenue from taxing capital income would fall by more than half as a consequence of more recent reforms providing more generous treatment of capital income. On the relationship between revenue collected from capital income taxation and measures of the effective tax rate on investment, see Gordon, Kalambokidis, and Slemrod (2004b).

[24] An additional consideration is the corporate income tax, examined in subsection 3.

[25] An important caveat is that the deductibility of interest payments combined with strategic tax avoidance behavior can lead to an opposing effect, as suggested by some of the evidence cited in note 23.

features on individuals' average intertemporal return to savings, the resulting interasset distortions are likely to be substantial.

2. Wealth Taxation[26]

Although sometimes viewed as a different sort of taxation, wealth taxes are, upon examination, simply a form of capital income taxation (see, for example, Atkinson and Stiglitz 1980). To demonstrate this, consider a wealth tax with a rate equal to $t_r r/(1+r)$. This tax may be imposed ex ante or ex post.

An ex ante wealth tax would apply this rate to period 1 savings, which equal $wl(1 - t) - c_1$, assuming for simplicity that there is a proportional labor income tax at rate t and no other taxation. For a given level of l and c_1, expenditures available for c_2 are given by

$$c_2 = \left[1 - \frac{t_r r}{1+r}\right][wl(1-t)-c_1](1+r) = [1+r(1-t_r)][wl(1-t)-c_1]. \quad (9.8)$$

After the first equal sign, the first term in brackets indicates the portion of period 1 savings that the individual has left after the ex ante wealth tax, the second term in brackets is the amount of the savings, and the final term indicates that this after-ex-ante-wealth-tax amount will grow at the (presumed untaxed) rate r. The expression on the right reflects simplification. To complete the argument about equivalence, simply observe that this final expression equals the value of c_2 implied by budget constraint (9.4) for the regime in which the tax rate t_r is applied to capital income (for the special case of a proportional income tax) and in which there is no ex ante wealth tax. Therefore, an ex ante wealth tax at the rate $t_r r/(1+r)$ is indeed equivalent to a capital income tax at the rate t_r.

For an ex post wealth tax—that is, a tax on savings plus interest, available for consumption in period 2, set at the rate $t_r r/(1+r)$—the result is the same. This conclusion can be verified by reinterpreting expression (9.8), where one simply supposes instead that the first term

---

[26] The subject of wealth transfer (estate and gift) taxation is treated separately, in chapter 10. As will be seen there, wealth and wealth transfer taxation are fundamentally different, even though they are often thought of as similar.

after the first equal sign refers to the portion available after an ex post wealth tax. The intuition for the equivalence of the two forms of the wealth tax is that, if the government is to take a given fraction of wealth, it does not matter whether it is taken ex ante (implicitly excluding the interest, which the government may earn itself by investing the ex ante tax proceeds) or ex post (where now the government collects the interest on what might be viewed as its share of the taxpayer's wealth). One can also think of this equivalence by reference to an ex ante wealth tax for which the bill is due ex post, with interest, or an ex post wealth tax that is prepaid, with the amount levied being adjusted for interest.

Because wealth taxation, ex ante or ex post, is equivalent to taxation of the return to capital, a subject that is analyzed in section A, little further comment is necessary. The primary difference between capital income taxes and wealth taxes is administrative: Wealth taxes require that the government assess individuals' levels of wealth, which is no easy task. However, capital income taxes impose similar requirements because measuring capital appreciation and depreciation requires valuation of capital. Furthermore, there is probably a good deal of overlap between assets that can be hidden from a wealth tax and assets that can have their capital gains as well as any dividends and interest concealed from a tax on capital income.[27]

3. Corporate Income Taxation

The analysis and applications up to this point consider a uniform tax on all returns to capital (or, equivalently, as just explained, on all capital). In practice, much capital taxation is nonuniform. An important instance is the corporate income tax, which in its classical, unintegrated variant is levied on equity investment undertaken in the corporate form. Corporations subject to this tax pay an income tax on their earnings, and individual taxpayers pay a further round of tax under the personal income

---

[27] A possible practical difference relates to the frequency of imposition of the taxes. Annually imposed wealth taxes place more demands on asset valuation, for example; however, capital income taxation that attempts to reach appreciation and depreciation as it accrues (rather than upon realization) also requires frequent valuation.

tax on dividend distributions.[28] (Individuals also pay tax on interest receipts, but interest payments are deductible by the corporation.) By contrast, equity investments through sole proprietorships, partnerships, and certain types of corporations are not subject to an entity-level tax; instead, income is attributed to owners who are taxed accordingly.

The corporate income tax—like other forms of nonuniform taxes and subsidies on capital income—adds a further layer to the foregoing analysis of capital taxation. It is clarifying to employ a similar approach to that used throughout this book, but taken one step further. Thus, just as one can determine whether capital taxation is efficient by holding the distribution of income constant, so one can assess intrinsic features of the corporate income tax most directly by considering its reduction, elimination, or expansion as part of a reform that keeps not only distribution but also the (average or overall) level of capital taxation constant. In this setting, the distinctive effects of a corporate income tax are its only effects. Specifically, capital invested in certain legal forms of business is subject to a higher level of tax than is capital invested in other forms. Moreover, as noted, because interest is deductible, the corporate income tax applies only to corporate equity. Such differential taxation tends to distort financial decisions, in the present context by discouraging operation in the corporate form, by encouraging the use of debt rather than equity, and perhaps also by discouraging dividend distributions, in each case relative to the levels that would be chosen for nontax reasons.[29]

The most fundamental question to ask is why corporations per se should be taxed at all. That is, what benefits might justify introducing the accompanying distortions? Most analysts, who emphasize that the

---

[28] A complete analysis would also need to account for the taxation of capital gains and losses when individuals sell shares.

[29] See generally Atkinson and Stiglitz (1980), Auerbach (2002), Bradford (1980, 1986), Graham (2003), Gravelle (1994), King (1977), and McLure (1979). Under the new (tax capitalization) view, the empirical validity of which is contested, distortion is limited to new equity. For recent work developing an agency theory of dividends, see Chetty and Saez (2007) and Gordon and Dietz (2007). Corporate income taxation also induces particular forms of avoidance behavior. Additionally, corporate income taxation raises more complex issues in the international setting.

burden of the corporate income tax (like that of any tax) is ultimately borne by individuals, are skeptical that good reasons exist. Presumably, if they do, they are to be found in the existence of some externality or in the ability of the corporate income tax to remedy some deficiency introduced by income taxation or, if efficient, capital taxation. One justification offered for the corporate income tax is that it prevents avoidance of the individual income tax on capital, for in the absence of a corporate income tax, individuals could invest in corporate form and defer taxes on capital income until they withdraw their funds, capturing the interest on the tax that would otherwise be due in the interim. Interestingly, most proposals for the repeal of the corporate income tax involve methods of integration that would eliminate the differential burden of the corporate income tax without making such deferral possible.[30] It is also suggested that corporations benefit from limited liability and thus should be taxed; however, the argument is a non sequitur (prices should equal marginal costs, which in the case of limited liability may be near zero, not benefits), the corporate income tax obligation is not directly related to any such benefits, and other limited liability entities are not subject to the tax. Various additional theories, based on different governmental benefits or on other grounds, have been offered—see, for example, the survey by Bird (1996)—but few relate closely to the form of the corporate income tax and most apply in principle to entities not subject to it. In sum, the corporate income tax, an important component of many tax systems, is difficult to rationalize when taking an integrated view of the optimal taxation problem.[31]

---

[30] Methods include treating the corporation as a pass-through entity, like other entities; giving corporations a deduction for dividends paid, like their deduction for interest; and giving shareholders a credit for corporate income taxes paid or an exclusion for dividend income (see, for example, American Law Institute 1989, 1993; McLure 1979; and U.S. Department of Treasury 1992). Most OECD countries provide some degree of integration, usually providing relief at the shareholder level (see, for example, Messere, de Kam, and Heady 2003).

[31] In developing countries, however, in which there are stricter limits on feasible tax instruments, taxing certain types of entities might be attractive.

C. Extensions

1. Uncertain Capital Income[32]

Uncertainty is central to capital income taxation because a substantial portion of the return to capital, notably regarding equity investments, consists of a risk premium. Furthermore, when income is uncertain, the taxation of risky returns provides implicit insurance, a sort of intrapersonal redistribution that is valuable because of the decreasing marginal utility of income.[33] (Compare subsection 5.E.2 on uncertain labor income.)

This understanding, however, is cast in a different light by Domar and Musgrave's (1944) seminal paper and subsequent work. Domar and Musgrave offer a partial equilibrium analysis in a model with two assets, one riskless and the other risky. Their basic insight is that taxes on the risky component of returns have no effect on individuals, who will simply gross up their initial investments in the risky asset to offset the effect of the tax.

To verify this claim, consider first a world in which only the riskless return, r, is taxed at the rate t_r. Suppose that, in this world, an investor would invest X in a risky asset that pays a gross return R_i (possibly less than X) in state of the world i. (For simplicity, ignore the rest of the investor's portfolio, assumed to be invested in a riskless asset; this investment both is held constant and is unaffected by the reform to be considered.) After risk is realized and tax is paid on the riskless return, a tax payment of $t_r r X$, the investor will have $R_i - t_r r X$, the gross return minus the tax on the riskless return to the initial investment.

---

[32] On taxation, risk, and household portfolio behavior more generally, see Poterba (2002).

[33] The concavity of the SWF, by contrast to the concavity of the utility function, is not as directly relevant if one adopts an ex ante, expected utility approach to measuring utility in the presence of uncertainty (see subsection 14.A.1.b on how this consideration pertains to whether the SWF should be utilitarian). In any event, the point in the text to follow regarding individuals' portfolio adjustments eliminating the apparent effect of taxation of risky returns renders moot any possible difference between ex ante and ex post assessments under a strictly concave SWF.

Now assume instead that all investment returns, including the risky component, are to be taxed at the rate t_r (in a fully symmetrical manner, allowing for complete deductibility of losses). The investor can offset the effect of this supplemental tax on risk by increasing his investment in the risky asset from X to $X/(1-t_r)$, borrowing the additional funds, $t_r X/(1-t_r)$, at the riskless rate r. After risk is realized, the loan (with interest) is repaid, and tax is paid, the investor will have

$$\frac{R_i}{1-t_r} - \frac{t_r X}{1-t_r}(1+r) - t_r\left[\frac{R_i - X}{1-t_r} - \frac{t_r X}{1-t_r}r\right]$$

$$= (1-t_r)\frac{R_i}{1-t_r} - \frac{t_r X}{1-t_r}(1+r-1-t_r r)$$

$$= R_i - \frac{t_r X}{1-t_r}r(1-t_r) = R_i - t_r rX. \tag{9.9}$$

In the first line of expression (9.9), the first term is the gross return on the investment of $X/(1-t_r)$, the second term is the repayment of the loan, $t_r X/(1-t_r)$, with interest, and the third term is the tax owed, the tax at rate t_r being levied now on the gross return net of the investment, with a deduction allowed for the interest payment on the loan. As can be seen after simplification, in every state (for any i), the investor's net return under this regime—having adjusted the initial level of investment—is $R_i - t_r rX$, which is identical to the net return under the initial regime that taxes only the riskless return to investment.

The foregoing result is often summarized by stating that income taxation and other forms of capital taxation in effect tax only the riskless return to capital and not the risk premium.[34] One implication is that capital taxation is less important than may appear because a tax on all returns is, accounting for portfolio adjustments, equivalent to a tax on only the riskless return, which is but a portion of the total return

---

[34] Closely related, the market value of the government's claim on risky returns in a perfect capital market is zero, which is unsurprising since the risk-adjusted value of the return to capital is just equal to the riskless rate (that is, by definition, the risk premium just compensates for the cost of bearing risk).

to capital. Furthermore, taxing risky returns does not, in the end, provide insurance since taxpayers' portfolio adjustments unwind this effect of taxation. Put another way, taxpayers wanting less risk could have invested in less risky portfolios in the absence of taxation; if subject to a system that automatically absorbs a portion of any risk they take, they simply gross up the extent of their pre-tax risk exposure in an offsetting manner.

This basic model has been qualified and extended in various ways. One set of work considers general equilibrium effects in asset markets and whether the government's budget is in balance in different states of the world (see Bulow and Summers 1984, Gordon 1985, and Kaplow 1994b). In basic settings, the foregoing analysis remains applicable. Relatedly, it can be demonstrated that various equivalences among taxes that hold in a world with certainty—notably, between a labor income tax and a consumption tax and between a capital income tax and an ex ante or ex post wealth tax—extend to the case of uncertain capital income (see Kaplow 1994b). Additional factors that may upset the results concerning the irrelevance of the taxation of risky returns are borrowing constraints, nonlinearities in the tax schedule (including limits on the ability to deduct investment losses), and limits on the ability to gross up certain types of investments. These and other considerations have implications for the efficiency of capital taxation when capital income is uncertain but do not, for the most part, have obvious implications for the problem of taxation and redistribution.[35]

---

[35] See, for example, Kaplow (1994b), MacKie-Mason (1990), and Weisbach (2004). Borrowing constraints are not obviously important for those holding most assets, assets obtained when grossing up might themselves be used as collateral, and constrained individuals can purchase assets with greater risk rather than personally borrowing to buy more assets of a given risk. Nonlinearities, notably limits on the deductibility of capital losses (which exist mainly to prevent selective realization of losses when taxation of capital gains and losses occurs only upon sale), may discourage risky investment. Grossing up is most difficult for unique, untraded assets where diversification is limited, such as when entrepreneurs start firms; if liquidity is limited because of moral hazard, forced diversification via taxation tends to be inefficient, whereas if liquidity is restricted due to adverse selection, the risk-sharing offered by taxation may well be efficient.

2. Capital Levies and Transitions[36]

One-time capital levies are traditionally viewed as an ideal sort of tax. Such a levy is imposed only on preexisting capital and, being one-time—with a presumed credible commitment never to be repeated—is nondistortionary.

There are three major problems with the argument in favor of a capital levy. First is the familiar point that the promise about the future may not be credible. The prospect of capital levies is a serious fear in many developing economies, which discourages foreign investment and induces residents to send capital outside the country. Any government that actually imposes a capital levy would not expect to be trusted anytime soon to avoid repetition of the levy. That most countries refrain from such actions reflects some mix of constitutional limitations, strong norms, and the fear that future capital flight would be more costly than any short-run, even if substantial, gain.[37]

Second, a capital levy must be unanticipated if it is to be nondistortionary. The difficulty with a long-anticipated capital levy is much like the problem of repetition: Beforehand, individuals will buy less capital (and engage in avoidance, such as through capital flight), which both causes distortion and erodes the ability of the levy to raise revenue. Eichengreen's (1990) reading of history is that largely unanticipated capital levies are extremely difficult to enact, particularly in modern democracies, since enactment of major reforms would ordinarily follow open, prolonged deliberation and political activity.[38] His exception that

---

[36] See Kaplow (1986, 1992a, 2003b, and especially 2007a) and also, on transitions, Shaviro (2000).

[37] For a classic statement of the dynamic commitment problem, which mentions capital levies as an illustration, see Kydland and Prescott (1977), and for a model with an infinitely repeated game in which the government's patience determines the success of de facto commitment, see Acemoglu, Golosov, and Tsyvinski (2006). It should be noted that, although explicit levies are uncommon, partial indirect levies—notably, through heightened (unanticipated) inflation—are more common and can generate the reputational problems associated with explicit capital levies.

[38] Eichengreen (1990) offers an interesting account of capital levies that were contemplated (with support by prominent economists, who wrote extensively on the subject), although not ultimately enacted, by many European countries following World War I.

proves the rule is the actual imposition of a levy by the occupying authorities in Japan shortly after World War II: Action was swift and unaccompanied by public discussion. (Additionally, it may not have given rise to a fear of repetition since it was imposed by outsiders, soon to depart, and was apparently motivated by a desire to expropriate from those believed to have promoted the war and to have profited from its execution.)

Third, there is a conceptual problem with the purported idyllic nature of a capital levy in developed economies that have an income tax.[39] Specifically, one could in principle raise sums distortion-free by reducing the grant component g of the income tax, even making it negative—that is, a uniform lump-sum levy. The primary deterrent to using this approach is not inefficiency but dislike of the distributive consequences. If a capital levy is a mere substitute for lowering g, and if g is already set optimally, then there is no benefit to a capital levy.

Further reflection suggests that a capital levy may nevertheless be welfare-increasing (setting aside problems of repetition and anticipation) because of its indirect tendency to redistribute the fruits of labor effort without distorting labor supply. At any given point in time, it is likely that ownership of the existing capital stock is distributed in a way that positively correlates with prior earnings and underlying earning ability, for individuals' savings are the product of prior accumulations that ultimately derive from labor income.[40] (The correlation will be highly imperfect due to differences in life-cycle stage, preferences, and other factors; some such confounding effects could be addressed, such as by making the levy age dependent.) Thus, a capital levy may be distributively appealing whereas reducing g would not be. Observe that this version of the argument is closely analogous to the notion that it would be ideal to impose future individualized lump-sum taxes based on ability as inferred from prior earnings or investments in human capital: The taxes would be nondistortionary in the future, and as long as

---

[39] Compare the discussion of Ramsey taxation in section 6.D.

[40] In some cases, the accumulations derive from inheritance, typically a product of parents' labor income, which also tends to be imperfectly correlated with individuals' earning ability.

this regime was not anticipated ex ante, society would not have suffered from prior distortions either.[41] If such an unanticipated, one-time imposition were possible, it would be optimal to fashion the redistributive tax as a function of revealed labor effort rather than imposing a uniform capital levy.

In light of the foregoing analysis, it is interesting to note that many contemplated fundamental tax reforms involve transitions that entail what is tantamount to a one-time capital levy (or grant). Most analyzed is the transition from an income tax to a consumption tax or simply the introduction of or raising the rates in a consumption tax: Unless there is transition relief for pre-enactment accumulations, the effect is to reduce the purchasing power of preexisting capital.[42] Thus, although a wage tax and a consumption tax may be equivalent in steady state, simulations of the transition to a consumption tax show greater efficiency gains than those that result from transition to a wage tax because the former contains a significant capital levy whereas the latter does not.[43] Of course, if the transition were anticipated, say, during years or decades of preceding debate, distortion would result and less revenue would be raised.[44]

Similar questions arise in other settings. For example, analyses of the efficiency of capital taxation in infinite-horizon models (see subsection A.1) often envision a world in which there is a preexisting capital stock without inquiring as to its origin—notably, as a consequence of prior earnings or of inheritance, which itself is the product of a donor's prior earnings, on which see chapter 10.[45] In such a model, the intertemporal inefficiency of taxing capital discussed in subsection A.1

---

[41] For a theoretical exploration of taxation based upon prior economic choices, see Roberts (1984) and the survey by Golosov, Tsyvinski, and Werning (2007).

[42] See, for example, Bradford (1996a, 1996b), Kaplow (2003b, 2007a), Sarkar and Zodrow (1993), and Shaviro (2000).

[43] See, for example, Auerbach and Kotlikoff (1987), Sarkar and Zodrow (1993), Auerbach (1996), and Altig et al. (2001).

[44] See, for example, the simulations in Howitt and Sinn (1989) that allow for a phase-in and those in Auerbach and Kotlikoff (1987) that consider early announcement of reforms.

[45] In addition, some work on the possible optimality of differential commodity taxation identifies potential benefits through implicitly taxing individuals' unobservable endowments (see note 14 in chapter 6), but the endowments are taken to be preexisting, so their likely origin in individuals' previous labor earnings is not considered.

will be counterbalanced by the advantage of the levy on preexisting capital. Therefore, it is not surprising that a dynamic analysis will suggest the optimality of maximal capital taxes initially but no capital taxation in the long-run steady state. All of this, of course, assumes that the enactment of the initially high capital tax is unanticipated and that the subsequent promise to eliminate capital taxation is credible after having just taxed income from existing capital at a 100% rate.

Likewise, negative capital levies—windfalls—would arise if, for example, corporate income taxation is reduced or eliminated. Thus, a key point concerning the desirability and appropriate form of integration of the corporate income tax concerns the fact that existing corporate equity would thereby be freed of future tax liability. This revenue loss is ordinarily seen as unaccompanied by any corresponding efficiency gain, although in a setting in which the possibility of integration may long be anticipated, an understanding that old equity would benefit would tend to have the effect of reducing pre-enactment distortion.

3. Human Capital

Human capital, taken here for simplicity to refer to the present value of earnings that individuals can produce, constitutes a substantial majority of all capital (see, for example, Davies and Whalley 1991 and Jorgenson and Fraumeni 1989). Furthermore, the returns to human capital—wages—are the direct or indirect source of most tax revenue. Accordingly, the relationship between human capital and taxation deserves attention. To illuminate the matter, it is useful to compare the tax treatment of human capital under an accrual income tax, which purports to tax capital income, with standard treatments of physical and financial capital, following Kaplow (1996b).[46] As is the case with capital taxation more generally, since we can contemplate distribution-neutral reforms, the focus is on efficiency.

The return to human capital consists of wages that under a traditional income tax are taxed only when realized, that is, when the wages

---

[46] For a complementary treatment of some of these issues, see Andrews and Bradford (1988, appendix).

are earned. To illustrate this point, consider an individual deciding between working slightly more in the present period or in a future period, in either case to fund a small increment to consumption in the future period.[47] Suppose further that the disutility of the incremental labor effort (discounted, as appropriate) is the same and that the present value, at the before-tax interest rate, of the earnings is also the same. Without taxes on capital, the individual would be indifferent between earning more now and earning more later. However, if income from physical and financial capital is taxed at the rate t_r, then the individual strictly prefers earning more later: The interest on present earnings, saved for future consumption, would be taxed, but if the individual instead funds future consumption from future wage income, there is no tax on what might be viewed as the implicit interest on human capital. Accordingly, capital taxation tends to favor shifting labor effort to future periods. Although this effect is distortionary, it tends to reduce the intertemporal distortion of consumption described in subsection A.1.

Viewed more broadly, a standard income tax (or any general tax on capital) treats human capital essentially on a realization basis by taxing wages when earned while ignoring changes in the value of an individual's stock of human capital. This is most apparent in an individual's last year of work: The year's wages are taxed, but the individual's stock of human capital will have fallen during the year by nearly the full amount of those wages (the present value at the outset equaling the year's wages with a slight time value discount) while no offsetting depreciation deduction is allowed, as would be the case under pure accrual income taxation. Under an idealized accrual system, the receipt of human capital (at birth) would be subject to tax, and each year's earnings would be partially offset by depreciation deductions that would be growing over time. Further taxation (including negative taxation for falls in human capital) would arise as uncertainty was resolved, just as with a physical or financial asset that produced a similar (yet equally uncertain) pattern

---

[47] If the proceeds were to be consumed in the present period in either case, the outcome would be the same because interest payments (negative interest receipts) on present borrowing against future earnings would be deductible under an accrual income tax.

of future cash flows.[48] Instead, both actual and ordinarily proposed methods of taxing human capital are realization based, producing a result closer to that under a consumption tax, tantamount to the exemption of returns to capital.

Under standard forms of capital taxation, investment in human capital may seem to be favored over investment in other capital because human capital is taxed only upon realization. As noted, however, there are no depreciation deductions for human capital and thus for incremental investments therein. Some investments in human capital, notably forgone earnings, are implicitly expensed (deducted immediately) since the forgone imputed income is never taxed, which is more favorable than depreciation (see Boskin 1977 and Heckman 1976).[49] Many direct investment expenditures, such as on education, are never deductible (although there are substantial public subsidies). Additionally, to the extent that the uncompensated labor supply elasticity is positive (negative), the reduction (increase) in labor effort due to labor income taxation will reduce (increase) the value of investments in human capital. Further influences on the return to human capital investment may arise because of general equilibrium effects on wages of the sort noted in subsection 5.E.3. The net effect of these (and other) factors is not entirely clear. Nevertheless, Trostel (1993) estimates that income taxes do significantly discourage investment in human capital, the primary channels being a consequence of the taxation of labor income, implying that a consumption tax or other

---

[48] Another way to understand the difference between accrual taxation of human capital and the realization-based approach implicit in taxing wages instead, with no adjustments for changes in the value of human capital, is to contemplate what sort of taxation at realization would serve as a proxy for accrual taxation. As a crude approximation, by analogy to Auerbach's (1991) scheme for realization-based taxation of capital gains that implicitly takes time value into account, any wage earnings could be subject to greater tax the longer the holding period, that is, the older the individual at the time the wages are earned. Thus, the effects of pure accrual taxation of human capital would be similar to those of applying to wage earnings a multiplier that grew over individuals' lifetimes. Such a multiplier would offset the favoritism for later earnings noted in the text.

[49] If such implicit deductions are taken in years in which marginal rates are low (due to rate graduation), the result could be less generous (see Nerlove et al. 1993).

schemes that did not tax capital income would have a similar effect. It does not follow, however, that all such effects involve inefficiencies: Taking as given that individuals, say, will work less because of labor income taxation, it is efficient for them to invest less in their human capital to that extent.[50]

---

[50] There may be externalities to investment in human capital, and general equilibrium effects also influence welfare, so such effects of taxation on human capital may still be of social consequence. One externality is caused by labor income taxation itself; because some of the benefit of augmenting human capital is captured by the government through taxation of wage income, individuals' tendency to reduce investment in human capital is socially excessive on this account. (In Hamilton's (1987) model, this factor favors some taxation of capital income because it is assumed that investment in human capital is financed entirely by forgone earnings that are implicitly expensed, with the result that capital taxation desirably shifts investment from physical and financial capital to human capital.) Also, if the tax-induced reduction in effective wages reduces labor supply, there is a further reduction to the return from investment in human capital (see, for example, Jacobs 2005). In addition, there may be a feedback effect whereby the reduction in human capital translates, ex post, into a lower wage, further reducing labor supply. Hence, the effects of labor income taxation would be greater than in the case in which wages were taken as given. On the other hand, general equilibrium effects resulting from changes in human capital investments at different skill levels may tend to dampen the effect of taxation on human capital (see Heckman, Lochner, and Taber 1999).

10

Taxation of Transfers

Private voluntary transfers, from one individual to another, may be subject to taxation under an income or consumption tax as well as under a tax regime aimed specifically at transfers. A typical income tax provides no deduction for donors' gifts, implicitly treating them as a form of consumption by donors, but excludes gift receipts from donees' tax base, which, as Simons (1938) argued, conflicts with the notion of comprehensively taxing "income." Under a cash-flow consumption tax, gifts could be deemed consumption of donors, donees, or both; the last option is not ordinarily proposed but nevertheless seems most consistent with the notion of taxing all "consumption," understood in the case of donors in accordance with revealed preference (by contrast to exhaustive use of resources).[1] Under a sales tax or VAT, gifts per se are not covered, with the result that only donees are taxed, when they use gifts to finance their own, direct consumption.

Independently, transfer taxation—levies on donors' gifts and bequests in the United States and on inheritances that donees receive in many other countries—is often applied to voluntary transfers involving fairly high levels of wealth. Note that, although sometimes considered together, the taxation of wealth transfers under any guise is qualitatively distinct from the taxation of wealth holdings, the latter having been examined in subsection 9.B.2 as a species of capital income taxation.[2]

---

[1] On the use of such tax base definitions as if they were normative principles, see section 15.F.

[2] To reinforce this point, note that on one hand it is possible for a donor to transfer resources every period yet to hold no wealth (that is, all earnings are consumed directly or transferred each period), and on the other hand an individual can amass large wealth early in

Analytically, it is helpful to ignore these differences among possible forms of transfer taxation and simply to consider what net tax or subsidy, if any, should be applied to voluntary transfers. For convenience, the baseline (relative to which a tax or subsidy is measured) employed here is a pure labor income tax regime, and any tax or subsidy on transfers is taken to be levied on the donor.[3]

The analysis begins by applying the framework of chapter 6 on commodity taxation. Own-consumption and gifts may be viewed as two different commodities available to prospective donors (hereafter, simply referred to as donors). Specifically, as before, it will be supposed that any contemplated change in the treatment of transfers is accompanied by an adjustment of the labor income tax schedule that holds donors' utilities constant. Framed in this manner, the question is whether donors at any given income level should be taxed more or less on account of giving an additional dollar to a donee rather than expending it on own-consumption.

If gifts were qualitatively similar to consumption of any other commodity, the benchmark result would be that no tax or subsidy is optimal. In addition to noting the standard qualifications, more extensive attention will be devoted to distinctive features of gifts. First, gifts ordinarily entail external effects regarding donees, both directly and also indirectly on account of donees' labor supply responses. Second, gifts have implications regarding donors' and donees' utility levels and marginal

---

life, hold it until retirement, and then consume it entirely, never making any transfers. Nor are these merely hypothetical considerations: A large portion of transfers involve sharing of contemporaneous earnings within the family, and a large portion of wealth holdings consists of life-cycle savings. As a consequence of this distinction, it is largely sufficient to consider transfer taxation in a static setting, even though transfer taxes are often seen in part as taxes on savings. To incorporate savings formally, one can imagine changing the level of transfer taxation while also adjusting not only the labor income tax, as noted in the text to follow, but also the tax on savings so as to keep the average effect of the latter constant, thereby isolating the question of optimal taxation of voluntary transfers. For further specification, see note 6.

[3] When taxes are nonlinear (and donors and donees may face different marginal tax rates), when there are different nonlinear systems potentially applicable to income and to transfers, or when utility functions are not insensitive to regime differences that have the same ultimate impact (see, for example, the discussion in subsection B.2), these simplifications may not capture all that is relevant.

utilities of consumption, which are pertinent to the marginal social value of redistribution.

The analysis then considers different transfer motives. Although the underlying impetus for consumption behavior ordinarily is irrelevant to optimal commodity taxation, in the case of voluntary transfers different motives imply different formulations of utility functions, which may affect the behavioral response to taxation as well as the welfare consequences of a given behavior. A final section will address other aspects of distribution (notably, intergenerational considerations), transfers of human capital in various forms, and charitable giving (in contrast to gifts to particular individuals, usually family members, which is the focus of most of the chapter). Some aspects of transfer taxation are further illuminated in chapter 12, on taxation of the family, since most voluntary transfers are between family members.[4] The presentation in the current chapter largely follows Kaplow (1998c, 2001a), where other issues are also examined.

A. Analysis

1. Taxation of Transfers as Differential Commodity Taxation

Consider a version of the model in chapter 6 in which each donor allocates disposable income, $wl - T(wl)$, between own-consumption c and gifts c_γ to some donee in order to maximize the donor's utility $u(c, c_\gamma, l)$.[5] The price of both commodities is normalized to one, the commodity

---

[4] When each adult and child is considered as a distinct individual (which is particularly appropriate in studying transfers), rather than viewing the family as if it were one person, a large portion of transfers consists of the support of minor children by parents and sharing between spouses. (Of course, most ordinary bequests and large explicit inter vivos transfers are also to relatives, often members of the donor's immediate family.) Furthermore, since many of these within-household transfers may be difficult to tax or subsidize as a practical matter even if such measures were optimal, differences in the tax and transfer program treatment of different family units can be viewed in part as a sort of presumptive taxation (or subsidization) of transfers within the family. See also note 14 in chapter 12.

[5] Until subsection B.3, c_γ will be taken to refer to true gifts, disallowing the possibility that a transfer is in exchange for donee services of some sort.

tax on own-consumption to zero, and the differential tax or subsidy on giving is t_γ. A donor's budget constraint is[6]

$$c + (1 + t_\gamma)c_\gamma = wl - T(wl). \tag{10.1}$$

For concreteness, it may be helpful to imagine some particular donor-donee pair, such as a parent and a child.

In this formulation, if donors' utility functions were weakly separable in labor, so that they could be expressed as $u(v(c, c_\gamma), l)$, the optimum would be $t_\gamma = 0$.[7] (This result ignores the effect of gifts on donees, a subject explored in subsection 2.) As in the standard optimal commodity tax problem, this conclusion is independent of the elasticities of demand for the two types of consumption. It also does not depend on whether individuals at different income levels engage in different relative levels of consumption—perhaps lower-income individuals devote a higher fraction of their income to own-consumption—because the income tax is taken to be adjusted to keep the distribution of utilities the same.

---

[6] If one wished to extend the model as mentioned in note 2 to the case in which transfers are given out of savings, one could instead consider a version of the two-period model in subsection 9.A.1, in which the utility function is now $u(c_1, c_2, c_\gamma, l)$, where c_1 is first-period own-consumption, c_2 is second-period own-consumption, c_γ is (second-period) giving, and l is (first-period) labor supply. In this case, the budget constraint (9.4) becomes

$$c_1 + \frac{c_2 + (1 + t_\gamma)c_\gamma}{1 + r(1 - t_r)} = wl - T(wl).$$

The optimal level of tax (or subsidy) on the return to capital, t_r, and on gifts, t_γ, could then each be determined, the former according to the prior analysis and the latter using the analysis to follow in the text. Relatedly, for any change in t_γ, one could change t_r in the opposite direction so as to keep constant the average tax on second-period consumption of both types and also adjust the labor income tax schedule to preserve the distribution of utility levels, so that the only effect of the change in t_γ would be on the relative treatment of own-consumption and gifts in the same (second) time period.

[7] As in chapter 6, this conclusion follows from Atkinson and Stiglitz (1976), as extended by Kaplow (2006c).

This conclusion is subject to the usual qualifications sketched in section 6.C. Notably, weak separability may well be violated. One possibility is that increasing gifts reduces the utility of leisure on account of the concomitant reduction in resources available for own-consumption, in which case a gift subsidy is optimal. Some gifts may have the opposite effect; perhaps transfers to grandchildren (in this case, inter vivos gifts rather than bequests) increase the relative value of leisure by raising the pleasure from spending time with them, in which case taxing gifts is optimal. Although potentially significant, this question has not been explored empirically. Perhaps the most important qualification to the no-differential-tax result in the present setting is that gifts typically generate externalities involving donees, which are considered next.

2. Externalities Due to Transfers

A gift inherently involves two parties, a donor and a donee. Subsection 1 focuses on donors. Consider now the situation of donees, who are assumed to choose labor effort to maximize $u(c,l)$ subject to the budget constraint

$$c = wl - T(wl) + \gamma, \tag{10.2}$$

where γ indicates the magnitude of the gift received.[8] (For a particular donor-donee pair, where each member does not give to or receive from anyone else, $\gamma = c_\gamma$.) As a consequence, donors' decisions give rise to externalities regarding donees. There is a direct, positive externality on donees and also an indirect, often negative externality on the public fisc.

a. Externality on donees. Gifts increase the utility of donees, which constitutes a positive externality to donors' gift decisions and thus, ceteris paribus, favors a gift subsidy, that is, $t_\gamma < 0$.[9] Observe that this is

---

[8] A more complete analysis might consider an overlapping-generations version of the model sketched in note 6, in which the same individuals both receive gifts, γ, in the first period of their lives and also make gifts, c_γ, in the second period.

[9] This point is noted in Atkinson (1971, p. 222, n. 1) and Stiglitz (1987, p. 1035) and is developed in Kaplow (1995b), who characterizes the optimal subsidy to gifts in a simplified

true even if the donor's gift is motivated by concern for the donee, as will be elaborated in subsection B.1 on altruistically motivated giving. A private–social divergence exists because the donee's utility enters the SWF in two ways: once, directly, because the donee is one of the individuals of concern, and a second time, indirectly, through the effect on the utility of the donor.[10] The donor considers the latter but not the former. Put another way, suppose that c_γ is the donor's (privately) optimal level of giving. If this level were increased slightly, the donor would suffer no first-order utility loss, but the donee would realize a first-order utility gain. Hence, the donor's chosen level of giving is less than is socially optimal.[11]

   b. Externality involving tax revenue. In the presence of a labor income tax (or many other forms of taxation), gifts also generally result in an externality on the public fisc. Ordinarily, the receipt of a gift will have an income effect that reduces the donee's labor supply.[12] Donees find such reductions privately optimal, given the gifts that they receive, but they do not bear the full cost of their behavioral adjustment on account of the labor income tax. For each dollar less that they earn, the fisc loses $T'(wl)$. To complete the argument, donors will be unconcerned about

---

setting in which there is no taxation (other than to finance the gift subsidy). A further positive externality arises through the benefits of gifts to donees' spouses and their families (see, for example, Nerlove, Razin, and Sadka 1986).

   [10] Some suggest that thus accounting for altruism in the SWF amounts to a double counting of the donee's utility. However, it is hard to see whose utility should not be counted. The donee is an individual in his/her own right and thus there is no basis for exclusion. For the donor, the utility achieved is real: Why should utility from giving, say, to one's children be ignored when it is revealed to be preferred to spending on own-consumption, the utility from which would be counted? Note that an implication of excluding such utility would be that those who give more would be deemed worse off rather than better off; moreover, under a strictly concave SWF, such individuals would deserve a greater allotment on that account. For further discussion, see subsection 13.B.3.

   [11] Unlike with typical externalities, moving the level of the gift toward the social optimum cannot in principle be accomplished in a way that generates a Pareto improvement because this manner of raising social welfare requires a different distribution of income.

   [12] For empirical evidence, see, for example, Holtz-Eakin, Joulfaian, and Rosen (1993), Imbens, Rubin, and Sacerdote (2001), and Joulfaian and Wilhelm (1994).

this effect on revenue when determining how much to give. Hence, there is a negative externality to donors' giving.[13]

Note that the extent of this tax revenue externality can be bounded from above by the donee's marginal income tax rate, $T'(wl)$. The reason is that in standard cases the income effect implies that the earnings reduction from receiving an incremental dollar will be less than a dollar. (If earnings fell by a full dollar, the marginal utility of consumption would be restored to its initial level whereas the marginal disutility of labor would decrease, which together imply that labor supply would have been reduced too much.) Accordingly, it would appear that the optimal level of taxation of transfers (even if positive) must be less than full taxation of the receipt of gifts at the donee's marginal tax rate—as proposed by Simons (1938) in order to tax income comprehensively, and as would arise under a cash-flow consumption tax if gifts were treated as consumption of both donors and donees. This suggestion combines the present result, that such a tax exceeds the level necessary to correct for the negative tax revenue externality, with the preceding results, that the simple benchmark involves no tax or subsidy on gifts

---

[13] One might wonder about an opposing externality involving donors' labor supply. If c_γ rises, c must fall. This adjustment implies a higher marginal utility of own-consumption, which would seem to induce an increase in donors' labor effort. Moreover, the external benefit of such an increase on the public fisc would be ignored by donors (this is just an alternative statement of the standard labor-leisure distortion). However, when an increase in c_γ is induced by a subsidy (a reduction in t_γ) and is accompanied in turn by an offsetting income tax adjustment, as presumed here, there is no net effect on donors' labor supply in the basic case. Indeed, as the text in subsection 1 indicates, from a donor's point of view, a tax or subsidy on expenditures on gifts is no different from a tax or subsidy on any other expenditure, so the analysis in chapter 6 is fully applicable. (Specifically, a subsidy on c_γ would be accompanied by an increase in marginal labor income tax rates, which has the effect of raising the net cost of earning income to spend on c that just offsets the extent to which expenditures on c have a higher marginal utility than before. Similarly, the lower effective cost of earning income to spend on c_γ—the combined effect of the higher marginal labor income tax rate and the subsidy on expenditures on c_γ—will just offset the reduction in the marginal utility from gifts. We know that this perfect offset must occur because, with weak separability of labor, the tax adjustment is set so as to maintain the same level of utility from a given level of labor earnings, presumed to be allocated optimally among different commodities in the pertinent regimes. See subsection 6.B.1.)

and that the positive externality on donees favors a subsidy. Of course, other considerations could alter this conclusion.

It need not be the case, however, that the tax revenue externality from gifts is negative. To the extent that gifts themselves represent investments in human capital that donees would not otherwise make (see subsection C.2) or serve to relax liquidity constraints and thereby permit donees to invest, say, in entrepreneurship, the resulting tax revenue externality may be positive, favoring a gift subsidy.[14]

3. Transfers' Effects on the Marginal Social Value of Redistribution

Differences in donors' and donees' utility functions and circumstances also influence the optimal taxation of transfers through their effects on the marginal social value of redistribution. In this regard, one might think of gifts as a sort of localized voluntary redistribution. On one hand, this suggests that giving should be favored since redistribution tends to raise social welfare, assuming that gifts are from higher- to lower-income individuals, which is usually the case. On the other hand, to the extent that some voluntary redistribution takes place, the marginal value of further redistribution via taxation may be reduced. The preceding analysis of externalities is highly pertinent to the former consideration. To incorporate the latter requires further attention to the effect of gifts on donors' and donees' marginal utilities of consumption and also (for strictly concave SWFs) on their utility levels.

First, consider donors, and suppose that there are two donors with the same income-earning ability who give different amounts. One possibility is that the donor who gives more does so on account of receiving greater utility from giving, that is, has a higher $\partial u/\partial c_\gamma$, ceteris paribus. For example, one donor may fortuitously have a spouse or child toward

---

[14] For empirical evidence on liquidity constraints, inheritance, and entrepreneurship, see, for example, Blanchflower and Oswald (1998), Cox (1990), and Holtz-Eakin, Joulfaian, and Rosen (1994a, 1994b). Donees' labor supply may also be affected for other reasons. There may be a reduction due to the Samaritan's dilemma, that is, if donees work less because they anticipate that altruistic donors will compensate through increased giving. Alternatively, there may be an increase if donees anticipate that donors view labor effort as virtuous and thus deserving of reward.

whom he has altruistic feelings, or the intensity of his altruism may be higher than that of the other donor. This donor will achieve a higher level of utility. Additionally, he will have a higher marginal utility of own-consumption because, as c_γ is increased, c must be reduced. The latter favors greater redistribution toward the higher-giving donor, which may be accomplished indirectly through subsidizing gifts. The former factor—the higher level of utility—would be immaterial to optimal redistribution under a utilitarian SWF but would favor less generosity, perhaps accomplished through less generous treatment of gifts, if the SWF were strictly concave. With sufficient concavity, this factor could dominate the opposing effect from higher marginal utility.[15]

These conclusions, however, are reversed if the donor gives more not on account of greater utility from giving but from a lower utility of own-consumption, that is, a lower $\partial u/\partial c$, ceteris paribus. In this case, we might imagine a donor who is less capable of enjoying the pleasures of ordinary consumption. This donor will achieve a lower level of utility and also will have a lower marginal utility of own-consumption. (Although as c_γ is increased, c must be reduced, which raises this marginal utility, it is the case that c_γ will not be raised sufficiently to offset the initially lower level of $\partial u/\partial c$, which is the force that drives the higher level of c_γ.)

Because donors' giving (when $t_\gamma = 0$) is determined by the first-order condition $\partial u/\partial c = \partial u/\partial c_\gamma$, any particular level of giving is consistent, for example, with both derivatives being high or both low, so the level of giving is not directly informative about which case is being observed. As with all redistributive judgments in the standard welfare economics framework, interpersonal comparisons of utility are required to move from observed circumstances to a distributive welfare judgment. It is not possible in the present setting, as is sometimes done, simply to stipulate that individuals' utility functions are the same; differences in giving behavior belie that assumption. However, there may be some practical basis for distinguishing among donors since we can also observe family configurations, the relationship between donors and their donees, and perhaps some other pertinent characteristics.[16]

---

[15] The possibility of such a tradeoff is introduced in subsection 3.B.3.

[16] The relevance of these features reinforces the importance of the previously noted connection between the present subject and that of taxation of families, explored in chapter 12.

Donees' circumstances also may vary. In the present framework, it is natural to consider two donees with the same income-earning ability who receive different levels of gifts. Here, suppose that the donees have the same utility functions and that the difference in gift receipts is due to the fortuity of the donor (if any) with whom each happens to be paired. Then the only effect of gifts is on the budget constraint. In the standard case, a donee receiving a higher gift has a higher utility level and also a lower marginal utility of consumption, which is the reason for the reduction in labor effort (in the standard case) identified in subsection 2.b. The existence of a higher utility level and a lower marginal utility of consumption favors less generous treatment under any standard SWF.

Combining these conclusions regarding donors and donees with each other and with those of the earlier subsections is rather complicated. For example, in the first case for donors, in which the marginal utility of own-consumption of those who give more is higher, under a utilitarian SWF giving should be favored somewhat more than otherwise on this account, but there is also an offsetting effect due to the lower marginal utility of consumption of donees. Furthermore, on account of transfers, individuals with the same income-earning ability may choose to earn different amounts, due to differences in utility functions or in opportunities for giving or receiving transfers. Thus, at any given income level, a single marginal tax rate must be applied to individuals who differ on multiple dimensions. Compare subsection 5.C.2 on heterogeneous preferences regarding consumption and labor effort. Formal analysis and simulations seem necessary to obtain a full appreciation of the problem of optimal taxation of voluntary transfers. One of the most important challenges in doing so is the need to specify the form of donors' utility functions, the subject of the next section.

B. Transfer Motives

Before considering particular transfer motives, it is useful to begin by asking why donors' motivations for private voluntary transfers are relevant. As noted earlier, it ordinarily is immaterial why an individual chooses to consume some good or service. The optimal differential tax rate does not depend, for example, on whether an individual chooses to go on vacation (rather than expend the same amount at home) because she prefers a change of pace, savors the beauty of the chosen destination, or cherishes revisiting a childhood haunt. With gifts, however, different motivations may imply differences in the functional forms for donors' or donees' utility that may be directly relevant to the welfare effects of gifts and also may carry behavioral implications for a tax or subsidy on transfers. For example, a tax on bequests will directly reduce the utility of altruistically motivated donors and also discourage their giving but will have neither effect on donors whose bequests are purely accidental (that is, due to leftover precautionary savings when complete annuitization is unavailable and there is no bequest motive). Also, a tax that reduces giving directly reduces the utility of donees who receive true gifts, but for those really exchanging services for apparent gifts, there is an offset to the extent that fewer services need to be provided.

Accordingly, it is important to consider the implications of different transfer motives. Observe, however, that even if the optimal treatment of each type of gift could be determined, normative implications for transfer policy remain uncertain for a number of reasons. Motives vary across donors in ways that are difficult to observe directly. (Thus, it may be optimal for transfer tax policy to treat differently inter vivos gifts and bequests, donor-donee pairs that have different relationships, gifts of human capital and cash, and so forth if these distinctions are correlated with different transfer motives, even though such distinctions may not per se be relevant.) Also, mixed motives may often be present for a single donor. Additionally, there is some evidence that donors' behavior is not entirely rational, perhaps in part because of a reluctance to contemplate and plan optimally for death.[17] These reasons undoubtedly contribute to the difficulty that researchers have had in determining actual transfer motives, despite substantial empirical investigation.[18]

---

[17] See, for example, Kopczuk and Slemrod (2005), who model the effects of denial of death on economic behavior, and Poterba (2001), who finds that many donors subject to heavy transfer taxation fail by a wide margin to take full advantage of inter vivos giving opportunities that would reduce tax burdens.

[18] See, for example, Arrondel and Masson (2006), Davies (1996), Masson and Pestieau (1997), and Stark (1995).

In the discussion to follow, the analysis will be simplified to avoid excessive repetition of material in section A and to focus on the differences between transfer motives. It will be useful to examine the case with weak labor separability and, specifically, to consider only donors' subutility functions, $v(c, c_\gamma)$, because transfer motives will be reflected there and because, with weak separability, the presumed adjustment to the income tax schedule will hold donors' labor supply constant in any event.[19]

1. Altruism

An altruistic donor's subutility function can be formulated as

$$v(c,c_\gamma) = \alpha\mu(c) + \beta\upsilon(c_\upsilon + c_\gamma, l_\upsilon), \tag{10.3}$$

where α and β are weights on self-regarding and altruistic utility, respectively, μ is the donor's utility from own-consumption, υ is the donee's utility function, c_υ is the donee's expenditure on consumption from after-labor-income-tax income, l_υ is the donee's labor effort, and w_υ will denote the donee's wage. Note that $c_\upsilon = w_\upsilon l_\upsilon - T(w_\upsilon l_\upsilon)$ and $c_\gamma = \gamma$, so that the donee's budget constraint (10.2) is now incorporated directly into the donee's utility function.

The analysis of the optimal tax or subsidy, t_γ, for this case follows closely that outlined in section A. To consider the externalities identified in subsection A.2, it is useful for concreteness to examine a utilitarian SWF. The contribution of the donor and donee to social welfare is given

---

[19] Implicitly, this construction assumes that it is possible to apply a different $T(wl)$ schedule to donors and to donees. Compare the general discussion of categorical income tax schedules in subsection 5.C.1 and the application to income transfer programs in section 7.C. If a single schedule must be employed, then, say, a gift subsidy would be associated with an adjustment to the income tax schedule that is less than that imagined in the foregoing analysis, implying that donors, subject to lower marginal tax rates than those that hold labor supply constant, would increase labor effort (assuming a positive uncompensated labor supply elasticity) and that donees, subject to higher marginal tax rates, would reduce labor effort relative to the adjustment discussed in subsection A.2.b. These effects would tend to be offsetting, though only by coincidence would they be precisely so, implying that some further subtle adjustment to the otherwise optimal transfer tax would be in order.

by $u(v(c,c_\gamma), l) + v(c_v + c_\gamma, l_v)$. In addition, we must consider any effect on tax revenue, weighted by the shadow price λ (see chapter 4).

The donor chooses c_γ to maximize u, with a marginal utility gain from increasing c_γ of $u_1\beta v_1$, where subscripts denote partial derivatives with respect to the pertinent argument. However, the direct contribution of an increase in c_γ to social welfare is $u_1\beta v_1 + v_1 = (u_1\beta + 1)v_1$. This illustrates the positive externality to giving, in that the altruistic donor considers the benefit to the donee only to the extent that it contributes to the donor's own utility, $u_1\beta v_1$, whereas society values this plus the direct benefit to the donee in her own right, v_1.

Next, consider the tax revenue externality. Because any differential tax or subsidy, the source of any inducement on the donor to change c_γ, is assumed to be financed by an income tax adjustment that has the effect of holding constant the donor's labor supply, we can confine our attention to the donee (for elaboration, see note 13). This adds to the social welfare maximization a term equal to $\lambda w_v T'(w_v l_v)(dl_v/dc_\gamma)$, which is a standard income effect. The term is the shadow price of tax revenue times $w_v T'(w_v l_v)$—the revenue effect of a one-unit increase in the donee's labor effort—times the change in the donee's labor effort, the latter being the same as the change in labor effort from any exogenous change in disposable income. Each component of this term is positive except the last, which is negative, so there is a revenue loss (in the ordinary case) that reduces social welfare. Furthermore, it is apparent from the foregoing that this effect is ignored by the donor when choosing c_γ.

2. Utility from Giving Per Se

Suppose that a donor is not motivated by altruism but instead receives utility from the act of giving itself. This utility may be due to an internal feeling of virtue from aiding others (what Andreoni (1990) terms a "warm glow"), a desire for prestige, or some other phenomenon. Such a donor's subutility can be expressed as

$$v(c,c_\gamma) = \alpha\mu(c) + \beta v(c_\gamma), \tag{10.4}$$

where v is now interpreted as the utility that the donor receives from giving per se rather than as the donee's utility, such as in the case of altruism displayed in expression (10.3).

Although this difference in the donor's subutility function has qualitatively different implications for behavior—notably, our present donor cares solely about how much he himself gives, not about other sources of consumption for the donee—analysis of the welfare effects of a tax or subsidy on giving is quite similar to that in the case of altruism. Again, the donor considers only the effect of his gift on his own utility, here $u_1\beta v'$, whereas social welfare also includes the effect of the gift on the donee in her own right. And, again, gifts affect the donee's labor supply, negatively affecting revenue.

Reflection on the hypothesis that the donor cares only about his own consumption sacrifice on behalf of the donee and not about the donee's overall situation suggests an alternative formulation of the present motive. Because the donor's actual sacrifice is measured by $(1+t_\gamma)c_\gamma$, not by c_γ alone, the donor's subutility might instead be taken as

$$v(c,c_\gamma) = \alpha\mu(c) + \beta v((1+t_\gamma)c_\gamma). \tag{10.5}$$

When t_γ is positive (negative), a gift of c_γ costs more (less) than c_γ and hence generates more (less) subutility. Consider the case in which there is a subsidy, that is, $t_\gamma < 0$. One can view the donor's gift as consisting only of $(1+t_\gamma)c_\gamma$, which is less than c_γ, with the difference, $-t_\gamma c_\gamma$, being provided to the donee by the government in the form of a matching grant. If the donor, unlike the altruist, is imagined not to care about what others give to the donee, then expression (10.5) reflects the assumption that the donor does not take personal credit for the $-t_\gamma c_\gamma$ portion of the donee's net receipt that is financed by the government.[20]

Under this version of the problem, the effect of a tax or subsidy on gifts is quite different. In addition to the effects described previously, raising a tax (subsidy) directly increases (decreases) the utility that the donor receives on account of a given level of gift, c_γ. From expression

---

[20] This interpretation is also potentially problematic, for if donors do not care about what is transferred to donees, a confiscatory tax levied on donees' gift receipts would not affect giving, which seems implausible. Obviously, further empirical exploration is required to obtain a more precise understanding of the phenomenon of donors receiving utility from giving per se.

(10.5), $\partial v / \partial t_\gamma = \beta v' c_\gamma$ (holding c_γ constant). It turns out that the effect of changing t_γ in the present case is to induce a redistribution between the fisc and donees, under which donors serve merely as the conduit. Specifically, donors choosing c_γ to maximize (10.5) select a level of c_γ that results in the same level of c and of $(1+t_\gamma)c_\gamma$—and accordingly of $v(c, c_\gamma)$—independent of t_γ. This follows from the donor's first-order condition for this case, which is $\alpha\mu' = \beta v'$. Thus, if one reduces t_γ, which is to say reduces the tax or increases the subsidy on giving, donors' utility is unaffected, and because the cost of giving falls, they increase c_γ in a manner that keeps their expenditures on gifts, $(1+t_\gamma)c_\gamma$, constant. Furthermore, this implies that, as the subsidy increases, donees' gift receipts increase by the amount that government expenditures on the subsidy increase. Thus, as stated, raising the subsidy on giving does indeed entail a transfer from the fisc to donees. The assessment of such a change depends purely on the desirability of such a redistribution—that is, on whether the pertinent donees' marginal utilities of income (weighted by the marginal welfare contributions of their utility, in the case of a non-utilitarian SWF) exceed the shadow cost of government revenue (taking into account effects of the redistribution on donees' labor supply as well).

In sum, when donors are motivated by the act of giving per se, the assessment of a tax or subsidy on transfers depends on how this motivation is formulated, notably, whether donors' utility benefit depends on their gross gift, c_γ, or on their net gift, the amount they actually give up in transferring c_γ to the donee, $(1+t_\gamma)c_\gamma$. To the extent that the act of giving per se is an important motive, it is necessary for empirical work to identify which of these variants (or what other formulation) is applicable.

3. Exchange

Now assume that the transfer of c_γ from donor to donee constitutes payment for services rendered.[21] Analysis of this case is straightforward and

---

[21] See, for example, Cox (1987) and, for a strategic analogue, Bernheim, Shleifer, and Summers (1985). Buchanan's (1983) argument that potential heirs engage in rent-seeking behavior to induce donors to make transfers is similar in this respect if such behavior involves

qualitatively distinct from the foregoing cases of true gifts. For the donor, c and c_γ simply represent two forms of ordinary consumption, so the analysis of subsection A.1, based on the standard differential commodity tax problem, is applicable: The optimum has $t_\gamma = 0$, subject to the standard qualifications, and there is nothing distinctive about the consideration of qualifications in the present case.

To complete the analysis, consider donees. Their receipt of γ (equal to the c_γ of their corresponding donor) is simply a form of labor income, albeit in an informal setting. Hence, it should be included (as part of wl) in determining total labor income subject to the tax schedule T. That some gifts in fact constitute payments for services was part of Simons's (1938) argument that gifts should be included in the income tax base of donees.

4. Accidental Bequests

Finally, consider donors who have no desire to make transfers but nevertheless leave bequests due to the incompleteness of annuity markets that may result from adverse selection.[22] In this case, although both aforementioned externalities—donees' utility gain in their own right and donees' reduction (or perhaps increase) in labor effort—are present, donors lack the affirmative motivation of altruistic donors or those who benefit from giving per se. Accordingly, t_γ would have no effect on their giving.[23] It is often suggested that, as a consequence of this final point, a

providing something of value to donors. Note further that gifts sometimes involve reciprocal exchanges for which determining motivation (for example, altruism versus exchange for services) may be difficult. Additionally, some reciprocal exchanges over time may involve loans and their repayment or informal insurance arrangements. See, for example, Kotlikoff and Spivak (1981) and Lucas and Stark (1985). These apparent transfers do not carry the same tax implications of either true gifts or exchanges for services.

[22] For empirical evidence on adverse selection in annuity markets, see, for example, Brown, Mitchell, and Poterba (2002) and Finkelstein and Poterba (2004).

[23] For empirical evidence suggesting that a substantial portion of bequests are intended, see, for example, Bernheim, Lemke, and Scholz (2004), finding that inter vivos transfers are responsive to expected estate taxes, and Kopczuk and Lupton (2007), finding that most of the elderly have bequest motives that account for half of their bequests; however, Hurd (2003) is more skeptical. Furthermore, it seems plausible that, even with incomplete annuity markets,

confiscatory transfer tax on accidental bequests would be optimal, but it is worth elaborating why this might be true. This result, after all, is not obvious since gifts still benefit donees; also, alternative schemes should be considered in light of the presumed imperfection in annuity markets.

To illustrate the benefits of a confiscatory tax, suppose that all prospective donees are identical ex ante, including that they are paired with identical donors. The only difference is that different donors randomly die at different ages and accordingly leave different bequests. In such a simple case, the optimal scheme for donees (donors are presumed to be indifferent) is complete insurance, wherein each bequest is shared equally by all donees. Such an insurance scheme can be seen as a 100% tax on bequests, with the proceeds distributed pro rata among donees. As a pure insurance scheme, this result could be extended to cases of ex ante heterogeneity of donee prospects by retaining the 100% tax but adjusting distributive shares to reflect expected bequests (assuming ex ante differences could be observed).[24]

Such arrangements, however, are not necessarily optimal as a matter of insurance or social welfare (taking into account the possibility of redistributing bequests in other than an actuarially fair manner). One important consideration is that donees whose respective donors die at different

---

many donors leaving accidental bequests derive some utility from the contemplation thereof. As in the preceding cases, however, only pure motives are under consideration in each subsection, with optimal treatment of mixed motivations presumably reflecting some combination of the separate analyses. Furthermore, it is important to distinguish accidental bequests—those by donors who wish to annuitize completely—from bequests by individuals who cannot bring themselves to engage in explicit planning. The latter group may nevertheless derive utility from anticipated bequests and also may be influenced by t_y, even if not in accord with complete maximization.

[24] Kopczuk (2003) advances the interesting alternative view that, seen entirely from the perspective of donors, estate taxation itself can be thought of as a government-provided annuity scheme. One can think of all donors paying an initial tax constituting their entire wealth and consuming an annual annuity stream until they die. An equivalent outcome is produced if instead they keep their wealth and perhaps receive an up-front wealth supplement (all of which one may think of as being held by the individual on behalf of the government, in its capacity as annuity provider), consume the same annual annuity stream, and hand over the remainder upon death. An estate tax exhibits traits of the latter.

ages may no longer be identically situated. For example, those whose parents die earlier may be worse off, so their higher inheritances (under a regime with no transfer tax rather than a confiscatory one) are compensatory.[25] As a matter of optimal insurance (and social welfare, under a utilitarian SWF), all that matters is donees' marginal utilities of income, so their different utility levels may be irrelevant. Under strictly concave SWFs, however, this compensatory feature of bequests would be beneficial. Furthermore, those whose parents die earlier tend to receive bequests at a younger age, and they may accordingly have a higher marginal utility of wealth on this account, due to liquidity constraints, a longer planning horizon, and the ability to spread the inheritance over a greater number of years, which would disfavor confiscatory taxation.

Possible remedies to the apparent failure in annuity markets should also be considered. Suppose incomplete annuitization is due entirely to adverse selection—that is, all prospective donors would wish to annuitize fully, say, at age 65, if this were possible at actuarially fair rates. Then it may be optimal for the government to force complete annuitization. If that were done, there would be no accidental bequests to tax.

C. Additional Considerations

1. Other Aspects of Distribution

Although discourse on transfer taxation often is greatly concerned with distributive issues, the foregoing discussion sets them aside. The reason is that distribution—in particular, the distribution of utility among donors—is understood to be held constant by an adjustment to the income tax schedule. As with many other subjects explored in this book, distribution is substantially orthogonal. Questions concerning the concentration

---

[25] If parents die substantially earlier, however, bequests would be lower, not higher. Note also that bequests may compensate not only for pure losses in utility but also for a reduction in inter vivos transfers that would otherwise have been received (although in some situations such transfers may have been negative).

of wealth are also ignored, in this case because taxation of wealth holdings is distinct from the present subject of taxation of wealth transfers,
as mentioned in the introduction to this chapter.[26]

There are, nevertheless, distributive consequences of giving even in
the present framework. Subsection A.3 considered the effects of giving
on the marginal social value of redistribution. There is also a further
distributive issue distinctly implicated by transfer taxation: Distribution
among donees and, more broadly, intergenerational distribution (see
also subsection 14.B.2).

Intergenerational issues can be examined using a two-period
overlapping-generations version of the model presented in section A.[27]
Many of the main ideas can be illustrated in a simple variant with just a
first generation of donors and a second generation of donees. For concreteness, suppose that all of the following are true: In the donor generation, high-income individuals make disproportionately large gifts;
taking the two generations as a whole, most giving is by individuals
with above-average income; and the typical recipient in the donee generation has less income than the corresponding donor but more than
the average second-generation member.

In the spirit of many prior discussions of this subject, consider first
the effect of transfers on living standards rather than on utility levels. By
this metric, the aforementioned pattern of giving reduces inequality
within the first generation (because the rich give disproportionately
more), increases inequality in the second generation (because the average recipient has above-average income), and reduces inequality in the

---

[26] Nevertheless, some favor heavy transfer taxation of the very wealthy because it reduces
concentrations of wealth over time, thereby limiting the extent to which a few individuals
wield disproportionate influence on government and society. However, taking this objective
as given, it is hardly clear why a wealthy individual induced to expend all his wealth during
his lifetime (for example, under the prospect of a confiscatory estate tax on large bequests)
reduces rather than increases the magnitude of such influence, by contrast to his spreading
the wealth over generations and among multiple individuals who are likely to have differing
agendas and also fewer resources with which to pursue them.

[27] See, for example, the sketch in notes 6 and 8 and also the analysis in Bevan and Stiglitz
(1979).

two generations as a whole (because typical recipients have lower incomes than their donors).[28] The latter result indicates that, on net, transfers constitute a sort of voluntary redistribution.[29]

Returning to the standard welfare economic framework, consider now the effect on the distribution of utility levels (which in the present setting are not unambiguously related to living standards, that is, own-consumption). Regarding donors, although gifts reduce their standard of living, true gifts necessarily increase their utility. If transfers thereby disproportionally augment the utility of better-off members of each generation, they plausibly increase inequality in the distribution of utilities, taking the two generations together. However, in the present context (as in others, on which see section 15.A), measures of inequality in isolation are incomplete and potentially misleading indicators of overall effects on social welfare. To see this, note that, in a world with no income taxation (and thus no income tax revenue externality), the transfers under consideration increase the utility of both donors and donees while affecting no one else. That is, permitting transfers—by contrast, say, to prohibiting them, such as through confiscatory taxation—results in a Pareto improvement, raising welfare under any standard SWF, even though inequality in utilities is increased. Put another way, the analysis in sections A and B already takes into account the welfare effects of transfers on both donors and donees (and on the public fisc), and any further distributive concerns are reflected in subsection A.3's consideration of how transfers affect the marginal social value of redistribution. That analysis would seem to exhaust distributive concerns from a welfarist perspective.[30]

---

[28] Depending on the precise pattern of giving and the measure of inequality, these characterizations need not be apt. For example, Wolff (2003) shows that, although richer households receive more private transfers than do poor households, transfers are a greater proportion of wealth holdings for the latter and thus help equalize the distribution of wealth; however, wealth transfers are essentially uncorrelated with lifetime earnings and thus do not equalize lifetime resources.

[29] As Bevan and Stiglitz (1979) and others have noted, it follows that analyses that confine attention to the steady-state extent of consumption inequality in an infinite, overlapping-generations model can be misleading. Such an approach is analogous to one that in the present example would measure inequality in the second generation alone.

[30] Farhi and Werning (2005) determine optimal income and estate taxation in an intergenerational context. They find that the average optimal estate tax rate is negative—a bequest

2. Human Capital

As noted in subsection 9.C.3, human capital constitutes a significant portion of all wealth yet is taxed very differently from the manner in which physical and financial capital is taxed. Likewise, contributions to human capital are a large fraction of all intergenerational transfers, broadly construed, but for the most part they are excluded from existing and proposed transfer tax schemes (and to some extent are additionally favored with income tax deductions or credits).

It should be apparent that parental transfers are indeed substantial determinants of children's human capital.[31] This is certainly true for innate ability, a product of parents' genes, and also holds for major environmental influences, including those within the home, in the neighborhood, and at school. In selecting residential locations or making expenditures on private provision, parents choose peer groups and the quality of formal instruction; they also are influential regarding postsecondary education and business opportunities. For all but the very wealthy, it seems likely that such factors are responsible for the lion's share of intergenerational wealth transmission. Nevertheless, it is not even imagined that most of these transfers might be subject to transfer taxation, and those that seem most plausible to tax (notably, payments for private education) are usually exempt as well.

The pertinent question for present purposes is whether transfers of human capital should be taxed or subsidized any differently from the treatment implied by the preceding generic analysis of gifts. A natural presumption is that they should not, for the analysis seems largely independent of the form of a gift, and, moreover, differential treatment tends to induce distortionary substitution.

There are, however, some pertinent differences. One concerns the tax revenue externality due to gifts. Although ordinarily negative, it was noted that this externality is positive when gifts contribute to donees' earnings and thus increase tax revenue. To this extent, human capital

---

subsidy—because parents' weight on their children's utility is less than the social weight and that this tax rate is rising (that is, the subsidy is falling) with the income of those in the donor (parent) generation for subtle reasons relating to relaxation of incentive-compatibility constraints.

[31] See, for example, Taubman (1996).

transfers should be subsidized relative to other transfers. Some such transfers may be directly identifiable; furthermore, it may be inferred that such transfers are most significant in the case of inter vivos gifts made early in the life cycle. Another possibility is that different sorts of transfers are associated with otherwise unobservable differences in transfer motives that would call for different levels of tax or subsidy. Perhaps human capital transfers are more likely to arise from altruism than to be offered in exchange for services. Additionally, accidental bequests do not for the most part augment human capital. Accordingly, there may be further justification for relatively favorable tax treatment of transfers of human capital.

3. Charitable Giving[32]

Charitable giving constitutes a substantial form of private transfer activity, which Andreoni (2006) reports to be approximately $240 billion in the United States in 2002. Although often viewed as sui generis, the subject of optimal taxation—or, as typically supposed, subsidization—of charitable contributions can readily be assimilated into the present framework. After all, charitable giving is a species of voluntary transfer. Donors presumably make contributions as a consequence of the utility they derive therefrom. And although donees are entities rather than people, in most cases the direct recipients may be viewed as representatives of groups of ultimate beneficiaries. Sometimes, charitable organizations are direct conduits, such as when their primary activity is to disperse donations to individuals in need. In other instances, this role is indirect, such as when donations are used to fund medical research that will benefit future individuals suffering from some disease. Accordingly, the foregoing analysis of donors giving to donees seems readily applicable to charitable giving. There are, however, a number of respects in which charitable gifts may differ.

First, consider direct gift externalities. The positive externality associated with gifts to identified individuals applies to charitable giving.

---

[32] See Andreoni (2006) for a survey and Bernheim and Rangel (2007) for a discussion emphasizing non-neoclassical treatments.

That is, an organization's beneficiaries count in their own right in assessing social welfare, in addition to any utility that the donor receives as a consequence of making a gift. Furthermore, to the extent that ultimate beneficiaries are substantially less well off than donors (compare gifts to aid the poor to contributions to the symphony), the contribution to social welfare on account of voluntary redistribution would be greater. In addition, with charitable contributions it seems important to consider another sort of positive externality, that gifts from one donor to a particular donee may simultaneously benefit other donors.[33] This possibility would arise, for example, if multiple donors were altruistic toward a single set of donees, say, the poor or future sufferers from some disease. By contrast, a warm-glow donor would not, by definition, benefit from others' gifts, although such a donor's gifts would benefit other donors who were altruistic toward the same donee. Therefore, the aggregate externality from charitable giving may vary greatly by context, both because of potentially large differences in the number of other concerned individuals and because of possible differences in those individuals' utility functions.[34]

Second, tax revenue externalities may be implicated. When a donee organization gives to those in need, the standard negative labor supply effect may arise (compare chapter 7's analysis of government transfer programs).[35] Other forms of charitable giving may have different effects

---

[33] See Saez (2004b), and also Karlan and List (2006), who offer evidence that individuals may be more motivated to give when others are as well (perhaps others' gifts provide information or affect the warm glow). This externality is also present with much individual giving, although to a more limited extent. One parent's transfers to children may benefit the other parent, and grandparents and other relatives as well. Parents' gifts to married children also tend to benefit grandchildren and the families of their children's spouses. These additional beneficiaries are ignored by the present model that looks at pairings of representative donors with representative donees.

[34] These factors, among others, should influence the extent to which one donor's giving crowds out or reinforces other donors' giving (including the case in which one donor is the government). See, for example, Bergstrom, Blume, and Varian (1986) and the survey by Andreoni (2006).

[35] Transfer programs generally have negative income and substitution effects, the latter due to the phasing out of transfers as income increases, tantamount to a higher marginal tax

on donees' labor supply. Improved medical research could reduce labor supply if it lowers the marginal utility of consumption in the future by reducing the cost of health care, but such gifts could increase marginal utility by making available more useful ways of spending disposable income or, by prolonging longevity, inducing individuals to work harder in anticipation of a longer retirement. Support of the symphony may make leisure more attractive to others who might attend performances, reducing labor supply. As with the direct (and ordinarily positive) externalities, there seems to be substantial heterogeneity regarding these additional effects of charitable contributions.

Third, different mixes of transfer motives should also be considered, especially because the unobservability of motives implies that transfer taxation must reflect averages for practically distinguishable categories of giving.[36] It was already observed that the mix of altruists and individuals gaining utility from giving per se may differ across types of charitable giving. In addition, exchange undoubtedly is often present and in varying degrees that may depend, in this case, on the form of the gift. Some contributions, such as for buildings to be named for the donor, have an aspect of purchasing a personal monument, and the charity's benefit may accordingly be significantly less than the face amount of the gift, the difference reflecting sums spent on gold-plating that may benefit the donor substantially more than the donee. Anonymous giving and contributions serving remote beneficiaries are less likely to fit the exchange model, although many donee organizations may provide their services in a form designed to be pleasing to donors even if less effective in helping donees. Finally, in contrast to the case of individual giving, purely accidental bequests seem unlikely because active estate planning is necessary to name charitable beneficiaries.

---

rate. For voluntary transfers, the analogy is the Samaritan's dilemma, mentioned in note 14 and analyzed in subsection 11.B.2 on social security.

[36] The observable dimensions differ between the two contexts. For individual giving, treatment may be dependent upon the relationship between the donor and donee, either individual's age, whether a transfer is a gift or bequest, and whether the transfer is of human capital (although the fungibility of money may make such transfers difficult to distinguish). For charitable giving, taxes or subsidies might vary by type of organization, number of other donors, whether gifts are anonymous, and whether and how they are restricted.

Fourth, charitable organizations' competition for contributions may dissipate resources in the attempt to attract gifts from donors.[37] Another consideration is that solicitations—rather than increasing prospective donors' utilities by making them aware of additional giving opportunities or augmenting the warm glow from giving—may reduce their utilities by inducing guilt feelings that are at best assuaged by any contributions they are induced to make.[38] It should be noted, however, that these phenomena are not distinctive to charitable giving but rather are analogous to those raised by Buchanan's (1983) depiction of individual donees' rent-seeking behavior (see note 21) in competing for particular donors' favor. In addition, these possibly negative features of charitable solicitation are shared more broadly with product advertising by competitors.

Taken together, the foregoing brief examination of charitable giving indicates that the subject is well illuminated by the present framework but that significant variation regarding most pertinent factors renders generalization difficult. In practice, many tax systems prefer charitable giving over giving to individual donees. In the transfer tax system, charitable contributions are often exempt (in the United States estate and gift tax, through a deduction, and in countries with an inheritance tax, through exempting charitable organizations), which favors such gifts over transfers to individuals but puts gifts on a par with own-consumption expenditures. Under the income tax in the United States and many other countries, there is also a charitable contribution deduction or credit (for inter vivos contributions), which favors such transfers over both own-consumption and ordinary gifts. For individuals with enough wealth to be subject to transfer taxation, the combined benefits provide a substantial preference for charitable over ordinary gifts. Typically, there is little effort to distinguish among types of charitable contributions.

A final important point, suggested by the discussion of positive externalities involving other donors, is that a complete analysis of chari-

---

[37] See, for example, Rose-Ackerman (1982).

[38] This factor and others lead Andreoni (2006) and Diamond (2006) to be wary of including utility that derives from giving per se (warm-glow utility) in the assessment of social welfare.

table giving requires that the alternative of direct government expenditure, the subject of chapter 8, also be integrated into the framework. In this regard, it should be noted that the objective is not properly formulated as inducing a given level of activity at the minimum cost to the fisc. First, if donors derive utility from giving, which itself may depend on how taxes on or subsidies to giving are formulated (see especially subsection 10.B.2 on alternative specifications of the utility from giving per se), social welfare may depend on who pays for public goods, independently of questions concerning the shadow cost of government funds.[39] Second, as section 8.C emphasizes, in the benchmark case the production costs of public goods determine their optimal provision, which implies as a first approximation that revenue costs as distinguished from resource costs are not the pertinent consideration.[40]

---

[39] See Diamond (2006) and Saez (2004b).

[40] For both of these reasons, the familiar view that the optimal subsidy (if any) for charitable contributions depends on the elasticity of charitable contributions is at best incomplete and is likely to be quite misleading. Regarding the latter reason noted in the text, recall from section 8.G that, as in the current chapter, it is appropriate to consider a policy experiment that is revenue and distribution neutral, so that the only effect is allocative. Thus, on reflection, it is not surprising that in the benchmark case the optimal Pigouvian tax (subsidy in the case of positive externalities) equals the marginal external effect and that this result is true without regard to the level of the demand elasticity.

11

Taxation and Social Security

A substantial fraction of taxation and expenditure in developed economies is devoted to social insurance, especially to finance consumption during years of retirement (including consumption of medical care). Systems typically impose a labor income tax—such as a flat-rate payroll tax—during working years to finance payments to retirees.[1]

This chapter first analyzes purely redistributive aspects of social security schemes in a setting in which individuals are taken to be rational, far-sighted utility maximizers not subject to liquidity constraints. Then these assumptions are relaxed for purposes of considering a central feature of social security, the forcing of a minimum level of savings. Finally, but briefly, some additional insurance dimensions are noted. A number of other important features of social security are not inherently related to the central themes of this book and therefore are omitted, including broader fiscal issues involving deficits and investment policy as well as political economy considerations, such as those related to pre-funding and the merits of privatization.[2]

---

[1] Many countries now mandate private retirement schemes in addition to or in lieu of government social insurance (see Bateman, Kingston, and Piggott 2001). A relevant distinction is that private retirement accounts tend to be actuarially fair by design. In any event, much of the analysis of this chapter is applicable to these programs as well.

[2] For broader treatments, see, for example, Diamond (1977, 2002, 2003, 2004), Feldstein (2005), and Feldstein and Liebman (2002b).

A. Redistribution

1. Labor Income Tax Comparison

To examine the purely redistributive element of social security, it is useful to set aside its other features and potential respects in which individual behavior may deviate from rational maximization of a standard utility function. Consider the simple two-period model employed in chapter 9 to analyze taxation of capital: Individuals work in only the first period and consume in both periods, with first-period savings earning interest (here assumed for ease of exposition to be untaxed). In addition to the redistributive labor income tax, now denoted $T^I(wl)$, individuals pay a social security tax of $T^S(wl)$ as well, and in the second period they receive social security benefits of $B^S(wl)$, which depend on their previous earnings. Modifying the budget constraint (9.3) and rearranging terms indicate that second-period consumption is given by

$$c_2 = \left[wl - T^I(wl) - T^S(wl) - c_1 \right](1+r) + B^S(wl). \qquad (11.1)$$

If social security were actuarially fair, we would have $T^S(wl)(1+r) = B^S(wl)$ for all wl. In allowing for redistributive social security, this equality is not imposed for any particular type of individual. One can, however, assume that $(1+r)\int T^S(wl) = \int B^S(wl)$. (This assumption, as will be apparent, is without loss of generality in the present model; the possibility of intergenerational redistribution in a setting with overlapping generations is considered in subsection 3.)

Define the net tax (transfer, if negative) imposed by social security as $T^N(wl) = T^S(wl) - B^S(wl)/(1+r)$. Using this expression to substitute for $T^S(wl)$ in (11.1) yields

$$\begin{aligned}
c_2 &= \left[wl - T^I(wl) - T^N(wl) - B^S(wl)/(1+r) - c_1 \right](1+r) + B^S(wl) \\
&= \left[wl - T^I(wl) - T^N(wl) - c_1 \right](1+r) \\
&= \left[wl - T(wl) - c_1 \right](1+r), \qquad (11.2)
\end{aligned}$$

where $T(wl) = T^I(wl) + T^N(wl)$, making use of the fact that the labor income tax and social security tax are both functions of (first-period) earnings. The last line in expression (11.2) is, of course, simply a rearrangement of the budget constraint (9.3) for the problem with no social security.

Accordingly, the existence of a redistributive social security system makes no difference in the present setting.[3] Any redistribution can be incorporated into the labor income tax and transfer scheme. Furthermore, that some of earnings must be set aside in period 1 for consumption in period 2 is immaterial because it is assumed here that individuals can borrow and lend, without constraint, at the rate r and that their decisions are fully rational. Therefore, it is not meaningful to ask how redistributive a social security scheme is or should be, unless political factors distinguish between economically equivalent systems or one introduces other features such as myopia, liquidity constraints, and forced savings, as is done in section B. Even in the latter case, it should not matter what portion (if any) of the payments that individuals at any income level are required to make in period 1, as a function of earnings, is nominally deemed to be part of the income tax or a separate social security tax. Nevertheless, following the practice employed throughout this book, it often will be convenient analytically to hold redistribution (in the entire fiscal system) constant in order to examine the optimal magnitude of an (actuarially fair) social security system, say, when individuals are myopic.

An implication of the foregoing discussion is that familiar claims regarding the efficiency consequences of marginal tax-benefit linkage in social security systems are potentially misleading. Linkage is said to be complete when $T^{S\prime}(wl) = B^{S\prime}(wl)/(1+r)$ (implying that $T^{N\prime}(wl) = 0$) and nonexistent when $T^{N\prime}(wl) = T^{S\prime}(wl)$ (implying that $B^{S\prime}(wl) = 0$, which means that benefits are uniform, independent of earnings). Moving, say, from no marginal linkage to complete linkage does reduce labor supply distortion, assuming that income taxes are unchanged. Note, however, that such a reform accomplished through changing the benefits formula necessarily entails a change from lump-sum benefits to benefits tied to earnings in a manner that has the same marginal incidence as the social security tax. If instead the tax formula is changed, it would need to be converted to a uniform lump-sum tax, to match the incidence of the benefits. In either case, the resulting reduction in distortion arises as a consequence of a concomitant reduction in redistribution. The

[3] For analyses of the extent of redistribution in the United States social security system and under various reform proposals, see Feldstein and Liebman (2002a) and Coronado, Fullerton, and Glass (2000).

increase in linkage is equivalent to reducing marginal tax rates in the income tax, funded by shrinking the lump-sum grant. That one can reduce distortion by reducing redistribution has nothing in particular to do with social security tax-benefit linkage. Furthermore, observe that if one wished to improve tax-benefit linkage within social security without changing overall redistribution, the income tax schedule would need to be adjusted in an offsetting manner. But in that case $T(wl)$ would be unchanged, and there would be no reduction in labor supply distortion.

2. Lifetime Income

Social security retirement benefits are ordinarily a function of individuals' earnings over the course of their working lives, which raises questions concerning optimal redistribution from a lifetime perspective. This problem is naturally analyzed using the optimal income taxation framework. As a first cut, Diamond (1977, 2003) suggests that one might reinterpret Mirrlees (1971) as addressing how lifetime taxes and transfers should depend on lifetime income. If individuals' earning abilities or utility functions vary over time, including in cases involving uncertainty (whether of earning ability, utility, or lifespan), further analysis is required.

Subsection 5.C.1 introduces the generalization involving group-specific income tax schedules $T(wl,\theta)$, where in the present setting θ might index individuals' ages. This formulation, represented in expression (5.1), is insufficient for present purposes because, for example, consumption at any given age—and thus both the marginal utility of consumption and the marginal contribution of utility to social welfare, W'—will in general depend on past earnings and consumption as well as on expected future earnings and consumption. Consequently, regarding the tax schedule itself, one may wish to interpret θ as a vector indicating not only age but also earnings history, so that a current period's taxes may depend on prior earnings as well as on current earnings and age per se (implicitly making possible any manner of lifetime income averaging, on which more later).[4]

---

[4] The analysis in this subsection implicitly assumes that the government commits to a tax schedule so that it is not possible ex post to extract more tax from individuals who, in prior periods, have revealed themselves to have high ability through their earnings. See the brief discussion in subsection 9.C.2 on capital levies and transitions.

This substantially more complex problem has received limited attention. As a matter of efficiency, one might suppose that marginal tax rates should be constant over time because distortion rises disproportionately with the marginal tax rate.[5] However, even with utility functions that are time separable and identical in each period, it need not be true that constant marginal rates minimize distortion in raising a given amount of revenue (in present value) from an individual whose earning ability varies over time.[6] As Heckman (1974) shows, individuals will tend to exert greater labor effort in periods in which their w is higher: Starting from a point of equal effort in each period, slightly raising effort in a high-w period and lowering effort by the same amount in a low-w period will have no first-order effect on the disutility of labor effort but will increase earnings.[7]

Given that both w and l will differ across periods (starting from a base case of identical tax functions in each period), it is hardly obvious that the labor supply elasticity will be the same in each period. In particular, the elasticity may be lower in high-w, high-l periods (that is, high-income periods).[8] If a given percentage increase in w raised l by a common

---

[5] The present suggestion brings to mind the well-known result of Barro (1979); however, his analysis simply assumed that the function relating distortion and taxation is the same in each period (the model is a reduced form pertaining to the economy as a whole), so the issues to be explored here did not arise.

[6] Note that the present problem is formally quite similar to a version of the problem of taxing a two-earner family considered in subsection 12.B.1.b. There, a case is examined in which two family members jointly choose labor effort and allocate consumption between themselves to maximize the sum of their utilities. The two different family members correspond to two different time periods (imagining now that an individual works and consumes in two periods), the allocation of consumption between the family members is governed by the same principles as the individual's allocation of consumption between the two periods, and the family members' choices of labor effort are governed by essentially the same first-order conditions as the individual's choices of labor effort in the two periods. Accordingly, the potential optimality of differentially taxing the earnings of the two family members is closely related to the potential optimality of tax rates varying across time periods in the present setting.

[7] Discussion in the text will abstract from complications arising from positive interest and (utility) discount rates. For example, a positive interest rate makes present earnings more valuable than future earnings, but one can interpret w as a time-adjusted (interest-rate-adjusted) effective wage for purposes of comparing wages across periods.

[8] This conjecture is suggestive at best because the result depends on the form of the utility function, the stipulated simplifying assumptions, and particularly on cross-effects

percentage even in high-w periods, the increase in lifetime consumption would be greater than for other, low-w periods, so marginal utility would fall more, requiring a greater reduction in labor effort to restore individuals' first-order conditions. (Note that higher optimized consumption in one period implies that labor supply falls in all periods: Saving and borrowing are used to equate marginal utility across periods, so changes in lifetime consumption can be thought of as changing a common marginal utility of consumption; when that marginal utility falls, individuals will find it optimal to reduce labor effort in all periods. See, for example, Heckman (1974) and MaCurdy (1981).) However, for a given elasticity, a higher w implies a lower optimal marginal tax rate because a given reduction in labor effort is more costly (recall the discussion of the denominator of expression (4.10)). These two potentially competing effects indicate that the question of the optimal lifetime pattern of marginal tax rates is complex; constancy may not be optimal, but the nature of the optimal deviation is not obvious. A further complication is that, in a system with earnings-history-dependent taxation, labor effort in any period will in general affect expected marginal tax rates in future periods, so the current effective marginal tax rate diverges from the rate nominally indicated by the tax schedule.

The discussion until this point does not exploit systematic patterns in age-earnings profiles. As noted in subsection 5.C.1, Kremer (2001) suggests that lower marginal rates on the young (particularly the very young, from ages 17–21) may be optimal. First, he offers evidence that their distribution of earnings is quite different: The ratio $(1-F)/f$ is much lower at low income levels because earnings are more concentrated there (compare the discussion of categorical assistance in subsection 7.C.1). Second, he offers some evidence that labor supply elasticities are higher. Both factors indicate that lower marginal income tax rates on young, low-earning individuals may be more efficient. Finally, there may also be some distributive benefit, which reflects the low correlation between early income and lifetime income. To a lesser extent, some of these

(the extent to which raising marginal tax rates in some periods increases revenue in other periods on account of individuals' raising labor effort in all other periods due to the increase in the marginal utility of consumption).

factors may also apply to older workers (and to women and some racial minorities). Although Kremer's analysis does not allow borrowing and savings and thus treats earnings each year as independent, the fact that age is a signal of the distribution of abilities and other considerations indicate that age-dependent taxation can raise social welfare.

Additional issues are presented by the introduction of uncertainty concerning earnings ability, utility, and lifespan. This problem, which is considered briefly in subsection 5.E.2 and in section C below, can now be imagined in a setting with many periods. Analyzing this case can be seen as encompassing unemployment insurance, disability insurance, medical insurance, and annuitization—the relevance of each depending on the availability of private insurance, as noted previously.

To examine how these various considerations relate to social security in particular, it is useful, as suggested in subsection A.1, to restate social security tax and benefit schemes as net taxes (or transfers, if negative) on labor income, which in turn can be viewed as part of the labor income tax per se. In the case in which benefits are a separable function of each year's earnings, this task is straightforward: The expression $T^N(wl) = T^S(wl) - B^S(wl)/(1+r)$ can be subscripted to refer to each period's earnings and taxes, where $B^S(wl)$ would refer to the component of ultimate benefits attributable to the corresponding period's earnings (and r could be restated to reflect the number of years of discounting required).

More generally, benefits may depend in a nonseparable manner on prior earnings. For example, they may be a nonlinear function of average earnings, or more weight may be given to years with higher earnings. In such cases, it would still be possible to state a function $T^N(wl)$ for each year, reflecting the difference between that year's social security–designated taxes and the net (present value) increment to benefits on account of that year's earnings—perhaps assuming hypothetically that the individual would have no future earnings, or maybe instead that future earnings would be constant at the current level. Clearly, the definition of $T^N(wl)$ in each year (except the last) would not be unique; moreover, the function would now need to be stated as $T^N(wl,\theta)$ because, in general, the net tax (transfer) would also depend on prior years' earnings. These two points are interrelated: An individual in a given year, when choosing labor supply, would take into account not only current taxes but also how current earnings would affect future taxes. In a world of certainty with known, fixed future tax schedules and benefit formulas, it would not matter which of the nonunique specifications was chosen because, as long as the net (present value) tax (or transfer) as a function of any annual earnings pattern for the individual was the same, behavior, utility, and revenue would also be the same. The relevant point is that, even when adding the complication of nonseparable benefits, one can view a social security system as tantamount to an adjustment to the labor income tax, in this case a time-dependent labor income tax that may be a function of prior as well as present earnings.

It follows, therefore, that, just as in the two-period model in section 1, there is little meaningful that can be said about the optimal social security system with regard to income redistribution, now viewed in terms of lifetime income. The foregoing analysis suggests that the optimal income tax problem in this setting is complex. Whatever solution emerges, it does not matter in the present setting what part of that scheme, if any, is designated as the social security system. Even if one introduces myopia or liquidity constraints, considered in section B, there will be no inherent relationship between the optimal social security system and lifetime redistribution, for the extent of redistribution is determined by the combined scheme, including the income tax and transfer system. Any degree of redistribution that incidentally arises in the social security system can be offset with the income tax.

Consider briefly some features of the existing social security retirement system in the United States (features shared, in varying degrees, by some other countries' systems). The use of a payroll tax (that is, a wage or labor income tax) that is constant over time might be viewed as a desirable feature because of the idea that time-invariant rates tend to minimize distortion. Qualifications to this view have already been noted, but in any event the description is inapt because it reflects an unintegrated view of the fiscal system in two important respects. First, the relevant marginal tax rate is not that of any specific tax but rather the aggregate net marginal rate from all taxes, including notably the income tax and phase-outs in transfer programs. With a nonlinear income tax-transfer system and income that varies over time, aggregate marginal tax rates are not constant.

Second, as subsection 1 emphasizes, the pertinent tax rate in viewing the social security system is not $T^S(wl)$ but $T^N(wl)$. Although the former applies a constant marginal tax rate (for earnings below the pay-roll tax ceiling), the latter does not because different periods' earnings have widely varying effects on future benefits. Some low-earning years contribute nothing to benefits (lowest-earning years are dropped), so $T^N(wl) = T^S(wl)$ in such years. But some high-earning years might con-tribute more to benefits than taxes paid, so not only does $T^N(wl) \neq T^S(wl)$, but we also have $T^N(wl) < 0$ in those years. Thus, the implicit values of $T^N(wl)$ and therefore probably the values of $T(wl) = T^I(wl) + T^N(wl)$ vary substantially across years, with significantly higher effective tax rates applied in low-earning years (assuming that marginal rate gradua-tion in the explicitly designated income tax is insufficient to offset the effect of varying $T^N(wl)$'s). Although the preceding analysis did not firmly endorse a presumption that marginal tax rates should be con-stant over time, in which case the existing scheme would be far from optimal, it also does not suggest that the existing pattern is likely to be appropriate. In particular, the direction of deviation from constancy, with higher marginal rates in low-w years typically involving very young workers, may not be correct. Furthermore, if one introduces uncer-tainty, it may be optimal to tax earnings in high-earning years at a higher rate than those in low-earning years, rather than employing the oppo-site pattern that is implicit in the current social security system.

Interestingly, although the pattern of rising marginal tax rates that is a common feature of observed income tax systems may not be opti-mal in a one-period setting, it may be beneficial in the present setting if it turned out to be optimal to tax individuals more in higher-earning years or if, as just discussed, social security systems viewed in isolation produce the opposite result. Nevertheless, an optimal overall system would allow taxes to depend on earnings history. Then there would be no need for the differentiation in marginal tax rates applicable to high versus low earnings across individuals in a given year to match the dif-ferentiation in marginal rates applicable to high versus low earnings by the same individual in different years.

Finally, it is instructive to consider how some of these consider-ations pertaining to the taxation of lifetime income relate to existing and proposed income and cash-flow consumption tax systems, which typically are based on annual earnings or consumption. If the system is linear, a constant marginal rate is applied in every period regardless of fluctuations in earnings (or expenditures), which, as already suggested, may not be optimal. In such cases, income averaging schemes—which, say, treat some income in high-earning years as though earned in low-earning years—are moot.

Furthermore, with a cash-flow consumption tax, to the extent that individuals smooth consumption over time, averaging also becomes irrelevant because, even with a nonlinear tax schedule, individuals would be at the same point on the schedule every year. In the hypothesized case, individuals use saving and borrowing to make it true in fact that consumption is equal every year, so there is no need for the tax system to undertake adjustments designed to treat individuals as if they had equal consumption every year.[9] The result is that individuals with different earnings patterns but the same present value of lifetime earnings—who in a no-tax world would enjoy the same utility and have the same marginal utility of consumption—will pay the same tax and face the same effective marginal tax rate on labor effort in each period (which, as noted, may not be optimal).

When a nonlinear, age-independent labor income tax is employed and wage rates vary over time (consider a simple, certainty case with a rising wage profile), individuals will face different marginal rates in different years. The efficiency consequences may be better or worse than with a constant marginal rate; they could be better, for example, if higher marginal rates apply to higher earnings and that situation indeed is optimal. Consider also that, under such a tax, individuals with different earnings patterns face different marginal tax rates in different periods and also will not generally realize the same level of utility or have the same marginal utility of consumption. In a commonly hypothesized case with no uncertainty, one individual is taken to have a constant lifetime wage and

---

[9] This statement, like the previous analysis in this subsection, abstracts from the effects of the interest rate and utility discount factors that, if not offsetting, would make the optimal consumption path nonconstant. In addition, in a nonlinear tax with falling marginal rates, individuals may fail to smooth consumption because unequal consumption over time would reduce the present value of tax payments. In either case, however, individuals' marginal tax rates on labor effort would be the same each period (because the allocation of incremental earnings, which determines the effective marginal tax rate, does not depend on the timing of the earnings).

another a fluctuating wage with the same average level.[10] If marginal
rates are rising (falling), the latter pays more (less) tax and also faces
higher (lower) marginal tax rates when wages are high.[11] On distributive
grounds, this outcome would not appear to be optimal; the efficiency
consequences are ambiguous, as already noted.

Vickrey (1939) proposed lifetime income averaging as a solution.[12]
The general sympathy for this approach is due to distributive considerations. The effect of such a scheme on marginal tax rates and thus on
labor supply distortion is not usually considered. On reflection, it should
be apparent that averaging in a nonlinear income tax regime has a similar effect to self-averaging (consumption smoothing) under a nonlinear
cash-flow consumption tax. In a simple world without uncertainty, the
marginal dollar earned in any period is subject to the same effective
marginal tax rate. That is, even if a current marginal dollar is taxed at a
higher or lower rate, future adjustments will produce the result that the
marginal distortion is the same in all periods. Once again, however, such
uniform treatment may not be optimal.

3. Intergenerational Redistribution

Social security retirement systems in developed economies commonly
operate largely on a pay-as-you-go basis rather than being pre-funded.

---

[10] As the earlier analysis suggests, the individual with fluctuating wages would actually
be better off. This individual would be equally well off if he worked the same amount each
period as the individual with a constant wage (abstracting, as is done throughout, from interest rate effects), but the individual will choose to work more (less) when wages are high (low),
thereby achieving a higher level of utility.

[11] Discussions of averaging usually consider the case of rising marginal rates, but falling
rates may be optimal and, as chapter 7 notes, are common at lower income levels due to the
phasing out of transfers.

[12] Under such a scheme, an individual's annual taxes are computed, for each year through
the present, as if lifetime income to date had been earned evenly, and from (the present value
of) this total tax obligation one subtracts (the present value of) all prior tax payments to
determine how much tax is owed. A major complication involves changing family status over
an individual's lifetime if tax schedules depend on family status, as they often do and, as
chapter 12 indicates, they optimally would in general. For a discussion of other averaging
schemes and of the merits of long-term averaging, see Goode (1980).

Specifically, schemes were implemented and benefits were increased so as to provide to older living generations significant net transfers that ultimately must be financed by succeeding generations. For generations still alive, this ongoing intergenerational redistribution could be partially or completely reversed through benefit cuts. Likewise, it would be possible in theory to tax some generations to produce a surplus out of which benefits could be paid to subsequent generations, producing intergenerational redistribution toward younger and future generations.

The subject of the optimal distribution between generations is considered in subsection 14.B.2. It may be noted that, as a practical matter, it is difficult to identify the extent of intergenerational redistribution on account of the baseline issue examined in section 8.E (implicitly in the intragenerational context) with regard to the redistributiveness of the entire existing fiscal system. Notably, it has been observed that although social security has redistributed from younger and future generations to those retiring in the latter half of the twentieth century, those recipients had previously engaged in substantial implicit redistribution toward future generations by fighting, funding, and making other sacrifices during wartime, creating infrastructure, undertaking research, providing for younger generations' education, and so forth. Of course, the extent of such redistribution depends on whether expenditures were financed currently or through issuing debt, a subject to be considered later.

The main point for present purposes is that, like those dimensions of redistribution considered previously in this section, the use of social security is not distinctive. Since the net social security tax is equivalent to an income tax schedule, income taxation could accomplish a similar result. This potential is most apparent if the income tax schedule is dependent on age or varies with birth cohort. In addition, even with an income tax schedule that in any given year depends only on current earnings, one could accomplish intergenerational redistribution by running current deficits or surpluses. In the short run, however, if one wished to redistribute more to a retired generation, something akin to a pay-as-you-go social security system would be required; specifically, benefits would have to be directed at current retirees. It should also be noted that, to the extent that the use of social security entails other effects, such as forced savings, it is useful to separate the differing objectives and utilize appropriate instruments. For example, if forced savings are undesirable (say, due to liquidity constraints), using the financing mechanism common for social security may not be the most efficient way to accomplish intergenerational transfers to existing retirees. Likewise, if forced savings are desirable but an intergenerational transfer is not, one could use a pre-funded social security system.

The direct efficiency costs of intergenerational redistribution should also be considered. To an extent, society could accomplish such redistribution without distortion, for example, by imposing uniform lump-sum taxes (equivalently, reducing $g = -T(0)$ in the income tax) on individuals in one generation and providing uniform subsidies (raising g) to members of another. However, if the optimal amounts paid and received were to depend on individuals' incomes, distortion would be involved in the ordinary fashion.

It is worth emphasizing that, despite the likely distortionary costs inherent in accomplishing whatever intergenerational redistribution is desired, intergenerational redistribution does not inherently raise questions of Pareto inefficiency. It is sometimes imagined that somehow everyone can be made better off, but such suggestions (and analyses) typically focus only on the steady state, ignoring the effect on transition generations.[13] The basic point is that, if society does wish to make a transfer to an existing, older generation, this payment must be funded in some manner. It can be paid for either by the current generation, presently, through reduced consumption (which would make them worse off), or through increased debt, which would make worse off the future generations who must then pay interest on the debt. If the debt could simply be extinguished, all future generations would gain, but obviously at a cost to those who held the debt.[14] As demonstrated by Breyer (1989), debt issued to finance the initial transfer cannot be retired without the

---

[13] Compare İmrohoroğlu, İmrohoroğlu, and Joines (2003, p. 769 n. 23), who explain that their results on time-inconsistent preferences show unfunded social security to be less attractive than is found in prior work because they ignore the transition and examine only the steady state. This problem is analogous to that identified in subsection 10.C.1 of assessing the policy toward private (typically intergenerational) transfers by examining only the recipient generation or the steady state, ignoring opposing effects on the original donor generation(s).

[14] Likewise, one might benefit future generations by cutting benefits to current retirees, as suggested for example in Smetters (2005), an approach that in some respects is analogous to the use of a one-time capital levy. On transitions and capital levies generally, see subsection 9.C.2.

generations who do so experiencing reduced consumption to that extent.[15] By analogy, an individual undertaking a current spending spree will need to reduce future consumption a corresponding amount, and there is no way to save one's way out of the situation; one can save more in lieu of current consumption, which reduces utility from consumption presently.

Note that the absence of a Pareto improvement through pre-funding (just as the impossibility of the individual raising utility from consumption in some periods without facing reductions in others) does not indicate that any given pattern is the social welfare (or lifetime utility) maximum. For example, it may be that societies with substantial unfunded social security retirement commitments (including those for medical care) would benefit from increasing national savings (which may be suboptimal due to capital taxation or other factors).[16] In that case, increasing the extent of pre-funding—say, through some mix of benefit reductions and current tax increases—may be desirable, assuming that neither the government nor individuals would undertake offsetting actions, such as through increased government spending and reductions in other taxes or through reduced private savings.

Once again, however, it does not matter in theory whether this shift is accomplished through changes in social security financing or through other action, notably, raising current taxes or curbing present spending to reduce national debt. Also, as has been previously noted, it may not be best to use social security (for example, entailing forced savings that may or may not be optimal) to implement policies that can be accomplished independently. Some of the debate about social security reform seems to reflect the belief that one or another approach is more likely to be successful on account of political economy considerations; for example, it may be easier politically to raise taxes to fund social security than to run a surplus, or it may be that creating private social security accounts would make it less likely that the government would subsequently

---

[15] See also the discussions in Diamond (2002) and Sinn (2000). The idea that moving to a higher-utility steady state is not ordinarily a pure matter of efficiency, due to the need for transitional sacrifices by some generations, was originally emphasized by Samuelson (1975).

[16] See, for example, Feldstein and Liebman (2002b). Observe that if savings are distorted, then in principle (in a model with identical individuals and other simplifications) a Pareto improvement is possible intragenerationally, through eliminating the distortion or otherwise achieving the results that would arise if the distortion were not present.

increase spending or cut other taxes, undercutting the attempt to increase national savings. Likewise, if individuals are myopic or their behavior otherwise deviates from that in the simple model employed in this section, otherwise equivalent actions may have different effects, which may bear on how social security should be formulated.

An additional intergenerational issue concerns risk-sharing. Given the incompleteness of futures markets, there is a potential role for the government to spread risk across generations, as examined in Gordon and Varian (1988), Gale (1990), Shiller (1999), Campbell and Nosbusch (2006), and Krueger and Kubler (2006). Risk-sharing might be accomplished through social security if retirees' benefits are a function not only of their own prior earnings but also of earnings by adjacent generations. Nominally, this is not done, in which case the effects of pay-as-you-go social security systems can be perverse. Specifically, if the obligation charged to younger generations is fixed by the benefit formula based on the earnings of the retiree generation, then when earnings are systematically low, younger workers need to pay higher tax rates since the base is small while the obligation is unchanged. Likewise, when earnings are high, tax rates fall. In practice, however, de facto risk sharing may be accomplished if there is a tendency to increase retiree benefits (retrospectively) when current workers' earnings are high and to trim benefits when they are low. In any event, a social security system is not the only means of spreading risk intergenerationally, and further analysis is necessary to identify how the optimal intergenerational arrangement depends on different generations' annual earnings and consumption.

4. Redistribution across Family Types

Social security systems may also redistribute across family types. In the United States, for example, spousal and other benefits result in substantial redistribution from single individuals to married couples and from two-earner families to one-earner families.[17]

As with other dimensions of redistribution through social security, it is helpful to separate the redistributive component ($T^N(wl)$ in the notation of subsection 1) and view it simply as part of the income tax.

---

[17] For explanations and documentation, see, for example, Boskin et al. (1987), Feldstein and Liebman's (2002b) survey, Feldstein and Samwick (1992), and Leimer (1999).

Here, however, benefit rules and thus T^N depend on family status, not just income. Nevertheless, the redistributive component can be assimilated into an income tax schedule that itself depends on family status, an approach that will be pursued in chapter 12 on taxation of families. It remains to consider whether social security's objectives are dependent on family status (for example, whether myopia leading to inadequate savings is a particular problem for married couples and whether the extent of any problem differs when there is only one earner). Nevertheless, even if they are, social security need not be redistributive on that account: The extent of forced savings could depend on family type, with future benefits funded on an actuarially fair basis. In any event, any distributive effect of social security can be augmented or offset through the income tax system to produce whatever overall distributive result is desired. Accordingly, the question of optimal redistribution across family types is largely separable in principle from that of the optimal design of social security.[18]

It is sometimes suggested that non-income-based intragenerational redistribution through social security is distortionary because effective marginal tax rates ($T^N(wl)$'s) differ significantly across individuals. It is generally correct that, ceteris paribus, distortion is greater when different individuals face different tax rates (since distortion rises disproportionately with marginal tax rates). If there is to be (income-based) redistribution between types, however, this cost is inevitable. As with standard redistribution, such distortion should in principle be traded off against whatever redistributive benefits are believed to result. Of course, if this sort of redistribution is believed to be undesirable, eliminating it would be doubly beneficial.

B. Forced Savings

Social security retirement provisions can be tantamount to schemes that force individuals to save a certain portion of their earnings in order to

---

[18] As always, political economy considerations, perhaps reflecting misunderstanding of how the system actually operates, may influence what sorts of redistribution are incorporated in a social security scheme rather than in the income tax and explicit transfer programs.

finance consumption during retirement. To focus on this feature, it is helpful to abstract from any redistribution and thereby consider actuarially fair systems, the only effect of which is to place a floor on savings. Such a floor is interesting only to the extent that it exceeds what (at least some) individuals would otherwise choose to save and that individuals do not offset the requirement through increased borrowing (either because that is impossible due to liquidity constraints or on account of aspects of their behavior that can generate inconsistencies, as will be mentioned).

This section first will analyze two primary rationales for forced savings—combating myopia and the Samaritan's dilemma—with particular attention to the effects of social security on labor supply and how those effects depend on the behavioral assumptions that may motivate forced savings.[19] Subsequent discussion will consider liquidity constraints, the importance of heterogeneity in savings behavior, and finally the relationship between forced savings and redistribution. A complete normative analysis of forced savings requires that other instruments also be considered. See, for example, subsection 9.A.2 on how myopia may bear on the optimal taxation of savings.

1. Myopia

It has long been suspected and recent work has investigated the possibility that individuals may not save adequately because of myopia (see, for example, Laibson 1996, 1997). Alternatively, if, as Bernheim (1994), Diamond (2004), and others suggest, the complexity of the retirement problem combined with inexperience puts it beyond the reach of typical workers, then a substantial fraction may err by saving too little (others

---

[19] To simplify the analysis and focus on the identified issues, this chapter largely relies on a two-period model in which individuals work only in the first period, thereby abstracting from endogenous retirement decisions, which might be incorporated by adding one or more intermediate periods in which individuals may choose to work and considering various ways in which subsequent benefits could depend upon earnings in different periods. This problem is examined extensively in Diamond (2002, 2003) and in a series of papers by Diamond and Mirrlees (summarized in Diamond 2003 and in Feldstein and Liebman 2002b and also noted in section C).

might save too much, but that will not help those who save too little). Empirical evidence is mixed regarding the extent to which individuals' savings upon reaching retirement either are inadequate or would be so but for the forced savings through social security.[20] In any event, it is widely accepted that a paternalistically motivated desire to force savings constitutes an important, and to some the most important, rationale for social security retirement systems.[21]

Assume that all individuals are identical and, on account of myopia, save too little for retirement. That is, in determining how much to consume, their decisional utility overweights the present. Savings levels are understood to be inadequate normatively because this weighting deviates from their utility as actually experienced. In such cases, the direct effect of forced savings, such as through social security, is to raise welfare by reducing this intertemporal misallocation of resources, and this beneficial effect will grow until the point at which the level of forced savings equals the level of savings individuals would have chosen if their savings decisions were rational.

This conclusion, however, ignores how forced savings would affect labor supply, a matter of particular concern since the labor income tax that finances forced savings exists on top of the distortionary labor income tax used for redistribution. A conjecture is that forced savings in the present setting would reduce labor supply: Considering a scheme that is actuarially fair, individuals would excessively discount the future benefits whereas taxes are paid presently; hence, although in fact $T^N(wl) = 0$, individuals are imagined to behave as if $T^N(wl) > 0$. Furthermore, given the preexisting labor supply distortion due to explicit income taxation, the hypothesized behavioral response would generate substantial additional distortion.

---

[20] See, for example, Kotlikoff, Spivak, and Summers (1982), Banks, Blundell, and Tanner (1998), Engen, Gale, and Uccello (1999), Moore and Mitchell (2000), Bernheim, Skinner, and Weinberg (2001), Aguiar and Hurst (2005), Scholz, Seshadri, and Khitatrakun (2006), and Smith (2006).

[21] If myopic individuals are also subject to standard-of-living effects under which present consumption influences the utility of future consumption (perhaps by reducing utility but raising marginal utility at any level of consumption), as in Diamond (2003), the welfare benefit of forced savings may be greater.

It is important to examine this conjecture explicitly. To do so, the analysis follows Kaplow (2006b). Consider again a simple, two-period model in which individuals work only in period 1 and allocate their after-tax earnings between the two periods. Two subcases will be distinguished: When individuals' labor supply decisions are subject to the same myopia that determines the allocation of consumption between periods, and when these decisions are rational in the sense that individuals not only understand that they will allocate their earnings myopically but also appreciate what their realized utility will actually be (that is, that such an allocation involves too high a level of first-period consumption, c_1). Both cases are of potential interest because myopic behavior is not very well understood and is context specific. For example, some individuals employ commitment devices (automatic contributions to retirement accounts, not purchasing types of food they know they will overeat), many fail to borrow (fully or at all) from increased home equity despite their tendency to consume all of their paychecks, and savings behavior may be influenced by modest changes in framing (such as when individuals' contributions to 401(k) retirement plans depend on what contribution, if any, is specified by the employer as the default).[22] Note further that, in practice, the effect of myopia on labor supply may depend on the nature of the decision in question: Decisions about whether to pursue higher education or what job to choose from among many that require different effort levels may perhaps be made nonmyopically, whereas the same individuals may forgo overtime opportunities because of the immediate temptation to spend time with friends or watch favorite television shows. For simplicity, the subsequent analysis focuses on the two pure cases.

To examine the effect of social security on labor supply, consider the following simplified model:

$$u(c_1,c_2,l) = \frac{c_1^{1-\rho}}{1-\rho} + \delta\frac{c_2^{1-\rho}}{1-\rho} - z(l), \tag{11.3}$$

where ρ is the coefficient of relative risk aversion (utility from consumption taking the constant-relative-risk-aversion form from expression (3.3),

---

[22] On the latter, see Madrian and Shea (2001) and Choi et al. (2004).

where it is understood that, when $\rho = 1$, utility from consumption c_i is instead given by $\ln c_i$), δ is the actual subjective discount factor, and z measures the disutility of labor effort, where $z' > 0$ and $z'' > 0$. (To clarify, δ is taken here to be a real trait of individuals' utility, for purposes of assessing social welfare; myopia will later be introduced separately.) Individuals are subject to a linear income tax, so their budget constraint is

$$c_1 + \frac{c_2}{1+r} = (1-t)wl + g. \tag{11.4}$$

To introduce myopia in a simple manner, suppose that, in allocating disposable income between c_1 and c_2, individuals behave as if they are maximizing the following variant of the utility function given by expression (11.3):

$$u(c_1, c_2, l) = \beta \frac{c_1^{1-\rho}}{1-\rho} + \delta \frac{c_2^{1-\rho}}{1-\rho} - z(l), \tag{11.5}$$

where the weight on first-period consumption β is taken to exceed 1.[23] The first-order condition for consumption by a myopic individual (which can be determined by solving the budget constraint (11.4) for c_2, substituting it into (11.5), and differentiating) is

$$\frac{\partial u}{\partial c_1} = \beta c_1^{-\rho} - \delta(1+r)c_2^{-\rho} = 0. \tag{11.6}$$

Because social security is assumed here to be actuarially fair, it has no effect on the budget constraint (11.4). The only effect of social security

---

[23] It would also be natural to weight the disutility of labor, z, by β because labor is supplied in the first period; including such a weight, however, would not materially affect the results (β would weight the z' term in expression (11.8) and appear implicitly in d^2u/dl^2 in the denominator of expression (11.9); nothing else, including any of the interpretations, would change). Note also that, instead of weighting first-period sources of utility by β, one could weight second-period utility from consumption by a fraction less than one. The results would be nearly identical, the difference between these two formulations being in the cardinalization of utility as a function of consumption. (Recall that the discount factor δ does not already reflect such a downward weighting of second-period consumption because δ is taken to be the true subjective discount rate, a feature of the normatively relevant utility function.)

in this model, therefore, is to force savings, so social security can be represented as placing an upper bound on c_1. For concreteness, this bound will be a stated fraction of disposable income, so the social security policy may be denoted by χ, the minimum required fraction of savings.[24] Accordingly, there is now the additional constraint

$$c_1 \leq (1-\chi)[(1-t)wl+g].$$ (11.7)

If the constraint is binding, this expression is satisfied as an equality, which in turn for any given level of l dictates the allocation of disposable income between c_1 and c_2.

a. Myopic labor supply. Consider the effect of social security, thus defined, on labor supply when the labor supply decision is also myopic in the sense that it is determined by maximizing utility as defined in expression (11.5) rather than as defined in expression (11.3).[25] The

----

[24] Two other formulations of social security can be considered, one in which the bound is a fraction of earnings, wl, and another in which the bound is a fraction of after-tax earnings, $(1-t)wl$ (which differ from disposable income on account of g). For any given tax rate t, these two formulations are equivalent to each other, and the effect of changing the bound differs between the two cases only in magnitude because raising the latter bound (on after-tax earnings) by one unit has a smaller effect than that of raising the former bound (on before-tax earnings) when $t > 0$. Analysis of these two cases yields results qualitatively similar to those of the case considered in the text. Note that including g in the quantity that is subject to forced savings, as is done here, has the effect that forced savings are a constant fraction of disposable income at all income levels, whereas the other formulations would make forced savings a rising fraction of disposable income (because the grant g, exempt from the forced-savings requirement in the alternative formulations, is a greater share of disposable income for low-income individuals). Alternatively, if the grant payment was divided between the two periods (and borrowing against it was impossible), these two alternative models would be even closer to the present model.

[25] Another variant would be to assume that individuals do not, when choosing labor supply, anticipate that they will misallocate consumption. In this case, however, they would not expect the social security forced-savings constraint to be binding (assuming that the constraint is not so strong as to force more second-period consumption than the nonmyopic optimum), so tightening that constraint would have no effect on labor supply. As a result, social security would raise welfare through improved consumption allocation and there would be no further effect on labor supply to be taken into account.

first-order condition for labor supply (when the forced-savings constraint (11.7) is binding) is

$$\frac{du}{dl} = \beta c_1^{-\rho}(1-\chi)(1-t)w + c_2^{-\rho}\delta(1+r)\chi(1-t)w - z' = 0. \qquad (11.8)$$

Differentiating this expression with respect to χ, rearranging terms, and making appropriate substitutions yield the following expression for the derivative of labor supply with respect to the forced-savings requirement:

$$l_\chi = \frac{(1-\rho)(1-t)w\left[\beta c_1^{-\rho} - \delta(1+r)c_2^{-\rho}\right]}{d^2u/dl^2}. \qquad (11.9)$$

To interpret this expression, note first that the denominator must be negative at the individual's optimum (and it can readily be shown to be strictly negative for all l in any event). Second, observe that the bracketed expression in the numerator equals $\partial u/\partial c_1$ from expression (11.6). Therefore, as the constraint just begins to bind, the effect on labor supply (in whichever direction it may be) will be negligible. (No matter how strong is the extent of myopia, individuals' consumption allocation decisions already reflect it; hence, at their unconstrained consumption optimum, they are indifferent to a marginal reduction in first-period consumption.) This result indicates that an actuarially fair tax on present disposable income to finance forced savings does not affect labor supply in a manner qualitatively or (in general) quantitatively similar to that of further raising the marginal tax rate on current earnings, even though individuals are assumed to be myopic.

As the constraint becomes tighter (as χ increases once the constraint binds), the term in brackets, $\partial u/\partial c_1$, becomes (more) positive. The reason is that this derivative reflects individuals' *perceived* marginal utility from raising c_1 rather than their actual marginal utility. When the social security forced-savings constraint is binding, c_1 is less than what individuals would choose, so the perceived marginal utility of raising c_1 would be positive. Accordingly, l_χ is negative (positive)—that is, tightening the forced-savings constraint reduces (increases) labor supply—if $\rho < 1$ ($\rho > 1$).

The intuition for this result regarding labor supply can be understood by decomposing two effects, indicated respectively by the "1" and the "$-\rho$" in the leading term $1 - \rho$. A direct effect arises from more forced savings. When labor supply decisions reflect the same myopia as do individuals' first-period consumption allocation decisions, forcing an incremental reallocation of consumption toward period 2 is viewed as undesirable. Hence, the perceived return to labor effort falls.

An indirect effect is due to changes in relative marginal utilities of consumption in the two periods. As χ is increased, the consumption reallocation toward period 2 makes the marginal utility of consumption higher in period 1 and lower in period 2. Because first-period rather than second-period consumption is perceived as too low, this reallocation changes the (perceived) marginal utility of consumption more in the first period than in the second. (Stated precisely, the third derivative of utility as a function of consumption is positive, so the magnitude of the second derivative is greater when consumption is (perceived to be) low, as it is here in the first period, than when it is high, as in the second period.) When relative risk aversion is low, specifically, when $\rho < 1$, this latter effect is smaller than the direct effect due to consumption being perceived to be less well allocated between the two periods, so the overall perceived marginal benefit of increasing labor effort falls. However, when risk aversion is high, $\rho > 1$, the latter effect dominates, so labor effort rises.[26] In other words, when $\rho > 1$, the fact that social security makes earnings seem less attractive is outweighed by the fact that the forced reduction in c_1 greatly increases the perceived marginal value of first-period consumption, which can only be raised, partially restoring it to its unconstrained level, by working more. When $\rho < 1$, this latter effect is present but is insufficient to outweigh the direct reduction in the value of consumption.

---

[26] Formally, this condition and analysis are close to that offered in subsection 12.A.1 on the question of how generous allocations should be to a two-person family when resources are shared unequally. On reflection, this coincidence is unsurprising: With myopia, it is often stated that individuals behave as if there are two selves (a present self and a future self); in the case of unequal sharing in the family, there literally are two persons, one of whom is given more weight than the other.

Further illumination can be gleaned by comparing l_χ to l_t, the derivative of labor supply with respect to the income tax rate. Sparing fairly tedious detail, as a very crude statement l_χ will for most values of ρ have the same sign as l_t, but its magnitude will tend to be closer to zero.[27] Recalling that $l_\chi = 0$ until after the point at which the forced-savings constraint begins to bind, one can now see more fully the respects in which increasing forced savings affects labor supply differently from the way that raising the tax rate does.

b. Nonmyopic labor supply. These results may be contrasted with the case in which labor supply decisions are not myopic in the sense that they maximize utility as defined by expression (11.3) rather than expression (11.5), although labor supply decisions take into account that, when it comes time to decide on consumption, the allocation will be given by the first-order condition for myopic consumption (11.6), except to the extent constrained by social security, expression (11.7).[28]

The analysis of this case is straightforward from the foregoing derivation, although the conclusions differ. The first-order condition for labor supply is again given by expression (11.8) and l_χ by expression (11.9), except that $\beta = 1$. The interpretation of (11.9) changes on account of the bracketed term. It still corresponds to $\partial u / \partial c_1$ from expression (11.6), now with $\beta = 1$. But when labor supply decisions are nonmyopic, and assuming that the social security parameter χ is in the range in which there is still overconsumption in period 1, the value of this

---

[27] See Kaplow (2006b). The expression for l_t differs in a number of respects from that for l_χ. The sign of the former does not depend simply on the sign of $1-\rho$; instead, ρ is weighted in each period by a fraction less than one, namely, the period's consumption minus the pertinent forced-savings share of the tax system's grant component g, all divided by the period's consumption. As a result, there will be a range of ρ somewhat in excess of one for which l_t is negative even though l_χ for the myopic case is positive. (See Chetty (2006) on how unearned income influences the values of ρ for which labor supply is upward sloping.) The tendency for the magnitude of l_χ to be closer to zero than that of l_t is due to the fact that, in the former case, the effects on each period's consumption are opposed to each other whereas, in the latter case, the effects on both periods' consumption work in the same direction.

[28] Paralleling the comment in note 25, one could also consider the case in which myopia is not anticipated when choosing labor supply, but then social security would have no effect on labor supply because the constraint would not be expected to bind.

expression is negative because c_1 has been raised past the point at which the nonmyopic first-order condition for consumption is satisfied.

One implication is that l_χ now has the same sign as $1 - \rho$, rather than the opposite sign. That is, as more savings are forced, labor supply will rise (fall) if ρ is less (greater) than 1. As before, the intuition has two components. First, when χ is increased, the proceeds of labor effort are better allocated, which encourages labor effort. Because the labor supply decision is taken to be rational, the value of social security—as a substitute device making it possible for individuals de facto to commit to consume less in period 1—is positive in fact and is perceived as such. On the other hand, as χ is increased, the reduction in consumption misallocation changes the marginal utility of consumption in each period, making it higher in period 1 and lower in period 2. Because of the curvature of utility as a function of each period's consumption, the latter effect is greater. When $\rho < 1$, this indirect effect is less than the direct effect due to consumption being better allocated between the two periods, so the overall marginal benefit of increasing labor effort rises. However, when $\rho > 1$, the indirect effect dominates, so labor effort falls. (One can also, as above, compare l_χ to l_t in the present case. Sparing the details, it is crudely true that l_χ will for most values of ρ have the opposite sign as l_t, and its magnitude will tend to be closer to zero.)

There is another notable difference between the present case and that with myopic labor supply. There, $l_\chi = 0$ as the forced-savings constraint just began to bind, whereas here this is not true: At that point, the marginal gain from consumption reallocation toward the future, which is taken into account in individuals' labor supply decisions, is at its greatest, and thus forced savings affect labor supply nontrivially (except when ρ or β is close to 1) from the moment the constraint begins to bind. This factor and, accordingly, the effect of forced savings on labor supply will equal zero not when the constraint just begins to bind, but rather when χ reaches the point at which the magnitude of forced savings just equals its optimal (nonmyopic) level (that is, when c_1 equals the value that satisfies the first-order condition (11.6), evaluated for $\beta = 1$). If χ were increased further, $\partial u / \partial c_1$ would reverse sign, becoming positive, and the sign of l_χ would reverse from whatever it had been when χ was lower.

To summarize, the effect of forcing additional savings on labor supply is qualitatively different in a number of respects from that of raising the (ordinary) marginal tax rate on labor income. Perhaps the clearest indication is that the sign of the effect (whatever it might be) is opposite for myopic and nonmyopic labor supply decisions. Additionally, in each case, the magnitude of the effect is determined differently. For myopic labor supply, the initial marginal effect is zero, whereas adding a small ordinary tax on top of a preexisting tax has a first-order effect. For non-myopic labor supply, the effect on labor supply tends to fall (rather than rise) as forced savings increase, reaching zero when forced savings equal the nonmyopic savings optimum.

An important part of the explanation for these differences between forced savings and taxation is that, even with significant myopia that leads to substantial overallocation of disposable income to c_1, the result is an increase in the actual and perceived marginal utility of c_2, suffi-ciently so that, at the unconstrained myopic optimum, the individual is indifferent about reallocations of consumption between the two periods (as noted earlier). Hence, forcibly reallocating some consumption to pe-riod 2 does not act at all like a tax, at least initially, even in the myopic labor supply case—and is viewed as a benefit in the nonmyopic labor supply case. Although these features change as the constraint tightens, they do not immediately vanish.

Finally, as a contrast with the foregoing analysis, consider briefly the possibility raised at the outset that individuals, rather than being myo-pic although nevertheless fully informed and calculating in their behav-ior, instead find the problem of intertemporal maximization too com-plex to solve effectively. To proceed further, it would be necessary to state explicitly how such individuals do behave, in particular when faced by a social security system. Perhaps some individuals overestimate and others underestimate the value of the benefits financed by their current social security tax obligations, in which case the distortion in labor sup-ply due to income taxation would be reduced for the former and in-creased for the latter. Or, because benefits are far in the future, they might be undervalued fairly generally, in which case an actuarially fair social security system would tend, to that extent, to have the same effect as an additional tax.[29] (It is important to distinguish the previously

---

[29] This possibility motivates proposals for providing taxpayers clearer annual statements explaining benefit accruals and for employing private accounts (which in the simplest case

analyzed case involving the discounting of future utility from the present one of discounting future dollar benefits.[30]) Another possibility is that individuals who are unable to calculate for themselves behave as if the government has (approximately) solved individuals' optimization problems and chosen the forced-savings rate accordingly; in this case, raising forced savings in an actuarially fair system would tend to increase labor supply.[31] Or individuals might not appreciate marginal effective tax rates and respond instead to average rates.[32] Clearly, further empirical work on individuals' behavior is necessary to determine the actual effects of social security on labor supply.

2. Samaritan's Dilemma

Social security's forced retirement savings requirement has also been rationalized by what Buchanan (1975) describes as the Samaritan's dilemma (see also Bernheim and Stark 1988, Bruce and Waldman 1990, Feldstein 1987, and Lindbeck and Weibull 1988). The notion is that individuals will have an incentive to undersave if they anticipate receiving transfers during retirement if, but only if, they are sufficiently destitute.

---

would be actuarially fair by construction and thus, one might suppose, would not be perceived as involving the imposition of any present effective tax). The latter and other forms of pre-funding have also been suggested as a response to perceived political risk that leads individuals not to believe that promised future benefits will actually be paid, on which see Dominitz, Manski, and Heinz (2003) (indicating that a substantial fraction of younger cohorts state that they do not expect to receive social security benefits upon retirement). See also Shoven and Slavov (2006), who compare political risk to investment risk.

[30] In the current case, if individuals were otherwise informed and rational, in the present model the effect on period 1 labor supply would be the same as that arising if one reduced the return to labor on the right side of the budget constraint (11.4). For example, if there were an additional tax of s on labor income and the proceeds financed actuarially fair benefits of which only $\alpha < 1$ were perceived, the right side of (11.4) would become $(1 - t - s)wl + g + \alpha[swl(1+r)]/(1+r) = [1 - t - (1 - \alpha)s]wl + g$.

[31] The intuition is that higher forced savings reduce present consumption, which both raises the marginal utility of present consumption and also, in the hypothesized setting, raises the perceived marginal utility of future consumption. This case and others are explored in Kaplow (2007c).

[32] Liebman and Zeckhauser (2004) refer to this possibility as well as to individuals' ignoring how present behavior affects future prices or tax rates as "schmeduling."

As a simple model of this phenomenon, suppose that in period 2 the government will pay a transfer equal to the shortfall between an individual's available resources, c_2, and a modest target level of consumption, c^*.[33] That is, the period 2 transfer is max$(0, c^* - c_2)$. Confronted by such a scheme, individuals who would receive any period 2 transfer would always receive the full c^*, for once in the range of eligibility for some transfer, savings are implicitly taxed at 100%, so individuals would not save at all. Moreover, some individuals who would otherwise have saved such that $c_2 > c^*$ will also choose not to save anything. Specifically, all individuals will compare their utility given the levels of l and c_1 that would be optimal in a world with no period 2 transfers to their utility if they consume all disposable income in period 1, c^* in period 2, and work the level of l that would be optimal conditional on that plan. In the present simple model, there will be some critical level of w below which individuals save nothing and above which individuals save as they would if there were no transfers.

Because we are focusing on actuarially fair schemes, it follows that individuals whom the government anticipates will save nothing based on their level of earnings (that is, those whose earnings are below those of the critical type) would be charged $c^*/(1 + r)$ in additional taxes.[34] (Although for individuals of very low ability, such a charge may seem too high to be optimal, keep in mind that any redistribution may be accomplished in the tax-transfer system; this degree of redistribution is taken to be unchanged in the analysis to follow.)

Now compare this period 2 transfer scheme to one that offers no transfers and forces individuals to save at least $c^*/(1 + r)$ in period 1.

---

[33] The Samaritan's dilemma extends to private transfers, notably from family or charities. That is, individuals may undersave because they anticipate support, say, from altruistic relatives. Forced savings likewise may be effective in this circumstance.

[34] There is not a unique actuarially fair scheme. The government could, as suggested in the text, charge $c^*/(1+r)$ to all whose earnings are below those predicted for the critical type w in a world with no transfers. However, if the government also imposed the charge on individuals with slightly higher earnings (w's), such individuals then would find it optimal to switch between the two types of optima, choosing to save nothing and receive the transfer c^* in period 2; note that in so doing the result is actuarially fair for them. This complication about uniqueness does not alter the fundamental character of the analysis and thus will be ignored.

Individuals who would have saved less than this amount in a world with no transfers or social security will be indifferent between this savings requirement and the transfers, for both regimes charge them $c^*/(1 + r)$ in period 1 and allow them to consume c^* in period 2. For individuals who would not be subject to the tax and transfer, this constraint will not be binding (their chosen savings exceed $c^*/(1 + r)$ by a nontrivial amount), so they too will be indifferent.

However, for individuals in the intermediate range, who would have saved at least $c^*/(1 + r)$ but whose w's are below the critical level, a forced-savings regime produces higher utility than does the tax and transfer regime. This utility gain arises because, under the transfer regime, these individuals were induced to consume less in period 2 than they would have found optimal in an unconstrained world. That is, their ideal level of savings exceeds $c^*/(1 + r)$ but is not so high as to deter them from saving nothing if this will qualify them for the period 2 transfer of c^* (which, once they have dominion over their disposable income, is available to them for free, the additional tax of $c^*/(1 + r)$ being a sunk cost when they make their savings decisions). The only effect of the transfer regime on them, given that it is actuarially fair, is to distort their savings behavior in the direction of too little savings. Switching to a regime of forced savings eliminates this distortion. Moreover, since by hypothesis these individuals would have saved more than $c^*/(1 + r)$, the forced-savings requirement is not binding on them. Note that this benefit from substituting forced savings for period 2 transfers involves an efficiency gain (a weak Pareto improvement), for no redistribution is involved.[35]

Consider now the effect of this sort of forced-savings requirement on labor supply, compared to a regime with no social security and no period 2 transfers. For all but the group for whom the forced-savings requirement of $c^*/(1 + r)$ is binding, there is no effect on labor supply. For individuals for whom the constraint is binding, period 2 consumption is

---

[35] Of course, in the present setting without myopia, forcing savings is itself inefficient, assuming, that is, that the government (and others) could commit not to make the period 2 transfers. Note further that the analysis in the present setting is analogous to that in others, such as when Medicaid, free health care, or other transfers are available only to individuals with no remaining assets (see subsection 7.B.3) or when disaster relief or a tax deduction mitigates losses but only to the extent that they are not covered by insurance.

simply c^*, and all incremental after-tax earnings are spent on period 1 consumption, that is, $c_1 = (1-t)wl + g - c^*/(1 + r)$. Accordingly, the first-order condition for labor supply is

$$\frac{du}{dl} = c_1^{-\rho}(1-t)w - z' = 0. \tag{11.10}$$

Differentiating this expression with respect to c^*, after some manipulation, yields

$$l_{c^*} = \frac{\rho c_1^{-\rho-1}(1-t)w/(1+r)}{-d^2u/dl^2}. \tag{11.11}$$

The numerator is the negative of the derivative of the marginal utility of consumption in the first period, where all incremental after-tax earnings are expended, weighted by the net-of-tax wage and also divided by $1+r$ because c^* is denominated in period 2 dollars. Clearly, l_{c^*} is positive, the intuition being that tightening the constraint reduces first-period consumption, the effect of which is to raise the marginal utility of consumption and thus the benefit of increasing labor supply.

Alternatively, one might, as in subsection 1, consider a constraint like that in expression (11.7) in which forced savings rise with disposable income (perhaps the pull of the Samaritan's dilemma is greater when individuals' pre-retirement consumption had been higher so that their fall in standard of living in the event of insufficient savings is greater). Again, the comparison is to a regime with no social security and no period 2 transfers. The first-order condition for labor supply is given by (11.8), and the effect of tightening the forced-savings constraint on labor effort is given by (11.9), each considered now for the case in which $\beta = 1$ (because in this subsection the phenomenon of forced savings is analyzed under the assumption of no myopia). The interpretation of expression (11.9) parallels that in the case of myopic labor supply (because in that case individuals' consumption and labor supply decisions would, in the absence of social security, be governed by the same utility function, as is the case here). Specifically, recall that the bracketed expression in the numerator equals $\partial u/\partial c_1$ from expression (11.6), again now for the case in which $\beta = 1$. Therefore, tightening the constraint makes this term more positive as c_1 is pushed further below its optimal level. Thus l_x is negative (positive)—that is, tightening the forced-savings constraint reduces (increases) labor supply—if $\rho < 1$ ($\rho > 1$), with the intuition decomposing the two effects paralleling that given previously.

Because in the present case no myopia is assumed to exist, there is no rationale for imposing forced savings at a level where the constraint is binding, except for fear of the Samaritan's dilemma, but the effects on labor supply in the preceding cases were by comparison to a regime without period 2 transfers. Although such a regime for remedying savings shortfalls is dominated by a pure forced-savings program in terms of the efficiency of consumption allocations, it is appropriate to consider the labor supply effects of this sort of transfer program as well. There are two sets of effects of raising c^* in such a scheme. First, for those who are already constrained, the effect on labor supply is positive and, indeed, is the same as in a regime of forced savings that finances c^* in period 2. (Recall that the difference between period 2 transfers and forced savings is that the former induces an additional, intermediate-ability group to reduce savings so as to become subject to the regime. Accordingly, this larger group is subject to the positive labor supply effects of raising c^*.) Second, as c^* increases, additional individuals will shift from their privately optimal levels of c_1 and c_2, as dictated by their first-order condition, to saving nothing beyond the implicit minimum savings mandate entailed by the actuarially fair funding requirement of $c^*/(1 + r)$. Their labor supply falls by a discrete amount. The reason is that the return to labor in terms of the marginal utility of consumption falls. Previously, the marginal utility of consuming in each period was equated, so it suffices to consider the marginal utility of period 1 consumption. After they shift regimes, if one supposes that labor supply remains the same, it must be that more is expended on period 1 consumption; hence, the marginal utility of consumption falls. Because the marginal disutility of labor supply is taken to be the same, the first-order condition does not hold and can be restored only by reducing period 1 consumption and labor effort.

In each of these regimes, therefore, there may exist costs or benefits due to labor supply effects, which can be significant given the preexisting labor supply distortion caused by redistributive labor income taxation. To assess the regimes, one must combine this consideration with the direct effects of the Samaritan's dilemma and its mitigation regarding individuals' allocations of consumption between periods in order to determine what sort of forced-savings regime is optimal.

3. Liquidity Constraints

The existence of liquidity constraints and their possible relevance to the redistribution problem were noted in subsection 5.E.1. Liquidity constraints also bear on the need for and desirability of forced savings (see, for example, Hubbard and Judd 1987). Liquidity constraints may inhibit undersavings on account of myopia (see Laibson 1997) or the Samaritan's dilemma. To the extent that individuals cannot borrow against future earnings, they are implicitly forced to save, at least until the time at which such earnings are realized. On the other hand, forcing liquidity-constrained individuals not subject to any infirmities to save a minimum amount reduces their long-run well-being. Of course, in the absence of externalities or irrationalities, forcing more savings than otherwise would be chosen is always distortionary; however, with liquidity constraints, the initial (say, zero) level of savings is already too high, so the marginal distortion from forced savings is greater than otherwise. Moreover, even minimal savings requirements will necessarily be binding on individuals who already are liquidity constrained.

Additional considerations further complicate the problem of determining the optimal extent (if any) of forced savings in the presence of liquidity constraints. One difficulty is empirical: Even if one can identify liquidity constraints (for references, see subsection 5.E.1), it may not be apparent whether such constraints are forcing individuals to underconsume relative to the optimum or instead are preventing even greater overconsumption that would otherwise occur. (Heterogeneity, considered in the next subsection, adds yet another dimension.) Another issue concerns externalities. Greater consumption by workers when they are relatively young may produce positive externalities to other family members, particularly children, relative to what would be produced by consumption in retirement (see chapters 10 and 12 on voluntary transfers and on taxation of the family). On the other hand, the Samaritan's dilemma, which as mentioned in note 33 may also involve family members, suggests that raising retirement consumption, especially when it is otherwise too low, may generate positive externalities.

Liquidity constraints and related factors bear on the optimal timing, as well as level, of savings and thus on the optimal structure of any forced-savings program. Many individuals have hump-shaped or rising wage profiles during their working years, although optimal consumption paths may be smooth; there exist early needs for funds to purchase consumer durables and housing (down payments) and also to finance investments in human capital; and consumption expenditures may produce greater benefits when children are present. Accordingly, it would be optimal for many to engage in little or no savings or to borrow in early to middle-age years and to save substantial amounts (including debt repayment) in later years. Typical forced-savings programs, by contrast, tend to take a constant fraction of earnings every year.

In principle, however, forced-savings regimes could vary by age. Other factors could also be reflected in tax and benefit rules. For example, for different earnings levels or occupational categories that are known, on average, to be associated with different lifetime earnings profiles, different schedules could be applied. Also, forced-savings requirements could be adjusted over the life cycle to reflect variations over time in the number of dependents. If liquidity constraints and these other factors are significant, substantial welfare gains could result from even modest departures from constant contribution rates (keeping in mind that if, say, consumption was already distorted downward in early years due to liquidity constraints, small additional savings requirements would impose first-order losses).

It is also important to consider how such changes in forced-savings requirements would affect labor supply. One instinct is that constant contribution rates are presumptively ideal because they minimize distortion. However, as noted in subsection A.2, the tax burden on account of social security is not given by the stated contribution schedule, $T^S(wl)$, but rather the net, $T^N(wl)$, which takes into account how the year's earnings affect future benefits. (Specifically, it was noted that, in the United States, flat contribution rates result in highly uneven net tax rates, often with the highest rates when individuals are youngest and low or negative rates in peak earning years.) In this section, we have been considering only actuarially fair schemes. As emphasized in subsections 1 and 2, however, when individuals may be myopic and, in any event when their savings behavior is constrained, labor supply responses may differ (in either direction, depending on the behavioral assumptions and parameters) from those of rational, unconstrained individuals. That analysis would need to be extended to a model with more than one period of work and time-varying wages, utility, or myopia to analyze the question properly. The main point, already noted, is that since a regime of forced savings, not pure taxation, is contemplated, it is not obvious a priori that constant (contribution) rates would tend to minimize labor supply distortion.

Because forced-savings regimes may be especially appealing when individuals are myopic, it is useful to contemplate additional effects that myopia may have on labor supply in a model with multiple periods of work. One possibility is that individuals' early investments in human capital will be influenced disproportionately by net earnings in early years. (This effect could be a product of myopia or limited information.) In that event, lower tax rates when young may be optimal because, in addition to reducing the current-period distortion in labor supply, there would be the additional benefit of reducing the downward distortion in human capital, which affects the wage rate in subsequent periods. Another possibility is that labor effort is subject to habituation: What effort seems normal, how one learns to live one's life outside work, and so forth may become set or at least shaped by early experiences.[36] In that case, there also may be benefits to reducing taxation in early years.[37] (Note that the magnitude of such effects may be influenced by shortsightedness; to the extent that higher future taxes are not anticipated, individuals will be more inclined to make investments in lifestyle that are best suited to their current level of labor effort.) This argument, in contrast to the previous one, refers to taxes rather than to contributions, which, as discussed, may have different effects on labor supply. Accordingly, these factors may bear more on the

---

[36] There are many possible channels. How exertion is experienced may itself reflect the extent to which effort deviates from one's norm. The enjoyment of some leisure activities is enhanced by investments of sorts; certain tastes are acquired and others remain undeveloped.

[37] The present argument depends on the uncompensated labor supply elasticity being positive. If it were zero, for example, lower present tax rates would not affect labor effort and thus would not affect habit formation, except that different average tax rates, or forced-savings rates, would influence present consumption levels, another channel by which habit formation may be influenced.

optimal redistributive income taxation problem than on that of optimal forced savings. In the taxation setting, the present argument does offer a reason to deviate from constant marginal tax rates over time.

This subsection has considered liquidity constraints and related matters that are relevant to forced savings viewed from a lifetime perspective. For a more complete understanding, this analysis should be combined with that in subsection A.2, which considers how social security retirement provisions are connected to the redistribution problem (which is abstracted from in the present section) when it is viewed over the life cycle rather than in the conventional one- (or two-) period setting.

4. Heterogeneity

Heterogeneity is likely to be important with regard to myopia and liquidity constraints, as well as savings preferences that reflect different wage profiles over the life cycle and differences in family composition. Moreover, many of the effects of forced savings are nonlinear and even asymmetric, so identifying average tendencies is insufficient in the determination of optimal policy. As previously noted, savings requirements will force upward the savings of those who save too little but not force downward the savings of those who save too much (which would not include the myopic but may include those who err when attempting to solve the lifetime maximization problem). Among the former, labor supply responses have opposite signs for individuals whose labor supply decisions are also myopic compared to those whose labor supply decisions are not. It was suggested that myopia may differentially affect different types of labor supply decisions (investment in human capital versus momentary overtime decisions), but obviously myopia may also vary greatly across individuals for the same types of decisions. The importance of liquidity constraints may depend on occupation, stage in the life cycle, family configuration, and other factors.

In trading off competing effects, the optimal forced-savings policy will also reflect variations in how marginal welfare consequences change with the tightness of the savings constraint. For individuals subject to myopia, the first dollar of consumption moved to the future will produce a first-order welfare gain, while the benefit falls to zero when the optimal intertemporal allocation is reached and becomes negative thereafter. As described in subsections 1 and 2, however, labor supply effects have different patterns. For individuals who are liquidity constrained—that is, assuming rational rather than myopic savings and borrowing behavior (and no externalities, notably, relating to the Samaritan's dilemma)—the first dollar moved to the future imposes a first-order welfare cost. For those who are not subject to infirmities or constraints, the first dollar of forced savings will not generally be binding and, as the constraint begins to bind (which it will at different points for different individuals, depending on preferences), there will initially be no first-order welfare loss.

Because some of the possible costs of forced savings involve first-order effects even at the outset, it is possible that the optimum involves no forced savings. Indeed, in such a case, most plausibly produced by significant liquidity constraints, making available additional borrowing may well be optimal. Regarding all of the identified effects (except possibly some regarding labor supply), marginal costs rise and marginal benefits fall as the forced-savings constraint is tightened, a typical pattern. It is worth emphasizing, as suggested in subsection 3, that the optimal scheme may be age dependent (and also a function of wage level, occupation, and family composition), perhaps with little or no forced savings for the young or those with children but with a positive savings requirement for others.[38]

5. Relationship to Redistribution

The present section has abstracted from any redistribution that may be embedded in forced savings through social security retirement schemes

---

[38] Externalities, notably arising in years in which children are present, introduce another dimension of heterogeneity that may favor differential forced-savings requirements for different family types. This feature of program design also interacts with the question of optimal redistribution among families, the subject of chapter 12. Nevertheless, the forced-savings issue has independent force: Holding the present value of redistribution across family types constant, forced reallocation of lifetime consumption by certain family types might raise social welfare. Note that a significant component of transfers that depend on the presence of children is the provision of free public education, a transfer that is received at a particular time in the life cycle and, because provided in kind, may well have the result of increasing the portion of a family's lifetime consumption (inclusive of government transfers of all types) that is expended on children (see section 7.E).

because, as discussed in section A, the redistribution problem is to a substantial extent separable in principle from other, more distinctive features of forced savings. Nevertheless, there are some considerations at the intersection of forced savings and redistribution.

First, as noted in subsection 2, if the Samaritan's dilemma takes a form under which the extent of second-period transfers is substantial relative to the low first-period earnings of low-skilled individuals, then actuarially fair funding of a second-period consumption floor could leave such individuals destitute in the first period. Put another way, if individuals (through the government or private transfers) have considerable sympathy for the elderly poor, addressing this concern through second-period payments or through forced savings may in itself make it optimal to depart from actuarially fair finance unless transfers to low-income individuals in the first period are already sufficiently generous.

Second, the analysis of liquidity constraints and of heterogeneity in subsections 3 and 4 suggests that the optimal degree of forced savings may well depend, among other factors, on individuals' levels of earnings (perhaps adjusted for stage in the life cycle and occupation). For example, myopia may be a greater problem for low-income individuals and may even contribute to low earning ability if it affects decisions to invest in human capital.[39] To be sure, merely allowing the relative degree of forced savings to vary by income does not entail redistribution. However, due to heterogeneity and the presence of liquidity constraints, forced-savings requirements inevitably impose welfare losses on some individuals and, more broadly, affect individuals' marginal utilities of consumption and utility levels. As a result, the optimal degree of redistribution—more precisely, the optimal income tax schedule

---

[39] Lawrance (1991) provides evidence that low-income, less-educated individuals appear to have a greater subjective discount rate, but evidence on consumption behavior does not distinguish between different underlying (true) preferences and differential susceptibility to myopia (or differential influence of the Samaritan's dilemma). The belief that undersaving is a greater problem for low-income individuals may explain why some social security programs, such as that in the United States, provide higher replacement rates (levels of funded retirement consumption relative to lifetime earnings) for lower-income individuals, although redistribution offers another possible explanation.

$T(wl)$—may well be affected by the problems examined in this section and the extent to which a policy of forced savings is employed to address them.[40]

C. Insurance

Social security schemes, in addition to incorporating various sorts of redistribution and forcing retirement savings, often contain additional features that involve insurance in some form. Annuitization, whether explicit or implicit (the latter through defined-benefit formulas), is often required. Annuitization tends to be desirable because of uncertainty over longevity (see Yaari 1965). Even when a bequest motive is present or incompleteness of other types of insurance makes precautionary savings rational, some degree of annuitization typically is optimal (see Davidoff, Brown, and Diamond 2005).

One rationale for mandating annuitization is the problem of adverse selection in annuity markets.[41] Another, emphasized by Diamond (2002, 2003), is that individuals may fail to appreciate the benefits of annuitization.[42] Furthermore, myopic individuals might consume their retirement

---

[40] This possibility can be illustrated using a natural extension of the two-period model with earnings and labor income taxation in only the first period. Consider a model in which there are many periods and also overlapping generations, with the income tax-and-transfer schedule applicable in every period. With no forced savings and many individuals subject to myopia, there will be many retired individuals living largely on the transfer g ($-T(0)$ in the nonlinear income tax scheme), and many of them may have very low abilities and labor supply elasticities, which could favor a higher g but even higher marginal tax rates at low income levels (assuming that the tax schedule is not age dependent) (compare the discussion in chapter 7). On the other hand, if the poorest individuals are not liquidity constrained, because they live largely off transfers, whereas a significant fraction of higher-ability individuals are liquidity constrained and a substantial portion of their earnings is subject to forced savings, then such individuals' marginal utilities would be higher as a consequence, which would tend to favor a less redistributive scheme.

[41] See, for example, Eckstein, Eichenbaum, and Peled (1985). For empirical evidence on adverse selection in annuities markets, see Brown, Mitchell, and Poterba (2002) and Finkelstein and Poterba (2004).

[42] Diamond argues that existing opportunities for annuitization appear to be underutilized despite substantial utility gains and that individuals generally fail to annuitize at

savings too soon if not forced to annuitize. A different sort of justification for compulsory annuitization is that the Samaritan's dilemma is also applicable to the timing of consumption during retirement; that is, individuals who rapidly deplete their savings may expect subsequently to receive greater public or private transfers as a consequence.

To a substantial extent, the merits of forced annuitization are unrelated to the optimal degree of redistribution across income levels. Annuitization does entail some horizontal redistribution among individuals with different life expectancies. When such differences are unknown at the time of annuitization, this is simply the provision of insurance; when differences are known (the source of adverse selection), there is no Pareto improvement but still a social welfare gain from forced annuitization. Life expectancies may be correlated with income, in which case forced annuitization would redistribute, on average, across income groups, but contribution rates or benefit levels—or the background income tax and transfer schedule—could be adjusted to offset any such effects.

Likewise, some of the important factors relating to the desirability of annuitization, particularly adverse selection, are unrelated to those bearing on forced savings. Annuitization could be desirable when requiring forced savings is not, and conversely.

As with forced savings, the effects of annuitization on labor supply have not been fully analyzed. Many similar considerations seem applicable. This is especially clear to the extent that myopia, misunderstanding, or the Samaritan's dilemma is relevant to annuitization. Even looking solely at adverse selection, the provision of otherwise unavailable insurance will in general affect the return (measured in expected marginal utility) to labor effort.[43] Although not a distortion considered in a vacuum, labor supply effects are important in light of the preexisting distortion due to redistributive labor income taxation.

Disability insurance is another significant feature of many social security systems.[44] Many of the same issues arise as with annuitization,

---

the optimal point in time, when young (when the extent of adverse selection may also be smaller).

[43] The direction and magnitude of the effect will depend on the curvature of individuals' utility functions.

[44] Unemployment insurance has similar characteristics, although the labor market search process and systematic risk may be more important than is the case with disability insurance.

including asymmetric information, myopia and other decision-making infirmities, and the Samaritan's dilemma.[45] These considerations in principle are largely independent of redistribution (the insurance can be actuarially fair). Requiring forced savings for retirement is also largely distinct, as reflected in the fact that public disability insurance and forced retirement savings are typically run as separate programs even if administered by a common government agency.

There are, however, important synergies, particularly since some disabilities are permanent, inducing retirement of sorts, and the skills and disutility associated with labor effort in many occupations tend to degrade during the years that individuals contemplate retirement. (Indeed, absent changes in utility or opportunities, many individuals might never retire.) This subject has received substantial attention, especially in a series of papers by Diamond and Mirrlees (1978, 1986, 2000).[46] It is understood that full insurance is not optimal because of moral hazard. Furthermore, it is necessary to carefully structure benefit levels for those not working and taxes and future benefits for those who continue to work in order to maintain work incentives over time. The failure to do so, especially in many European countries, is thought to contribute to the significant rise in earlier retirement (see Gruber and Wise 1999).

Another major feature of some social security systems, notably in the United States, is the provision of medical insurance for individuals beyond a certain age. In many other countries, the government provides health care for everyone, although one can conceptualize such systems as forced insurance paid for by workers currently, with supplemental payroll taxes constituting prepayment for insurance during retirement years. Due to the high and rising cost of health care, particularly for older individuals, medical expenditures for retirees are quite large. Such health care provision raises essentially all of the issues considered in this chapter pertaining to redistribution, forced savings, and insurance and thus can be analyzed similarly.

---

[45] The prevalence of private disability insurance is substantially greater than private annuitization, suggesting that these problems may be less significant for many individuals.

[46] For summaries and further discussion, see Diamond (2003) and Feldstein and Liebman (2002b).

12

Taxation of Families

🏃

Tax schedules and transfer programs can and often do depend on family structure, notably, on whether there are one or two adults and on the number of children. How taxes and transfers should depend on such family characteristics has proved controversial, and the treatment of different family types exhibits substantial variation among programs, across countries, and over time.[1]

This chapter analyzes taxation of families as an extension of the optimal income taxation framework. It begins by considering a simplified setting in which only distribution across families is at issue, thereby abstracting from labor effort and the endogeneity of family structure. For families that consist of more than one individual, social welfare is taken here to depend on the utilities of each family member viewed as a distinct individual. These individual utilities—and, as will be seen, marginal utilities—depend on intrafamily allocations, economies of scale, the nature of utility interdependencies among family members, and differences in the cost of producing utility between family members (children compared to adults). Accordingly, analysis of the purely distributive dimension of the taxation of families requires a careful microeconomic examination inside the black box of family units.

It should be emphasized that the distributive considerations examined in this chapter are in an important sense orthogonal to the standard distributive focus in this book, which is concerned with differences in earning ability, as indicated by differences in income.[2] The

---

[1] See, for example, Dingeldey (2001, table 1) on different systems for taxing married couples in Europe.

[2] See Schelling (1984, pp. 18–21).

present question is: As between two different types of families with the same income, how much income should be transferred and in which direction? Or, put another way, what income difference would have to prevail between two family types for the distribution between them to be optimal? Yet another formulation is to take as given how much revenue will be raised from (or transferred to) a group of families of similar income or standard of living and to ask how that aggregate burden (or benefit) should be allocated among them. Articulating the question of distribution across family types in this manner exposes the confusion behind the common belief that it may be too expensive, say, to fix the marriage tax (if it indeed is broken) or to provide generous family-size adjustments; after all, a given degree of relative generosity to various family types can be achieved by reducing their taxes, including below zero, or by raising those on other types—or (the present suggestion) by a combination of the two that is revenue neutral.

The difference between this distributive inquiry and the standard (so-called vertical) one can be seen by noting that, until one answers the foregoing questions, one cannot say who is richer or poorer and thus what direction of transfer flow would "increase redistribution." Furthermore, as will be seen, the problem is more complicated than this point suggests because, unlike in the standard setting, the optimal direction of redistribution is not always from better-off to worse-off families. The possibility that redistribution may optimally favor the better-off (at least under some standard SWFs) will be most apparent in the analysis of economies of scale in subsection A.2. Another instance arises with children, the subject of subsection A.4. To illustrate this idea, suppose that there are two otherwise identical married couples who each want a child and that only the first succeeds; moreover, the child is healthy and is happier than either of its parents. At this point, the utility of each member of the three-person family will exceed that of each in the two-person family. Nevertheless, it may well be optimal for redistribution to flow from the latter to the former, and indeed this is the typical pattern of redistribution.

The primary motivation for beginning the analysis with the pure distributive question is that the problem of optimal taxation of families is complex, so it is helpful to isolate particular factors as a first step. The across-family-type distributive dimension makes questions about the optimal taxation of families distinctive, and, even taken alone, this aspect poses significant analytical challenges. In addition, this area is one of the few in this book in which even qualitative results—about the direction of optimal redistribution—may depend on the form of the SWF. Accordingly, distributive questions will be addressed before incorporating additional aspects of the problem.

The latter portion of this chapter takes up incentive concerns, first, involving labor effort, the focus of most optimal income tax analysis, and, second, involving family structure, an instance of endogenous categorization, a general problem examined briefly in subsections 5.C.1 and 7.C.3.[3] The more complete version of the problem is quite challenging and has not been studied intensively, so this part of the analysis will be more preliminary and speculative than that focused on distribution alone.

A. Distribution

The framework and analysis of family taxation as a pure distribution problem, with labor effort and family composition taken as given, will follow Kaplow (1996c).[4] In the model, the government allocates a fixed amount of resources, C, between two households, a two-person family and a single individual. Interpreting the two members of the family as adults illuminates the distributive problem between singles and couples, whereas interpreting the two members as a representative parent and a representative child indicates how the optimal distribution is affected by the presence of children.

Social welfare is determined by the final allocation, not the taxes and transfers themselves. The two-member family receives c (in total)

---

[3] One topic not addressed is that, taking a lifetime perspective, most individuals will spend time in different types of family units and in different positions within such units, which further complicates the optimal tax problem, particularly when one accounts for individuals' optimization over the life cycle.

[4] Kaplow (1996c) derives the supplemental properties that are merely asserted herein and also examines further variations.

and the single individual $C-c$. Because it often will be of interest to consider the value of the single individual's consumption relative to that of the family, it is convenient to denote this individual's consumption as ωc, where $\omega = (C-c)/c$, the ratio of the single individual's allotment to the family's total allotment. Choosing an optimal consumption allocation is thus equivalent to determining the optimal value of ω, with c an implicit function of ω, that is, $c = C/(1+\omega)$. Note that a useful benchmark is the value $\omega = \frac{1}{2}$, indicating that the single individual's allocation equals the per capita allocation to members of the two-person family. Lower (higher) values of ω imply that the family is given a more (less) generous per capita allotment than that given to the single individual.

The actual allocation within the family may not involve an equal division of its resources c. Instead, the family itself determines the intrafamily allocation. It is assumed here that the government cannot directly observe or influence this allocation. This restriction is obviously an oversimplification, one that is explored in some other parts of this book.[5] However, there are limits to the ability of the government to monitor and regulate intrafamily allocations of resources, so it is important to explore the implications of this assumption. This feature is part of what makes the problem of family taxation different from one that simply introduces heterogeneous utility functions for each family type.[6] (Relatedly, when labor effort is not fixed, one family member's consumption in general depends on others' labor effort, adding to the interdependencies among individuals in a family.) In most of the models examined later, however, analysis will be performed for (or will implicitly encompass) the case in which the family's allocation is assumed to maximize family welfare—which could be imagined to result from family members' preferences, bargaining, or government intervention.

---

[5] Some transfers between family members are observable, in which case the analysis in chapter 10 on transfer taxation is applicable (see note 4 in chapter 10 and note 14 here). In addition, even if transfers are unobservable, it may still be possible to influence the intrafamily allocation of resources. For example, if the government wishes to increase the share going to children, it may provide free public education or in-kind transfer programs at levels higher than what parents would otherwise allocate to their children (see subsection 7.E), or it may use commodity taxes and subsidies.

[6] See Apps and Rees (1988).

For concreteness and simplicity, a utilitarian SWF will be employed. It will usually be obvious how the results generalize since most depend on the concavity of individuals' utility functions and a more concave SWF will tend to have implications similar to those of more concave utility functions (on which see section 3.B).

As noted, the SWF is taken to be individualistic, that is, a function of each individual's utility. Accordingly, in the present model, social welfare will be the sum of three individuals' utilities rather than the sum of some family utility function for the two-member family and the single individual's utility function. To be sure, with a utilitarian SWF there would be no difference as long as the family's utility function was taken to be the sum of the utilities of its two members. However, reduced-form family utility functions that may be used in other literatures to describe behavior need not and often do not take this form, so the present point is worth emphasizing.

As a simple illustration of the possible deviation between the two approaches, consider the case in which there is a de facto household dictator who determines the intrafamily allocation (such as in some of the examples that follow). This dictator's utility function will describe the family's behavior, but if this utility function were used in the SWF to represent the family's utility, a practice employed in some literature, the utility of other family members would thereby be excluded.[7] The present explicit approach of inserting each individual's utility into the SWF and maximizing the SWF constructed in this manner also differs from one that would define an equivalence scale and attempt, say, to equalize equivalent income across families.[8] It will become clear (most transparently in subsection 2 on economies of scale) that this alternative method is not tantamount to maximizing any standard SWF, except by coincidence. An important reason is that equivalence scales focus on utility levels whereas marginal utility is highly relevant (solely relevant for a utilitarian SWF) to optimal distribution, and with heterogeneous family types there is often a disjunction between utility levels and marginal

---

[7] Compare the discussion of gift externalities in subsection 10.A.2.a, especially note 10 on altruism, and the treatment of altruism in subsection 13.B.3.

[8] See, for example, Deaton and Muellbauer (1986) and Gronau (1988).

utility. For prior criticism of the use of equivalence scales for welfare analysis, see, for example, Pollak and Wales (1979).

Before proceeding with the analysis, it is helpful to have in mind a simple baseline scenario. Consider the case in which each person's utility as a function of consumption is the same, there are no economies of scale, there are no utility interdependencies, and the two-member family shares its allocation equally. The optimum clearly involves each person receiving an equal per capita share (which implies that $\omega = \frac{1}{2}$), an outcome that mirrors Edgeworth's (1897) egalitarian result for the case in which there are only single individuals (and, as assumed in this section, there are no incentive effects of redistribution). A familiar feature of this allocation is that resources, utilities, and marginal utilities are all equalized. By contrast, in the cases to be examined in which various of these baseline assumptions are relaxed, equal resources do not generally imply equal utilities, equal utilities do not generally imply equal marginal utilities, and the optimal distribution of resources does not ordinarily involve equating resources, utilities, or even marginal utilities (the latter because they may not be equated within the two-member family).

1. Unequal Sharing

Because social welfare depends on individuals' utilities and individuals' utility functions are strictly concave in consumption, unequal sharing of resources in the two-member family will adversely affect social welfare. Furthermore, the optimal allocation between the two-member family and the single individual (the optimal ω) may well depend on how sharing operates within the family. Indeed, the appropriate tax treatment of the family is thought by many to depend on whether or not resources are shared equally.[9]

---

[9] A common view is that unitary treatment of married couples is premised on equal sharing, so many who believe that sharing is in fact unequal favor treating married couples as two separate individuals for tax purposes. This view is problematic on its face because it seems more based on a metaphor (treat the couple as a family if and only if they behave as an idealized, equal-sharing family) than on how varying the sharing assumption affects the impact of the two different regimes on welfare. Notably, one needs to determine whether individualized or family treatment is more generous in the presence of unequal sharing, whether

To examine unequal sharing, modify the baseline scenario so that the two family members share resources in some fixed ratio. The first member's share is denoted by ϕ, taken without loss of generality to exceed ½ (and also to be less than 1). Social welfare is therefore equal to $u(\phi c) + u((1-\phi)c) + u(\omega c)$, the sum of the utilities of the two family members and of the single individual. Differentiating with respect to c (keeping in mind that ω is implicitly a function of c) yields the following condition for the utilitarian optimum:

$$\phi u'(\phi c) + (1-\phi)u'((1-\phi)c) = u'(\omega c). \tag{12.1}$$

This first-order condition, as one would expect, sets the sum of the two family members' marginal utilities from an additional dollar allocated to the two-member family (taking account of how much of the dollar each member actually will consume) equal to the marginal utility of an additional dollar allocated to the single individual. The first term on the left side indicates the benefit from the fraction ϕ of a dollar allocated to the family going to the first member, whose marginal utility reflects the consumption share ϕ. The second term likewise indicates the benefit from $1-\phi$ of a dollar going to the second member. The right side is the single individual's marginal utility of a dollar.

In general, it is indeterminate whether the optimal ω exceeds, equals, or is less than ½. On one hand, allocations to the family are less valuable because more of an incremental dollar goes to the member with the lower marginal utility. On the other hand, such allocations are more valuable because (starting from $\omega = ½$), the person with the highest marginal utility (of the three, including the single individual) thereby benefits. Which effect is greater depends on the curvature of the utility function, as will now be elaborated.

To explore this tradeoff concretely, it is helpful to consider the case in which each person (the two family members and the single individual) has the same constant-relative-risk-aversion utility function introduced in subsection 3.B.1, expression (3.3). It is then straightforward to show that the optimal ω is less than ½ (greater generosity to the family)

---

more or less generosity is optimal in light of unequal sharing, and how the different forms of treatment may themselves affect the intrafamily allocation of resources.

if and only if the coefficient of relative risk aversion exceeds 1. The claim is easiest to see in the threshold case in which the coefficient of relative risk aversion equals 1, which, as expression (3.3) indicates, is the case in which $u(c) = \ln c$. Then, $u'(c) = 1/c$, the left side of (12.1) equals $1/c + 1/c$ (that is, $2/c$), and the right side equals $1/\omega c$, so $\omega = \frac{1}{2}$.

The intuition relating the result to concavity is as follows. The more concave is the utility function, the more rapidly the marginal utility of consumption falls with consumption, so the greater is the extent to which the lowest-consumption individual's (member 2's) marginal utility exceeds that of the others, notably, that of the single individual. Accordingly, when the utility function is sufficiently concave, the inequality effect—the benefit of allocating more resources to family member 2—dominates. Note that this result holds even though the benefit to member 2 must be accomplished by giving even more resources to member 1, the individual with the lowest marginal utility of income.

Interestingly, in the high-concavity case, member 1—who would be the best-off individual even if resources were allocated between the family and the single individual in equal per capita shares ($\omega = \frac{1}{2}$)—is doubly rewarded by the optimal allocation ($\omega < \frac{1}{2}$): The two-member family receives additional resources on account of the inequality in sharing, and member 1 is assumed to consume a disproportionate share of the greater allotment. Note further that if the SWF were strictly concave rather than utilitarian, this effect would tend to be accentuated because the plight of member 2 would receive even greater weight. This phenomenon reflects the second-best nature of the problem, the government having been assumed to be unable to affect intrafamily allocations.

In the low-concavity case, the single individual would receive a higher per capita consumption allotment than would the family under a utilitarian SWF. A more concave SWF would, once again, relatively favor the family because member 2 is the least-well-off individual. Therefore, if the concavity of u is low, a utilitarian SWF would have $\omega > \frac{1}{2}$ (per capita resources favor the single individual), whereas a sufficiently concave SWF would have $\omega < \frac{1}{2}$ (per capita resources favor the family), illustrating that even the direction of optimal redistribution may depend on the SWF (a general possibility first raised in subsection 3.B.3).

The foregoing analysis stipulates a fixed sharing ratio, ϕ. If, instead, the share of the more advantaged member rises (falls) with available consumption, treatment of the two-member family should be less (more) generous than implied by expression (12.1) because the marginal dollar favors the advantaged member more (less) than does the average dollar, and it is the average (more precisely, the total) that determines individuals' marginal utilities of consumption.

A more complete analysis of unequal sharing requires that shares not merely be stipulated but rather determined from some model of intrafamily behavior, which would include an analysis of bargaining and how it may be influenced by changes in taxes and transfers. Some further variations in intrafamily allocations will be considered in subsections 3 and 4, but no comprehensive analysis that links to the literature on household behavior is attempted.[10]

2. Economies of Scale

It is commonly suggested that two can live cheaper than one (translation: two can live cheaper than two ones).[11] Furthermore, economies of scale are often thought to justify less generous (per capita) treatment of couples than of single individuals, for example, the practice in the United States that a married couple's tax liability typically exceeds the combined tax liability of two single individuals each of whom earns half the couple's income.

To analyze scale economies, return to the baseline scenario with equal sharing and suppose that the two-member family's consumption

---

[10] Surveys of household behavior include Behrman (1997) and Bergstrom (1997). Note that when family structure is taken to be endogenous, the tax treatment of single individuals may affect intrafamily sharing because such treatment affects family members' outside options. This interaction further complicates the family taxation problem because of the benefits of influencing intrafamily sharing, which affects social welfare but cannot be set directly by the government.

[11] As will be discussed further in subsection B.2.a with regard to family formation, the abstract analysis in the text does not indicate whether the two-person family is a married couple, cohabiting individuals in a long-term personal relationship, or two individuals who share housing merely to save resources. Due to differing levels of trust and commonalities in preferences, it may be that the extent of scale economies varies among such household types (see Pollak 1985).

c is effectively worth $\beta(c) > c$. That is, each family member's utility is $u(\beta(c)/2)$. For concreteness, consider first the linear case: $\beta(c) = \beta c$, where $\beta > 1$. The first-order condition for the utilitarian optimum is:

$$\beta u'(\beta c/2) = u'(\omega c). \tag{12.2}$$

On the left side, the leading β indicates that a marginal dollar is worth more to the two-member family than to the single individual, which favors more generous treatment of the family (see Kondor 1975). On the other hand, because the argument of u' is $\beta c/2$ rather than simply $c/2$ and, moreover, $\beta > 1$, the marginal utility per unit of effective consumption for the family is lower than that for the single individual, which favors less generous treatment of the family. (This latter effect corresponds to conventional wisdom on the subject.)[12]

It is straightforward to show that whether the optimal ω exceeds, equals, or is less than $\frac{1}{2}$ depends simply on whether the relative risk aversion of u (evaluated at $\beta c/2$) exceeds, equals, or is less than 1. Just as in the case of unequal sharing, the point is illustrated by the threshold case in which the coefficient of relative risk aversion equals 1, so $u(c) = \ln c$ and thus $u'(c) = 1/c$. The left side of (12.2) equals $2/c$ and the right side equals $1/\omega c$, so $\omega = \frac{1}{2}$.

The intuition is that, when concavity is high, the reduction in each family member's marginal utility of effective consumption due to the higher standard of living achieved on account of scale economies exceeds the benefit that each actual dollar is translated into β effective dollars. Relatedly, a more concave SWF will relatively favor the single individual. Therefore, just as in the case with unequal sharing, it is possible that the direction of redistribution will depend on the concavity of the SWF. However, the results in the present case are reversed: Here, low concavity (of the utility function and of the SWF) favors a greater allocation to the family and high concavity favors giving relatively more to the single individual.

The case with economies of scale also demonstrates very directly how the pattern of resources, of utilities, and of marginal utilities may differ

---

[12] Compare the tradeoff examined in Sheshinski and Weiss (1982) regarding whether families will allocate more or fewer resources to their more able children.

from each other. For example, when $\omega = \frac{1}{2}$ is optimal, resources are equal per capita, the utilities of each member of the two-person family exceed that of the single individual, and the marginal utility of a dollar (but not that of an effective dollar) is equated between the family members and the single individual. If $\omega > \frac{1}{2}$ is optimal (less generosity to the family), per capita resources favor the single individual, the utilities of each family member are nevertheless higher than that of the single individual, and the marginal utility of a dollar (although not of an effective dollar) is equated.

Consider briefly nonlinear scale economies. In the first-order condition (12.2), the first factor becomes $\beta'(c)$ rather than the constant β: The marginal scale economy effect determines how efficiently the family converts an additional dollar into an effective unit of consumption, but the extent to which each family member's marginal utility of effective consumption is reduced depends on the average (total) effect, $\beta(c)/2$. For example, if marginal scale economies fall with income, the ratio of the marginal effect to the average effect will fall with income, implying that ω should rise with income—that is, relative generosity toward the family should fall with income.[13]

3. Intrafamily Transfer Motives

In the preceding two subsections, the family's allocation was taken to be divided between its two members according to stipulated shares. No reference was made to how that decision is determined. This division is not ordinarily made (and here it is assumed cannot be made) by the government. Nor is it the case that each family member's consumption is wholly dictated by what he or she earns, net of any taxes paid to or transfers received from the government. Spouses usually share income to some extent, and children receive transfers from parents. Intrafamily transfers require some motivation, and whatever the underlying impulse, the existence of sharing suggests the presence of interdependencies and interactions among family members that may be relevant in assessing social welfare.

---

[13] For evidence that scale economies rise with income, see, for example, Donaldson and Pendakur (2003) and Koulovatianos, Schröder, and Schmidt (2005).

As noted briefly in chapter 10 on the taxation of voluntary transfers, there is a close connection between that subject and taxation of the family given that a significant portion of transfers are among family members. Accordingly, it is natural to revisit the motivations for intrafamily transfers that were examined in section 10.B. There, the purpose was to see how the optimal tax or subsidy on identified transfers depends on transfer motives. Here, by contrast, it is assumed that transfers are not observed.[14] Nevertheless, the distribution among families is to be optimized in light of the intrafamily transfers that are understood to occur and the motives that produce them.

a. Altruism. Suppose first that each family member is altruistic toward the other. Specifically, family member i's total utility is given by $u_i + \psi_i u_j$, $i \neq j$, where ψ_i is the strength of member i's altruism toward member j. Beginning with the case of equal sharing, the family's total utility entering into the utilitarian SWF will be $(1 + \psi_2)u(c/2) + (1 + \psi_1)u(c/2)$. The social first-order condition is:

$$\left(1 + \frac{\psi_1 + \psi_2}{2}\right)u'(c/2) = u'(\omega c).$$ (12.3)

The optimal allocation is more favorable to the family ($\omega < \frac{1}{2}$) to an extent that increases with the degree of altruism. (As one would expect from the analysis of prior cases, the extent of the added generosity is lower as the concavity of utility is higher.) The intuition, like that in the examination of unidirectional altruism in subsection 10.B.1, is that each individual's own-consumption generates utility both for him- or herself and also for the other family member.[15]

---

[14] In practice, exceptionally large transfers, transfers to individuals no longer part of the immediate family (including grown children), and bequests are most likely to be observable whereas routine intrafamily transfers, some of which are implicit in the sharing of capital goods, are probably the most difficult to measure. To that extent, the present chapter can be seen as addressed to the latter case (involving what may be viewed as a sort of presumptive taxation or subsidy on intrafamily transfers), and chapter 10 on estate and gift taxation can be understood as applicable to the former. See also note 4 in chapter 10.

[15] See note 10 in subsection 10.A.2 and subsection 13.B.3 on the concern that this statement entails some inappropriate sort of double counting.

Equal sharing may not, however, prevail, and in particular it is worth inquiring what sharing rule is implied by altruism. Suppose that shares are chosen to maximize total family welfare, in the spirit of Samuelson (1956). In the family's optimization problem, the first-order condition equates the aggregate marginal utility of a unit of consumption to each member: $(1+\psi_2)u'(\phi c) = (1+\psi_1)u'((1-\phi)c)$. When the expression for social welfare is differentiated with respect to c and the appropriate substitution is made from this first-order condition, one of the equivalent ways to express the first-order condition for social welfare maximization is

$$(1+\psi_2)u'(\phi c) = u'(\omega c). \tag{12.4}$$

(The parameter ψ_1 implicitly enters, in a manner that proves to be symmetric, through the determination of ϕ in the family's first-order condition.) It can be demonstrated that, as one would expect, greater altruism favors more generosity toward the family ($\omega < \frac{1}{2}$). (This result is easiest to see when $\psi_1 = \psi_2 > 0$, in which case $\phi = \frac{1}{2}$, which clearly requires that $\omega < \frac{1}{2}$.)

Suppose instead that shares are chosen to maximize the welfare of family member 1, who alone is altruistic, as in Becker (1974). In this case, the optimal treatment depends on the intensity of member 1's altruism. When $\psi_1 = 1$, that is, when member 1 gives equal weight to his or her own utility and that of member 2, equal sharing will result, a special case of when equal sharing was stipulated (that is, the case reflected in expression (12.3), with $\psi_1 = 1$ and $\psi_2 = 0$), wherein more generous treatment of the family ($\omega < \frac{1}{2}$) is optimal. For lower values of ψ_1, the result is more complex. Like the cases of unequal sharing examined in subsection 1, greater generosity toward the family results in a majority of the additional resources going to member 1, who already has consumption in excess of the social optimum, but the resources going to member 2 are particularly valuable because of his or her higher marginal utility of consumption—and here, also because the gains to member 2 will augment the utility of member 1. However, one must also account for the fact that member 2's share will depend on the two-member family's allocation.

b. Utility from sharing per se. Suppose that member 1 (a parent) views transfers to member 2 (a child) as a form of direct personal consumption so that member 1's utility is given by $u(\phi c) + v((1-\phi)c)$, where v indicates the consumption benefit of the transfer (which here is assumed to constitute the totality of member 2's resources). The social first-order condition—for the case in which, for simplicity, ϕ is independent of c—is

$$\phi u'(\phi c) + (1-\phi)v'((1-\phi)c) + (1-\phi)u'((1-\phi)c) = u'(\omega c). \qquad (12.5)$$

This condition differs from expression (12.1), for the simple case of unequal sharing, on account of the additional term, $(1-\phi)v'((1-\phi)c)$, on the left side, which implies that the optimal allocation in this case will be more generous toward the family.[16] This result depends on the assumption that member 1's utility from own-consumption, $u(\phi c)$, is the same as that of a single individual with the same level of consumption, which need not be the case (one can imagine that it would be higher or lower).

To further explore the subject of transfers as sharing, consider the case in which (at the personally maximizing allocation ϕ, taken here to be a fixed share of the family's resources) member 1 receives the same utility as would a single individual who had the family's total resources. That is, member 1's utility is $u(c)$. (This utility implicitly depends on ϕ; transfers to member 2 can be analogized to expenditures on a second commodity, and $u(c)$ for member 1 denotes the utility achieved when c is allocated optimally between own-consumption and transfers to member 2.) Perhaps the single individual would spend additional resources on entertainment rather than on a child; the assumption here is that (when consumption is allocated optimally by each) the parent's incremental expenditures on a child would augment the parent's utility by the same amount as would the single individual's incremental expenditures on entertainment. The social first-order condition for this case is

$$u'(c) + (1-\phi)u'((1-\phi)c) = u'(\omega c). \qquad (12.6)$$

---

[16] This implication can also be seen from the fact that member 1's optimal choice of ϕ satisfies the first-order condition $u' = v'$. Accordingly, the first two terms on the left side of (12.5) together equal $u'(\phi c)$, which replaces $\phi u'(\phi c)$ in expression (12.1) for the simpler case of unequal sharing.

The optimal allocation is clearly such that $\omega < 1$, which implies that family member 1 will be better off than the single individual. For further illumination, recall again from expression (3.3) the case of constant relative risk aversion where the coefficient of relative risk aversion equals 1. Then $u(c) = \ln c$, and $u'(c) = 1/c$, so the left side of (12.6) equals $1/c + 1/c$ (that is, $2/c$), and the right side equals $1/\omega c$, so $\omega = \frac{1}{2}$. When the risk aversion coefficient is greater (less) than 1, the social optimum is such that $\omega < \frac{1}{2}$ when ϕ is high (low) and $\omega > \frac{1}{2}$ when ϕ is low (high). The intuition is that when, say, the concavity of utility is high and ϕ is high, the dominant factor is the benefit of increasing consumption to family member 2, so the optimal allocation to the family is generous. The present case can be viewed as involving a combination of unequal sharing (to a greater degree when ϕ is high) and a sort of scale economies (to a greater extent when ϕ is low), the latter because resources given to member 2 count twice in social welfare. Furthermore, recall that high concavity has opposite implications for optimal generosity toward the family in these two cases, favoring greater generosity when sharing is more unequal but favoring less generosity when scale economies are greater.

    c. Exchange. Assume that member 1 controls the family's resources and gives a share to member 2 in exchange for some services. As in the preceding case, member 1's utility may be given by $u(\phi c) + v((1 - \phi)c)$, where v now indicates the consumption benefit that is received in exchange from member 2. Accordingly, the analysis for this case may appear to be no different.

    A distinction does arise, however, if one takes into account the effort that member 2 must exert to perform the services, taken to be a form of labor effort, which is generally being ignored in this section. For purely distributive purposes, this source of disutility would be relevant to the extent that it affected member 2's marginal utility of consumption. With a strictly concave rather than utilitarian SWF, the effect of labor effort on member 2's utility level also would matter.

4. Children

As indicated at the outset, one interpretation of the two-member family is that member 1 is a representative parent and member 2 a representative child, so in many respects the effect of children on optimal distribution has already been addressed. When one family member is a child, however, it seems particularly appropriate to consider the case in which member 2's utility function differs, specifically by requiring fewer resources to achieve a given level of utility. (For example, clothing may be less expensive, needs for space lower, and simple pleasures more appealing.) Specifically, assume that member 2's utility is given by $u((1-\phi)c/\zeta)$, where $\zeta < 1$. Member 1, taken as a representative adult, continues (as in the benchmark scenario) to have the same utility function and thus to achieve the same level of utility for a given level of consumption as does the single individual.

First, consider a case where the family's sharing equalizes the utility levels of the two family members. This requirement implies that $\phi = 1/(1+\zeta)$. The first-order condition for social welfare maximization is

$$\frac{2}{1+\zeta}u'\left(\frac{c}{1+\zeta}\right) = u'(\omega c). \tag{12.7}$$

Because $\zeta < 1$, the leading component on the left side of expression (12.7) exceeds 1. Accordingly, it must be that the optimum entails $1/(1+\zeta) > \omega$. Furthermore, because $\phi = 1/(1+\zeta)$, we have $\phi > \omega$. That is, consumption and thus the utility of family member 1 exceeds that of the single individual. Recalling that family members 1 and 2 have the same utility level as each other, we can see that the optimal distribution entails that both family members are better off than is the single individual. This result arises because member 2 is a more efficient generator of utility.

The present case is analogous to that with economies of scale: Here, they are realized only by member 2, but due to the posited intrafamily sharing rule, their benefits are implicitly shared with member 1. Recall that with scale economies, although it is not necessarily true that $\omega < \frac{1}{2}$ at the optimum, it is nevertheless true that the family members enjoy a higher utility level than does the single individual. Furthermore, as with scale economies, the concavity of the utility function is relevant to the socially optimal distribution: The greater is the degree of concavity, the more the family members' diminishing marginal utility opposes the efficiency effect, so the less is the relative generosity toward the family.

Second, suppose instead that the family's allocation maximizes the sum of their utilities, which entails equating (effective) marginal utilities rather than utility levels. This intrafamily allocation will be relatively more advantageous to member 2 compared to the preceding case because, at the point at which members 1 and 2 have equal utility levels, member 2's effective marginal utility is greater by a factor of $1/\zeta$, which exceeds one, reflecting member 2's relative marginal efficiency in producing utility. After substituting the family's first-order condition for its own utility maximization problem into the first-order condition for the social optimization, the result is

$$u'(\phi c) = u'(\omega c). \qquad (12.8)$$

This result obviously implies that, at the socially optimal distribution of resources, $\phi = \omega$, that is, that the resources and thus the utility levels of family member 1 and the single individual are equated. Member 2's utility will, of course, be greater. The intuition is as follows: The family equates each member's marginal utility of resources. The social authority equates the marginal utility of a dollar to the family—which at the family's optimum equals the marginal utility of either member—to the marginal utility of the single individual. Hence, in this case the marginal utilities of all individuals are equated, but their total utilities (and their resource allotments) are not.

The two foregoing cases suggest that, on distributive grounds, the optimal allotment to a family unit should be significantly greater if there are children, ceteris paribus, unless the children are such efficient utility generators that they can be brought to the same utility level as adults with negligible additional resources. (That is, in the prior two cases, $\omega \leq \phi$, so unless ϕ is near 1, the single individual should not receive nearly as many resources as the adult who also has a child.[17]) In practice,

---

[17] Observe that a natural benchmark in the present case with children is $\omega = \phi$ (the single individual's allocation equals what is consumed by the adult family member) rather than $\omega = \frac{1}{2}$ because a child is not on a par with an adult. Also note that the caveat in the text regarding the child who is a highly efficient utility generator is inapplicable in the second case (when the family's allocation maximizes rather than equalizes the members' utilities) if the concavity of the utility function is very low; in that case, even when ζ is very low, the family will allocate a high share to the child (because marginal utility falls slowly, the child's greater efficiency in consumption is dominant), so the requirement that $\omega = \phi$ in this case implies that the single individual's optimal allotment is still significantly below that of the family.

the tax adjustments for children in most countries are relatively modest, although transfer programs aimed at the poor reflect more substantial relative generosity in the presence of children. In assessing this question, however, government expenditures on goods and services should be taken into account (see chapter 8); free or highly subsidized public education involves a substantial allocation of resources toward families with children.

5. Distributive Shares as a Function of Income

The model employed in this section considers a pure distribution problem between a two-person family and a single individual, abstracting from different initial income levels, among other things. Although direct consideration of differences in earning ability and thus income is deferred to subsection B.1, it is worth noting that the qualitative results in this section are largely independent of income levels (that is, of the level of resources C to be allocated). For example, in the case of fixed, unequal sharing or linear economies of scale, whether ω exceeds, equals, or is less than ½ in the optimal allocation depends only on whether the coefficient of relative risk aversion exceeds, equals, or is less than 1, and thus is entirely independent of C in the case of a constant-relative-risk-aversion utility function. Likewise, the conclusions that more generous treatment of the family is optimal in basic cases of altruism and when children are more efficient utility generators do not depend on the level of C.

To further explore how these results depend on the level of resources, consider again constant-relative-risk-aversion utility functions (see expression (3.3)). In that case, virtually all of the social first-order conditions that determine the level of ω (and not merely, for example, whether it exceeds ½) can be shown to be independent of c and thus of C.[18]

---

[18] The only exception is condition (12.5), for the first subcase involving utility from sharing per se, which contains the term $(1-\phi)\upsilon'((1-\phi)c)$. If the functional form of υ is of the same type (constant relative risk aversion), then this condition is also independent of c. (It is not immediately obvious that condition (12.4) is independent of c for this case because ϕ in that expression depends on the family's optimization; however, in their optimization problem, it turns out that ϕ is also independent of c.)

Accordingly, the relative degree to which the family or the single individual should be favored does not in these simple cases depend on whether rich or poor families are involved. This independence, however, does not hold in general, as noted, for example, in the case in which sharing is a function of income.

To the extent that the optimal distribution across family types is independent of resource levels, it seems to be in tension with the fact that many tax systems provide adjustments that are constant in absolute amount or even phased out as income rises (for example, in the United States), rather than constituting, say, a fixed proportion of income. As explained in the introduction, such adjustments need not raise concerns about revenue or ordinary ("vertical") distributive matters as is sometimes suggested, for one can adjust the relative treatment of different types of families by increasing generosity to some and decreasing it to others, in a manner that is both revenue neutral and ordinary-distribution neutral. Whether this possible divergence between potentially optimal and typically provided treatment of families can be rationalized on incentive grounds is a central subject of the next section.

B. Incentives

In most of the analysis to follow, it is assumed that taxation optimally depends on family structure for distributive reasons, although for the most part the particular dependency and its basis need not be specified. The question addressed is how distributive and incentive considerations should be combined. Labor effort and endogenous family structure will be examined separately; presumably, the optimal scheme will reflect some sort of compromise among the pertinent results.

1. Labor Effort

a. One-worker families. Consider families with only one (potential) worker. This case is of direct interest and also provides insight into the more complex case in which there are two (potential) workers. To analyze this problem, it is helpful to recall the modification of the first-order condition introduced in subsection 5.C.1 on ability taxation and employed in section 7.C to examine categorical tax and transfer schemes. That modification, contained in expression (5.1) (for the simplified case without income effects), allowed the distribution and density functions, F and f, to vary across groups, indexed by the variable θ. Here, the variable θ can be taken to indicate the number of adults in a household, the number of children, or any combination thereof. In the present context, it is necessary to introduce a further generalization in which utility functions also may depend on θ. For this case, the re-expressed first-order condition is

$$\frac{T'(w^* l^*, \theta)}{1 - T'(w^* l^*, \theta)} = \frac{1 - F(w^*, \theta)}{\xi^*(\theta) w^* f(w^*, \theta)} \cdot \frac{\int\limits_{w^*}^{\infty} \left(1 - \frac{W'(u(w, \theta)) u_c(\theta)}{\lambda}\right) f(w, \theta) dw}{1 - F(w^*, \theta)}.$$

(12.9)

Note that when the utility function may depend on θ, it also follows that the labor supply elasticity and hence ξ^* depends on θ as well.[19]

Now suppose that the worker chooses labor effort and shares after-tax earnings so as to maximize total family utility and that the SWF is utilitarian. Accordingly, although the worker's labor effort is distorted by the marginal tax rate, T', just as in the standard optimal income tax problem, there are no further complications.[20] For each type of family (one-worker families with, say, different numbers of children, and also single individuals), corresponding to a value of θ, the first-order condition (12.9) will be applicable. The function u in this expression can be

---

[19] Note that θ could also vary by age (both that of adults, to allow different rates for the elderly, and that of children, since infants, younger children, and teenagers may have different utility functions). Furthermore, as noted in earlier chapters, u could depend on other characteristics, such as physical disabilities. Indeed, disabilities might be analyzed similarly to economies of scale in subsection A.2, except that one would not vary the number of members in the household and it would be natural to consider cases in which $\beta < 1$ (so that more rather than less disposable income is required to achieve a given utility level).

[20] The analysis of labor effort throughout subsection 1 ignores that there may be an externality involving dependents, as discussed in subsection 7.D.3. This externality arises, recall, because even altruistic parents do not value the targets of their altruism to the same extent as society does when the SWF is individualistic (see subsections 10.A.2.a and 13.B.3).

taken as the sum of utilities in the family and u_c as the increment to total family utility as total family consumption is increased.

Differences in u were the focus of section A. Suppose that there are two types of families and that one of them, at a given c, has a higher total marginal utility per dollar, u_c (it does not much matter which types of families or for what reason). Ignoring other factors, if this difference would be eliminated by a constant adjustment to disposable income, independent of the initial level of consumption, the optimum would have tax schedules that differed only in their grant, which difference would be fully compensatory. That is, if earnings and marginal tax rates at all incomes were the same, the different types of families would have the same total marginal utility.

As subsection A.5 indicates, however, it seems plausible that the absolute amount of any adjustment would vary with disposable income. For concreteness, suppose that the family type with higher marginal utility requires a constant proportion of earnings (rather than a constant absolute amount) as a supplement to reach the point of equal marginal utility. To achieve such a result, it would be necessary to reduce that type of family's marginal tax rate by the same amount at each level of earnings.[21] Such an adjustment, however, is unlikely to be optimal. Examining expression (12.9), under the stated assumptions the integral in the second term would be equal across the two groups at each level of earnings, as would all of the other terms on the right side (for the moment, adhering to the ceteris paribus assumption). But the left sides would, under the posited assumption, differ systematically, being lower at every level of earnings for the favored group that is subject to the schedule with lower marginal tax rates. This suggests, very crudely, that the optimum in this case would tend to involve an adjustment of marginal rates in the direction suggested, but not to an extent that fully

---

[21] A more plausible, although still artificial, example would require that disposable income (rather than earnings) be increased by a constant fraction in order to equalize marginal utilities. This would require a proportionately higher grant in addition to a reduction in marginal tax rates at each level of income, the combined effect of which would be to raise the net-of-tax earnings rate by the same proportion (an adjustment that would differ from that described in the text unless the preexisting tax schedule were linear). The simpler version in the text is employed for expositional convenience.

equalizes the two family types' marginal utilities (at a given ability level)—that is, there would be a compromise between optimal distribution by family type and the otherwise optimal mix of labor incentives and ordinary (vertical) distributive concerns. This heuristic argument provides an intuitive explanation for the result in Cremer, Dellis, and Pestieau (2003) that, if families with different numbers of children are each subject to separate linear income tax schedules, families with more children should be subject to lower marginal tax rates.

These simple examples suggest that different tax schedules, including possibly different grants and marginal rates, may be optimal for different family types on account of the sorts of distributive considerations examined in section A. Typically, one would expect that the optimal adjustments will provide incomplete compensation because they will require a departure from the otherwise second-best optimal tax schedule (although this is not necessarily the case, as indicated by the first example in which grant adjustments alone would suffice). Other bases for adjustment include those previously examined in section 7.C: If F and f differ across families, both grants and marginal rates will be affected. Also, as alluded to previously, when utility functions differ, ξ^* may differ as well, although no obvious pattern can be identified.[22]

A complete analysis of the problem would also have to address the initial simplifying assumptions. If the individual choosing labor effort is maximizing his or her own utility and not that of the family, then the distortion caused by marginal tax rates is not the only wedge between the private and social optima. For example, lowering marginal tax rates

---

[22] It might appear that the substitution effect and thus the compensated labor supply elasticity would be larger for families with higher need, say, families with more children, reflected in a higher u_c. When a given level of disposable income is shared among more people, individuals are each at earlier points on their utility curves and thus have higher marginal utilities. For standard utility functions, however, the magnitude of u_{cc}, which appears in the denominator of the substitution effect, is also greater. To illustrate, for a constant-relative-risk-aversion utility function (with separable disutility of labor effort), the ratio cu_{cc}/u_c is constant, so it does not seem that any systematic effect of this sort of difference in utility on the substitution effect can be readily predicted. (The relationship between substitution effects, income effects, and the curvature of the utility function is explored further in Chetty (2006).)

relative to what would be optimal in the single-individual case, by raising work effort, may increase the amount of consumption allocated to other family members who are given more weight in the SWF than in the individual decision-maker's utility function. On the other hand, higher grants may be optimal for similar reasons, which may require higher marginal tax rates (assuming that the cost of the higher grants is not funded entirely by other groups). Furthermore, if the SWF was strictly concave rather than utilitarian, one could not simply add family members' utilities but would instead have to treat each member's utility separately, which would alter the distributive prescriptions in section A, as previously discussed, and may introduce a further disparity between working individuals' and society's maximands.

   b. Two-worker families. For family units with two (potential) workers, the preceding analysis of incentives must be supplemented. Setting aside the now more complicated problem of who is (are) the decision-maker(s) in the family and what is the (their) maximand(s), we confine attention to the case in which both workers' labor effort is chosen jointly, along with the intrafamily sharing rule, to maximize the sum of family members' utilities (and assume again that the SWF is utilitarian). The primary additional complication in this case is that the elasticity term, ξ^*, in expression (12.9) will now refer to a weighted average elasticity. If, as will be explored further, primary earners have similar elasticities to those of single individuals and second earners have higher elasticities, optimal marginal tax rates on two-(potential)-worker families would seem to be lower than those on single-worker families (and, due to the resulting reduction in marginal utilities of consumption, optimal grants would be lower as well). Implicit in this framework is that the tax schedule, $T(wl,\theta)$, is taken to be a function of the family's combined income.[23]

   An alternative, analyzed and advocated by many analysts and reflected in many countries' tax systems, is that each worker be subject to a separate tax schedule (so-called individual filing). This system represents a

---

[23] The interpretation of the argument wl must be amended; income refers to total income, so w might be interpreted as a weighted average wage and l as total labor effort.

special case of the more general formulation $T(w_1 l_1, w_2 l_2, \theta)$, that is, a tax schedule that may depend on each worker's earnings, considered independently.[24] The feasibility of such individualized schemes requires that earned income for each family member can be distinctly observed, which seems plausible except primarily for cases with jointly operated family businesses.[25]

Separate schedules are thought to be efficient because of the generally believed empirical proposition that second earners in married couples have a higher labor supply elasticity, which makes it optimal to employ lower marginal tax rates. Some of the evidence was presented in subsection 5.A.1, which also discussed caveats, including Blau and Kahn's (2007) finding that married women's labor supply elasticities have fallen substantially in recent decades, their labor supply behavior in many respects converging toward that of married men. In addition, if married women with higher elasticities also have lower wages, there is a countervailing effect: The denominator of the first-order condition (12.9) contains both the elasticity and the wage rate.

Boskin and Sheshinski (1983) analyze this problem and present simulations suggesting that optimal marginal tax rates on second earners should perhaps be only half to a third as high as those on primary earners. A pertinent aspect of the problem is the extent to which the two spouses' abilities (wage rates) are correlated—that is, the extent of assortative mating by skill level. Boskin and Sheshinski assume a close connection, which one supposes helps explain their results because raising the marginal tax rate on the first earner's income and lowering the rate on the second's, in contributing to efficiency, does not detract much from ordinary (vertical) redistribution (see also Apps and Rees 1999).

In considering the argument for differential rates on account of differences in labor supply elasticities, it is important to investigate why the elasticities differ, for these reasons may bear on optimal tax treatment.[26]

---

[24] Solving this general problem is technically challenging because it involves multidimensional screening. For preliminary analysis, see Kleven, Kreiner, and Saez (2006).

[25] Other problems of separate filing concern the attribution of permitted deductions and unearned income (notably, from savings), where manipulation may be easier to undertake.

[26] In addition to the factors considered in section A that influence family members' utility functions, including interdependencies, and also whatever factors may underlie intrafamily

The matter has been little explored. It may be that second earners' higher elasticity is due primarily to the participation decision (where nonparticipation is more of an option in two-earner families), when fixed costs are often assumed to be present. However, the high prevalence of part-time work, including among second earners, raises questions about the extent to which this is the dominant explanation.[27] Additionally, the presence of fixed costs does not have clear implications for the elasticity. Differences in labor supply elasticities could also reflect different preferences (whether innate, a product of socialization, or due to specialization in child care), but no such simple explanation suffices because different degrees of utility from leisure do not in a straightforward manner imply different elasticities.[28]

Another explanation may derive from the existence of differential earning abilities in a context with intrafamily sharing, making note of the fact that sharing creates a link between the family members' marginal utilities of consumption. Suppose, for example, that a two-earner couple jointly chooses each member's labor effort, l_1 and l_2, and allocates consumption between them to maximize the sum of identical utility functions, each a function of the respective member's consumption allocation and labor effort.[29] Furthermore, assume that $w_1 > w_2$ and that both members are subject to the same marginal tax rate. Observe that there will be an advantage to the higher-ability member working relatively

---

sharing rules (which, construing the intrafamily bargaining process more comprehensively, include rules about labor supply to the market and to home production), the household formation process (see subsection 2) may also be relevant.

[27] Blundell et al. (1999) indicate that part-time employment at all levels is very common for both single mothers and women in couples in the United Kingdom. In addition, Blundell and Walker (2002) present evidence for the United Kingdom that a substantial proportion of child care obtained by single parents involves the use of friends and relatives and that the marginal cost of child care rises with hours of work, as cheaper forms of child care are exhausted first.

[28] Compare the discussion in subsection 5.C.2 of heterogeneous preferences for consumption or labor effort.

[29] As mentioned in note 6 of chapter 11, this problem is formally similar to that of a single individual choosing labor supply in different time periods when wages vary; accordingly, the life-cycle labor supply analysis in, for example, Heckman (1974) and MaCurdy (1981) is informative. The heuristic argument in the text parallels that in subsection 11.A.2.

harder than the other: Beginning at $l_1 = l_2$, slightly raising l_1 and lowering l_2 by the same amount would cause no direct first-order loss in the sum of utilities on account of the disutility of labor effort but would raise c.

These factors suggest that the labor supply elasticity of the high-wage, high-labor-supply spouse (member 1) will be lower. Suppose, on the contrary, that a given percentage increase in the net-of-tax wage would cause the same percentage (uncompensated) labor supply response by each family member. Given that the two members' marginal utilities of consumption are equated as a result of sharing, any differential effect on the members' marginal utilities of consumption will be due to a difference in the change in disposable income, which has two components: the change in net-of-tax wage multiplied by the level of labor effort and the change in labor effort multiplied by the net-of-tax wage. Under the stipulation of equal (uncompensated) elasticities, all of these components are smaller for the lower-wage member. (Recall that this member's labor effort is initially lower; in addition, the two change components refer to equal percentage changes and hence smaller absolute changes.) Because disposable income rises less when the second member's wage rises by a given percentage, the marginal utility of income falls by a smaller amount. This consideration implies that this member's labor effort must increase relatively more to restore the first-order condition.[30] Recall, however, that even supposing that member 2's elasticity is higher, this elasticity is multiplied in the first-order condition (12.9) by the wage rate, which here is stipulated to be lower. Hence, if this is the explanation for differing elasticities, it does not have the ordinarily supposed implication regarding optimal differential income tax rates.

Finally, suppose that it does turn out to be optimal to apply a schedule with lower marginal tax rates on secondary earners, defined here as

---

[30] If this analysis underlies the observed difference in elasticities, elasticity differences should increase with the difference in earning abilities, which in turn is correlated with the difference in spouses' incomes. Note that there are other possible influences. (For example, because the two members begin at a different level of labor effort and, from a counterfactual point of equal elasticities, have labor supply responses that differ in magnitude (versus percentage), it is possible that there will be differences on account of the degree of change in the disutility of labor effort. In a simple case with additively separable utility and the disutility of labor effort proportional to the square of effort, the pertinent second derivative is constant, and it can be shown that the effects mentioned in the text make up the complete story.)

those with a lower ability (wage) and (unless the tax rate is much lower and the labor supply elasticity is very high) lower earnings. Merely providing for separate filing does not necessarily accomplish this result, much less to the optimal extent. For example, if the income tax schedule is linear and separate filers pay the same marginal tax rate as joint filers, there is no efficiency effect of separate filing. It is commonly supposed that separate filing produces lower marginal rates on second earners because it is imagined that the tax schedules would have graduated rates, although the analysis in chapter 4 reveals that there is no presumption that optimal marginal tax rates rise with income. Indeed, optimal marginal rates may fall, in which case separate schedules would result in a higher marginal rate being applicable to the second earner—assuming that the marginal rate applicable to each member's earnings is the rate applicable to twice the earnings on the joint schedule. (And, as noted in chapter 7, marginal rates inclusive of phase-outs do fall at low levels of income.) If, however, separate schedules were consciously designed with the foregoing efficiency argument in mind, one could apply higher marginal rates to primary earners and lower marginal rates to secondary earners, each compared to the otherwise optimal marginal rates if joint income was subject to a single schedule.[31]

2. Endogenous Family Structure

a. Marriage. As suggested in subsection 7.C.3, when different categories of individuals are subject to different tax and transfer schedules,

---

[31] The greater the difference in marginal tax rates between two spouses, the larger will be the distortion in their relative labor supply, which reduces the optimal extent of differentiation. For example, in Schroyen's (2003) two-type model, spouses' efforts devoted to household production are perfect substitutes, so a couple with two high-earning spouses may have an incentive for one spouse to reduce market labor supply to benefit from lower taxes, making up the difference by producing more at home, while the other spouse increases market labor effort. Note, however, that for many purposes household production need not be considered explicitly: A general specification for how various combinations of each spouse's leisure (in combination with consumption purchases in the market) are converted into utility can equivalently be interpreted as involving household production as an intermediate step or as reflecting a direct translation of leisure into ultimate utility. A complication does arise, however, if individuals vary not only in earning ability but also in household production ability (see Apps and Rees 1999).

categorization may be endogenous. Tax treatment that is more or less generous to different types of families creates incentives for family formation and dissolution. For many tax systems, the pertinent rewards or penalties pertain to marriage and divorce, although tax systems can depend on any type of family arrangement, including various forms of cohabitation (which at various times and places has been considered relevant under transfer programs).

One way that some systems influence incentives for marriage is by employing income splitting: treating a couple with differential earnings as if each member earned half the total. Such a scheme reduces taxes when rates are graduated (which they often are in developed countries for middle- and upper-income taxpayers) but raises taxes in the reverse situation (which arises for low-income individuals when there are high phaseouts of transfer programs followed by a range of lower marginal tax rates).[32] Independently, marriage is penalized when higher taxes are levied on married couples, often rationalized by the existence of economies of scale.

The analysis in section A, although not providing a clear justification for existing systems, does provide a number of reasons why it may be optimal on distributive grounds to treat some family types more generously than others. Only by a most unlikely coincidence would all the factors net to zero at all income levels for all family configurations. Accordingly, a scheme that is ideal on distributive grounds is likely to influence marriage decisions.

Because inducing changes in decisions that otherwise would be privately optimal is ordinarily inefficient, this consideration tends to favor reducing differentiation from the level suggested by the analysis in section A to an extent that depends on the pertinent elasticity.[33] In the present context, however, the possibility that marriage and divorce entail externalities, especially in the presence of children, needs to be considered. For example, positive externalities to marriage would, ceteris paribus,

---

[32] As noted just before, some of these features may not be optimal. In any event, neither effect should be assumed to be inherent in income splitting.

[33] For a survey of empirical evidence on the effect of tax and transfer programs on marriage decisions, see Alm, Dickert-Conlin, and Whittington (1999).

justify more favorable treatment to an extent that also depends on the elasticity of response (here, a higher elasticity might favor greater differentiation) and on the magnitude of the externality.[34]

b. Procreation. Taxation that depends on the number of children in a family influences incentives for procreation (and, more broadly, for adoption and other forms of taking in dependents who are recognized by the tax system).[35] Most tax and transfer schemes are more generous (in absolute rather than per capita or other terms) toward larger families, the magnitude of generosity often being relatively larger for low-income individuals eligible for transfer programs. The analysis in section A suggests that significant family size adjustments might be optimal on distributive grounds.

Once again, if one indulges the usual presumption that taxation should not alter private behavior, the implication is that the degree of generosity should be mitigated to an extent that reflects the procreation elasticity.[36] Regarding children, however, the potential importance of externalities is especially notable. First, as noted in section A, parents' concern for children reflects how children enter parents' utility functions, whereas social welfare additionally counts children's utilities in their own right. Second, procreation affects population size, which has potentially far-reaching positive and negative externalities. High- (low-)

---

[34] Another sort of externality to marriage may arise on account of the creation of positive utility interdependencies, which neither party fully takes into account, and the voluntary sharing of resources that results. The magnitude of the latter effect would, however, be mitigated to the extent of positive assortative mating, on which see the survey by Lam (1997). Note that adjustments may also be in order if, instead of externalities, marriage has self-control benefits or costs that myopic individuals underappreciate.

[35] There are indirect effects as well. For example, the effect of taxation on second earners' labor supply may affect incentives to procreate; conversely, bearing children will have a feedback effect on their labor supply.

[36] For empirical evidence, see Schultz (1994) on the effect of welfare and Whittington, Alm, and Peters (1990) on the effect of income tax exemptions. Because the analysis in section A raises the possibility that more significant adjustments may be optimal than are typically provided, especially at middle and upper income ranges, it is possible that currently hard-to-detect effects may turn out to be significant. See, for example, Milligan (2005), finding that a large fertility subsidy in Quebec strongly increased procreation.

ability children—whose expected earning abilities are correlated with parents' abilities—are likely to cause positive (negative) fiscal externalities over their lifetimes, reflecting the differences between taxes paid and the cost of transfers and other government services received. In addition, there may be agglomeration or congestion effects (see, for example, Robinson and Srinivasan 1997). More broadly, it is controversial how an SWF should reflect variations in population size (in contrast to comparisons in which the relevant population is fixed), on which see Mirlees (1972), Nerlove, Razin, and Sadka (1986), and subsection 14.B.3.

PART V: DISTRIBUTIVE JUSTICE AND SOCIAL WELFARE

13

Welfare

*

In the standard welfare economic framework sketched in chapter 3 and used thereafter, policies are assessed by reference to a social welfare function (SWF) that aggregates the effects of policies on each individual's well-being (utility). Chapter 14 will consider the process of aggregation itself. The present chapter focuses on what social welfare is taken to be a function of. Considered first is the doctrine referred to as welfarism, under which social welfare is taken to depend on individuals' levels of well-being and on nothing else. Then attention shifts to the meaning of the concept of well-being and an examination of various factors that some analysts believe require modifications of individuals' utilities if they are to serve as proper arguments of an SWF. These two subjects are of more than abstract academic interest: Some economists, including Sen (discussed in subsection B.4), advance views that appear to call for wholesale deviations from welfarism; certain prominent tax equity norms, including some of those examined in chapter 15, conflict with welfarism; and important proposed extensions to optimal tax analysis, for example, those designed to account for interdependent preferences (see section 5.D), are controversial because of disagreement about the proper normative stance regarding the notion of individuals' well-being.[1]

---

[1] Much of the content in part V draws extensively on the mid-1990s draft of the earlier version of this book mentioned in the preface, and most of the ideas in this chapter, especially those in section A on welfarism, were substantially developed in connection with the writing of Kaplow and Shavell (2002).

A. Welfarism

1. Definition

As stated in subsection 3.B.1, an individualistic SWF—so called because social welfare depends only on individuals' utility or well-being—is a real-valued function of individuals' utility levels. Thus, for the case of a finite population, we can write $SW(x) = W(u_1(x), \ldots, u_n(x))$, where x is the social state or regime. By contrast, a nonindividualistic SWF may be written as $SZ(x) = Z(u_1(x), \ldots, u_n(x), x)$, where Z depends nontrivially on its final argument. The difference between these two formulations is that SW depends on x only through the effect of x on each of the u_i's, whereas SZ at least sometimes depends on x independently of—or in addition to—its effect on the u_i's.

Suppose, for example, that adherence to a specific governmental decision-making process is held to be an intrinsic social good, which is to say that it is deemed to contribute to social welfare independently of the quality of the decisions produced or of how individuals' utilities may be affected by participation in the process itself. (It may well be that following the process tends to improve decisions or to please individuals directly, but these possible benefits are not all that is deemed to matter.) Then the value of SZ would be higher in a state in which the process was followed more often, ceteris paribus.

An equivalent way to state the difference between individualistic and nonindividualistic SWFs is in terms of their information requirements. Knowledge of how a regime x affects each individual's level of well-being $u_i(x)$ is always sufficient to form an assessment under SW but is not always sufficient under SZ. That is, if for two regimes x and x', $u_i(x) = u_i(x')$ for all i, it is necessarily true that $SW(x) = SW(x')$, but it is sometimes true that $SZ(x) \neq SZ(x')$.[2] Continuing with our example, suppose that the specified decision-making process is followed more often in x' than in x, but that other distinctive features of x' precisely offset

---

[2] If there were never such an inequality in assessments, then each profile of the u_i's would—regardless of the state x that produced it—be associated with a unique real number, so it would be possible to express SZ as an individualistic SWF. (Conversely, if it is sometimes true that, even though everyone's utility is the same in two states, the social assessment differs, then it is impossible to express the SWF in the individualistic form SW.)

the effect of this difference on each individual's utility. The individualistic SWF, SW, would judge the two states indifferent, whereas SZ would value x' more highly.

Welfarism is the doctrine that social judgments should be in accord with an individualistic SWF. Although this doctrine is largely accepted by economists, there are notable deviations, some of which are explored later in this chapter and others in chapter 15. For example, much work on inequality measurement and most on horizontal equity is inconsistent with welfarism. Furthermore, most twentieth-century moral philosophers and many principles of common morality oppose welfarism; more specifically, many critiques of utilitarianism involve attacks on welfarism (rather than objections to the use of an additive function for purposes of aggregation).[3] Accordingly, the following subsections consider the rationale for welfarism and offer some perspectives on the pertinent debates.

2. Basis for Welfarism

Controversy over welfarism primarily concerns the insistence that the SWF must depend *exclusively* on individuals' well-being. Although this requirement may seem unduly stringent, it is justified by two considerations. First is the lack of an affirmative rationale for giving weight to anything that is truly unrelated to well-being (especially given the encompassing definition of well-being, elaborated in subsection B.1).[4] Singer (1988, p. 152) asks, "But how can something *matter* if it does not matter *to anyone*, or to any group of beings?" Second is the cost of giving

---

[3] See the arguments of Williams (1973) in the well-known collection *Utilitarianism: For and Against* and also the essays in *Utilitarianism and Beyond* (Sen and Williams 1982). Kaplow and Shavell's (2002) defense of welfarism addresses most of the subjects in this chapter in greater depth as well as other critiques of welfarism. See also Ng (2000a) and, for a defense by a moral philosopher, Hare (1981).

A comment on terminology is in order. Most debates in moral philosophy distinguish between consequentialism—the doctrine that only consequences (whether for individuals' well-being or otherwise) of actions or policies matter—and nonconsequentialism (usually deontological views). Welfarism is a species of consequentialism, and utilitarianism is the most discussed form of welfarism. However, as noted, much debate about utilitarianism concerns welfarism (or often consequentialism) more broadly.

[4] It is difficult to elaborate the point concerning lack of justification in the abstract. Later discussion of particular nonwelfarist criteria will consider the matter in more detail.

weight to other aims: If additional objectives are credited, some tradeoff with, that is, reduction in, well-being is required. Smart (1973, p. 5) presents "a persuasive type of objection" to nonwelfarist principles, namely, the existence of cases in which they "prescribe actions which lead to avoidable human misery."

To develop these points, it is useful to consider a simple series of hypothetical societies. First, imagine a populace that consists of only a single individual. There it would seem difficult to resist welfarism, for what basis could be offered for sacrificing that individual's well-being? Next, suppose that there are n individuals, each identically situated. There may be any manner of interaction among them; it is merely assumed that, say, each individual spends the same amount of time in any particular role and is affected in precisely the same manner as is any other individual. In this case, principles regulating human intercourse, whether informally or through government or other institutions, are potentially applicable. Nevertheless, since each person is affected identically by any regime, it is literally true that what is good for one is good for all. Again, nonwelfarist principles seem hard to justify; giving them weight would entail making everyone worse off. Yet, if a nonwelfarist SWF was correct, it would be applicable to such a society and thus require making everyone worse off whenever it diverged from welfarism.

The notion that nonwelfarist assessment violates the Pareto principle is demonstrated formally by Kaplow and Shavell (2001).[5] The argument is as follows: Beginning with $SZ(x)$, a nonindividualistic SWF, we know from the previous discussion that there exists x and x' such that $u_i(x) = u_i(x')$ for all i but $SZ(x) \neq SZ(x')$. Assume (without loss of generality) that $SZ(x) > SZ(x')$. Assume further that SZ is continuous with respect to some good and that this good has the property that, if each person has more of it, then each person is better off.[6] Now construct x'' from x' by increasing everyone's amount of this good from the levels in

---

[5] Sen (1970) previously demonstrated a conflict between the Pareto principle and a particular nonwelfarist principle involving (an arguably contentious notion of) libertarian rights. For discussions that relate Sen's argument to the ideas discussed in subsection 3, see, for example, Hardin (1986) and Kaplow and Shavell (2002).

[6] Note that full continuity of SZ, such as with respect to the degree of satisfaction of various nonwelfarist principles, is not required.

x' by a small positive amount. If this increment is sufficiently small, by continuity we have $SZ(x) > SZ(x'')$. However, by construction of x'', it is also true that $u_i(x'') > u_i(x')$ for all i. Combined with the premise that $u_i(x) = u_i(x')$ for all i, this implies that $u_i(x'') > u_i(x)$ for all i. Thus, if the (weak) Pareto principle is satisfied, it must be that $SZ(x'') > SZ(x)$, a contradiction.

The intuition for this result is that a nonindividualistic SWF must give weight to some factor independent of its effect on individuals' well-being. Accordingly, we can compare a social state to another that is identical except in two respects: It is inferior with respect to the nonutility factor, and every individual is ever-so-slightly better off (due to having a bit more of some good). As long as the weight ascribed to the nonutility factor is positive, we can make each individual's utility benefit sufficiently small such that the nonindividualistic SWF favors the state in which everyone is worse off.

The affirmative warrant for nonwelfarist social assessment is thus difficult to comprehend. The puzzle is deepened by the fact that most moral theorists claim to ground their nonwelfarist views in concern for the individual, often under the rubric of freedom, autonomy, or fairness. Yet it is hard to understand to whom any nonwelfarist principle is being fair when all potential subjects of concern may be made worse off by application of that principle. Furthermore, the conflict with the Pareto principle means not only that nonwelfarist prescriptions would fail to command unanimous assent, but also that there exist situations in which there would be unanimous dissent; hence, nonwelfarist views seem inherently to be in tension with notions of freedom and autonomy as well.

3. Perspectives on Welfarism

As noted, many philosophers adhere to nonwelfarist views, and some economists advance nonwelfarist ideas, including in the assessment of taxation and redistribution. Additionally, various norms of common morality deviate from pure welfarism. For example, breaking promises is often regarded to be wrongful independently of whether doing so is socially detrimental. And many feel that rewards and punishments should reflect merit or desert aside from any incentive benefits from their doing so.

How can the appeal of nonwelfarist principles be reconciled with the contrary arguments and the lack of any explicit, affirmative rationale? Why do we have moral intuitions in particular contexts that seem to support rules that would, upon reflection, sometimes operate to everyone's detriment? A number of perspectives on these questions have been offered through the ages.[7]

a. Two-level moral theory. It is important to distinguish two different levels at which a moral theory might operate. At the fundamental level, the question addressed is: What is the ultimate criterion of the social good? Advancing individuals' well-being—welfarism—is one possible answer to this question. (It is a partial answer because the SWF must be specified further.) This is the level at which the foregoing analysis is conducted.

At the practical level, the question is: What constitution, regime, policies, or rules should be implemented, in light of how society actually operates, to best advance the fundamental notion of the social good? One particularly interesting aspect concerns the personal character traits and other dispositions that would be best to inculcate in individuals, given what we know about human nature.

This distinction between levels of moral analysis has a long lineage. Hare (1981) traces it to Aristotle, Plato, and the classical utilitarians. Mill's (1861) famous essay, *Utilitarianism*, devotes its longest chapter (a third of the total) to this subject—which is ironic given that subsequent critics often advance the very arguments that Mill addressed therein, without acknowledging his response. Prominent twentieth-century exponents of two-level theory include the economist Harrod (1936) (writing in a philosophy journal), Rawls (1955) (preceding his more well-known work), the psychologist Baron (1994), and, most extensively, Hare (1981).[8]

---

[7] For detailed discussion and references to pertinent literatures, see Kaplow and Shavell (2002).

[8] The two-level distinction is related to the well-known debate between act- and rule-utilitarians. In that setting, however, the distinction between levels is often confused. Ultimately, most agree that act-utilitarianism is correct regarding how an act should be assessed against the ultimate criterion of the social good. The problem in much of the debate is that the question under consideration (level of moral thought) is ambiguous. For example,

This distinction helps to explain a wide range of human institutions. Formal organizations, notably government (but also corporations and other entities), are often best governed by rules (some embodied in constitutional "rights," including the right to "due process") that limit actors from freely maximizing the true, fundamental, social objective for fear that if permitted to do so they would not, producing less good in the end. Bentham's (1822–1823) lengthy (and less-known) constitutional writing develops this idea in detail. In similar spirit, Mill ([1861] 1998, p. 93) observed, "We should be glad to see just conduct enforced and injustice repressed, even in the minutest details, if we were not, with reason, afraid of trusting the magistrate with so unlimited an amount of power over individuals."

Also significant is the use of rules in the realm of common morality, to regulate individuals' informal interactions in everyday life. The sanctity of promises is one example; others are norms of fair division, which reduce conflict, and the principle of retribution, which deters aggression. Such notions are usually more than mere rules of thumb designed to economize on information and costs of calculation. Rather, they carry their own behavior-influencing force, both internally, through emotions such as guilt, and externally, through social sanctions such as disapprobation. Thus, individuals may refrain from breaking promises even when doing so would otherwise be to their advantage. Such norm potency helps to modulate self-interested behavior, thereby promoting cooperation and restraining opportunism. The significance of these norms, emphasized by Hume (1751), Mill (1861), Darwin (1874), and Sidgwick (1907), has

---

if it is asked whether, in a highly unusual circumstance, a teacher should strike a student even though there is a rule—and a good rule, for the sorts of reasons discussed in the text to follow—against corporal punishment, two different answers may be given, both correct but each responsive to a different question. If striking the student would in fact (taking into account all subsequent, indirect effects) produce more good than harm, then, at the fundamental level, it would be "good" if the teacher struck the child. But if instead the question is something like "would we like our children to be taught by teachers who showed no compunction about striking the child" or "would we like teachers, instead of being presented with a hard-and-fast rule against striking their students, to be encouraged to exercise discretion on the matter, knowing that it often will be exercised in the heat of the moment"—both directed to the practical level—then the answer would be negative. There is no real inconsistency, but in some discourse on the matter these two types of questions—corresponding to two different levels of moral inquiry—are not clearly differentiated.

been increasingly emphasized by economists, such as Becker (1996), Frank (1988), and Hirshleifer (1987), and other social scientists and natural scientists, including Alexander (1987), Baron (1993), Campbell (1975), Daly and Wilson (1988), and E.O. Wilson (1980).

The distinction between the fundamental criterion of the good and the practical question of what rules and norms are best to guide human affairs helps to reconcile the tension between welfarism and competing principles. The suggestion is that welfarism, in its pure form, is indeed the appropriate ideal for assessing the social good, whereas competing notions that sometimes conflict with welfarism (and thus also with the Pareto principle) are practical, intermediate norms that may be related to common morality or the restraint of government power. Accordingly, the latter are not truly inconsistent with welfarism as long as their proper role is understood. This view is elaborated in the subsections that follow.

b. Moral intuitions. Well-socialized individuals, whether contemplating how to act toward others or engaging in philosophical reflection on proper conduct, will understandably have intuitions regarding what is morally correct. This is particularly likely on account of the aforementioned emotional and social consequences of various norm-related behaviors.

To the extent that intuitive normative principles—including notions of equity that seem applicable to tax policy and income redistribution—have their roots in common morality, a number of implications follow. First, because of the distinction between the two levels of moral theory, it is possible, indeed likely, that practical principles (even optimal ones, given constraints of the human condition) will deviate from the fundamental criterion of the good. This is simply the truism that the optimal, second-best rule in the presence of constraints generally will not implement the first best. Hence, as suggested, the apparent conflict between welfarism and competing criteria can be reconciled.

Second, within the practical level, different sorts of principles are often appropriate in different contexts. Norms regulating conduct within families, between friends, and among coworkers may differ from one another. Even greater is the difference between any of these sets of norms and those that should regulate relationships between different agencies of government (courts versus legislatures) and between government and the governed. For example, broken promises among friends, breached contracts between firms, and transgressed rules regulating interactions between police and citizens are subject to different forms of dispute resolution and different sanctions. Even more, the underlying rules themselves should and do differ. This contrast is important for understanding the appropriate role of notions of fairness and equity for tax policy. Norms of fair division or those dictating equality in human social interaction have functions and modes of enforcement that differ greatly from those appropriate to a tax authority. To be sure, there will be underlying similarities of purpose (just as there are among rules involving understandings between friends, between firms, and between citizens and police). But the differences across contexts are sufficiently great that we should anticipate that our internal sense of equity, developed in the realm of everyday social interaction, would at best be suggestive of how government fiscal affairs should be structured.[9]

Third, the weight of common morality suggests that its precepts may sway our judgment even when their use is inappropriate. Treating others unfairly or inequitably makes us feel guilty and raises, even if subconsciously, concerns about how others will react. And the prospect that individuals would treat us improperly arouses anger. These feelings are difficult to ignore as we contemplate subjects outside of everyday interaction, such as the formulation of tax policy, because of the existence of apparent similarities. Even when reasoned analysis suggests, for example, that violations of horizontal equity—the command that equals be treated equally—are not of concern in a particular realm, such violations may still feel wrong.

At least the first two of these implications are familiar from the increasing attention to the teachings of cognitive psychology.[10] Regarding

---

[9] For example, norms of fair division may have evolved to assist cooperation (dividing meat from the hunt) or to avoid conflict (focal points may provide useful boundaries). And norms respecting the "rights" of current possessors (of food or land) may similarly avert hostilities. Although related concerns may impose practical, political constraints on government, these norms are addressed to a substantially different question from the fundamental inquiry into the proper criterion of the social good, as applied to questions regarding the overall distribution of income.

[10] See, for example, Baron (2000), Hogarth and Reder (1987), Kahneman, Slovic, and Tversky (1982), Nisbett and Ross (1980), and Rabin (1998).

ideal theory versus practical rules of conduct, we are aware of the many respects in which human decision-making heuristics conflict with normative decision theory. It is acknowledged that this inconsistency does not imply the existence of any defects in the latter—that is, the discrepancy does not make decisions that fail to maximize our objective normatively compelling. Rather, it is recognized that our decision-making heuristics and biases are, at best, optimal adaptive responses for the environment in which they evolved.[11]

Furthermore, the practical decision rules we actually use are better suited to some contexts than others. A heuristic may lead to approximately optimal decisions in the realm in which it was developed but to very poor outcomes in some other settings presented, say, by recent technological advances. Nevertheless, despite these important context differences, we often err by overgeneralization and may continue to follow our habits even when their deficiencies have previously been brought to our attention.

The connection between decision heuristics and biases both in general and in the particular realm of moral decision-making has been emphasized, among others, by Baron (1993, 1998).[12] In addition to identifying the connection and exploring how some of the same errors are at work, particular infirmities in the context of moral reasoning have been identified. Moral intuitions, however, may differ with regard to the third implication concerning the emotional and social weight associated with deviation from norms of common morality. As noted, this feature suggests that we may find it even more difficult than in the case of, say, decision-making under uncertainty, to engage in the proper, ideal normative analysis (welfarism), unswayed by our everyday decision rules (common morality).

---

[11] See, for example, Gigerenzer and Selten (2001).

[12] "What is the causal connection between something being morally right and our intuition that it is right? It is easier to understand our intuitions as arising from overgeneralizations of learned principles, or from the emotions that evolution gave us. . . ." Baron (1998, p. 152). Philosophers have long emphasized the limitations of moral intuitions as sources of illumination of the ultimate good (see, for example, Mill 1861, Sidgwick 1907, Westermarck 1932, and Hare 1981).

c. Relevance of nonwelfarist principles under welfarism. To round out an account of the apparent conflict between nonwelfarist principles and welfarism, it is useful to state clearly the relevance of the former under the latter. First, as suggested by the discussion of two-level moral theory, it is clear that, even if the fundamental criterion of the good admits only consideration of individuals' well-being, various principles that on their face are nonwelfarist are likely to be appropriate at the practical level, for the regulation of human interaction and of government. For example, the norm of equal treatment of equals that underlies horizontal equity and notions of due process that are implicitly invoked in some critiques of utilitarianism (see subsection 14.A.1.b) are well understood as useful constraints on the behavior of public officials and institutions. Even in this context, however, such principles must be applied carefully. What process should be due obviously depends on the context (determining who is next in line at the post office compared to who should be subject to severe punishment). Insistence on equal treatment needs to be moderated (perfect equality is often impossible and near perfection may be excessively costly), and context is relevant (random enforcement, such as with tax audits, violates equal treatment, but if selection is truly random, the potential for abuse may be limited). In all cases, determination of optimal policies requires reference to the proper objective function, which, as suggested here, is purely welfarist.

Second, nonwelfarist principles may serve as proxy instruments for policy analysis. When various equity norms are violated, there may well be an underlying problem, something indicating that welfare is not being maximized. This is apparent with notions of merit and desert because rewards and punishments in accord with such concepts tend to encourage productive effort and deter misbehavior. Further examples involving horizontal equity will be discussed in section 15.B. However, understood as proxy instruments, nonwelfarist principles have their limits. They may motivate inquiry, but they are not part of the ultimate social objective that, in the end, is invoked to determine optimal policy. In discussing critiques of utilitarianism, Mirrlees (1982) offers the observation, so familiar in ordinary economic analysis, that counterintuitive findings do call for explanation but do not per se warrant rejection. After all, if our initial intuitions are never wrong, what is the point of analysis? This message is particularly apt regarding optimal taxation, where the analysis is complex and subtle and important results, such as those pertaining to the shape of the optimal income tax schedule, are often unexpected. Furthermore, as observed in subsection b, we know that our modes of decision-making are often mistaken, involving oversimplified heuristics that, in addition, may be erroneously extended to contexts in which their performance is poor. Hence, divergences between the results of careful tax policy analysis and our intuitions concerning ideal taxation should be reasonably frequent; if they are not, our analysis has probably been too casual. An important lesson is that, when considering familiar notions of tax equity—as with all intuitions, moral or otherwise—it is valuable to determine their underlying basis. Once their (usually intermediate, instrumental) relationship to welfare is identified, they can guide policy analysis more effectively, and it will be more apparent when their usefulness has been exhausted.

Third, because of our attachment to nonwelfarist principles—as explained, they are not mere rules of thumb but maxims that carry emotional freight—they may have weight under welfarist analysis because they are a component of welfare itself.[13] That is, we may have tastes regarding, say, how vicious criminals are punished or how income is distributed. Indeed, preferences regarding income redistribution were the subject of section 5.D, extending the analysis of optimal income taxation. Whether and to what extent nonwelfarist notions should be credited on this ground is an empirical question, quite distinct from whether the notions have any standing as fundamental criteria of the social good. (A separate question is whether, even if such tastes exist, they should be counted, a subject examined further in subsection B.3.)

---

[13] Understanding individuals' moral sense as akin to tastes dates at least to Hutcheson (1725–1755) and Hume (1751). Furthermore, Mill ([1861] 1998, p. 83) observed that individuals can develop tastes even for rules that begin as merely means to an end: "What was once desired as an instrument for the attainment of happiness, has come to be desired for its own sake. In being desired for its own sake it is, however, desired as *part* of happiness."

B. Well-Being

1. Definition

It is familiar to economists that well-being or utility (the terms are used interchangeably throughout) is a broad, subjective notion, not one limited to material pleasures, hedonistic enjoyment, or any other a priori class of pleasures and pains. Resources, often measured in monetary units, are means to obtain goods and services; these, in turn, are means to generating utility, which may be derived directly from goods or indirectly and intangibly, such as through fulfillment, sympathetic feelings for family and friends, aesthetic enjoyment of art or the environment, and so forth. What counts, and how much it counts, for each individual in society depends on that individual's mind, not on any analyst's view of what should constitute well-being.[14]

It is common for outsiders to welfare economics (particularly critics thereof) to suppose that utility is a narrower concept—paralleling attacks on utilitarianism—but this view reflects a misinterpretation.[15] Although minimal exposure to economics may leave the impression that only money or goods are thought to be important, their intermediate role is well understood within the profession, as indicated, for example, by Lancaster's (1966) framework in which goods are inputs that yield characteristics that in turn produce utility, Michael and Becker's (1973) household production function approach, and the wide range of objects

---

[14] Modern philosophical treatments, which vary in how closely they adhere to subjectivist accounts similar to those used in welfare economics, include Griffin (1986), Nussbaum and Sen (1993), and Sumner (1996). Among others, Mill (1861) is sometimes associated with the view that higher (intellectual) pleasures are superior to more basic (sensual) pleasures, although there is some dispute about the extent to which he believed this in principle rather than as an empirical proposition about human nature.

[15] Regarding criticism of classical utilitarians, Bentham ([1781] 1988, p. 33) explicitly includes among the "simple pleasures" the pleasures of skill, amity, a good name, piety, benevolence, imagination, and association. And Mill (1861, pp. 55–56) not only took a broad view himself but also lamented that followers of the Greek philosopher Epicurus were unfairly characterized as holding a narrow orientation toward pleasure.

of human concern that are addressed by economists. In any event, what should be deemed to constitute well-being for normative purposes is not a matter of stipulation or interpretation of economists' practices. Instead, well-being should be construed in a manner that connects to the ultimate motivation for welfarism, which deems individuals' well-being and only their well-being to be relevant to social welfare. As will be seen, this point illuminates the questions examined in the subsections that follow.

2. Limited Information and Other Decision-Making Infirmities

It has long been understood that individuals' decisions may not always be in their own best interests, a point that is receiving increased attention in work at the intersection of economics and psychology.[16] Individuals may lack pertinent information or suffer from cognitive biases, myopia, addiction, and so forth.[17] In such situations, what may be termed decisional utility—corresponding to expressed preferences as indicated by actual behavior—differs from experienced utility—the actual subjective states arising as a consequence of decisions.

The standard view, accepted here, is that at least in principle it is experienced utility that corresponds to subjective well-being, which is taken to be of normative significance. Thus, Sidgwick (1907), Harsanyi (1955), and Mirrlees (1982), among others, argue that social welfare should be assessed by reference to individuals' rational, fully informed preferences when they conflict with revealed preferences. What is desirable for individuals should be understood "supposing the desirer to possess a perfect forecast, emotional as well as intellectual, of the state of attainment or fruition," in the words of Sidgwick ([1907] 1981, p. 111).

---

[16] See, for example, the literature cited in note 10, and recent work on neuroeconomics, surveyed by Camerer, Loewenstein, and Prelec (2005).

[17] A particularly interesting case involves imperfect information about one's own future preferences and the possibility of changing one's preferences (see, for example, Cyert and De Groot 1975 and Weizsäcker 1971). Stigler and Becker (1977) suggest that one can analyze all such cases as ones involving stable tastes but possibly changed circumstances or limited information.

The basis for this view can be seen most clearly in cases of misinformation. Suppose that an individual desires to step forward in order to attain a better view from a mountaintop (and will do so unless restrained) but is unaware that the footing is insecure, so that the result would be a catastrophic fall. Utility is deemed to be lower, not higher, if the individual's stated preference is satisfied, for it is the actual consequence that is taken to matter.

The policy implications of this view are somewhat limited for familiar reasons emphasized by Bentham (1781) and Mill (1859), namely, that the government often lacks the information and may not have the right incentives to improve on individuals' imperfect situations. In certain areas, such as safety regulation, gains may be possible. Regarding tax and expenditure policy, in-kind provision of goods and services (public housing, free and compulsory public education) is sometimes offered in lieu of cash for these reasons, although, as explained in section 7.E, it may be that externalities and other explanations are the more weighty considerations. Another important application involves social insurance systems, often justified on grounds of individuals' myopia (see subsection 11.B.1).

Finally, mistakes may have a distributive incidence that affects the optimal extent of redistribution. In particular, deficient decision-making may be concentrated among the poor, in significant part because myopia and other infirmities may partially explain their poverty. One could model such infirmities analogously to subsection 12.A.2's model of economies of scale within the family (though the effect is opposite in direction). In the notation of that model, we can simply examine the case in which the lower is income, the lower is β, where $\beta = 1$ at the highest level of income. Then we can write individuals' utility functions (focusing, as there, only on consumption) as $u(\beta c)$. The marginal utility of consumption is $\beta u'(\beta c)$. The leading coefficient indicates that low-β individuals make less effective use of each dollar and hence have a lower marginal utility on this account. However, β also multiplies c as the argument of u', implying that low-β individuals' marginal utility is higher because they are at a lower level of effective consumption. Which effect is larger depends, as in subsection 12.A.2, on the curvature of u. If individuals' relative risk aversion is greater (less) than one, overall marginal utility of low-β individuals would be higher (lower) because the latter effect would be more (less) significant than the former. Additionally, there is the straightforward point that utility levels of low-β individuals will be lower, so if the SWF is strictly concave, greater redistribution would be optimal on this account.

3. Other-Regarding Preferences

Some economists and philosophers argue that certain sorts of preferences should not be credited in assessing social welfare. In analyzing redistribution, the most relevant preferences include both positive preferences toward others, such as altruism, and negative preferences, such as envy.[18] Before discussing these specific possible sources of utility, it is useful to consider the broader category of other-regarding (or external) preferences, which Dworkin (1981a), Harsanyi (1977, 1988), and Nozick (1974), among others, suggest should be ignored altogether.[19]

First, preferences should be distinguished from beliefs or viewpoints. For example, one who regards utilitarianism as the proper normative stance does not necessarily—in fact, is quite unlikely to—have personal preferences that weight all individuals in society equally, whether oneself, immediate family members, neighbors, or distant strangers. The arguments of a welfarist SWF are individuals' utilities—their subjective well-being, not their normative theories—so beliefs or viewpoints should indeed be disregarded when assessing the level of social welfare under a given regime.

Second, if actual preferences are involved, it is prima facie problematic to omit particular components of utility. The normative basis for welfarism depends on individuals' actual well-being and does not discriminate among its sources. It is not clear why any preferences should not count or how a list of objectionable preferences might be determined. Furthermore, because ignoring elements of well-being

---

[18] See section 5.D (preferences regarding redistribution), chapter 10 (taxation of transfers; especially section 10.B on transfer motives and subsection 10.C.3 on charitable giving), and chapter 12 (taxation of families).

[19] The topics in this subsection and pertinent literature are considered more fully in Kaplow and Shavell (2002).

constitutes a formal violation of welfarism, the demonstration in sub-section A.2 indicates that all individuals may be made worse off as a result (which is demonstrated later for altruism and envy).

Third, it is unclear what it means to censor a preference. The implication is that the pertinent individuals would be treated as if they had a different utility function, so in principle it would be necessary to specify that alternative utility function. Yet an infinity of functions (not subject to censorship conditions) are possible. None of them is the actual utility function of the individuals in question, so it is hard to see the basis for making a selection. Perhaps more important, it is unclear what would be the normative force of maximizing such a utility function for a person who does not experience utility in accord with it.

Fourth, the suggestion that other-regarding preferences are a problematic class is, upon reflection, alarming. After all, much of what individuals value regards others, including the love of family members, companionship of friends, fulfillment from participation in teams or social groups, and appreciation of performing artists.[20] Perhaps one could distinguish between inward and outward concern for others, so that it would be acceptable to enjoy a friend's jokes or the play of one's children but not to get any utility from their well-being, but it is not clear that our feelings always draw such distinctions or that those distinctions should matter.

Turn now to the pertinent specific positive and negative other-regarding preferences that have been subject to challenge. Although crediting positive preferences, notably, altruism, in assessing matters pertaining to taxation and redistribution may seem unexceptional, Harsanyi (1988) and others object on the ground that doing so would violate equality because social welfare assessments would thereby give more weight to some individuals (subjects of others' altruism) than to others or that it would involve some sort of double counting.[21] The foregoing comments,

---

[20] Note that the case of performing artists includes instances of what may be viewed as negative other-regarding preferences since onlookers' pleasure may derive from performers' acts that involve their suffering pain.

[21] This objection was addressed briefly in note 10 in chapter 10 on taxation of transfers and was mentioned in chapter 12 on taxation of families because of the relevance of altruism (and other positive preference interdependencies) to those analyses.

of course, are fully applicable to the present case in which individuals derive positive utility from others' well-being. Note further that if such preferences receive no weight, then in principle one should prohibit many acts of caring and kindness within the family and toward others, a prohibition that would typically make both the altruist and the beneficiaries worse off. Suppose, for example, that all individuals were in pairs, one gaining altruistic utility from the other, that all started with equal resources, and that the altruists in each pair give gifts or otherwise bestow benefits on the others. From an initial point of equal resources, such transfers would reduce total utility if the altruistic utility is ignored (for the transfers are disequalizing and let us assume that otherwise the individuals have identical utility functions exhibiting diminishing marginal utility). Yet restricting gifts would reduce everyone's actual utility.

The particular objections to admitting altruism also are weak on their own terms. When altruism is credited, no one's utility or marginal utility in its own right counts more than anyone else's. To be sure, subjects of altruism may be lucky because they are likely to benefit from others' concern. But so are individuals whose talents happen to be highly in demand on account of others' preferences. (Performing artists' incomes vary wildly depending on what is in fashion.) To be sure, individuals who command more resources for whatever reason will thereby have a lower marginal utility of income (and a higher level of utility, relevant for a strictly concave SWF), which will be taken into account when maximizing the SWF. See, for example, subsection 10.A.3 on the effect of private voluntary transfers on the marginal social value of redistribution. The double-counting objection also is untenable. It suggests, in the case of a gift, that the donor's or the donee's utility should be ignored. But the donee does consume the resources and thus has a higher utility, and as an individual distinct from the donor, the donee should be counted in his or her own right. Likewise, the donor in fact receives distinctive utility—by revealed preference, more than if the resources had been used on own-consumption; to ignore it would be inconsistent with a concern for the donor's actual subjective well-being.

Basing social welfare judgments regarding distributive issues on negative other-regarding preferences, such as envy, seems more problematic than crediting altruism. First, satisfying such preferences usually reduces utility overall, for others' utility losses are ordinarily larger than any gain to the envious. Second, society may well be better off if individuals did not have such preferences (whereas altruistic preferences generally permit a higher level of social welfare to be achieved with given resources).[22] This latter argument, however, needs to be articulated more fully. To satisfy an individual's negative preference requires making others worse off. If the preference could be extinguished, the individual could be made as well off as before without making the other individuals worse off, making possible gains in well-being, ceteris paribus. Furthermore, it might be supposed that a social policy of discrediting preferences would help to alter them over time. For example, Becker (1996) and Frank (1985) are among the many who suggest that antidiscrimination laws may have influenced people's discriminatory attitudes. Note, however, that this sort of justification for ignoring certain negative preferences is instrumental: The preferences are ignored not because the individuals' actual well-being does not matter, but instead because the social act of ignoring them will lead to a superior state of affairs. (Note that this analysis exemplifies the sort of two-level reasoning and critical examination of moral intuitions that is discussed in subsection A.3.[23])

Perhaps these functional explanations underlie our reluctance to credit negative preferences, whether involving envy, racism, or sadism. We might believe that satisfying such preferences is rarely, if ever, desirable (even assuming that the preferences are permanent) and doubt that we could identify any exceptions, and we may also believe that closing

---

[22] Altruistic preferences are not entirely unproblematic because of difficulties like the Samaritan's dilemma (see, for example, Bernheim and Stark 1988). In addition, not all negative preferences lead to lower social welfare. For example, individuals' desire to see wrongdoers punished leads them to cooperate with authorities and to engage in social ostracism, the prospect of which deters misbehavior (although the retributive urge can also be excessive, leading to undesirable consequences).

[23] This explicit, welfarist account of why it may not be best for society to base policy on certain negative preferences offers grounds for determining which preferences are objectionable and what prescription follows from the judgment, unlike the typical objections to other-regarding preferences found in the pertinent literatures.

our eyes to such preferences or even denouncing them will contribute to the problems' dissolution. If instead negative preferences were strong, widely held, permanent, and could be satisfied at little direct cost, it is hardly clear that they should be ignored. Suppose that, beyond some point, additional income directly increased each individual's utility only slightly and actually contributed much more to everyone else's suffering on account of negative preferences. Then a policy that trimmed incomes would make everyone better off. Such a hypothetical example may not seem powerful because it is so fanciful—our imaginations cannot really find credible the premise that all actually would be better off if everyone's standard of living were reduced, so the conclusion seems less compelling. If, however, we transform the example, it seems plainly correct: Suppose that the negative preferences derive not from others simply having the added income, but from the fact that all use it to hold noisier parties that bother their neighbors. This "tangible" externality would be counted, yet such externalities are like envy in that they influence utility through complex neural activity that we are only beginning to understand.[24]

In sum, it seems difficult to articulate the actual meaning of preference censoring or to identify a convincing rationale for ignoring, as a matter of first principles, certain sorts of preferences. Nevertheless, it may be good social policy to set aside certain negative preferences, including envy. In any event, it is hardly clear that such preferences exist in sufficient strength to have a meaningful impact on the optimal income taxation problem. For example, in Boskin and Sheshinski's (1978, p. 599) analysis of how individuals' concern for relative status affects optimal redistribution, they cautioned the reader that empirical evidence for an extremely strong concern, which is often taken for granted, is "virtually nonexistent, let alone convincing."

---

[24] To take another, lighter example, suppose that a group of individuals greatly enjoy practical jokes, that the butt of any particular joke suffers only a little, and that each is at the suffering end equally often. Satisfying these negative preferences makes everyone better off, and it is hard to see why this source of utility should be ignored—that is, in the absence of additional effects such as an influence on character that would adversely affect other behaviors (in which case the preferences would not be irrelevant but instead would be outweighed).

4. Capabilities, Primary Goods, and Well-Being[25]

In considering the subject of redistribution, some economists and philosophers would not assess individuals' situations by reference to well-being. Instead, Sen (1985a, 1985b, 1997) examines capabilities and functionings, such as nourishment, shelter, physical mobility, and the ability to take part in the life of the community, and Rawls (1971, 1982) considers primary goods, including rights and liberties, opportunities and powers, and income and wealth.[26] According primacy to such means of fulfillment rather than to fulfillment itself, however, seems difficult to justify and (unsurprisingly, in light of the argument in subsection A.2) may well lead to everyone being worse off.

In many respects, these constructs are problematic on their face. Most primary goods and capabilities are patently instrumental rather than intrinsically valuable to individuals, just as the commodities in Michael and Becker's (1973) theory of household production and the characteristics in Lancaster's (1966) consumer theory are means of generating utility. Perhaps some primary goods and capabilities are ends, but in that case they constitute elements of well-being rather than its totality.

Additionally, many questions regarding these theories remain unanswered: Whether viewed as means, ends, or some combination thereof, how is the list of primary goods or capabilities to be determined? How can the same list be employed for heterogeneous individuals who face differing circumstances? Additionally, since multiple means are admitted, how are they to be aggregated to produce an overall assessment of individuals' situations?[27] Welfare economics answers such questions by reference to individuals' utility functions. Any resulting list, of course, may vary across individuals and states. If well-being is not the guide and if uniformity is imposed, then some substantial justificatory apparatus is required, but none has been offered.[28]

---

[25] This section draws on Kaplow (2007f).

[26] See also Dworkin (1981b), who focuses on equality of resources, which he contrasts with equality of welfare.

[27] Critics of Rawls's notion have suggested that this index problem is insurmountable (see Blair 1988, Gibbard 1979, and Plott 1978).

[28] Proponents of alternatives to well-being rely on the reader's intuition and seem to suggest that their theories, once revealed, are self-evident. They also sometimes make reference

Assuming these obstacles could be overcome, the result—whatever it may be—will conflict with the Pareto principle.[29] If all individuals were identical, all would be worse off if the social allocation of goods was that dictated by the alternative theory because (except by coincidence) individuals would receive more of some goods and less of others than the levels that would maximize their utilities. If individuals' utility functions varied, then the theory's allocation would be welfare-reducing for all (except possibly for a subset, by coincidence—although even then, if the theory's allocation were abandoned, a redistribution of benefits from the others would make possible a Pareto improvement). Moreover, in this case, individuals would wish to trade with each other in order to align their allocation of goods more closely with their actual preferences. To prevent the theory's dictates from being undermined, such Pareto-improving trade would have to be prohibited. As suggested in subsection A.2, such anti-Paretian results are troublesome for moral theories that purport to ground themselves in such notions as consent, freedom, and autonomy, which is the case for both Sen and Rawls.[30]

How, then, can one explain the attraction of such alternative theories? As with the other issues explored in this chapter, on reflection it appears that what are being treated as ends in themselves are better understood instrumentally. Well-being—especially in the presence of preference heterogeneity—is difficult to measure objectively and uncontroversially, so as a practical matter it may make sense to focus on specific, tangible indicators. Furthermore, one may be concerned about an excessive tendency

---

to a concern about individuals having expensive tastes (see Rawls 1982, pp. 168–169, and Sen 1997, pp. 197–198). As noted in Kaplow (2006a), however, they ignore that individuals have a disincentive (rather than the implicitly assumed affirmative incentive) to develop tastes that by definition reduce their well-being, ceteris paribus.

[29] For more formal statements, see Kaplow (2007f). Relatedly, Gibbard (1979) shows that Rawls's approach is incompatible with the Pareto principle when individuals are heterogeneous, on account of the price index problem (which arises even when the only primary good is income because prices of different underlying goods can vary across regimes).

[30] Sen (1985b) uses the terms "agency" and "freedom" in his title, and the concepts are central to his argument there and elsewhere in advancing his notions of capabilities and functionings. Rawls (1971), as is well known, imagines that individuals in an original position would unanimously consent to his framework (of which primary goods is a component), and his primacy of liberty makes clear that freedom is a central concept for him as well.

to focus on money, thereby omitting other important constituents of well-being. Interestingly, Sen's (1985a) book developing his capabilities-based approach features two appendixes, one showing how capability-based measures differ in practice from using per capita GNP and another showing how differences in the treatment of men and women are obscured unless one pays attention to capabilities.[31] Both discussions suggest that his work may be motivated by the need to provide a more nearly complete depiction of well-being, especially in considering developing countries, although the more conceptual body of the book and his other writings on the subject have more of an anti-welfarist flavor.

Primary goods or capabilities may best be understood as ways of gauging well-being rather than as substitute concepts, but in that event the answers to the questions posed at the outset of this subsection are empirical and contingent on the individuals involved and their circumstances. As a practical matter, taxation and income redistribution are largely undertaken in terms of money, and individuals are not generally distinguished on account of possible differences in their utility functions; to the extent that this approach is followed, Sen's and Rawls's approaches may not have implications that diverge sharply from welfarism's focus on well-being. However, as subsection 2 notes, some transfers are in-kind, and the government directly provides goods and services, often including public education. Furthermore, utility differences are pertinent to the taxation of private transfers and the taxation of families, discussed in chapters 10 and 12, respectively, and in the case of physical disabilities. In these realms, it may matter whether society cares about individuals' well-being or something else.[32]

---

[31] Rawls (1971, p. 95; 1982, p. 159) likewise offers practical arguments in support of his notion of primary goods.

[32] Regarding physical disabilities, for example, a capability deficit may, ceteris paribus, indicate a well-being deficit. It would not make sense to remedy the capability deficit directly, such as by providing expensive transportation services and other costly accommodations to individuals, if they could be made better off (and at lower cost) by being given money that could be spent otherwise. For example, some disabled individuals might prefer cheaper home entertainment to a toilsome journey to the opera, which would not be enjoyed on account of the exhaustion involved in getting there. Not all disabled individuals will have the goal of emulating the movements and other activities of those who are not disabled; treating them as if they do or should, regardless of their actual wishes, is avoided (at least in principle) when the social objective is denominated in terms of well-being.

14

Social Welfare Function

Chapter 13 presents the rationale for the SWF to be a function of individuals' utilities (and of nothing else). This chapter considers two remaining questions. First, how should individuals' utilities be aggregated? In subsection 3.B.1, it was noted that optimal income tax analysis often considers SWFs of an isoelastic form (see expression 3.2), where the parameter e indicates society's degree of aversion to inequality in utility levels: $e = 0$ corresponds to the utilitarian SWF and higher levels of e to strictly concave SWFs. (The limiting case, as e approaches infinity, yields the maximin formulation suggested by Rawls (1971), placing all weight on the least-well-off individual.) Even if this functional form were accepted, it would remain necessary to select a value of e.

Second, whose utilities are to be included as arguments in the SWF? A standard response is to count all citizens in the nation while excluding all others. Some of the fundamental normative issues regarding this view will be examined, although briefly and tentatively.

A. Aggregation

This section begins by examining two frameworks that have been suggested for choosing an SWF. Then some concerns are addressed.

1. Frameworks

a. Original position. Although most often associated with Rawls (1971), the notion that distributive judgments should be derived from individuals' choices in some sort of "original position" behind a "veil of ignorance" had previously been advanced by Vickrey (1945) and Harsanyi (1953), among others.[1] Specifically, they suggested that individuals consider what regime they would favor if they had an equal chance of being any member of society, in which case a utilitarian SWF would be employed.

Taking the case of a finite population of n individuals, each individual is postulated to have a $1/n$ probability of taking the role and thus experiencing the utility $u_i(x)$ of each individual i, where, as in chapters 3 and 13, x denotes the regime or social state. Hence, an individual would choose x to maximize expected utility, given by

$$\sum \frac{1}{n} u_i(x), \tag{14.1}$$

where summations are over i, from 1 to n. Obviously, maximizing an individual's expected utility, expression (14.1), is equivalent to maximizing

$$\frac{1}{n} \sum u_i(x), \tag{14.2}$$

that is, maximizing average utility over the population. Furthermore, for a given population (see subsection B.3), maximizing expression (14.2) is equivalent to maximizing

$$\sum u_i(x), \tag{14.3}$$

that is, maximizing total utility over the population. Therefore, as explored in section 3.B, the SWF would exhibit a (possibly significant) preference for equalizing resources, but with this utilitarian SWF, that preference would depend entirely on the concavity of individuals' utility

---

[1] See also Fleming (1952) and Strotz (1958). The motivation for this framework is that it embodies impartiality. In these respects, it is similar to the Golden Rule (commanding that individuals treat others as they would wish others to treat themselves), Kant's (1785) categorical imperative (insisting that individuals choose principles for themselves as if the principles would be generalized to the entire population), and Lewis's (1946) suggestion that individuals imagine that they would rotate through all positions in society.

functions—corresponding to the rate at which individuals' marginal utility declines, which is equivalent to their degree of risk aversion.

Vickrey and Harsanyi thereby presented a basic normative framework in which the problem of choosing an SWF was formally equivalent to the problem of individual choice under uncertainty. Rawls (1971) embraced this general approach but resisted the utilitarian implication. He insisted, in essence, that individuals in the original position would maximize the minimum value of utility, with the now familiar implication that society should reduce the entire population to misery if this would improve the lot of the least-well-off individual infinitesimally.

The reasons for Rawls's (1971) conclusion remain obscure and contested. He acknowledged Harsanyi's work and endorsed the view that individuals should be rational, as that concept is understood in decision theory. Nevertheless, he insisted that individuals' "risk aversion" in the original position and other considerations would lead them to choose a maximin SWF.[2] A useful clarification is offered in Arrow's (1973, p. 256) book review of Rawls (1971):[3]

> When I first wrote on this matter [Arrow 1951], I . . . denied the welfare relevance of the expected-utility theory. But the Vickrey-Harsanyi argument puts matters in a different perspective; if an individual assumes he may with equal probability be any member of society, then indeed he evaluates any policy by his expected utility, *where the utility function is specifically that defined by the von Neumann–Morgenstern theorem.* Rawls therefore errs when he argues that average utilitarianism assumes risk neutrality . . . ; on the contrary, the degree of risk aversion of the individuals is already incorporated in the utility function.[4]

---

[2] Rawls's approach differs in other respects not obviously pertinent to the concavity of the SWF, including his use of primary goods rather than utility (on which see subsection 13.B.4), his reference to the least-well-off group rather than individual, and his emphasis especially in later writings on political (as distinct from moral) theory.

[3] See also Hare's (1973) review.

[4] Sen (1979) suggests that Harsanyi does not establish that the SWF must be linear because, in essence, one could apply a nonlinear SWF to transformed von Neumann–Morgenstern (VNM) utility functions (see also Weymark 1991). For example, if one squares individuals' VNM utilities, the corresponding SWF would first take the square root of each

b. Social rationality. Another framework that can be used to narrow the range of admissible SWFs is one that imposes rationality requirements. This approach also was pioneered by Harsanyi (1955, 1977). He makes three sets of assumptions. First, individuals' preferences are assumed to conform to the standard rationality postulates of decision theory—namely, completeness, transitivity, continuity, and monotonicity—which implies that they can be represented by a von Neumann–Morgenstern utility function. Second, the SWF is assumed to respect the same rationality postulates. To this, Harsanyi adds a third set of explicitly value-laden assumptions, tantamount to welfarism, positive responsiveness, and equality (equivalently, symmetry or anonymity).

The first two sets of assumptions plus welfarism imply that the SWF is linear in individuals' von Neumann–Morgenstern utilities. The analysis parallels that for individual decision-making under uncertainty. The main difference is that the probabilities of individual decision analysis are replaced by weights, which in the abstract could be arbitrary. The linear SWF is further specified by positive responsiveness (that is, social welfare is increasing rather than decreasing in individuals' well-being) and equal-weighting, which brings us to the utilitarian SWF. It should be emphasized that the linearity result is produced not by the final set of value judgments but rather by the rationality postulates. Thus, to favor a standard, strictly concave SWF ($e > 0$), it is necessary to reject at least one of the rationality requirements.

In a brief, provocative comment, Diamond (1967, p. 766) offers an example that he suggests illustrates a shortcoming of Harsanyi (1955), namely, that in addition to final states "society is also interested in the process of choice." As explained in subsection 13.A.3, however, two-level moral theory allows welfarism (and, accordingly, utilitarianism) to

---

individual's utility function before summing them. This point, however, carries no implication: The result of transforming both the VNM utilities and the SWF in a precisely offsetting fashion is a nullity. (Note also that squared VNM utilities are not themselves proper VNM utilities for the individuals in question because the VNM utility function may only be subject to linear transformations.) Furthermore, regarding both the present derivation of utilitarianism and that presented in the next subsection, there is no doubt that Harsanyi and others refer to individuals' VNM utility functions, so the meaning of the statement that the SWF must be linear in individuals' utilities is unambiguous (see, for example, d'Aspremont and Gérard-Varet 1991).

accommodate this apparently competing consideration.[5] Indeed, as noted there, for both Bentham and Mill a concern for government process was a chief instance in which optimal pragmatic rules and institutions would likely deviate from a full, direct realization of normative first principles. To accept that the SWF should be utilitarian does not imply, for example, that one must give a tax collector wide discretion in the choice of audit targets. Furthermore, concern for abuse should motivate attention to governmental processes independently of whether the SWF that should guide design of the income tax schedule is linear or strictly concave.

Two further perspectives reinforce the suggestion that a rational SWF must be linear. The first draws on the Pareto principle, which might have been thought inapplicable to distributive questions. Suppose, following Kaplow (1995a), that under a proposed reform each individual's expected utility is higher, but the resulting distribution of utilities has a greater variance than in the status quo. The latter feature would reduce social welfare under a strictly concave SWF. Moreover, if the increase in each individual's expected utility is sufficiently small (holding the increase in variance constant), the inequality effect would dominate and the reform would be deemed to lower social welfare. Yet, by assumption, each individual's expected utility is higher under the reform. Thus, any strictly concave SWF sometimes violates the Pareto principle.

Relatedly, Hammond (1983), Myerson (1981), and Ng (1981) have noted that only a linear SWF satisfies a time consistency property relating ex ante and ex post welfare assessments. In the foregoing example, a strictly concave SWF offers a different assessment if, instead of assessing the ex post outcome, one inserts as arguments individuals' ex ante expected utilities. To illustrate the problem, elaborate the prior example by assuming specifically that nine individuals will gain and one will lose under the reform, and each individual has an equal chance of being the loser. An ex ante assessment favors implementation (because by hypothesis each individual's expected utility is higher under the reform). Once implemented, there are (with certainty) nine winners and one loser, and the strictly concave SWF judges the ex post situation worse than the preexisting

---

[5] For further discussion of Diamond's example, see Broome (1984), Harsanyi (1975), Mirrlees (1982), and Ng (1981).

status quo. Thus, if feasible, the reform should be repealed immediately. Once repealed, however, the SWF would favor re-implementation, that is, if ex ante (expected) utilities were the arguments. And so on.[6]

2. Concerns

a. Interpersonal comparisons of utility. The use of an individualistic SWF in optimal income tax analysis (or otherwise) implicitly involves interpersonal comparisons of utility. For concreteness, consider a utilitarian SWF. In choosing among the admissible representations of each individual's von Neumann–Morgenstern utility function (which is only unique up to a linear transformation), one is deciding how units of one individual's utility function compare to units of others' utility functions.[7]

During the mid-twentieth century and to an extent thereafter, interpersonal utility comparisons were eschewed in welfare economics, following the argument of Robbins.[8] It appears, however, that he was misinterpreted from the outset. As Robbins (1935, pp. vii–x) clarified

---

[6] To avoid such circularity, the SWF would have to use only ex post distributions of utilities—which, as noted previously, creates a conflict with the Pareto principle.

[7] This requires what is referred to as cardinal unit comparability (see, for example, Sen 1977). For a strictly concave SWF, one needs cardinal full comparability, which includes comparisons of utility levels as well. The extreme case of the maximin SWF requires only level comparability. It had been believed that this requirement is different from and, in some respects, less demanding than, cardinal unit comparability. However, cardinality derives from the von Neumann–Morgenstern axioms, which are independent of comparability. Furthermore, given cardinality, level comparability implies unit comparability, but not vice versa (see Ng 1984a). The intuition is that one can take any unit of one individual's utility—say the unit from 1 util to 2 utils—and, using level comparability, find the corresponding util measures on any other individual's utility function, at which point one knows how many utils of any other individual's utility correspond to one unit of the first individual's utility.

[8] This subject is related to the apparent paradox involving the use of the standard class of individualistic SWFs in spite of Arrow's (1951) famous impossibility theorem that seems to rule out all SWFs. The resolution is that individualistic SWFs are possible when one relaxes one of Arrow's assumptions, specifically, to allow the domain of social choice procedures to consist of individuals' utilities rather than just their orderings. (Note that orderings do not permit unit or level comparability; see note 7.)

in the second edition of *An Essay on the Nature and Significance of Economic Science* and in a subsequent essay (Robbins 1938), his argument was not that interpersonal comparisons should not be made—indeed, they were inevitable—but rather that they involve value judgments rather than scientifically verifiable statements.

Much modern welfare economics has pursued analysis of SWFs that depend on individuals' utilities and not just orderings because preference intensities matter and interpersonal comparisons of utility are required if distributive judgments are to be made.[9] A number of observations have been offered regarding the feasibility of interpersonal comparisons (even if such comparisons are contestable). First is the fact that comparisons are regularly made, whether in everyday interaction when deciding how to treat children or allocate burdens between spouses, in emergency rooms when conducting triage, or in the policy realm when setting priorities for assistance. We also make analogous intrapersonal comparisons, such as when deciding whether to change occupations, get married, or have children—comparisons that are based in part on our observations of others' analogous experiences. Interpersonal judgments may be grounded on the underlying similarity of members of the human species but also may take account of observable differences in individuals' constitutions, circumstances, and expressions. A further argument advanced by Binmore (1998) is that we have evolved to have some capacity to make interpersonal comparisons, for this ability is useful in social interactions. Additional support is provided by modern scientific research on humans' ability to register others' psychological states.[10] One might

---

[9] In very basic settings, little information is required. Lerner (1944) showed that allowing individuals' utility functions to differ in unobservable ways does not upset the conclusion that a utilitarian SWF is maximized by an equal allocation of resources (in a setting with lump-sum transfers and no labor supply). See also Sen (1973b), extending the result to all concave SWFs. However, when incentive tradeoffs are necessary, as in the optimal income taxation literature, further information about the distribution of utility functions is required, at which point the analysis may proceed allowing for such heterogeneity (see subsection 5.C.2).

[10] See, for example, Wicker et al. (2003), showing that one individual's facial expression of disgust activates a neural representation of the same experience in observers' brains, and Preston and de Waal (2002), exploring how empathy operates in the nervous system and discussing its adaptive features.

further speculate that, independently of any such internal mechanisms, advances in brain science may ultimately provide a scientific basis for measuring individuals' utility in an interpersonally comparable fashion.[11] Even well short of such knowledge, however, the need for and existence of at least some basis for interpersonal utility comparisons have led to a broader acceptance thereof.[12]

b. Weight on equality. Some analysts wonder whether the SWF derived in one of subsection 1's frameworks or in some other fashion gives appropriate weight to equality.[13] It is unclear, however, what implication, if any, follows from any deviation between our intuitions about the weight of equality or degree of redistribution that seems correct and the implications of whatever SWF emerges from analysis of compelling moral constructions.

First, as the analysis in subsection 13.A.3.b warns, our moral intuitions are likely to be unreliable, and counterintuitive results should be anticipated. This seems all the more likely given the nature of the redistribution problem. As chapters 4 and 5, among others, make clear, the optimal extent of redistribution—even for a given SWF—depends on a complex array of subtle factors, including various traits of utility functions, the distribution of skills, available tax instruments, general equilibrium effects, considerations of administration and enforcement, and so forth. The shape of the optimal income tax schedule is counterintuitive, and the optimal degree of redistribution is highly contingent,

---

[11] It seems no coincidence that the ordinalist revolution in economics roughly coincided with behavioralism in psychology, at a time when our limited knowledge rendered activity within the human brain almost entirely beyond our comprehension.

[12] See, for example, Brandt (1979), Hare (1981), Harsanyi (1975, 1982), Little (1957), Mirrlees (1982), Scitovsky (1951), and Sen (1973a).

[13] A prominent example is Sen's (1973a, p. 16) objection that utilitarianism should not be regarded as sufficiently egalitarian (or egalitarian at all) because it is unconcerned with the distribution of utility levels per se. Instead, Sen advances what he refers to as a "weak equity axiom," which requires that an individual (say, A) who receives lower utility for any given income level than another must receive a larger allocation of income. However, this axiom may be more extreme than is maximin: Consider the case in which the incentive effects of implementing such a scheme so reduce productivity as to make even individual A far worse off than under less radical schemes.

the concavity of the SWF being just one factor. Furthermore, all standard SWFs favor complete equality in the simple resource allocation problem (without labor supply considerations), and in most optimal income tax simulations, all SWFs, including a utilitarian one, favor substantial redistribution, reflecting the nontrivial concavity of utility as a function of income. It is unclear how we could have reliable intuitions that would indicate whether any particular result entailed too much or too little weight on equality.[14]

Consider also the various meanings of equality. Under perhaps the most basic understanding of the notion, that everyone should be treated in the same manner, all standard SWFs adhere perfectly to the concept, for every individual is treated symmetrically. (In Harsanyi's second derivation of utilitarianism, recall that the linearity of the SWF was due to the rationality postulates; a separate value judgment of equality was invoked to yield the result that each individual's utility is to be weighted equally in the summation.) It is a property of a utilitarian SWF that individuals' marginal utilities count equally, whereas changes in utility levels per se are irrelevant. (As suggested with regard to the derivation from the original position in note 1, equating contributions to marginal utility across individuals is entailed by maxims such as the Golden Rule, which commands us to treat others as we would wish others to treat ourselves.) Under maximin, utility levels count equally, but marginal utility is immaterial. For other strictly concave SWFs, the result is in between; neither individuals' marginal utilities nor their utility levels matter equally even though utility functions enter the SWF symmetrically.

B. Membership in Society

Under welfarism, social welfare is taken to be a function of individuals' utilities. Which individuals should be included, however, is not self-evident. Questions of membership in society are among the most

---

[14] An additional problem is that our basic intuitions about redistribution probably pertain to the distribution of resources (income), which is what we observe being redistributed, not utils, which are the unit of measure of the arguments of the SWF.

challenging ones that must be confronted in developing a complete theory of distributive justice. This section considers, in a limited manner, the spatial dimension (national boundaries), the intertemporal dimension (intergenerational considerations, such as discounting), and the endogeneity of population size (requiring welfare comparisons between societies of different populations with differing membership).[15]

Some preliminary notes are in order. First, most of the analysis in the rest of the book is unaffected by the resolution of these issues because that analysis pertains to how to maximize an individualistic SWF, regardless of the population involved. Nevertheless, there are exceptions, notably some issues raised in chapter 10 on transfer taxation and in chapter 12 on taxation of the family. Second, these issues are largely independent of the form (concavity) of the SWF, although it will sometimes be convenient to refer to a utilitarian SWF for concreteness.[16]

1. National Boundaries

From a normative perspective, it is difficult to adopt other than a universal view on membership in society if redistribution is to be contemplated at all. National boundaries, the most commonly assumed demarcations of populations for purposes of redistributive income taxation and other government programs, have practical and political significance, but no clear, a priori ethical relevance in determining whose utility should count in formulating an SWF.[17] The self-interest of members of a

---

[15] There is also an important species dimension, particularly concerning the weight to be accorded to nonhuman sentient beings. Just as welfarism tends to favor an inclusive view along the dimensions considered in the text, welfarists including the classical utilitarians (see Sidgwick 1907, referring as well to Bentham, Mill, and utilitarians generally) would include all sentient beings, a view favored by such moderns as Singer (1975) and Regan (1983).

[16] Nor are these issues pertinent only under welfarism. For example, in any rights-based scheme, one needs to determine which individuals (foreigners? the unborn?) are to be accorded rights.

[17] See, for example, Singer (2004). Practically, enforcement of compulsory taxation may be limited by national boundaries, and the ability to administer transfers in other jurisdictions may be inferior, but such restrictions pertain to which policies maximize the SWF, not to what the SWF should be taken to be. National boundaries may also correspond to the reach of citizens' altruism and to who votes and thus has the political power to insist

nation or a union of nations, however vast or narrow its scope, in not having to redistribute to others seems little different normatively from that of a smaller jurisdiction (say, a rich suburb) or even a particular high-income individual seeking an exemption from redistribution. In an original position behind a veil of ignorance, individuals would not know their national identity any more than they would know their relative position within their nation; hence, they would favor international redistribution. This point is particularly important in light of the fact that a substantial majority of global inequality involves income differences between nations rather than within them.[18]

Nevertheless, national boundaries may retain significance to the problem of optimal redistributive taxation because of incentive considerations. To some extent (how much and in which instances is very hard to say), differences in well-being across nations reflect differences in prior investments and their outcomes. In a consistent intertemporal framework, it would be optimal to protect winners' claims to some degree. As explored in subsection 9.C.2's analysis of capital levies and transitions, although it may seem appealing ex post to tax accumulations from prior efforts, this opportunistic approach is unlikely to be an optimal long-run strategy.

Preliminary insight into this problem may be gleaned from the models surveyed in subsection 5.E.2 on uncertain labor income and in subsection 9.C.3 on human capital. One view would be that individuals who moved to and established themselves in different regions made investments that had uncertain payoffs in terms of future wage rates. In some regions, resulting wages turned out to be high; in others, low. In that case, the income tax operates to a degree as insurance, and some redistribution is optimal. However, to the extent that many individuals had accepted preexisting wages in their region of origin and did not make such investments in human capital, the optimal extent of redistribution

---

on inclusion. There is, however, great variation in the extent to which national boundaries in any country and at any point in history have these and other pertinent characteristics (in part since such boundaries are often accidents of history, the results of war, or the dictates of former colonial rulers). In any event, such considerations are beyond the purview of this book.

[18] See, for example, Kopczuk, Slemrod, and Yitzhaki (2005) and Sala-i-Martin (2002).

from investors to noninvestors—in contrast to redistribution between successful and unsuccessful investors—is further limited because of the distortion of ex ante incentives (as well as the distortion of ex post labor supply, which occurs in either case).[19]

A further complication is that present beneficiaries are often many generations removed from those who made the pertinent investments and took the risks. It does not follow, however, that a consistent dynamic perspective would ignore that current beneficiaries' high wages may be attributable to ancestors' investments, the payoffs from which consisted perhaps in significant part of bequests of human capital and a favorable working and living environment. In analyzing the taxation of transfers generally, subsection 10.C.1 explained how focusing only on inequality in the donee generation provides an incomplete and significantly misleading view of the problem. Stated more concretely, it is clear that many immigrants make large sacrifices that are substantially motivated by the prospect of benefits to their descendants, so the prospect of their descendants' gains being taxed away would reduce immigrants' incentives, in addition to reducing immigrants' well-being, itself a component of social welfare.

Another consideration is the role of immigration in global redistribution. This book concentrates on taxation and transfers. In the international setting, however, the potential distributive effect of labor mobility is great. Immigration raises a number of qualitatively different issues because, even ignoring that an immigrant may become subject to a different tax-transfer system, movement may affect the individual's wage

---

[19] In another variation, in which investors face, say, either a high wage outcome or death (due to starvation or disease in a new settlement), they face no prospect of receiving transfers in the adverse state, so the optimal degree to which an ideal scheme would tax their labor income in the favorable state is lower, although some taxation would nevertheless be optimal (since, starting from a zero rate, there is a first-order redistributive gain in light of such individuals' low marginal utilities of income). One can analogize this scenario to the problem of compensating wage differentials that offset nonpecuniary job disamenities (that is, part of wage payments offsets a sort of negative income that is not observed, so individuals receiving compensating differentials are implicitly misclassified with higher-ability types and thus are overtaxed, inefficiently discouraging employment in sectors with disamenities) (see subsection 5.C.2 and note 50).

and impose a variety of positive and negative externalities on the countries of origin and destination.[20] Additionally, even accepting an inclusive SWF, the foregoing analysis indicates that it is hardly obvious that optimal redistribution across nations corresponds to the application of a given country's tax-transfer scheme to immigrants. Finally, when there exist different tax-transfer systems in different countries, there will be inefficient incentives for cross-country mobility (by the poor, to high-transfer jurisdictions, and by the rich, to jurisdictions having less redistributive tax systems, the latter being more important to the extent that some countries compete for their residence).

2. Future Generations

Intergenerational distributive justice involves an additional, intertemporal dimension often presented as the question of whether (and, if so, how much) to discount the lives or utility of future individuals.[21] To motivate the anti-discounting view, it is common to present an illustration like that of Parfit (1984), who notes that a 5% annual discount rate makes one present life more valuable than one hundred thirty lives a century from now, two million in three centuries, and nearly forty billion (the entire human race?) in five hundred years. The question of how to weight present versus future lives can be considered more explicitly using the frameworks outlined in section A.

In the original position, a person ignorant of which generation he or she would be born into (and placing an equal probability on becoming each possible individual, regardless of generation) would accord equal weight to the utility of different individuals in different generations just as equal weight would be accorded to individuals within

---

[20] See, for example, Bhagwati and Wilson (1989).

[21] It also raises the difficult practical challenge of determining the intergenerational distribution under various regimes, for one needs to account not only for observable transfers such as through social security systems and national debt but also for effective transfers through infrastructure and other long-lived tangible assets, knowledge, institutions (including, for example, wars and revolutions that created lasting peace or threaten future conflict), as well as more familiar yet complex matters involving natural resource depletion and environmental degradation.

a given generation.[22] A similar view is suggested by reasoning in accord with the Golden Rule and related constructs.[23] Different generations under this view would be treated differently on account of actual differences in circumstances—for example, if a future generation had a lower probability of existing, its utility would be discounted accordingly—but there would be no discounting of lives or utility per se.

The argument from social rationality, recall, produced equal weighting by stipulation (the rationality postulates implying only linearity). In the intergenerational setting, one could similarly stipulate equal weighting of utilities—or one might stipulate otherwise, although the normative basis for doing so is unclear. Considering the case of overlapping generations, it seems hard to justify distinguishing utilities across simultaneously existing individuals of different cohorts; by extension, there would be no discounting even across generations that did not overlap.

An additional set of issues, pertaining especially to resource depletion and environmental quality (for example, climate change), is often examined from a perspective of intergenerational justice. Upon analysis, however, such issues are not qualitatively different from the pure distributive question, as it might be addressed through social security, debt policy, or other fiscal measures. Specifically, environmental and all other intergenerational problems can be separated into questions of efficiency and distribution, just as is true intragenerationally, following the approach developed primarily in chapters 2, 6, and 8. That is, one can address the

---

[22] See, for example, Mueller (1974). When Rawls (1971) addressed intergenerational justice, he assumed that only a single generation occupied the original position. Although individuals do not know which generation they belong to, there is the unraveling problem that each would rationally take as given that prior generations have—or have not—been generous, and concern for future generations would be dependent on the extent of altruism. For criticism, see, for example, Barry (1977, 1989). In responses to such criticisms, Rawls (1993, p. 274) presents a revised view.

[23] "It seems, however, clear that the time at which a man exists cannot affect the value of his happiness from a universal point of view . . ." (Sidgwick [1907] 1981, p. 414). Consider also, for example, Lewis's (1946) idea that individuals should be imagined to rotate among all roles. Relatedly, Cowen (1992) argues that social welfare should be viewed as unaffected if an individual is moved from one generation to another, assuming that the individual receives the same utility in either case and that no one else's utility is affected (see also Broome 1992 and Parfit 1984).

question of intergenerational distributive justice in a simple world in which such complications are absent—that is, one with an environment that stays constant and the only question is how much money to transfer among generations—and, whatever its resolution, determine which policies are efficient.[24]

Externalities and public goods of all sorts (including goods like infrastructure that have long lives) can be thought of as vectors with different components indexed by time or cohort, just as in the case of commodities (compare the treatment of capital taxation in chapter 9).[25] Accordingly, as chapter 8 indicates (see section 8.G on regulation in particular), it is optimal in the basic case to set policy (other than purely redistributive policy) using efficiency criteria alone.[26] The idea of employing a distribution-neutral income tax adjustment, introduced in chapter 2, can be extended so as to keep utilities constant not only across individuals implicitly taken to be of a given generation but also across individuals of different generations. As before, moving in a distribution-neutral manner to more efficient policies generates a surplus that can be distributed to produce a Pareto improvement, in this case including members of all relevant generations.

Because the experiment under consideration is distribution neutral, this argument holds regardless of how the question of intergenerational justice (that is, the extent of any intergenerational discount) is resolved. If more weight is placed on future generations, ceteris paribus, it is likely that better environmental protection will be optimal, but this will be due to an income effect that does not distinguish the environment from any other type of investment. (For example, optimal R&D for consumer goods would also probably be higher on this account.) One complication is that the costs of some investments may be incurred in a different (earlier) generation from their benefits. All this means is that the earlier

---

[24] The ideas that follow are developed in greater detail in Kaplow (2007b).

[25] The SWF can index individuals similarly, applying equal weights or otherwise. And, following subsection 5.C.1, the variable θ in a group-conditioned income tax schedule can also index time or cohorts; alternatively, if the same schedule must apply to each generation, then all generations would be represented by a single density function f.

[26] Qualifications were noted (see section 6.C); however, they are essentially orthogonal to the intergenerational dimension.

generation should make the necessary investments—whether they are in environmental regulation, infrastructure, R&D, machines, or whatever else—financing them by debt that may be carried forward (relative to whatever financial path was otherwise contemplated). All such investments should be undertaken to the point at which the marginal unit breaks even, at a common discount rate corresponding to the return on capital.[27] Holding constant how much or little one generation expects to benefit another, future generation, this benefit should be conferred in the most efficient manner. The surplus can be divided to the advantage of both generations.

There is a substantially equivalent way to state the same argument, one that first converts everything (lives, utility) into dollars and then applies ordinary discounting.[28] Begin, say, with an amenity in a future generation F. Using ordinary techniques for valuing amenities, this can be given a monetary value in time F dollars. That value, in turn, can be discounted back to present generation P dollars using ordinary discounting of money. Finally, this amount can be converted to the original type of amenity in the present generation P using the valuation of the current generation. Taking this sequence together, future amenities (or, more broadly, utility) are translated to present amenities (or utility).[29] This approach is dictated by efficiency for essentially the reason given previously: If one followed any other rule, a deviation in the direction dictated by this valuation and discounting method, accompanied by a

---

[27] It may be noted that the equilibrium discount rate may well depend on the prevailing intergenerational distribution of income, but that distribution is being held constant in the contemplated policy experiment. For elaboration on this and other factors bearing on the market discount rate, see, for example, Arrow et al. (1996), Kaplow (2007b), Lind et al. (1982), and Nordhaus (1994).

[28] Aspects of this variation are suggested in a variety of prior writing. See, for example, Arrow et al. (1996), Revesz (1999), and Viscusi (1995).

[29] The argument in the text does not require that the translation be one for one, or in any other stipulated ratio. As the foregoing discussion indicates, the question of intergenerational distribution (which may, for example, be framed as a statement of how utility in one generation is to be traded off against utility in another) is resolved independently. The present argument simply takes the present distribution (which will influence the discount rate, see note 27) as given.

distributively offsetting adjustment in the intergenerational flow of money, would yield a gain that could be allocated to both generations.

Consider briefly some additional factors that may influence the intergenerational allocation of resources. First, it is sometimes conjectured that future generations will be ever richer on account of technological advance. (Analogous reasoning is applicable to the case in which increasing scarcity, congestion, and pollution have the opposite effect.) In that case, the marginal social value of dollars in the future would be lower on account of the diminishing marginal utility of consumption. Note, however, that this is not necessarily the case. Suppose, in particular, that technology benefits future generations by enabling them to make more effective use of resources in a manner that is formally analogous to economies of scale in the family, analyzed in subsection 12.A.2. In this case, a value of $\beta > 1$ would indicate that an individual in the future generation obtains more effective consumption per unit of resource (say, measured in present value in the current generation) than does an individual in the present generation. The pure efficiency effect raises the effective marginal utility of consumption, which works in the opposite direction of the more familiar diminishing marginal utility effect that reduces effective marginal utility. As before, for linear (constant-with-income) economies and a utilitarian social welfare function, it is optimal (ceteris paribus) to distribute more (less) to the future generation, relative to the otherwise optimal equal division, if relative risk aversion is less (greater) than one.[30]

Second, suppose that income levels in future generations are uncertain. In this case, the allocation across generations can be understood by analogy to the problem of precautionary savings by individuals of a given generation who face intertemporal income uncertainty. Another question concerns the possibility raised by Barro (1974) that individuals' private intergenerational transfers will offset the government's (Ricardian equivalence). Such substitution is unlikely to be fully operative for all families; to the extent that it is, it applies only within a certain range. Therefore, such private behavior may, to a degree that

---

[30] One can analogize this problem to intrapersonal allocations over time, where the curvature of the utility function influences the sign of the elasticity of saving with respect to the rate of return.

varies across the population, partially inhibit intergenerational redistributive efforts.[31]

3. Population Size

There remains the question of how to compare social welfare between populations of different sizes.[32] This question is exemplified by the debate between classical utilitarians who would maximize total utility and those (including many moderns) who would maximize average utility. For example, the total view would deem as superior a regime that would result in a population of 10 with utilities of 100 each to one with 9 individuals with utilities of 110 each, whereas the average view would favor the latter. Note that this issue is not distinctive to utilitarianism per se; under a strictly concave SWF, the same question would be faced, requiring a determination whether social welfare should be normalized to population size.[33]

Two arguments seem to favor the total view. One is from the original position, assuming that individuals do not know for certain that they will necessarily be one of the individuals who exist under either regime (to allow otherwise would inject precisely the partiality that the original-position framework is designed to eliminate).[34] In the foregoing

---

[31] Recall from the discussions in subsections 10.B.1 and 12.B.2.b that the weight that individuals place on descendants on account of altruism (or otherwise, as a matter of preference) is less than the social weight, so the existence of intergenerational transfers does not imply that their level is socially optimal.

[32] One aspect of the problem is that comparisons involving different population sizes necessarily involve, to an extent, different individuals being alive. This feature, however, is not distinct to population size issues because any difference in regimes will, especially in the long run, result in different individuals being born. (Even the slightest change may cause some individuals to procreate an instant sooner or later, which in turn will have ripple effects into the future.) This issue is explored by Parfit (1984), who suggests the irrelevance of such differences in identity in assessing the social good.

[33] Consider examples in which utility is distributed equally (or in which full equalization is optimal because there are no incentive considerations), in which case the concavity of the SWF has no obvious relevance.

[34] Rawls (1971) favors the average view precisely by supposing that individuals in the original position would know that they would exist for certain in the lower-population regime. This move is criticized, for example, by Hare (1973) and Sumner (1978).

example, therefore, one might suppose that, behind the veil, there are 10 hypothetical beings who might with equal likelihood be one of the 10 actual individuals in the first regime, whereas for the second regime they each have a 90% chance of being one of the actual individuals and a 10% chance of not existing. Rational maximization would, under this construct, favor the total view.

Another argument is based on a sequential construction of the sort developed at length by Parfit (1984). Suppose we begin with a world of 10 individuals, each with a utility of 100. (Total utility is 1000; average utility is 100.) Next, suppose we could implement a regime that would raise the utility of each existing individual to 105 and also create an additional individual who would have a utility of 28 (assumed to be above the threshold that the life would be worth living, that is, preferable to not living). (Total utility is now 1078; average utility is 98.) A variation of the Pareto principle suggests that this regime involves higher social welfare, for all individuals who are alive under either regime prefer the latter. This is true despite average utility being lower in the latter regime. As a final step, suppose that it is possible to implement a further reform that equalizes utility for all individuals at an average level that is one unit higher than that in the intermediate regime. (Specifically, suppose that total utility is now 1089; average utility is 99). This step raises total utility and also distributes it more equally, which raises social welfare under any standard SWF (utilitarian or strictly concave).

Combining these steps, we have moved from a population of 10 with a utility of 100 each to a population of 11 with a utility of 99 each, having a higher total utility but a lower average. If each step involves an increase in social welfare, then so must the combination. Moreover, we can imagine repeating this process again and again, resulting in a very large population with a very low average utility.[35] Parfit (1984) deems this result the "repugnant conclusion." Despite his dismissal of criticisms that

---

[35] The only caveat is that the additional member in step one must have a utility that is not below the level at which life is worth living. Of course, if it were below such a level, then total utility—measured relative to the appropriate origin—should be deemed to fall on account of the existence of this individual.

would interfere with the argument, he adheres to the view that the result is intrinsically repugnant, leaving it to future thinkers to develop the theory that can explain why this is so.[36] Of course, it is easy to understand why many analysts and readers sympathize with Parfit, for we all know that we are among the currently existing lives, and following the logic of his construct suggests that, in an ideal world, we would be far worse off. But just like the argument from the original position that assumes individuals are not fully behind a veil of ignorance and instead know that they will be the lucky ones to experience life in the small total but high average utility world, this reaction is obviously one from self-interest.[37]

Our reluctance to believe that the optimal population size is tremendously large may also arise from other considerations.[38] Notably, at some point, the negative externalities of additional lives, due to congestion, pollution, and resource depletion, may well outweigh any positive externalities from agglomeration or otherwise. Such considerations, however, are relevant under both the total and the average view and do not obviously bear on which formulation of the SWF is normatively correct. In either case, they suggest that utilities will tend to fall further as population increases, reducing the population level at which total or average utility is maximized. Note that, in the relevant range, such externalities suggest that individuals' incentives to procreate may be too high. However, as discussed with regard to altruism in subsections 10.B.1 on transfers and 12.B.2.b on incentives to procreate, parents' weight on

---

[36] Ng (1989) argues that no such rescuing theory can exist and that the large-population outcome may not really be repugnant, although he does suggest a modification of the total view. Cowen (1996) similarly argues that it is impossible to reconcile the repugnant conclusion with other basic ethical intuitions, but argues that some of the latter might best be relaxed. For alternative views, see, for example, Blackorby, Bossert, and Donaldson (1995), Broome (1996), Dasgupta (1994), and Hurka (1983).

[37] Parfit (1984) also notes that, under the average view, a tiny population, even one with only a single individual, would be deemed superior to a large population with a high average utility, as long as that average was below that of the tiny (or singleton) population. Others have previously voiced this criticism of the average view (see, for example, Sumner 1978).

[38] See, for example, Hare (1988).

their children's welfare is in one important respect systematically lower than the social weight (because parents consider how children contribute to the parents' own utility, which is but one of the channels, and the indirect one at that, by which children's utility contributes to social welfare).[39] Hence, even in a world in which population increases generate net negative externalities (aside from the benefit to the additional individuals themselves), it is possible that individuals' procreation incentives are still suboptimal.

---

[39] See also subsection 13.B.3 on the question whether other-regarding utility should be included in social welfare.

15

Other Normative Criteria

For purposes of assessing taxation and redistribution, chapters 13 and 14 present a complete framework. That is, once it is decided that social welfare should depend exclusively on individuals' utilities, what the functional form of the SWF is, and whose utilities count, it would appear that there is no room for further normative analysis, much less for additional and potentially conflicting normative criteria.

This approach to distributive justice and social welfare, however, became established in applied work only with the emergence of the literature on optimal income taxation in the 1970s. Before then, more informal, intuitive notions of tax equity had an important role. Moreover, as section 3.A indicates, many such notions continue to be invoked today, perhaps in part because optimal income tax analysis is complex and its application to a wide range of subsidiary questions is not immediately obvious. For some of these other normative concepts, there exists a substantial technical literature developing measurement indexes—for example, there are two handbooks on income inequality per se, Atkinson and Bourguignon (2000) and Silber (1999)—and they are often employed in applied policy analysis as a supplement to or substitute for an SWF.

All such normative criteria are prima facie problematic. If the welfare economic framework is accepted, either competing measures must be proxy indicators for aspects of social welfare or they register something else, the pursuit of which inevitably entails the sacrifice of social welfare. In fact, both elements are often present. The continuing appeal of the other normative criteria seems in part attributable to their resonance with intuitions about distributive justice. The analysis in subsection 13.A.3 explains, however, that such intuitions are unreliable and can lead us astray, especially because the context of application differs substantially from that in which the intuitions originate. As will be seen, the residual usefulness of these various tax equity criteria as proxy principles varies greatly and may require that they be used differently from the manner suggested in the pertinent literatures.

A. Inequality, Poverty, Progressivity, Redistribution

Economists have developed indexes of inequality and poverty in a society and of the progressivity and redistribution associated with part or all of the fiscal system.[1] These measures are often employed to offer a normative assessment of taxation, the standard implication being that regimes exhibiting less inequality and poverty and tax schemes involving more progressivity and redistribution are superior.[2] As shown in Kaplow (2005), however, the literature does not offer an affirmative basis for this approach, and it does not appear that any justification can be provided. For concreteness, the reasoning will be presented for the case of inequality indexes, where the literature is most developed, and then briefly applied to measures of other traits of policies or outcomes.

Many inequality indexes are incomplete and ungrounded. Unless one distribution of income dominates another (that is, individuals below any given percentile level have more income under one income distribution than under another), inequality measures generally conflict. Some may satisfy certain axioms, but those in turn need justification—in principle, grounded in an SWF. For many measures, there exist inequality-reducing reforms that raise welfare under some SWFs but lower welfare under others. Most measures do not indicate the weight to be placed on inequality, so it is unclear how much a society should

---

[1] See, for example, on inequality: Atkinson and Bourguignon (2000), Cowell (1995), Lambert (2001), and Silber (1999); on poverty: Atkinson (1987), Clark, Hemming, and Ulph (1981), Lambert (2001), Ravallion (1994), Ruggles (1990), Sen (1976), and Silber (1999); and on progressivity and redistribution: Jakobsson (1976), Kakwani (1977), Lambert (1999, 2001), Musgrave and Thin (1948), and Suits (1977).

[2] The indexes also have descriptive uses, which raise different issues (see Kaplow 2005).

sacrifice to increase equality by any specified amount. Furthermore, many indexes are based on the distribution of incomes, but the meaning of income differences depends on individuals' utility functions. (For example, resolution of the question of whether inequality should be deemed constant if all incomes increase by the same proportion would presumably depend on the curvature of individuals' utilities as a function of income.)

To address such problems, Dalton (1920) argued that inequality measures had to be related to economic welfare, in essence that they needed to be based explicitly on an SWF. The most prominent such measure—associated with Atkinson (1970), Kolm (1969), and Sen (1973a)—is constructed in four steps. First, an SWF must be chosen; typical is the isoelastic reduced form introduced in expression (3.4) in subsection 3.B.1:

$$SW(x) = \int \frac{y^{1-\gamma}}{1-\gamma} f(y) dy, \text{ for } \gamma \neq 1, \tag{15.1}$$

where for simplicity all that is taken to matter in a regime x is each individual's disposable income, here denoted y following convention, and γ indicates the degree of aversion to inequality (which, recall, in this formulation is a sort of composite of the curvature in individuals' utility functions and in the social welfare function).[3] Second, using information on the density of the income distribution, $f(y)$, social welfare is calculated using (15.1). Third, one computes what is referred to as the equally distributed equivalent level of income, denoted y_e, which has the property that, if everyone had income at that level, social welfare would be the same as that computed in step 2. For the stated SWF (15.1), this can readily be determined as follows:

$$\frac{y_e^{1-\gamma}}{1-\gamma} = SW(x) = \int \frac{y^{1-\gamma}}{1-\gamma} f(y) dy, \text{ or}$$

$$y_e = \left[\int y^{1-\gamma} f(y) dy \right]^{1/(1-\gamma)}. \tag{15.2}$$

---

[3] The analysis to follow could be replicated for the case in which $\gamma = 1$ using $\ln y$.

Fourth and finally, we construct the index of inequality, I, as follows:

$$I = 1 - \frac{y_e}{y_\mu}, \tag{15.3}$$

where y_μ refers to mean income. The ratio of equivalently distributed income to mean income, y_e/y_μ, indicates the portion of actual income that would be necessary to achieve the existing level of social welfare if instead that income were distributed equally. Therefore, the inequality index I indicates how much income could in principle be destroyed while leaving social welfare unchanged if only the remaining income were distributed equally.

Reflection upon this derivation, however, reveals that there is little possible use for the resulting inequality measure I. The index, of course, tells only part of the story; it must be combined with additional information to produce a full assessment of any regime x. Yet the full assessment was already obtained in step 2, when social welfare was calculated. In other words, to produce the partial indicator I, one must first derive the complete measure of social welfare and then perform further operations to strip away relevant information. Furthermore, no shortcut is possible. In particular, there is no way to derive I without first specifying an SWF and determining the level of social welfare under the pertinent regime. Different SWFs will produce different measures of I; furthermore, it was the very need to provide a normative grounding for inequality measurement that motivated the SWF-based approach. Because this approach does not allow construction of an inequality index based upon partial information, it is difficult to identify how the resulting measure can be useful.

Nevertheless, as noted at the outset, inequality indexes are often used to grade policies and governments. It should be apparent that such assessments are inherently incomplete and potentially misleading. Ceteris paribus, what inequality indexes omit—mean income—is in the relevant range negatively related to what is measured. This is the familiar equity-efficiency tradeoff. Knowing that a policy increases (or reduces) inequality or that one country's inequality is higher (lower) than another's does not indicate that the policy is detrimental (desirable) or that the government's performance is subpar (or superior).

The primary justification for the normative use of inequality measures is as a corrective to comparisons that focus excessively on per capita GDP, ignoring the distribution of income. Assessing policies or governments based purely on GDP in settings in which distribution is not held constant is similarly incomplete and misleading. Nevertheless, rather than supplementing GDP data with an inequality measure, which cannot be obtained without choosing an SWF and measuring social welfare, it would be superior to provide the social welfare assessment that had to be computed in step 2 along the way to generating the inequality measure. One of this book's themes, developed initially in section 3.A, is that explicit reference to the social objective is necessary. Consideration of inequality measures reinforces this view.

Poverty indexes may be analyzed similarly. For a normative measure to be policy relevant, it must be based on an SWF. Indeed, some poverty indexes are essentially truncated normative inequality indexes. The main differences are that poverty measures are even more incomplete and also are sensitive to the arbitrary judgment involved in drawing a poverty line and to the manner of determining how to assess the circumstances of individuals who fall below it. Attention to poverty is understandable, for if there is sufficient concavity in either utility functions or the SWF, the situation of individuals at the bottom of the income distribution will significantly influence the optimal design of redistribution policies. This fact, however, does not make it necessary to derive separate poverty measures, for the assessment provided by the SWF itself will by definition have already taken the importance of low-income individuals' situations into account—and will also reflect the impact of policies on other individuals, including those just above the poverty line, whose situations are also likely to be relevant.[4]

Indexes of progressivity and redistribution have similar shortcomings. In some instances, the connection is especially close, such as when the degree of redistribution is defined by the difference between the level

_____

[4] For purposes of designing some transfer programs, there may be an administrative need for a cutoff, which might be set at some threshold. Yet the ideal level of such a cutoff for any particular program is the outcome of the optimization process, not an input or a constraint.

of inequality before and after tax, measured by an inequality index.[5] And progressivity, in turn, may be measured by the extent of redistribution. (If not, the measure is even more arbitrary, such as when one looks at ratios of average tax rates but not their magnitude; for example, very low rates, even if applied only to the very rich, might be quite progressive by some measures yet still be of little import.) In any event, to be of normative relevance, the measures must be derived from an SWF, but once the SWF is specified and social welfare is measured, a complete assessment already exists.[6]

B. Horizontal Equity

Horizontal equity, one of the basic notions of tax fairness advanced by Musgrave (1959), is the seemingly uncontroversial command that equals be treated (taxed) equally. Economists have generated a variety of indexes of horizontal inequity.[7] Typically, these indexes measure the extent of inequality of treatment of individuals under a tax reform whose incomes were equal prior to the reform (or in the pre-tax distribution of income or some other benchmark setting). Such horizontal inequity is viewed negatively, suggesting the need to trade it off against social welfare, the latter presumably defined by reference to a standard SWF. As developed in Kaplow (1989, 1995a, 2001b), however, this normative recommendation lacks affirmative justification and accordingly results

---

[5] Also, the literature engaging in explicit normative measurement derives indexes from an SWF, often drawing directly on Atkinson (1970).

[6] Some advocates directly assess taxation (sometimes the entire system, sometimes a single tax instrument) by reference to whether it is progressive or proportional. For example, Blum and Kalven's (1952, 1953) well-known essay criticizes sacrifice theories as well as other principles and concludes that taxes should be proportional, but as Bankman and Griffith (1987) and Groves (1974), among others, have noted, their conclusion rests on little more than a presumption in favor of proportionality. (Furthermore, since Blum and Kalven would allow exemptions and do not restrict how tax proceeds may be spent, they implicitly allow progressivity in the standard economic sense of rising average rates and also substantial redistribution, which seems inconsistent with most of their critique.)

[7] See, for example, Aronson and Lambert (1994), Auerbach and Hassett (2002), Atkinson (1980), Feldstein (1976), King (1983), Musgrave (1990), and Plotnick (1981).

in a needless sacrifice in welfare, possibly everyone's welfare. The intuitive appeal of horizontal equity, moreover, may be understood by the manner in which it serves as a proxy indicator for other possible sources of welfare reduction, although standard indexes are not well suited for this surrogate function.

To begin, horizontal equity has familiar definitional problems. What if few individuals (or none) are precise equals in the benchmark distribution? What is the basis for seemingly ad hoc judgments about how pre-reform individuals are to be grouped and post-reform differences are to be weighted? Are rank reversals, which may or may not involve unequal treatment of pre-reform equals, similarly problematic? And finally, can indexes that address some of these and other challenges still be properly understood as measures of horizontal inequity? Some attempts to address these questions offer decompositions of standard SWFs, wherein one component is deemed to be a measure of horizontal inequity. However, the basis for such decompositions seems largely semantic, and the purpose for distinguishing certain influences on social welfare is unclear.

The shortcomings of horizontal inequity indexes are similar to those of the inequality and related indexes examined in section A. For example, if one needs to specify an SWF and have complete information on its determinants, there seems no good reason to undertake further computations (some of which require further information) to produce an index that represents merely an aspect of social welfare. More worrisome is the suggestion, often explicit but sometimes implicit, that one component of social welfare should be given more weight than another. Why should a one-util shortfall to individual i count more than some other one-util shortfall to the same individual i because the former is classified as one particular form of inequity? The literature does not attempt to answer this basic question or, relatedly, indicate why a distinct measure of horizontal inequity is required in the first instance.[8]

---

[8] Many measures of horizontal inequity have further defects. For example, most define the equals who should be treated equally by reference to a pre-reform status quo. However, once a reform that reduces horizontal equity is implemented, the resulting regime becomes the status quo; hence, repeal can only further reduce horizontal equity, and under most indexes it ordinarily would. One might add more broadly that reforms are motivated by the existence of defects in the status quo, which would seem to contraindicate placing a negative value on departures from the status quo per se. These problems can be avoided by specifying

Furthermore, it follows from the general discussion of nonwelfarist principles in subsection 13.A.2 that giving any weight to horizontal inequity conflicts with the Pareto principle.[9] Consider, for example, a society of two individuals, identical in all respects ex ante, and a reform that raises one individual's utility and lowers the other's by a smaller amount, with each individual having an equal chance of occupying each position. Ex ante expected utility rises with the reform, so both would favor it. If, however, any weight is put on the violation of horizontal equity (the equals will not be treated equally), there exist cases—where the expected utility increase is sufficiently small (one can reduce the mean but maintain the variance)—in which the reform will be opposed.[10]

Despite these deficiencies in horizontal equity indexes, the maxim that equals should be treated equally has intuitive appeal, and this attraction can readily be explained. The discussion in subsection 13.A.3 suggests that we often have moral intuitions that arise in contexts distinct from the setting of optimal tax design but that nevertheless seem compelling and may have a proxy role even though they are not independent moral principles to be pursued at the expense of individuals' well-being. Most directly, in ordinary settings, if it maximizes social welfare to subject individual i to treatment X rather than Y, and if individual j is identical in all relevant respects to i, then j also should receive treatment X. If we observe that i receives X and j receives Y, it is likely that a mistake has been made. In other words, optimization

---

some idealized distribution as the benchmark rather than the status quo, but why only deviations involving unequal treatment of equals should matter—or why they should matter differently from other deviations—is obscure. Why would we not evaluate any regime or reform by reference to the objective function (SWF) from which the idealized distribution was derived? These sorts of difficulties reinforce the suggestion that the literature has developed multiple, conflicting indexes without first specifying the purpose of measurement.

[9] There are a number of ways to see that measures of horizontal inequity are nonwelfarist. If not all utils are weighted in the same manner, then information on each individual's utility level obviously is insufficient to form a social judgment. Also, most indexes make reference to the pre-reform income distribution, the pre-tax distribution, or some other benchmark, indicating that information other than individuals' utilities in the actually prevailing state is relevant.

[10] This is essentially the same example (from Kaplow 1995a) used in subsection 14.A.1.b.

typically implies equal treatment, so unequal treatment typically signifies a failure to optimize.[11] In such instances, it is necessary to identify the mistake (is j being treated suboptimally, or i, or possibly both?) and correct it. The value of such correction is already indicated by the SWF. Moreover, correction of mistreatment is valuable even if there exists no other individual who was already being treated correctly.

Unequal treatment of equals sometimes indicates particular sorts of welfare reductions. It may suggest the existence of greater income inequality (for example, a reform may not seem to affect the income distribution when data consists of decile averages, but dispersion within deciles might have increased).[12] Similarly, as suggested by the foregoing example involving a violation of the Pareto principle, horizontal inequity may correlate with exposure to risk, which is welfare reducing, ceteris paribus. Another sort of concern involves the possibility of corruption and various other abuses of power, which in important instances involve unequal treatment (racial discrimination, government favors to political allies).[13] Indeed, this problem probably best explains the intuitive force of the equal treatment principle.

The question remains how best to analyze these issues. Income inequality and risk are already fully assessed under a standard SWF, applied to the resulting distribution of income. Abuse of power, by contrast, might be detected by searching for deviant decisions or discrimination across pertinent classifications (race, political affiliation). None of these and other concerns, however, seem well captured by standard indexes of horizontal inequity, which compare certain components of dispersion between, say, the income distribution before and after imposition of a tax reform that applies generally to a large, otherwise anonymous population.

---

[11] There are subtle exceptions, such as in the case of nonconvexities, see Stiglitz (1982b), or when randomization is optimal (for example, with tax audits). Additionally, it is sometimes the case that otherwise sensible policies will result in incidental unequal treatment of individuals on account of their preference heterogeneity. See subsection 6.C.4 and also the analysis in subsection 5.C.2 of the implications of different preferences for consumption and leisure for the optimal income tax problem.

[12] See Atkinson (1980).

[13] See, for example, Mirrlees (1982) and Stiglitz (1982b).

Consideration of horizontal equity may seem orthogonal to most of the issues considered in this book, but this is not always the case. Appeals to horizontal equity are made, for example, when tax base concepts are elevated to evaluative norms (see section F) in order to resolve myriad issues such as tax base design (income versus consumption taxation), when uniform commodity taxation is favored independently of the applicability of economic arguments, including those that may justify deviations, and when it is argued that certain family types should be treated in the same manner as others. Horizontal equity is also invoked in addressing more detailed design questions, such as whether a deduction should be allowed for medical expenses, and in matters of administration and enforcement. Again, as a proxy principle, there may be some value (generally speaking, differences in treatment do need justification). Ultimately, however, direct use of the welfare economic approach is both necessary and sufficient.

Consider, for example, the problem of the taxation of families (chapter 12), where horizontal equity is often employed in attempts to resolve disputes about proper relative taxation. By definition, horizontal equity cannot tell us which groupings of individuals are the "equals" who are supposed to be treated equally, for that begs the very question at issue.[14] Confining attention to matters of distribution, the optimal treatment of various family configurations was seen to depend on a number of subtle factors that could be analyzed only by making explicit reference to an SWF (or a class of SWFs). Additionally, whatever would be optimal on distributive grounds must be adjusted in light of incentive considerations that may differ by family type for reasons largely unrelated to distributive considerations. The concept of horizontal equity does not contribute to these inquiries.

Furthermore, the apparently clear guidance that horizontal equity seems to offer in other settings may turn out to be misleading, if not mistaken. For example, it is fairly widely accepted that consideration of horizontal equity favors a tax deduction for medical expenses and casualty losses on the ground that individuals suffering from such bad luck should be compared to individuals not suffering such misfortune but

---

[14] This point about the notion of equal treatment is quite general, as emphasized by Westen (1990).

whose incomes are otherwise lower by the extent of such losses. This conclusion, however, ignores ex ante incentives, including the incentive to obtain insurance, which may well make a tax deduction counterproductive.[15] In sum, even the proxy role for horizontal equity should be viewed cautiously.

C. Sacrifice Theories

For centuries, a prominent view has been that taxpayers should make equal sacrifices in contributing to the cost of government activity.[16] There is disagreement about whether there should be equal absolute sacrifice (the rich and the poor should suffer the same absolute decline in utility), equal proportional sacrifice, or equal marginal sacrifice. For the most part, this view expresses an intuition rather than an implication of a developed theory of distributive justice. The exception is that the equal marginal sacrifice principle, advanced by Edgeworth (1897) and Pigou (1928), is a corollary of utilitarianism for the familiar reason that maximizing total utility implies equating individuals' marginal utilities (in the first best).

The intuition favoring equal sacrifice, like other moral intuitions examined in subsection 13.A.3.b, can be understood as being useful in the informal settings in which it probably arose—such as by serving as a focal point in organizing contributions to a group activity—while serving at best as a proxy indicator for an aspect of social welfare maximization in the context of the design of government policy. Regarding the latter, sacrifice theories purport to be applicable to how public goods are financed and are silent regarding other taxation, notably for redistributive purposes. Yet as long as redistributive taxation is unconstrained—suppose that the income tax may be freely adjusted to maximize a given SWF—it is immaterial how tax rates are provisionally set to meet a revenue requirement that covers the cost of public goods.[17]

---

[15] See, for example, Kaplow (1992b).

[16] On the history of thought relating to this principle, see Musgrave (1959).

[17] Nor can this difficulty be avoided by deeming redistribution—for example, expenditures on transfer programs—to be a public good, for it makes no sense to talk of equal sacrifice by both the rich and the poor when net payments involve a flow from the rich to the poor.

If instead the entire tax system must adhere to a sacrifice principle—that is, if (perhaps following a libertarian view) the only permissible use of taxation is to finance public goods—then the implications of sacrifice theories for redistribution have a substantially arbitrary character. The reason is that the sacrifice theories specify the distributive properties of taxation independently of the distributive incidence of the public goods being financed.[18] To take a simple example, suppose that there is some project that will provide a uniform benefit of $100 per capita. Further, imagine that the market could provide this benefit at a cost (and would charge a price) of $90 per capita. The government, by contrast, can provide the benefit at a cost of $89 per capita (charging no price). Finally, assume that under the prevailing equal sacrifice norm, the required tax would charge the rich $300 and the poor $30 in taxes if the government were to undertake the project.[19] Obviously this equal sacrifice tax redistributes income relative to a world in which the good is privately provided. The rich pay $300 for a benefit worth $100, for a net loss of $200, whereas the poor pay $30 for a benefit worth $100, for a net gain of $70. With private provision, each individual would have a net gain of $10. To reinforce this point, suppose that the technology changes so that market provision becomes more efficient—say, the market cost drops to $88 per capita—and it is therefore decided that the government should cease providing the benefit. Now, each individual pays $88 for a benefit of $100, a net gain of $12 per capita.

This example illustrates that the norms of equal sacrifice may call for substantial redistribution or none (one could also construct examples of negative redistribution, that is, net transfers to the rich) depending on the distributive incidence of public goods and, for example, on small differences in technology that have nothing to do with any plausible normative principle governing redistribution. Put another way, once one accounts for the distributive incidence of expenditures, which

---

[18] This is the mirror image of the situation examined in section 8.A in which the distributive incidence of a public good was taken as given and different income tax adjustments were considered (see figures 8.2A–8.2C).

[19] For any of the equal sacrifice norms except equal marginal sacrifice (which would require virtual equality), one could state utility functions and initial levels of income such that the tax payments postulated in the text would satisfy the pertinent norm.

chapter 8 emphasizes is critical, the norms do not have the implications one would expect. After all, how can one say that the rich and the poor make equal sacrifices when, as in the initial example, the rich have a net loss and the poor a net gain? In sum, the notion of equal sacrifice, despite its intuitive appeal in certain settings, is not a helpful guide in addressing the problem of taxation and redistribution. Accordingly, it is not surprising that it no longer receives significant attention.

D. Benefit Principle

The benefit principle (already examined in section 8.F on benefit taxation) is like the equal sacrifice norms in that it is limited to the question of how public goods should be financed and hence does not seem to address the question of redistributive taxation. It differs from the equal sacrifice norms in that it dictates that the incidence of taxes used to finance public goods should match the distributive incidence of the public goods being financed. Therefore, if all taxation had to be in accord with the benefit principle, no redistribution would occur. However, if redistributive taxation is permitted, then, like the sacrifice theories, it is essentially moot.

As explored previously, the benefit theory of taxation nevertheless receives some attention in modern public economics writing. There is controversy over the correct notion of benefit taxation although the purpose of such a canonical formulation is not apparent. Moreover, there is interest in whether benefit taxation is progressive, a concern that seems immaterial since, whatever is the incidence of benefit taxation, one might presume that it tends to offset the incidence of the public goods being financed. Finally, sections 8.E and 8.F raised the baseline problem: Are the benefits of public goods to be measured relative to a hypothetical state of anarchy or, if not, against what other benchmark? As explained there, no such baseline is required under the welfare economic framework either to decide which public goods should be provided or to determine how redistributive taxation should optimally be configured.

Under certain libertarian views, by contrast, redistribution is impermissible and only benefit taxation would be allowed. Accordingly, it would be necessary to state a baseline, for the distribution prevailing in that state is the one deemed to be normatively required under a just regime of taxation. A baseline of anarchy is problematic; even if it could be defined, it would preserve the advantages of the strong who successfully prey on the weak, the core injustice designed to be prevented by the libertarian minimal state. Also, there remains the question of how to allocate the surplus (which may constitute nearly all existing value) in moving from anarchy to a just regime. A contrary baseline with rightful behavior yet no public sector is problematic because, if individuals are entitled to their allotment in that state, no one would have to pay taxes. Finally, a baseline with rightful behavior and the minimal state in place begs the question of what tax regime, which is part of the minimal state, is normatively required. Some might insist that taxes be proportional—or satisfy one of the equal sacrifice theories—but any such stipulation appears arbitrary.

E. Ability to Pay

The notion that tax burdens should reflect individuals' "ability to pay" is commonly used in arguments about the ideal tax base and rate structure.[20] Just as with the norms of equal sacrifice and the benefit principle, however, the concept of ability to pay seems literally to be addressed only to the question of how to raise revenue to finance government programs, ignoring the question of redistribution to which it is often applied. After all, why would we ask what the poor are able to pay when we intend for them to receive?[21] Setting that basic problem aside, the concept nevertheless remains elusive. Anyone is *able* to pay any amount that he possesses (although if he starves as a result, he will not be able to pay anything in the next tax period), but this says nothing about what individuals *should* pay. Those suggesting that taxes be in accord with

---

[20] Musgrave (1959) traces this principle to the sixteenth century and identifies among its prominent supporters Rousseau and John Stuart Mill.

[21] And, as with the equal sacrifice norms, even regarding the finance of public goods, the distributive incidence of the public goods being financed is ignored, even though this incidence importantly influences the net distributive effect.

ability to pay obviously have in mind that the rich should pay more than the poor. But this uncontroversial dictate does not tell us how much more, what this difference may depend upon (rate of diminution in the marginal utility of income? elasticity of labor supply?), or why this is so. In sum, the underlying justification is unstated and the prescription is so imprecise as to render the principle of little use—or, reflecting actual practice, to leave it so open-ended as to mean whatever a proponent wishes it to mean (see Vickrey 1947, pp. 3–4, 374–375).

F. Definitions as Norms

Particularly in addressing questions about the appropriate tax base, various definitions are often treated as if they constitute normative principles of tax equity. For example, the familiar Haig-Simons definition of income—the sum of an individual's consumption plus change in wealth—has been taken by many as the test of an ideal tax base. A notable example is Simons (1938) himself, but one must include much subsequent advocacy of comprehensive income taxation and analogous arguments in favor of a comprehensive consumption tax. Also related are debates about the merits of the tax expenditure concept, which is often taken to suggest that any deviations from the idealized tax base are presumptively inappropriate.[22]

Definitions of income and the like are necessary for communication and sometimes are clarifying (for example, standard definitions make apparent that costs of producing income need to be subtracted from gross receipts). Nevertheless, it is apparent that such definitions are not in themselves normative principles. Moreover, as with many of the other normative criteria examined in this chapter, they are incomplete. For example, they do not indicate how much value is lost on account of various departures from the supposedly ideal base, information that is necessary whenever tax administration and enforcement are not costless.

---

[22] This idea is most associated with Surrey (1973). For a range of views, see, for example, Bittker (1969), Griffith (1989), Shaviro (2004), Surrey and McDaniel (1985), and Weisbach and Nussim (2004).

Furthermore, many particular debates—such as concerning transfer taxation and taxation of the family—raise ambiguities or are not addressed by such definitions. Of course, even when the definitions are clear, one can always argue over which of various definitions to adopt as a guide in determining the tax base. Accordingly, it is not surprising that the once-widespread practice of using definitions as norms, although still of some significance, is waning.

16

Conclusion

The theory of taxation and public economics is usefully conceptualized in terms of a core framework. The setting is the world of the two fundamental theorems of welfare economics, modified to include an income tax to accomplish redistribution in light of the infeasibility of distortion-free individualized lump-sum taxes. The analysis is characterized by explicit attention to the social objective of welfare maximization in determining how multiple instruments are best used to achieve it.

The presence of the income tax and the related second-best problem involving the tradeoff of distribution and labor supply distortion have a substantial qualitative influence on how distinct forms of taxation and other tools of government policy are optimally employed. The analytical task is further complicated by the difficulty of the optimal nonlinear income tax problem, even standing alone. Frequently, however, it is possible to construct reform packages that are distribution neutral as a whole by choosing an offsetting income tax adjustment. This technique enables a streamlined yet rigorous analysis of many subjects.

As stated in the introduction, the proposed approach not only is attractive a priori but also yields substantial concrete dividends. This chapter brings together some of the results that appear throughout in order to illustrate these payoffs. In considering various examples, it is useful to bear in mind that the central insights—some of which depart substantially from existing understandings—are obtained directly as a consequence of following the suggested path of inquiry.

As noted, a number of topics are examined using a distribution-neutral policy experiment in which the income tax is adjusted to offset the distributive effects of altering the particular instrument under consideration. To perform this adjustment, it is not necessary either to determine what income tax is optimal or to stipulate that the preexisting income tax is set optimally. Rather, the creation of a distribution-neutral reform package moots distributive concerns and, as it turns out, also holds labor supply constant in the benchmark case with utility weakly separable in labor. All that remains are what might be deemed the distinctive effects of the instrument under examination. In important contexts, this approach yields results that diverge from those in the literature, an implication of which is that (often implicit) redistribution was a confounding factor in prior analyses.

The most basic application of distribution-neutral analysis is to commodity taxation. Atkinson and Stiglitz's (1976) result that uniform commodity taxation is optimal (with weak labor separability) is reproduced, extended, made more intuitive, and formulated in a manner that facilitates its application to other subjects. Their conclusion that Ramsey tax principles are nullified in the presence of an income tax, which exists in developed economies, is reinforced. This conclusion casts into question the widespread practice of differential treatment of luxuries and necessities, such as the exemption of food purchases from VATs and sales taxes. Literature that relaxes the separability assumption finds that, since raw food purchases (in contrast to prepared foods) are leisure complements and thus optimally should be taxed relatively heavily on second-best grounds, existing contrary policies may well be highly inefficient. Such policies are motivated on distributive grounds, but the distribution-neutral framework teaches us that it would be more efficient to achieve any desired distributive effects through adjustment of the income tax and transfer system.

The distribution-neutral approach, by focusing on the distinctive effects of commodity taxation, highlights both the relevance of various qualifications to the uniformity result and the irrelevance in principle of direct distributive effects to optimal commodity taxation. Likewise, although the presence of important qualifications should serve to direct further research, it should not be taken as a reason to abandon the uniformity result as a benchmark for analysis, reverting to Ramsey-based models or others that ignore the presence of the income tax or in other respects do not properly take into account the tradeoff between distribution and labor supply distortion. This injunction has important ramifications for much of the literature on capital taxation.

Additional subjects are similarly cast in a new light. Previous research on the optimal provision of public goods and on the regulation of externalities has considered how traditional first-best principles—the Samuelson cost-benefit test and the Pigouvian prescription to set corrective taxes and subsidies equal to marginal external effects—should be modified in light of distributive effects or on account of the preexisting labor-leisure distortion due to income taxation. Under the distribution-neutral approach, both second-best complications are incorporated, and again in the benchmark case simple efficiency tests give proper guidance. Both of these subjects can be understood in terms of the analysis of commodity taxation: Deviations from the Samuelson rule (thought of by reference to Lindahl pricing) and from the internalization command (where external effects are priced along with direct production costs) are formally similar to departures from uniformity of commodity taxation. The distribution-neutral approach also illuminates additional questions that have proved difficult in the past: determining how the provision of public goods feeds back on the question of optimal redistribution through income taxation, measuring the distributive incidence of public sector activity, and choosing among conflicting conceptions of benefit taxation. In each case, the conclusions obtained supplement or in certain respects supplant prevailing views.

Yet another example of the power of the distribution-neutral approach is seen in the examination of transfer (estate and gift) taxation. Much analysis and debate over this controversial form of taxation concerns revenue and distributive effects and also effects on savings. Yet, a distribution-neutral policy reform (which may be augmented to hold the direct burden on savings constant as well) has no immediate impact on any of these considerations. The distinctive feature of transfer taxation is that it taxes (or, in principle, subsidizes) transfers, so the analysis focuses on the question whether, at a given level of income, an individual should be taxed more or less as a consequence of giving a marginal dollar to a donee rather than consuming it directly. Thus stated, this problem is yet another that looks like a version of the optimal differential commodity tax problem. One of the most important qualifications to the uniformity result involves externalities. As explored, with private transfers there are two: a positive externality that the donor confers on the donee and a negative externality (in the basic case) due to the income effect that leads the donee to work less (which is inefficient due to the preexisting labor-leisure distortion caused by income taxation). The results are extended to consider charitable contributions; many of the determinants of the optimal subsidy turn out to be different from those usually examined. Both subjects raise important empirical questions that are not addressed in existing literature.

The value of the distribution-neutral construct is great even with regard to reforms that will not in fact be distribution neutral. In such cases, one can construct a simple two-step decomposition of the actual reform proposal: the distribution-neutral version of the substantive reform, followed by what is a purely redistributive adjustment to the income tax. The first step is analyzed precisely as already described, and the second step presents the standard optimal redistributive income tax problem, which is analyzed by other means. Note that the latter analysis is generic; the problem is largely the same, independent of the policy to which the redistribution is linked. (When benchmark assumptions are relaxed, there can be interactions, as discussed, but these too are clarified by the decomposition that employs the distribution-neutral approach as the first step.) Moreover, separation of the first step enables analysts of myriad subjects in public economics to specialize, focusing on distinctive features of the instruments they choose to study. Comparability of different analyses of a given policy is greatly facilitated if all of the studies hold distribution constant.

Although the distribution-neutral approach enables the problem of optimal income taxation to be set aside when examining many policy instruments, the topic does remain a central one in public economics. Several chapters of this book directly investigate optimal redistributive taxation. In addition to examining the existing formal treatments of optimal income taxation along with simulations—with some attention to key assumptions and the interpretation of conflicting results—a number of extensions are considered, many of which have received only limited attention in recent research despite their potential importance to the fundamental problem.

The primary limitation of optimal income taxation is the presumed unobservability of individuals' differences in income-earning ability. There are, however, a number of ways in which ability or other proxies might be measured, and suggestions are offered about how further analysis might be conducted. No matter how imperfect such alternatives might be, it is plausible that some use of them would be optimal, and such use already exists with respect to categorical transfer programs, including provision for the disabled.

Greater attention to the structure of individuals' preferences is also warranted. If individuals vary (unobservably) in their marginal utility of consumption or disutility of labor, a given level of observed income no longer signals a particular degree of underlying earning ability. Examination of these cases yields some unexpected conclusions, due in significant part to the fact that standard intuitions neglect how individuals optimally adjust their labor supply in light of differences in their utility functions. Preferences that depend on others' situations, including altruism, envy, and related concerns about relative position, may also affect optimal redistribution. These sorts of preferences have attracted increased attention, but there has been little work relating them directly to optimal income taxation, and preliminary analysis suggests that the implications may deviate from conventional wisdom on the subject.

Other important extensions of the optimal income taxation problem are noted to varying degrees. The centrality of administrative and enforcement concerns is difficult to overstate, especially given the serious problems of avoidance and evasion of income and other taxes and the fact that information limitations determine the feasibility of different tax instruments. Optimal taxation over the life cycle introduces its own complications due to liquidity constraints, myopia and other behavioral characteristics that may affect intertemporal optimization, and life-cycle variations in wage rates. These considerations are important in extending the optimal income tax problem over time, in determining the optimal taxation of capital (savings), and in designing social insurance schemes (the existence of which is often justified by reference to some of these complications). Certain implications are familiar, others are more novel and subtle (such as the relevance of nonconstant wage profiles), and yet others are counterintuitive. For example, with myopia—under which individuals discount future social security benefits relative to the present wage taxes that finance them—the sign, magnitude, and direction of the rate of change of labor-supply effects of social security forced-savings rules are quite different from those of a tax levied on top of a preexisting distortionary tax (the labor income tax). In addition, the nature of these effects depends on how myopia in consumption relates to possible myopia in labor supply, the latter subject not yet having benefited from significant empirical attention. Also discussed are general equilibrium effects of income taxation on relative wages, which may be changing over time with the skill mix in the economy and available technology, and nontax distortions that may have a first-order effect on labor supply and thus interact significantly with income taxation in determining the overall magnitude of labor supply distortion.

A helpful but underutilized application of optimal income taxation analysis is to the design of public transfer programs. Since transfer programs are in principle part of the income tax schedule, optimal income tax results should provide a complete depiction of optimal transfers. Nevertheless, much analysis of transfer programs is performed separately, focusing only on the target population. Yet we know that the primary benefit of raising the marginal income tax rate at a low level of income (say, in the phase-out range of a welfare program) is the revenue gain from all individuals with higher incomes, for whom the change is inframarginal.

The implications of directly employing optimal income tax analysis are seen most clearly in the investigation of categorical assistance, wherein some individuals (say, the disabled or single parents with young children) receive more generous transfers than do others. It appears that optimal marginal tax rates should be lower on such groups, which differs from the practice of employing higher rates on account of there being more welfare benefits to phase out. Existing and proposed work inducement programs also do not seem to be designed optimally. Some such schemes presume the observability of certain information (hours worked), but then do not take full advantage of this information in program design. Current structures might be partially rationalized by very large net positive externalities to work, yet substantial new empirical work is necessary to support this justification. More broadly, welfare programs often are not evaluated explicitly in terms of a social welfare function (SWF), the need for which is another major theme of the present study.

A standard SWF was at the heart of Mirrlees's (1971) seminal investigation and is centrally featured in this book. Attention is devoted to elaborating the welfarist foundations for this approach and to examining the bases for choosing a particular form for the function. Here, attention will be confined to emphasizing the importance of employing an SWF in the analysis of particular subjects, in addition to those already mentioned (notably, the importance of incorporating the welfare effects of distribution when it is not being held constant).

Determining the optimal allocation of tax obligations and transfer payments across different family types poses a particularly subtle and challenging instance in which explicit use of an SWF is required. The reason is due to possible differences in utility functions and interdependencies among individuals in a family unit. For example, in simple cases in which there is unequal sharing of resources within a family unit or economies of scale, more or less generosity toward the family might be warranted, depending on the concavity of individuals' utility functions. Interestingly, when unequal sharing favors greater generosity, scale economies favor less generosity, and vice versa. The present approach also illuminates the question of how differential treatment across family types (say, greater generosity to families with more children) should vary as a function of income; it may well be that, a priori, proportionality is a good approximation, whereas many systems provide benefits that are constant in absolute terms or even decreasing with family income.

The incentive effects of different tax treatments of the family, with a focus on labor effort, are considered as well. The idea that lower-earning spouses (typically women) should be taxed more lightly due to their higher labor supply elasticity is explored. A difficulty is that the source of any differing elasticity is not well understood. This gap in knowledge is problematic because differences in utility functions not only bear on labor supply but also directly on welfare. Furthermore, because spouses' labor supply is interdependent, the optimization problem differs from one in which isolated single individuals might have (observably) different labor supply elasticities. Regarding all of these issues, empirical evidence is limited, perhaps due to a lack of prior recognition of the ways in which certain aspects of behavior are relevant to the social optimization problem.

Direct attention to individuals' utility functions and an SWF is also important in examining the taxation (or subsidization) of private transfers. Because two individuals are involved and each counts in a standard, individualistic SWF, the welfare effects of gifts are qualitatively different from those of ordinary expenditures on own-consumption. As mentioned, two sorts of externalities are involved. In addition, transfer motives, a subject of substantial empirical study, bear not only on behavior but also directly on welfare, for different motivations imply different formulations of the utility function. Indeed, even for a single type of motive—utility from giving per se—it is shown that two different variants have quite different implications for optimal transfer taxation. Moreover, there are subtle distributive considerations in light of the fact that giving affects both donors' and donees' marginal utilities of consumption and hence the marginal social value of redistribution.

At a more abstract level, implications for the proper criteria in the assessment of taxation and other policies are also considered. A purely welfarist approach is defended on a number of grounds, including importantly that giving weight to any other type of criterion sometimes entails a conflict with the Pareto principle. For example, approaches to distributive justice that pay attention to individuals' capabilities and functionings or to primary goods, as suggested by Sen and Rawls respectively, in principle make everyone worse off than they would be under purely welfare-based distributive decisions. On a different front, measures of inequality, poverty, progressivity, and redistribution need to be grounded in an SWF in order to have normative significance, and when they are, they turn out to be unnecessary and misleading if employed in policy assessment. Horizontal equity and other traditional tax equity criteria like the notion of ability to pay are also unhelpful and, when they have bite, conflict with the Pareto principle. In sum, normative approaches that deviate from the pure welfarism of the standard welfare economic framework are found to be untenable. The continuing appeal of some of these approaches, and on occasion their practical usefulness, can be explained by their tendency in some settings to serve as proxy indicators for whether social welfare is being maximized. These conclusions come into focus when such alternative criteria are compared explicitly to the direct and exclusive use of a standard SWF.

Having reviewed the book's major themes and illustrated the value of a unified conceptual approach, it is worth reflecting on the enterprise as a whole. As stated in the introduction, most work on issues of taxation and related questions in public economics is inevitably specialized, for familiar and compelling reasons. The suggestion motivating this book is that, on occasion, there is value in stepping back and considering explicitly the relationships among the parts. What is learned can then be used to refocus, redirect, or even wholly realign subsequent research on particular subjects. In some cases, new questions requiring further analytical work are raised, and in virtually every instance additional hypotheses and parameters requiring empirical investigation are identified. In others, certain complications are determined to be more important and potentially more problematic than generally perceived. Here, the distribution-neutral approach has substantial value because it provides a manner of incorporating the income tax and addressing second-best considerations involving distribution and labor supply distortion without having to solve the optimal nonlinear income tax problem.

Another benefit of consistently and methodically employing the proposed framework is cross-fertilization. Problems as seemingly different as capital income taxation, public goods provision, externality regulation, and transfer taxation are revealed to have important common elements. Moreover, each of their distinctive features is highlighted when their similarities are crisply defined and then, using the distribution-neutral approach, stripped away. Constructs that enable complicating factors to be held constant generally facilitate progress. And when such factors—here, distribution and labor supply distortion—are not held constant, one is reminded that they all need to be taken into account in an ultimate welfare analysis of a contemplated reform.

Just as with the two fundamental theorems of welfare economics, it is extremely useful to relate analysis to a common, well-understood, core model, even when important assumptions are violated. When one begins at the foundations, rigor is enhanced, effort is economized, understanding is deepened, and communication is facilitated. In addition, it is often easier to see which qualifications to the standard story should most command our attention. Accordingly, it should be kept in mind that the sometimes stark results presented here—such as the optimality of uniform commodity taxation, use of an unmodified cost-benefit test for public goods, and pure Pigouvian taxation—are offered as benchmarks for thinking, not as one-size-fits-all prescriptions for policy.

The purpose of this book is not to champion particular policies or analytical results but rather to urge a new way of thinking. The general conceptual approach and some of the particular lines of inquiry— notably, the use of a distribution-neutral construct in various settings— are claimed to have merit. This view is defended on abstract grounds and, at much greater length, through analyses of particular subjects that serve to illustrate the virtues of the proffered framework. Ultimately, however, it is the course of future research that will indicate the value of the theory of taxation and public economics that is advanced here.

References

Aarbu, Karl O., and Thor O. Thoresen. 2001. Income Responses to Tax Changes—Evidence from the Norwegian Tax Reform. *National Tax Journal* 54:319–335.

Aaron, Henry, and Martin McGuire. 1970. Public Goods and Income Distribution. *Econometrica* 38:907–920.

———. 1976. Reply to Geoffrey Brennan, "The Distributional Implications of Public Goods." *Econometrica* 44:401–404.

Acemoglu, Daron, Michael Golosov, and Aleh Tsyvinski. 2006. Markets versus Governments: Political Economy of Mechanisms. Working Paper No. 12224, NBER Working Paper Series. Cambridge, Mass.: National Bureau of Economic Research.

Acs, Gregory, Norma Coe, Keith Watson, and Robert I. Lerman. 1998. Does Work Pay? An Analysis of the Work Incentives under TANF. Occasional Paper No. 9. Washington, D.C.: Urban Institute.

Aguiar, Mark, and Erik Hurst. 2005. Consumption versus Expenditure. *Journal of Political Economy* 113:919–948.

Ahmed, Shaghil, and Dean Croushore. 1996. The Marginal Cost of Funds with Nonseparable Public Spending. *Public Finance Quarterly* 24:216–236.

Akerlof, George A. 1978. The Economics of "Tagging" as Applied to the Optimal Income Tax, Welfare Programs, and Manpower Planning. *American Economic Review* 68:8–19.

Albanesi, Stefania, and Christopher Sleet. 2006. Dynamic Optimal Taxation with Private Information. *Review of Economic Studies* 73:1–30.

Alesina, Alberto, and Philippe Weil. 1992. Menus of Linear Income Tax Schedules. Working Paper 3968, NBER Working Papers Series. Cambridge, Mass.: National Bureau of Economic Research.

Alesina, Alberto, Edward Glaeser, and Bruce Sacerdote. 2006. Work and Leisure in the United States and Europe: Why So Different? In *NBER Macroeconomics Annual 2005*, edited by Mark Gertler and Kenneth Rogoff, vol. 20, pp. 1–64. Cambridge, Mass.: MIT Press.

Alexander, Richard D. 1987. *The Biology of Moral Systems*. Hawthorne, N.Y.: A. de Gruyter.

Allen, Franklin. 1982. Optimal Linear Income Taxation with General Equilibrium Effects on Wages. *Journal of Public Economics* 17:135–143.

Allgood, Sam, and Arthur Snow. 1998. The Marginal Cost of Raising Tax Revenue and Redistributing Income. *Journal of Political Economy* 106:1246–1273.

Allingham, M. G. 1975. Towards an Ability Tax. *Journal of Public Economics* 4:361–376.

Alm, James, and Sally Wallace. 2000. Are the Rich Different? In *Does Atlas Shrug? The Economic Consequences of Taxing the Rich*, edited by Joel B. Slemrod, pp. 165–187. New York: Russell Sage Foundation.

Alm, James, Stacy Dickert-Conlin, and Leslie A. Whittington. 1999. The Marriage Penalty. *Journal of Economic Perspectives* 13, no. 3:193–204.

Altig, David, Alan J. Auerbach, Laurence J. Kotlikoff, Kent A. Smetters, and Jan Walliser. 2001. Simulating Fundamental Tax Reform in the United States. *American Economic Review* 91:574–595.

American Law Institute. 1989. *Federal Income Tax Project, Reporter's Study Draft, Subchapter C (Supplemental Study)*. (Reporter's Study by William D. Andrews.) Philadelphia: American Law Institute.

———. 1993. *Federal Income Tax Project, Integration of the Individual and Corporate Income Taxes*. (Reporter's Study of Corporate Tax Integration by Alvin C. Warren.) Philadelphia: American Law Institute.

Andreoni, James. 1990. Impure Altruism and Donations to Public Goods: A Theory of Warm-Glow Giving. *Economic Journal* 100:464–477.

———. 2006. Philanthropy. In *Handbook of the Economics of Giving, Altruism and Reciprocity*, edited by Serge-Christophe Kolm and Jean Mercier Ythier, vol. 2:1201–1269. Amsterdam: North-Holland.

Andreoni, James, Brian Erard, and Jonathan Feinstein. 1998. Tax Compliance. *Journal of Economic Literature* 36:818–860.

Andrews, William D. 1974. A Consumption-Type or Cash Flow Personal Income Tax. *Harvard Law Review* 87:1113–1188.

Andrews, William D., and David F. Bradford. 1988. Savings Incentives in a Hybrid Income Tax. In *Uneasy Compromise: Problems of a Hybrid Income-Consumption Tax*, edited by Henry J. Aaron, Harvey Galper, and Joseph A. Pechman, pp. 269–300. Washington, D.C.: Brookings Institution.

Antel, John J. 1992. The Intergenerational Transfer of Welfare Dependency: Some Statistical Evidence. *Review of Economics and Statistics* 74:467–473.

Apps, Patricia F., and Ray Rees. 1988. Taxation and the Household. *Journal of Public Economics* 35:355–369.

———. 1999. Household Production, Human Capital and Optimal Linear Income Taxation. In *Regulation Strategies and Economic Policies: Essays in Honour of Bernard Corry and Maurice Peston*, edited by Sami Daniel, Philip Arestis, and John Grahl, vol. 3:105–124. Cheltenham, U.K.: Edward Elgar.

Aronson, J. Richard, and Peter J. Lambert. 1994. Decomposing the Gini Coefficient to Reveal the Vertical, Horizontal, and Reranking Effects of Income Taxation. *National Tax Journal* 47:273–294.

Arrondel, Luc, and André Masson. 2006. Altruism, Exchange or Indirect Reciprocity: What Do the Data on Family Transfers Show? In *Handbook of the Economics of Giving, Altruism and Reciprocity*, edited by Serge-Christophe Kolm and Jean Mercier Ythier, vol. 2:971–1053. Amsterdam: North-Holland.

Arrow, Kenneth J. 1951. *Social Choice and Individual Values*. New York: Wiley.

————. 1973. Some Ordinalist-Utilitarian Notes on Rawls's Theory of Justice. *Journal of Philosophy* 70:245–263.

Arrow, K. J., W. R. Cline, K.-G. Maler, M. Munasinghe, R. Squitieri, and J. E. Stiglitz. 1996. Intertemporal Equity, Discounting, and Economic Efficiency. In *Climate Change 1995: Economic and Social Dimensions of Climate Change,* edited by James P. Bruce, Hoesung Lee, and Erik F. Haites, pp. 125–144. Cambridge: Cambridge University Press.

Aschauer, David Alan. 1985. Fiscal Policy and Aggregate Demand. *American Economic Review* 75:117–127.

Atkinson, Anthony B. 1970. On the Measurement of Inequality. *Journal of Economic Theory* 2:244–263.

————. 1971. Capital Taxes, the Redistribution of Wealth and Individual Savings. *Review of Economic Studies* 38:209–227.

————. 1973. How Progressive Should Income Tax Be? In *Essays in Modern Economics,* edited by Michael Parkin with A. R. Nobay, pp. 90–109. London: Longman.

————. 1980. Horizontal Equity and the Distribution of the Tax Burden. In *The Economics of Taxation,* edited by Henry J. Aaron and Michael J. Boskin, pp. 3–18. Washington, D.C.: Brookings Institution.

————. 1983. *The Economics of Inequality.* 2nd ed. Oxford: Clarendon Press.

————. 1987. On the Measurement of Poverty. *Econometrica* 55:749–764.

Atkinson, Anthony B., and François Bourguignon, eds. 2000. *Handbook of Income Distribution,* vol. 1. Amsterdam: Elsevier.

Atkinson, Anthony B., and Agnar Sandmo. 1980. Welfare Implications of the Taxation of Savings. *Economic Journal* 90:529–549.

Atkinson, Anthony B., and Nicholas H. Stern. 1974. Pigou, Taxation and Public Goods. *Review of Economic Studies* 41:119–128.

Atkinson, Anthony B., and Joseph E. Stiglitz. 1972. The Structure of Indirect Taxation and Economic Efficiency. *Journal of Public Economics* 1:97–119.

————. 1976. The Design of Tax Structure: Direct versus Indirect Taxation. *Journal of Public Economics* 6:55–75.

————. 1980. *Lectures on Public Economics.* New York: McGraw-Hill Book Company.

Auerbach, Alan J. 1985. The Theory of Excess Burden and Optimal Taxation. In *Handbook of Public Economics,* edited by Alan J. Auerbach and Martin Feldstein, vol. 1:61–127. Amsterdam: North-Holland.

————. 1991. Retrospective Capital Gains Taxation. *American Economic Review* 81: 167–178.

————. 1996. Tax Reform, Capital Allocation, Efficiency, and Growth. In *Economic Effects of Fundamental Tax Reform,* edited by Henry J. Aaron and William G. Gale, pp. 29–81. Washington, D.C.: Brookings Institution Press.

————. 2002. Taxation and Corporate Financial Policy. In *Handbook of Public Economics,* edited by Alan J. Auerbach and Martin Feldstein, vol. 3:1251–1292. Amsterdam: Elsevier.

Auerbach, Alan J., and Kevin A. Hassett. 2002. A New Measure of Horizontal Equity. *American Economic Review* 92:1116–1125.

Auerbach, Alan J., and James R. Hines, Jr. 2002. Taxation and Economic Efficiency. In *Handbook of Public Economics,* edited by Alan J. Auerbach and Martin Feldstein, vol. 3:1347–1421. Amsterdam: Elsevier.

Auerbach, Alan J., and Laurence J. Kotlikoff. 1987. *Dynamic Fiscal Policy.* Cambridge: Cambridge University Press.

Auten, Gerald, and Robert Carroll. 1995. Behavior of the Affluent and the 1986 Tax Reform Act. National Tax Association Proceedings, Eighty-Seventh Annual Conference: 70–76.

———. 1999. The Effect of Income Taxes on Household Income. *Review of Economics and Statistics* 81:681–693.

Ballard, Charles L., and Don Fullerton. 1992. Distortionary Taxes and the Provision of Public Goods. *Journal of Economic Perspectives* 6, no. 3:117–131.

Bankman, Joseph, and Thomas Griffith. 1987. Social Welfare and the Rate Structure: A New Look at Progressive Taxation. *California Law Review* 75:1905–1967.

Banks, James, Richard Blundell, and Sarah Tanner. 1998. Is There a Retirement-Savings Puzzle? *American Economic Review* 88:769–788.

Barnett, William A. 1979. The Joint Allocation of Leisure and Goods Expenditure. *Econometrica* 47:539–563.

Baron, Jonathan. 1993. *Morality and Rational Choice.* Boston: Kluwer Academic Publishers.

———. 1994. Nonconsequentialist Decisions. *Behavioral and Brain Sciences* 17:1–10.

———. 1998. *Judgment Misguided: Intuition and Error in Public Decision Making.* New York: Oxford University Press.

———. 2000. *Thinking and Deciding.* 3rd ed. New York: Cambridge University Press.

Baron, Jonathan, and Edward J. McCaffery. 2006. Masking Redistribution (or Its Absence). In *Behavioral Public Finance,* edited by Edward J. McCaffery and Joel Slemrod, pp. 85–112. New York: Russell Sage Foundation.

Barro, Robert J. 1974. Are Government Bonds Net Wealth? *Journal of Political Economy* 82:1095–1117.

———. 1979. On the Determination of the Public Debt. *Journal of Political Economy* 87:940–971.

Barry, Brian. 1977. Justice between Generations. In *Law, Morality and Society: Essays in Honour of H. L. A. Hart,* edited by P. M. S. Hacker and J. Raz, pp. 268–284. Oxford: Clarendon Press.

———. 1989. *Theories of Justice.* Berkeley: University of California Press.

Barsky, Robert B., F. Thomas Juster, Miles S. Kimball, and Matthew D. Shapiro. 1997. Preference Parameters and Behavioral Heterogeneity: An Experimental Approach in the Health and Retirement Study. *Quarterly Journal of Economics* 112:537–579.

Bateman, Hazel, Geoffrey Kingston, and John Piggott. 2001. *Forced Saving: Mandating Private Retirement Incomes.* Cambridge: Cambridge University Press.

Becker, Gary S. 1974. A Theory of Social Interactions. *Journal of Political Economy* 82:1063–1093.

———. 1996. *Accounting for Tastes*. Cambridge, Mass.: Harvard University Press.

Behrman, Jere R. 1997. Intrahousehold Distribution and the Family. In *Handbook of Population and Family Economics*, edited by Mark R. Rosenzweig and Oded Stark, vol. 1A:125–187. Amsterdam: Elsevier.

Bennett, John. 1987. The Second-Best Lump-Sum Taxation of Observable Characteristics. *Public Finance* 42:227–235.

Bentham, Jeremy. [1781] 1988. *The Principles of Morals and Legislation*. [First published as *An Introduction to the Principles of Morals and Legislation*.] Amherst, N.Y.: Prometheus Books.

———. [1822–1823] 1990. *Securities Against Misrule and Other Constitutional Writings for Tripoli and Greece*, edited by Philip Schofield. New York: Oxford University Press.

Bergstrom, Theodore C. 1997. A Survey of Theories of the Family. In *Handbook of Population and Family Economics*, edited by Mark R. Rosensweig and Oded Stark, vol. 1A:21–79. Amsterdam: Elsevier.

Bergstrom, Theodore, Lawrence Blume, and Hal Varian. 1986. On the Private Provision of Public Goods. *Journal of Public Economics* 29:25–49.

Bernheim, B. Douglas. 1994. Personal Saving, Information, and Economic Literacy: New Directions for Public Policy. In *Tax Policy for Economic Growth in the 1990s*, pp. 53–78. Washington, D.C.: American Council for Capital Formation, Center for Policy Research.

———. 2002. Taxation and Saving. In *Handbook of Public Economics*, edited by Alan J. Auerbach and Martin Feldstein, vol. 3:1173–1249. Amsterdam: Elsevier.

Bernheim, B. Douglas, and Antonio Rangel. 2007. Behavioral Public Economics: Welfare and Policy Analysis with Nonstandard Decision-Makers. In *Behavioral Economics and Its Applications*, edited by Peter Diamond and Hannu Vartiainen, pp. 7–77. Princeton: Princeton University Press.

Bernheim, B. Douglas, and Oded Stark. 1988. Altruism within the Family Reconsidered: Do Nice Guys Finish Last? *American Economic Review* 78:1034–1045.

Bernheim, B. Douglas, Robert J. Lemke, and John Karl Scholz. 2004. Do Estate and Gift Taxes Affect the Timing of Private Transfers? *Journal of Public Economics* 88:2617–2634.

Bernheim, B. Douglas, Andrei Shleifer, and Lawrence H. Summers. 1985. The Strategic Bequest Motive. *Journal of Political Economy* 93:1045–1076.

Bernheim, B. Douglas, Jonathan Skinner, and Steven Weinberg. 2001. What Accounts for the Variation in Retirement Wealth among U.S. Households? *American Economic Review* 91:832–857.

Besley, Timothy, and Stephen Coate. 1995. The Design of Income Maintenance Programmes. *Review of Economic Studies* 62:187–221.

Bevan, D. L., and J. E. Stiglitz. 1979. Intergenerational Transfers and Inequality. *Greek Economic Review* 1, no. 1:8–26.

Bhagwati, Jagdish N., and John Douglas Wilson, eds. 1989. *Income Taxation and International Mobility.* Cambridge, Mass.: MIT Press.

Binmore, Ken. 1998. *Game Theory and the Social Contract II: Just Playing.* Cambridge, Mass.: MIT Press.

Bird, Richard M. 1996. Why Tax Corporations? Working Paper 96-2, International Centre for Tax Studies. Toronto: University of Toronto.

Bittker, Boris I. 1969. Accounting for Federal "Tax Subsidies" in the National Budget. *National Tax Journal* 22:244–261.

Blackorby, Charles, and David Donaldson. 1988. Cash versus Kind, Self-Selection, and Efficient Transfers. *American Economic Review* 78:691–700.

Blackorby, Charles, Walter Bossert, and David Donaldson. 1995. Intertemporal Population Ethics: Critical-Level Utilitarian Principles. *Econometrica* 63:1303–1320.

Blair, Douglas H. 1988. The Primary-Goods Indexation Problem in Rawls's *Theory of Justice. Theory and Decision* 24:239–252.

Blanchflower, David G., and Andrew J. Oswald. 1998. What Makes an Entrepreneur? *Journal of Labor Economics* 16:26–60.

———. 2004. Well-being over Time in Britain and the USA. *Journal of Public Economics* 88:1359–1386.

Blau, Francine D., and Lawrence M. Kahn. 2007. Changes in the Labor Supply Behavior of Married Women: 1980–2000. *Journal of Labor Economics* 25:393–438.

Blomquist, Glenn C., Mark C. Berger, and John P. Hoehn. 1988. New Estimates of Quality of Life in Urban Areas. *American Economic Review* 78:89–107.

Blomquist, N. Sören. 1984. The Wage Rate Tax—An Alternative to the Income Tax? *Scandinavian Journal of Economics* 86:269–285.

Blum, Walter J., and Harry Kalven, Jr. 1952. The Uneasy Case for Progressive Taxation. *University of Chicago Law Review* 19:417–520.

———. 1953. *The Uneasy Case for Progressive Taxation.* Chicago: University of Chicago Press.

Blumkin, Tomer, and Efraim Sadka. 2005. A Case for Taxing Education. Working Paper No. 1440, CESifo Working Paper Series. Munich: CESifo.

Blundell, Richard, and Thomas MaCurdy. 1999. Labor Supply: A Review of Alternative Approaches. In *Handbook of Labor Economics,* edited by Orley Ashenfelter and David Card, vol. 3A:1559–1695. Amsterdam: Elsevier.

Blundell, Richard, and Ian Walker. 1982. Modelling the Joint Determination of Household Labour Supplies and Commodity Demands. *Economic Journal* 92:351–364.

———. 2002. Working Families' Tax Credit: A Review of the Evidence, Issues and Prospects for Further Research. *Economie Publique — Etudes et Recherches* 11:77–127.

Blundell, Richard, Alan Duncan, Julian McCrae, and Costas Meghir. 1999. Evaluating In-Work Benefit Reform: The Working Families Tax Credit in the UK. Working Paper No. 160, JCPR Working Papers. Chicago: Northwestern University/University of Chicago Joint Center for Poverty Research.

Boadway, Robin, and Michael Keen. 1993. Public Goods, Self-Selection and Optimal Income Taxation. *International Economic Review* 34:463–478.

Boadway, Robin, Maurice Marchand, and Pierre Pestieau. 1994. Towards a Theory of the Direct-Indirect Tax Mix. *Journal of Public Economics* 55:71–88.

Boadway, Robin, Maurice Marchand, Pierre Pestieau, and Maria del Mar Racionero. 2002. Optimal Redistribution with Heterogeneous Preferences for Leisure. *Journal of Public Economic Theory* 4:475–498.

Bös, Dieter. 1985. Public Sector Pricing. In *Handbook of Public Economics*, edited by Alan J. Auerbach and Martin Feldstein, vol. 1:129–211. Amsterdam: North-Holland.

Boskin, Michael J. 1977. Notes on the Tax Treatment of Human Capital. In *Conference on Tax Research 1975*, Office of Tax Analysis, Department of the Treasury, pp. 185–195. Washington, D.C.: Department of the Treasury.

Boskin, Michael J., and Eytan Sheshinski. 1978. Optimal Redistributive Taxation When Individual Welfare Depends upon Relative Income. *Quarterly Journal of Economics* 92:589–601.

———. 1983. Optimal Tax Treatment of the Family: Married Couples. *Journal of Public Economics* 20:281–297.

Boskin, Michael J., Laurence J. Kotlikoff, Douglas J. Puffert, and John B. Shoven. 1987. Social Security: A Financial Appraisal across and within Generations. *National Tax Journal* 40:19–34.

Bound, John, Charles Brown, Greg Duncan, and Willard Rodgers. 1989. Measurement Error in Cross-Sectional and Longitudinal Labor Market Surveys: Results from Two Validation Studies. Working Paper 2884, NBER Working Paper Series. Cambridge, Mass.: National Bureau of Economic Research.

Bovenberg, A. Lans, and Lawrence H. Goulder. 2002. Environmental Taxation and Regulation. In *Handbook of Public Economics*, edited by Alan J. Auerbach and Martin Feldstein, vol. 3:1471–1545. Amsterdam: Elsevier.

Bradford, David F. 1980. The Economics of Tax Policy toward Savings. In *The Government and Capital Formation*, edited by George M. von Furstenberg, pp. 11–71. Cambridge, Mass.: Ballinger Publishing Co.

———. 1986. *Untangling the Income Tax*. Cambridge, Mass.: Harvard University Press.

———. 1996a. Consumption Taxes: Some Fundamental Transition Issues. In *Frontiers of Tax Reform*, edited by Michael J. Boskin, pp. 123–150. Stanford: Hoover Institution Press.

———. 1996b. *Fundamental Issues in Consumption Taxation.* Washington, D.C.: American Enterprise Institute Press.

Bradford, David F., and U.S. Treasury Tax Policy Staff. 1984. *Blueprints for Basic Tax Reform*. 2nd ed. Arlington, Va.: Tax Analysts.

Brandt, Richard B. 1979. *A Theory of the Good and the Right*. New York: Oxford University Press.

Brannon, Gerard M. 1980. Tax Expenditures and Income Distribution: A Theoretical Analysis of the Upside-Down Subsidy Argument. In *The Economics of Taxation*, edited by Henry J. Aaron and Michael J. Boskin, pp. 87–98. Washington, D.C.: Brookings Institution.

Brennan, Geoffrey. 1973. Pareto Desirable Redistribution: The Case of Malice and Envy. *Journal of Public Economics* 2:173–183.

Brennan, Geoffrey. 1976a. The Distributional Implications of Public Goods. *Econometrica* 44:391–399.

———. 1976b. Public Goods and Income Distribution: A Rejoinder to the Aaron-McGuire Reply. *Econometrica* 44:405–407.

Brett, Craig. 1998. Who Should Be on Workfare? The Use of Work Requirements as Part of an Optimal Tax Mix. *Oxford Economic Papers* 50:607–622.

Breyer, Friedrich. 1989. On the Intergenerational Pareto Efficiency of Pay-as-you-go Financed Pension Systems. *Journal of Institutional and Theoretical Economics* 145:643–658.

Brito, Dagobert L., and William H. Oakland. 1977. Some Properties of the Optimal Income-Tax. *International Economic Review* 18:407–423.

Broome, John. 1984. Uncertainty and Fairness. *Economic Journal* 94:624–632.

———. 1992. *Counting the Cost of Global Warming*. Cambridge: White Horse Press.

———. 1996. The Welfare Economics of Population. *Oxford Economic Papers* 48:177–193.

Brown, Jeffrey R., and Amy Finkelstein. 2004. The Interaction of Public and Private Insurance: Medicaid and the Long-Term Care Insurance Market. Working Paper 10989, NBER Working Paper Series. Cambridge, Mass.: National Bureau of Economic Research.

Brown, Jeffrey R., Olivia S. Mitchell, and James M. Poterba. 2002. Mortality Risk, Inflation Risk, and Annuity Products. In *Innovations in Retirement Financing*, edited by Olivia S. Mitchell, Zvi Bodie, P. Brett Hammond, and Stephen Zeldes, pp. 175–197. Philadelphia: University of Pennsylvania Press.

Browning, Edgar K. 1993. The Marginal Cost of Redistribution. *Public Finance Quarterly* 21:3–32.

———. 1994. The Non-tax Wedge. *Journal of Public Economics* 53:419–433.

Browning, Edgar K., and William R. Johnson. 1984. The Trade-Off between Equality and Efficiency. *Journal of Political Economy* 92:175–203.

Browning, Martin, and Costas Meghir. 1991. The Effects of Male and Female Labor Supply on Commodity Demands. *Econometrica* 59:925–951.

Bruce, Neil, and Michael Waldman. 1990. The Rotten-Kid Theorem Meets the Samaritan's Dilemma. *Quarterly Journal of Economics* 105:155–165.

———. 1991. Transfers in Kind: Why They Can Be Efficient and Nonpaternalistic. *American Economic Review* 81:1345–1351.

Buchanan, James M. 1959. Saving and the Rate of Interest: A Comment. *Journal of Political Economy* 67:79–82.

———. 1975. The Samaritan's Dilemma. In *Altruism, Morality, and Economic Theory*, edited by Edmund S. Phelps, pp. 71–85. New York: Russell Sage Foundation.

———. 1983. Rent Seeking, Noncompensated Transfers, and Laws of Succession. *Journal of Law & Economics* 26:71–85.

Bulow, Jeremy I., and Lawrence H. Summers. 1984. The Taxation of Risky Assets. *Journal of Political Economy* 92:20–39.

Camerer, Colin, George Loewenstein, and Drazen Prelec. 2005. Neuroeconomics: How Neuroscience Can Inform Economics. *Journal of Economic Literature* 43:9–64.

Cameron, Stephen V., and Christopher Taber. 2004. Estimation of Educational Borrowing Constraints Using Returns to Schooling. *Journal of Political Economy* 112:132–182.

Campbell, Donald T. 1975. On the Conflicts between Biological and Social Evolution and between Psychology and Moral Tradition. *American Psychologist* 30:1103–1126.

Campbell, John Y. 1996. Understanding Risk and Return. *Journal of Political Economy* 104:298–345.

Campbell, John Y., and Yves Nosbusch. 2006. Intergenerational Risksharing and Equilibrium Asset Prices. Working Paper 12204, NBER Working Paper Series. Cambridge, Mass.: National Bureau of Economic Research.

Cancian, Maria, and Arik Levinson. 2006. Labor Supply Effects of the Earned Income Tax Credit: Evidence from Wisconsin's Supplemental Benefit for Families with Three Children. *National Tax Journal* 59: 781–800.

Carruth, Alan A. 1982. On the Role of the Production and Consumption Assumptions for Optimum Taxation. *Journal of Public Economics* 17:145–155.

Casler, Stephen D., and Aisha Rafiqui. 1993. Evaluating Fuel Tax Equity: Direct and Indirect Distributional Effects. *National Tax Journal* 46:197–205.

Chamley, Christophe. 1986. Optimal Taxation of Capital Income in General Equilibrium with Infinite Lives. *Econometrica* 54:607–622.

Chetty, Raj. 2006. A New Method of Estimating Risk Aversion. *American Economic Review* 96:1821–1834.

Chetty, Raj, and Emmanuel Saez. 2007. An Agency Theory of Dividend Taxation. Working Paper 13538, NBER Working Paper Series. Cambridge, Mass.: National Bureau of Economic Research.

Choi, E. Kwan, and Carmen F. Menezes. 1992. Is Relative Risk Aversion Greater Than One? *International Review of Economics and Finance* 1:43–54.

Choi, James J., David Laibson, Brigitte C. Madrian, and Andrew Metrick. 2004. For Better or for Worse: Default Effects and 401(k) Savings Behavior. In *Perspectives on the Economics of Aging*, edited by David A. Wise, pp. 81–121. Chicago: University of Chicago Press.

Christian, Charles W. 1994. Voluntary Compliance with the Individual Income Tax: Results from the 1988 TCMP Study. *IRS Research Bulletin* 1993/1994:35–42.

Christiansen, Vidar. 1981. Evaluation of Public Projects under Optimal Taxation. *Review of Economic Studies* 48:447–457.

———. 1984. Which Commodity Taxes Should Supplement the Income Tax? *Journal of Public Economics* 24:195–220.

Clark, Stephen, Richard Hemming, and David Ulph. 1981. On Indices for the Measurement of Poverty. *Economic Journal* 91:515–526.

Coase, R. H. 1960. The Problem of Social Cost. *Journal of Law & Economics* 3:1–44.

Coate, Stephen. 1995. Altruism, the Samaritan's Dilemma, and Government Transfer Policy. *American Economic Review* 85:46–57.

Cochrane, John H. 1991. A Simple Test of Consumption Insurance. *Journal of Political Economy* 99:957–976.

Corlett, W. J., and D. C. Hague. 1953. Complementarity and the Excess Burden of Taxation. *Review of Economic Studies* 21:21–30.

Coronado, Julia Lynn, Don Fullerton, and Thomas Glass. 2000. The Progressivity of Social Security. Working Paper 7520, NBER Working Paper Series. Cambridge, Mass.: National Bureau of Economic Research.

Cowell, Frank A. 1990. *Cheating the Government: The Economics of Evasion.* Cambridge, Mass.: MIT Press.

———. 1995. *Measuring Inequality.* 2nd ed. London: Prentice Hall/Harvester Wheatsheaf.

Cowen, Tyler. 1992. Consequentialism Implies a Zero Rate of Intergenerational Discount. In *Justice between Age Groups and Generations,* edited by Peter Laslett and James Fishkin, pp. 162–168. Philosophy, Politics, and Society, sixth series. New Haven: Yale University Press.

———. 1996. What Do We Learn from the Repugnant Conclusion? *Ethics* 106:754–775.

Cox, Donald. 1987. Motives for Private Income Transfers. *Journal of Political Economy* 95:508–546.

———. 1990. Intergenerational Transfers and Liquidity Constraints. *Quarterly Journal of Economics* 105:187–217.

Cox, Donald, and Tullio Jappelli. 1993. The Effect of Borrowing Constraints on Consumer Liabilities. *Journal of Money, Credit, and Banking* 25:197–213.

Cremer, Helmuth, and Firouz Gahvari. 1994. Tax Evasion, Concealment and the Optimal Linear Income Tax. *Scandinavian Journal of Economics* 96:219–239.

Cremer, Helmuth, Arnaud Dellis, and Pierre Pestieau. 2003. Family Size and Optimal Income Taxation. *Journal of Population Economics* 16:37–54.

Cremer, Helmuth, Firouz Gahvari, and Norbert Ladoux. 1998. Externalities and Optimal Taxation. *Journal of Public Economics* 70:343–364.

Cremer, Helmuth, Pierre Pestieau, and Jean-Charles Rochet. 2001. Direct versus Indirect Taxation: The Design of the Tax Structure Revisited. *International Economic Review* 42:781–799.

Currie, Janet. 1994. Welfare and the Well-Being of Children: The Relative Effectiveness of Cash and In-Kind Transfers. In *Tax Policy and the Economy,* edited by James M. Poterba, vol. 8:1–43. Cambridge, Mass.: MIT Press.

Cutler, David M., and Jonathan Gruber. 1996. Does Public Insurance Crowd Out Private Insurance? *Quarterly Journal of Economics* 111:391–430.

Cyert, Richard M., and Morris H. DeGroot. 1975. Adaptive Utility. In *Adaptive Economic Models,* edited by Richard H. Day and Theodore Groves, pp. 223–246. New York: Academic Press.

Dahan, Momi, and Michel Strawczynski. 2000. Optimal Income Taxation: An Example with a U-Shaped Pattern of Optimal Marginal Tax Rates: Comment. *American Economic Review* 90:681–686.

———. 2004. The Optimal Asymptotic Income Tax Rate. Discussion Paper No. 2004.15, Bank of Israel Discussion Paper Series. Jerusalem: Research Department, Bank of Israel.

Dales, John H. 1968. *Pollution, Property, and Prices.* Toronto: University of Toronto Press.

Dalton, Hugh. 1920. The Measurement of the Inequality of Incomes. *Economic Journal* 30:348–361.

Daly, Martin, and Margo Wilson. 1988. *Homicide.* New York: A. de Gruyter.

Darwin, Charles. [1874] 1998. *The Descent of Man.* Reprint of 2nd ed. Amherst, N.Y.: Prometheus Books.

Dasgupta, Partha. 1994. Savings and Fertility: Ethical Issues. *Philosophy and Public Affairs* 23:99–127.

Dasgupta, Partha, and Peter Hammond. 1980. Fully Progressive Taxation. *Journal of Public Economics* 13:141–154.

D'Aspremont, C., and L. A. Gérard-Varet. 1991. Utilitarian Fundamentalism and Limited Information. In *Interpersonal Comparisons of Well-Being*, edited by Jon Elster and John Roemer, pp. 371–386. Cambridge: Cambridge University Press.

Davidoff, Thomas, Jeffrey R. Brown, and Peter A. Diamond. 2005. Annuities and Individual Welfare. *American Economic Review* 95:1573–1590.

Davies, James B. 1996. Explaining Intergenerational Transfers. In *Household and Family Economics*, edited by Paul Menchik, pp. 47–82. Boston: Kluwer Academic Publishers.

Davies, James B., and Michael Hoy. 2002. Flat Rate Taxes and Inequality Measurement. *Journal of Public Economics* 84:33–46.

Davies, James B., and John Whalley. 1991. Taxes and Capital Formation: How Important Is Human Capital? In *National Saving and Economic Performance*, edited by B. Douglas Bernheim and John B. Shoven, pp. 163–200. Chicago: University of Chicago Press.

Deaton, Angus. 1979. Optimally Uniform Commodity Taxes. *Economics Letters* 2: 357–361.

Deaton, Angus, and John Muellbauer. 1986. On Measuring Child Costs: With Applications to Poor Countries. *Journal of Political Economy* 94:720–744.

De Wulf, Luc. 1975. Fiscal Incidence Studies in Developing Countries. *International Monetary Fund Staff Papers* 22:61–131.

Diamond, Peter A. 1967. Cardinal Welfare, Individualistic Ethics, and Interpersonal Comparison of Utility: Comment. *Journal of Political Economy* 75:765–766.

———. 1968. Negative Taxes and the Poverty Problem—A Review Article. *National Tax Journal* 21:288–303.

———. 1975. A Many-Person Ramsey Tax Rule. *Journal of Public Economics* 4:335–342.

———. 1977. A Framework for Social Security Analysis. *Journal of Public Economics* 8:275–298.

———. 1980. Income Taxation with Fixed Hours of Work. *Journal of Public Economics* 13:101–110.

———. 1998. Optimal Income Taxation: An Example with a U-Shaped Pattern of Optimal Marginal Tax Rates. *American Economic Review* 88:83–95.

———. 2002. *Social Security Reform.* Oxford: Oxford University Press.

———. 2003. *Taxation, Incomplete Markets, and Social Security: The 2000 Munich Lectures.* Cambridge, Mass.: MIT Press.

Diamond, Peter A. 2004. Social Security. *American Economic Review* 94:1–24.

———. 2006. Optimal Tax Treatment of Private Contributions for Public Goods with and without Warm Glow Preferences. *Journal of Public Economics* 90:897–919.

Diamond, Peter A., and James A. Mirrlees. 1971. Optimal Taxation and Public Production II: Tax Rules. *American Economic Review* 61:261–278.

———. 1978. A Model of Social Insurance with Variable Retirement. *Journal of Public Economics* 10:295–336.

———. 1986. Payroll-Tax Financed Social Insurance with Variable Retirement. *Scandinavian Journal of Economics* 88:25–50.

———. 2000. Adjusting One's Standard of Living: Two-Period Models. In *Incentives, Organization, and Public Economics: Papers in Honour of Sir James Mirrlees*, edited by Peter J. Hammond and Gareth D. Myles, pp. 107–122. New York: Oxford University Press.

Diamond, Peter A., and Eytan Sheshinski. 1995. Economic Aspects of Optimal Disability Benefits. *Journal of Public Economics* 57:1–23.

Dickert, Stacy, Scott Houser, and John Karl Scholz. 1994. Taxes and the Poor: A Microsimulation Study of Implicit and Explicit Taxes. *National Tax Journal* 47:621–638.

Dingeldey, Irene. 2001. European Tax Systems and Their Impact on Family Employment Patterns. *Journal of Social Policy* 30:653–672.

Dixit, Avinash. 1975. Welfare Effects of Tax and Price Changes. *Journal of Public Economics* 4:103–123.

———. 1985. Tax Policy in Open Economies. In *Handbook of Public Economics*, edited by Alan J. Auerbach and Martin Feldstein, vol. 1:313–374. Amsterdam: North-Holland.

Dodge, David A. 1975. Impact of Tax, Transfer, and Expenditure Policies of Government on the Distribution of Personal Income in Canada. *Review of Income and Wealth* 21:1–52.

Domar, Evsey D., and Richard A. Musgrave. 1944. Proportional Income Taxation and Risk-Taking. *Quarterly Journal of Economics* 58:388–423.

Dominitz, Jeff, Charles F. Manski, and Jordan Heinz. 2003. "Will Social Security Be There for You?": How Americans Perceive Their Benefits. Working Paper 9798, NBER Working Papers Series. Cambridge, Mass.: National Bureau of Economic Research.

Donaldson, David, and Krishna Pendakur. 2003. Equivalent-Expenditure Functions and Expenditure-Dependent Equivalence Scales. *Journal of Public Economics* 88:175–208.

Drèze, Jean, and Amartya Sen. 1989. *Hunger and Public Action*. Oxford: Clarendon Press.

Drèze, Jean, and Nicholas Stern. 1987. The Theory of Cost–Benefit Analysis. In *Handbook of Public Economics*, edited by Alan J. Auerbach and Martin Feldstein, vol. 2: 909–989. Amsterdam: North-Holland.

Duesenberry, James S. 1949. *Income, Saving, and the Theory of Consumer Behavior*. Cambridge, Mass.: Harvard University Press.

Duncan, Greg, Martha Hill, and Saul Hoffman. 1988. Welfare Dependence within and across Generations. *Science* 239:467–471.

Dupor, Bill, and Wen-Fang Liu. 2003. Jealousy and Equilibrium Overconsumption. *American Economic Review* 93:423–428.

Dworkin, Ronald. 1981a. What Is Equality? Part 1: Equality of Welfare. *Philosophy and Public Affairs* 10:185–246.

———. 1981b. What Is Equality? Part 2: Equality of Resources. *Philosophy and Public Affairs* 10:283–345.

Easterlin, Richard A. 1973. Does Money Buy Happiness? *Public Interest* 30:3–10.

———. 1974. Does Economic Growth Improve the Human Lot? Some Empirical Evidence. In *Nations and Households in Economic Growth: Essays in Honor of Moses Abramovitz*, edited by Paul A. David and Melvin W. Reder, pp. 89–125. New York: Academic Press.

———. 2001. Income and Happiness: Towards a Unified Theory. *Economic Journal* 111:465–484.

Eaton, Jonathan, and Harvey S. Rosen. 1980a. Labor Supply, Uncertainty, and Efficient Taxation. *Journal of Public Economics* 14:365–374.

———. 1980b. Optimal Redistributive Taxation and Uncertainty. *Quarterly Journal of Economics* 95:357–364.

———. 1980c. Taxation, Human Capital, and Uncertainty. *American Economic Review* 70:705–715.

Ebert, Udo. 1988. Optimal Income Taxation: On the Case of Two-Dimensional Populations. Graduate School of Economics, University of Bonn. Discussion Paper No. A-169. Bonn, Germany.

———. 1992. A Reexamination of the Optimal Nonlinear Income Tax. *Journal of Public Economics* 49:47–73.

Eckstein, Zvi, Martin Eichenbaum, and Dan Peled. 1985. Uncertain Lifetimes and the Welfare Enhancing Properties of Annuity Markets and Social Security. *Journal of Public Economics* 26:303–326.

Economic Report of the President. 1996. Washington, D.C.: United States Government Printing Office.

Edgeworth, Francis Y. 1897. The Pure Theory of Taxation. *Economic Journal* 7:46–70, 226–238, 550–571.

Eichengreen, Barry. 1990. The Capital Levy in Theory and Practice. In *Public Debt Management: Theory and History,* edited by Rudiger Dornbusch and Mario Draghi, pp. 191–220. Cambridge: Cambridge University Press.

Eissa, Nada, and Hilary Williamson Hoynes. 2006a. Behavioral Responses to Taxes: Lessons from the EITC and Labor Supply. In *Tax Policy and the Economy*, edited by James M. Poterba, vol. 20:74–110. Cambridge, Mass.: MIT Press.

———. 2006b. The Hours of Work Response of Married Couples: Taxes and the Earned Income Tax Credit. In *Tax Policy and Labor Market Performance*, edited by Jonas Agell and Peter Birch Sørensen, pp. 187–227. Cambridge, Mass.: MIT Press.

Eissa, Nada, and Jeffrey B. Liebman. 1996. Labor Supply Response to the Earned Income Tax Credit. *Quarterly Journal of Economics* 111:605–637.

Ellwood, David T. 2000. The Impact of the Earned Income Tax Credit and Social Policy Reforms on Work, Marriage, and Living Arrangements. *National Tax Journal* 53:1063–1105.

Engen, Eric M., William G. Gale, and Cori E. Uccello. 1999. The Adequacy of Household Saving. *Brookings Papers on Economic Activity* 1999, no. 2:65–187.

Farhi, Emmanuel, and Iván Werning. 2005. Inequality, Social Discounting and Estate Taxation. Working Paper 11408, NBER Working Paper Series. Cambridge, Mass.: National Bureau of Economic Research.

Feenberg, Daniel R., and James M. Poterba. 1993. Income Inequality and the Incomes of Very High-Income Taxpayers: Evidence from Tax Returns. In *Tax Policy and the Economy*, edited by James M. Poterba, vol. 7:145–177. Cambridge, Mass.: MIT Press.

Feldstein, Martin S. 1972. Equity and Efficiency in Public Sector Pricing: The Optimal Two-Part Tariff. *Quarterly Journal of Economics* 86:175–187.

———. 1973. On the Optimal Progressivity of the Income Tax. *Journal of Public Economics* 2:357–376.

———. 1974. Distributional Preferences in Public Expenditure Analysis. In *Redistribution through Public Choice*, edited by Harold M. Hochman and George E. Peterson, pp. 136–161. New York: Columbia University Press.

———. 1976. On the Theory of Tax Reform. *Journal of Public Economics* 6:77–104.

———. 1978. The Welfare Cost of Capital Income Taxation. *Journal of Political Economy* 86, no. 2, pt. 2:S29–S51.

———. 1987. Should Social Security Benefits Be Means Tested? *Journal of Political Economy* 95:468–484.

———. 1995. The Effect of Marginal Tax Rates on Taxable Income: A Panel Study of the 1986 Tax Reform Act. *Journal of Political Economy* 103:551–572.

———. 1999. Tax Avoidance and the Deadweight Loss of the Income Tax. *Review of Economics and Statistics* 81:674–680.

———. 2005. Rethinking Social Insurance. *American Economic Review* 95:1–24.

Feldstein, Martin S., and Daniel Feenberg. 1996. The Effect of Increased Tax Rates on Taxable Income and Economic Efficiency: A Preliminary Analysis of the 1993 Tax Rate Increases. In *Tax Policy and the Economy,* edited by James M. Poterba, vol. 10: 89–117. Cambridge, Mass.: MIT Press.

Feldstein, Martin S., and Jeffrey B. Liebman, eds. 2002a. *The Distributional Aspects of Social Security and Social Security Reform.* Chicago: University of Chicago Press.

———. 2002b. Social Security. In *Handbook of Public Economics,* edited by Alan J. Auerbach and Martin Feldstein, vol. 4:2245–2324. Amsterdam: Elsevier.

Feldstein, Martin, and Andrew Samwick. 1992. Social Security Rules and Marginal Tax Rates. *National Tax Journal* 45:1–22.

Finkelstein, Amy, and James Poterba. 2004. Adverse Selection in Insurance Markets: Policyholder Evidence from the U.K. Annuity Market. *Journal of Political Economy* 112:183–208.

Fleming, Marcus. 1952. A Cardinal Concept of Welfare. *Quarterly Journal of Economics* 66:366–384.

Foley, Duncan K. 1970. Lindahl's Solution and the Core of an Economy with Public Goods. *Econometrica* 38:66–72.

Fortin, Bernard, Michel Truchon, and Louis Beauséjour. 1993. On Reforming the Welfare System: Workfare Meets the Negative Income Tax. *Journal of Public Economics* 51:119–151.

Frank, Robert H. 1984a. Are Workers Paid Their Marginal Products? *American Economic Review* 74:549–571.

———. 1984b. Interdependent Preferences and the Competitive Wage Structure. *RAND Journal of Economics* 15:510–520.

———. 1985. *Choosing the Right Pond: Human Behavior and the Quest for Status.* New York: Oxford University Press.

———. 1988. *Passions within Reason: The Strategic Role of the Emotions.* New York: Norton.

———. 1999. *Luxury Fever: Money and Happiness in an Era of Excess.* Princeton: Princeton University Press.

Frey, Bruno S., and Alois Stutzer. 2002. *Happiness and Economics: How the Economy and Institutions Affect Well-Being.* Princeton: Princeton University Press.

Fuchs, Victor R., Alan B. Krueger, and James M. Poterba. 1998. Economists' Views about Parameters, Values, and Policies: Survey Results in Labor and Public Economics. *Journal of Economic Literature* 36:1387–1425.

Fullerton, Don. 1991. Reconciling Recent Estimates of the Marginal Welfare Cost of Taxation. *American Economic Review* 81:302–308.

Fullerton, Don, and Diane L. Rogers. 1993. *Who Bears the Lifetime Tax Burden?* Washington, D.C.: Brookings Institution.

Gale, Douglas. 1990. The Efficient Design of Public Debt. In *Public Debt Management: Theory and History,* edited by Rudiger Dornbusch and Mario Draghi, pp. 14–47. Cambridge: Cambridge University Press.

Gallup, George H. 1976. Human Needs and Satisfactions: A Global Survey. *Public Opinion Quarterly* 40:459–467.

Garfinkel, Irwin. 1973. Is In-Kind Redistribution Efficient? *Quarterly Journal of Economics* 87:320–330.

———, ed. 1982. *Income-Tested Transfer Programs: The Case For and Against.* New York: Academic Press.

Gemmell, Norman. 1985. The Incidence of Government Expenditure and Redistribution in the United Kingdom. *Economica* 52:335–344.

Giannarelli, Linda, and Eugene Steuerle. 1995. The Twice-Poverty Trap: Tax Rates Faced by AFDC Recipients. Working Paper. Washington, D.C.: Urban Institute.

Gibbard, Allan. 1979. Disparate Goods and Rawls' Difference Principle: A Social Choice Theoretic Treatment. *Theory and Decision* 11:267–288.

Giertz, Seth H. 2004. Recent Literature on Taxable-Income Elasticities. Technical Paper No. 2004-16, Congressional Budget Office Technical Paper Series. Washington, D.C.: Congressional Budget Office.

Giertz, Seth H. 2006. The Elasticity of Taxable Income During the 1990s: A Sensitivity Analysis. Working Paper No. 2006-03, Congressional Budget Office Working Paper Series. Washington, D.C.: Congressional Budget Office.

Gigerenzer, Gerd, and Reinhard Selton, eds. 2001. *Bounded Rationality: The Adaptive Toolbox.* Cambridge, Mass.: MIT Press.

Gillespie, W. Irwin. 1965. Effect of Public Expenditures on the Distribution of Income. In *Essays in Fiscal Federalism*, edited by Richard A. Musgrave, pp. 122–186. Washington, D.C.: Brookings Institution.

Gokhale, Jagadeesh, Laurence J. Kotlikoff, and Alexi Sluchynsky. 2002. Does It Pay to Work? Working Paper 9096, NBER Working Paper Series. Cambridge, Mass.: National Bureau of Economic Research.

Goldberg, Kalman, and Robert C. Scott. 1981. Fiscal Incidence: A Revision of Benefits Incidence Estimates. *Journal of Regional Science* 21:203–221.

Golosov, Mikhail, and Aleh Tsyvinski. 2006. Designing Optimal Disability Insurance: A Case for Asset Testing. *Journal of Political Economy* 114:257–279.

Golosov, Mikhail, Narayana Kocherlakota, and Aleh Tsyvinski. 2003. Optimal Indirect and Capital Taxation. *Review of Economic Studies* 70:569–587.

Golosov, Mikhail, Aleh Tsyvinski, and Iván Werning. 2007. New Dynamic Public Finance: A User's Guide. In *NBER Macroeconomics Annual 2006*, edited by Daron Acemoglu, Kenneth Rogoff, and Michael Woodford, vol. 21, pp. 317–363. Cambridge, Mass.: MIT Press.

Goode, Richard. 1980. Long-Term Averaging of Income for Tax Puposes. In *The Economics of Taxation*, edited by Henry J. Aaron and Michael J. Boskin, pp. 159–178. Washington, D.C.: Brookings Institution.

Goolsbee, Austan. 1999. Evidence on the High-Income Laffer Curve from Six Decades of Tax Reform. *Brookings Papers on Economic Activity* 1999, no. 2:1–64.

———. 2000a. It's Not About the Money: Why Natural Experiments Don't Work on the Rich. In *Does Atlas Shrug? The Economic Consequences of Taxing the Rich*, edited by Joel B. Slemrod, pp. 141–158. New York: Russell Sage Foundation.

———. 2000b. What Happens When You Tax the Rich? Evidence from Executive Compensation. *Journal of Political Economy* 108:352–378.

Gordon, James P. F. 1989. Individual Morality and Reputation Costs as Deterrents to Tax Evasion. *European Economic Review* 33:797–805.

Gordon, Roger H. 1985. Taxation of Corporate Capital Income: Tax Revenues versus Tax Distortions. *Quarterly Journal of Economics* 100:1–27.

Gordon, Roger H., and Martin Dietz. 2007. Dividends and Taxes. In *Institutional Foundations of Public Finance: Economic and Legal Perspectives*, edited by Alan J. Auerbach and Daniel Shaviro (forthcoming). Cambridge, Mass.: Harvard University Press.

Gordon, Roger H., and James R. Hines, Jr. 2002. International Taxation. In *Handbook of Public Economics*, edited by Alan J. Auerbach and Martin Feldstein, vol. 4:1935–1999. Amsterdam: Elsevier.

Gordon, Roger H., and Wei Li. 2005. Tax Structure in Developing Countries: Many Puzzles and a Possible Explanation. Working Paper 11267, NBER Working Paper Series. Cambridge, Mass.: National Bureau of Economic Research.

Gordon, Roger H., and Joel Slemrod. 1988. Do We Collect Any Revenue from Taxing Capital Income? In *Tax Policy and the Economy*, edited by Lawrence H. Summers, vol. 2:89–130. Cambridge, Mass.: MIT Press.

———. 2000. Are "Real" Responses to Taxes Simply Income Shifting between Corporate and Personal Tax Bases? In *Does Atlas Shrug? The Economic Consequences of Taxing the Rich*, edited by Joel B. Slemrod, pp. 240–280. New York: Russell Sage Foundation.

Gordon, Roger H., and Hal R. Varian. 1988. Intergenerational Risk Sharing. *Journal of Public Economics* 37:185–202.

Gordon, Roger H., Laura Kalambokidis, and Joel Slemrod. 2004a. Do We *Now* Collect Any Revenue from Taxing Capital Income? *Journal of Public Economics* 88:981–1109.

———. 2004b. A New Summary Measure of the Effective Tax Rate on Investment. In *Measuring the Tax Burden on Capital and Labor*, edited by Peter Birch Sørensen, pp. 99–128. Cambridge, Mass.: MIT Press.

Gordon, Roger H., Laura Kalambokidis, Jeffrey Rohaly, and Joel Slemrod. 2004. Toward a Consumption Tax, and Beyond. *American Economic Review (AEA Papers and Proceedings)* 94, no. 2:161–165.

Goulder, Lawrence H., ed. 2002. *Environmental Policy Making in Economies with Prior Tax Distortions*. Cheltenham, U.K.: Edward Elgar.

Graham, John R. 2003. Taxes and Corporate Finance: A Review. *Review of Financial Studies* 16:1075–1129.

Gravelle, Jane G. 1994. *The Economic Effects of Taxing Capital Income*. Cambridge, Mass.: MIT Press.

Green, Christopher. 1967. *Negative Taxes and the Poverty Problem*. Washington, D.C.: Brookings Institution.

Green, Jerry, and Laurence J. Kotlikoff. 2007. On the General Relativity of Fiscal Language. In *Institutional Foundations of Public Finance: Economic and Legal Perspectives*, edited by Alan J. Auerbach and Daniel Shaviro (forthcoming). Cambridge, Mass.: Harvard University Press.

Greenwood, Jeremy, and Guillaume Vandenbroucke. 2005. Hours Worked: Long-run Trends. In *The New Palgrave Dictionary of Economics*, 2nd ed., edited by Lawrence E. Blume and Steven N. Durlauf (forthcoming). London: Palgrave Macmillan.

Griffin, James. 1986. *Well-Being: Its Meaning, Measurement, and Moral Importance*. Oxford: Clarendon Press.

Griffith, Thomas D. 1989. Theories of Personal Deductions in the Income Tax. *Hastings Law Journal* 40:343–395.

Grogger, Jeffrey, and Lynn A. Karoly. 2005. *Welfare Reform: Effects of a Decade of Change*. Cambridge, Mass.: Harvard University Press.

Gronau, Reuben. 1988. Consumption Technology and the Intrafamily Distribution of Resources: Adult Equivalence Scales Reexamined. *Journal of Political Economy* 96:1183–1205.

Grossman, Sanford J., and Oliver D. Hart. 1983. An Analysis of the Principal-Agent Problem. *Econometrica* 51:7–46.

Groves, Harold. 1974. *Tax Philosophers: Two Hundred Years of Thought in Great Britain and the United States.* Madison: University of Wisconsin Press.

Gruber, Jon, and Emmanuel Saez. 2002. The Elasticity of Taxable Income: Evidence and Implications. *Journal of Public Economics* 84:1–32.

Gruber, Jonathan, and David A. Wise, eds. 1999. *Social Security and Retirement around the World.* Chicago: University of Chicago Press.

Gruber, Jonathan, and Aaron Yelowitz. 1999. Public Health Insurance and Private Savings. *Journal of Political Economy* 107:1249–1274.

Guyton, John L., John F. O'Hare, Michael P. Stavrianos, and Eric J. Toder. 2003. Estimating the Compliance Cost of the U.S. Individual Income Tax. *National Tax Journal* 56:673–688.

Hagerty, Michael R., and Ruut Veenhoven. 2003. Wealth and Happiness Revisited— Growing National Income *Does* Go with Greater Happiness. *Social Indicators Research* 64:1–27.

Hall, Robert E. 1986. Comment on Hubbard and Judd, "Liquidity Constraints, Fiscal Policy, and Consumption." *Brookings Papers on Economic Activity* 1986, no. 1:51–53.

Hamilton, Jonathan H. 1987. Optimal Wage and Income Taxation with Wage Uncertainty. *International Economic Review* 28:373–388.

Hammond, Peter. 1983. Ex-post Optimality as a Dynamically Consistent Objective for Collective Choice under Uncertainty. In *Social Choice and Welfare*, edited by Prasanta K. Pattanaik and Maurice Salles, pp. 175–205. New York: Elsevier Science Pub. Co.

Hardin, Russell. 1986. The Utilitarian Logic of Liberalism. *Ethics* 97:47–74.

Harding, Ann. 1995. The Impact of Health, Education, and Housing Outlays upon Income Distribution in Australia in the 1990s. *Australian Economic Review* 111:71–86.

Hare, Richard M. 1973. Rawls' Theory of Justice—I. *Philosophical Quarterly* 23:144–155.

———. 1981. *Moral Thinking: Its Levels, Method, and Point.* New York: Oxford University Press.

———. 1988. Possible People. *Bioethics* 2:279–293.

Harrod, R. F. 1936. Utilitarianism Revised. *Mind* 45:137–156.

Harsanyi, John C. 1953. Cardinal Utility in Welfare Economics and in the Theory of Risk-Taking. *Journal of Political Economy* 61:434–435.

———. 1955. Cardinal Welfare, Individualistic Ethics, and Interpersonal Comparisons of Utility. *Journal of Political Economy* 63:309–321.

———. 1975. Nonlinear Social Welfare Functions: Do Welfare Economists Have a Special Exemption from Bayesian Rationality? *Theory and Decision* 6:311–332.

———. 1977. *Rational Behavior and Bargaining Equilibrium in Games and Social Situations.* New York: Cambridge University Press.

————. 1982. Morality and the Theory of Rational Behavior. In *Utilitarianism and Beyond,* edited by Amartya Sen and Bernard Williams, pp. 39–62. New York: Cambridge University Press.

————. 1988. Problems with Act-Utilitarianism and with Malevolent Preferences. In *Hare and Critics: Essays on Moral Thinking,* edited by Douglas Seanor and N. Fotion, pp. 89–99. Oxford: Clarendon Press.

Hausman, Jerry A. 1981. Labor Supply. In *How Taxes Affect Economic Behavior,* edited by Henry J. Aaron and Joseph A. Pechman, pp. 27–72. Washington, D.C.: Brookings Institution.

Heckman, James J. 1974. Life Cycle Consumption and Labor Supply: An Explanation of the Relationship between Income and Consumption over the Life Cycle. *American Economic Review* 64:188–194.

————. 1976. A Life-Cycle Model of Earnings, Learning, and Consumption. *Journal of Political Economy* 84, no. 4, pt. 2:S11–S44.

————. 1993. What Has Been Learned about Labor Supply in the Past Twenty Years? *American Economic Review (AEA Papers and Proceedings)* 83, no. 2:116–121.

————. 1996. Comment on Nada Eissa, "Labor Supply and the Economic Recovery Tax Act of 1981." In *Empirical Foundations of Household Taxation,* edited by Martin Feldstein and James M. Poterba, pp. 32–38. Chicago: University of Chicago Press.

Heckman, James J., Lance Lochner, and Christopher Taber. 1999. Human Capital Formation and General Equilibrium Treatment Effects: A Study of Tax and Tuition Policy. *Fiscal Studies* 20:25–40.

Hellwig, Martin F. 2004. Optimal Income Taxation, Public-Goods Provision and Public-Sector Pricing: A Contribution to the Foundations of Public Economics. Working Paper No. 2004/14, Max Planck Institute for Research on Collective Goods Working Paper Series. Bonn: Max Planck Institute for Research on Collective Goods.

Helpman, Elhanan, and Efraim Sadka. 1978. Optimal Taxation of Full Income. *International Economic Review* 19:247–251.

Henderson, J. Vernon. 1982. Evaluating Consumer Amenities and Interregional Welfare Differences. *Journal of Urban Economics* 11:32–59.

Hepner, Mickey, and W. Robert Reed. 2004. The Effect of Welfare on Work and Marriage: A View from the States. *Cato Journal* 24:349–370.

Hines, James R., Jr. 2000. What Is Benefit Taxation? *Journal of Public Economics* 75:483–492.

Hirsch, Fred. 1976. *Social Limits to Growth.* Cambridge, Mass.: Harvard University Press.

Hirshleifer, Jack. 1987. On the Emotions as Guarantors of Threats and Promises. In *The Latest on the Best: Essays on Evolution and Optimality,* edited by John Dupré, pp. 307–326. Cambridge, Mass.: MIT Press.

Hochman, Harold M., and James D. Rodgers. 1969. Pareto Optimal Redistribution. *American Economic Review* 59:542–557.

Hoehn, John P., Mark C. Berger, and Glenn C. Blomquist. 1987. A Hedonic Model of

Interregional Wages, Rents, and Amenity Values. *Journal of Regional Science* 27:605–620.

Hoff, Karla, and Andrew B. Lyon. 1995. Non-Leaky Buckets: Optimal Redistributive Taxation and Agency Costs. *Journal of Public Economics* 58:365–390.

Hogarth, Robin M., and Melvin W. Reder, eds. 1987. *Rational Choice: The Contrast between Economics and Psychology*. Chicago: University of Chicago Press.

Holtz-Eakin, Douglas, David Joulfaian, and Harvey S. Rosen. 1993. The Carnegie Conjecture: Some Empirical Evidence. *Quarterly Journal of Economics* 108:413–435.

———. 1994a. Entrepreneurial Decisions and Liquidity Constraints. *RAND Journal of Economics* 25:334–347.

———. 1994b. Sticking It Out: Entrepreneurial Survival and Liquidity Constraints. *Journal of Political Economy* 102:53–75.

Hotz, V. Joseph, and John Karl Scholz. 2003. The Earned Income Tax Credit. In *Means-Tested Transfer Programs in the United States*, edited by Robert A. Moffitt, pp. 141–197. Chicago: University of Chicago Press.

Howitt, Peter, and Hans-Werner Sinn. 1989. Gradual Reforms of Capital Income Taxation. *American Economic Review* 79:106–124.

Hubbard, R. Glenn, and Kenneth L. Judd. 1986. Liquidity Constraints, Fiscal Policy, and Consumption. *Brookings Papers on Economic Activity* 1986, no. 1:1–50.

———. 1987. Social Security and Individual Welfare: Precautionary Saving, Borrowing Constraints, and the Payroll Tax. *American Economic Review* 77:630–646.

Hubbard, R. Glenn, Jonathan Skinner, and Stephen P. Zeldes. 1995. Precautionary Saving and Social Insurance. *Journal of Political Economy* 103:360–399.

Hume, David. [1751] 1998. *An Enquiry Concerning the Principles of Morals*. Edited by Tom L. Beauchamp. Oxford: Clarendon Press.

Hurd, Michael D. 2003. Bequests: By Accident or by Design? In *Death and Dollars: The Role of Gifts and Bequests in America,* edited by Alicia Munnell and Annika Sundén, pp. 93–118. Washington, D.C.: Brookings Institution Press.

Hurka, Thomas. 1983. Value and Population Size. *Ethics* 93:496–507.

Hurst, Erik, and Annamaria Lusardi. 2004. Liquidity Constraints, Household Wealth, and Entrepreneurship. *Journal of Political Economy* 112:319–347.

Hurst, Erik, and James P. Ziliak. 2006. Do Welfare Asset Limits Affect Household Saving? Evidence from Welfare Reform. *Journal of Human Resources* 41:46–71.

Hutcheson, Francis. [1725–1755] 1994. *Philosophical Writings*, edited by R. S. Downie. London: Everyman Library.

Hylland, Aanund, and Richard Zeckhauser. 1979. Distributional Objectives Should Affect Taxes But Not Program Choice or Design. *Scandinavian Journal of Economics* 81:264–284.

Imbens, Guido W., Donald B. Rubin, and Bruce I. Sacerdote. 2001. Estimating the Effect of Unearned Income on Labor Earnings, Savings, and Consumption: Evidence from a Survey of Lottery Players. *American Economic Review* 91:778–794.

Immonen, Ritva, Ravi Kanbur, Michael Keen, and Matti Tuomala. 1998. Tagging and Taxing: The Optimal Use of Categorical and Income Information in Designing Tax/Transfer Schemes. *Economica* 65:179–192.

İmrohoroğlu, Ayşe, Selahattin İmrohoroğlu, and Douglas H. Joines. 2003. Time-Inconsistent Preferences and Social Security. *Quarterly Journal of Economics* 118:745–784.

Internal Revenue Service. 1996. Federal Tax Compliance Research: Individual Income Tax Gap Estimates for 1985, 1988, 1992. Publication 1415. Washington, D.C.: Internal Revenue Service.

———. 2005. Tax Gap Facts and Figures. Washington, D.C.: Internal Revenue Service. http://www.irs.gov/pub/irs-utl/tax_gap_facts-figures.pdf.

Iorwerth, Aled ab, and John Whalley. 2002. Efficiency Considerations and the Exemption of Food from Sales and Value Added Taxes. *Canadian Journal of Economics* 35:166–182.

Ireland, Norman J. 1998. Status-Seeking, Income Taxation and Efficiency. *Journal of Public Economics* 70:99–113.

———. 2001. Optimal Income Tax in the Presence of Status Effects. *Journal of Public Economics* 81:193–212.

Jacobs, Bas. 2005. Optimal Income Taxation with Endogenous Human Capital. *Journal of Public Economic Theory* 7:295–315.

Jakobsson, Ulf. 1976. On the Measurement of the Degree of Progression. *Journal of Public Economics* 5:161–168.

Jencks, Christopher, and Kathryn Edin. 1990. The Real Welfare Problem. *American Prospect* 1, no. 1:31–50.

Jorgenson, Dale W., and Barbara M. Fraumeni. 1989. The Accumulation of Human and Nonhuman Capital, 1948–84. In *The Measurement of Saving, Investment, and Wealth*, edited by Robert E. Lipsey and Helen Stone Tice, pp. 227–282. Chicago: University of Chicago Press.

Joulfaian, David, and Mark O. Wilhelm. 1994. Inheritance and Labor Supply. *Journal of Human Resources* 29:1205–1234.

Judd, Kenneth L. 1985. Redistributive Taxation in a Simple Perfect Foresight Model. *Journal of Public Economics* 28:59–83.

Juhn, Chinhui, Kevin M. Murphy, and Robert H. Topel. 1991. Why Has the Natural Rate of Unemployment Increased over Time? *Brookings Papers on Economic Activity* 1991, no. 2:75–142.

Juster, F. Thomas, and Frank P. Stafford. 1991. The Allocation of Time: Empirical Findings, Behavioral Models, and Problems of Measurement. *Journal of Economic Literature* 29:471–522.

Kahneman, Daniel, Paul Slovic, and Amos Tversky, eds. 1982. *Judgment under Uncertainty: Heuristics and Biases*. New York: Cambridge University Press.

Kakwani, N. C. 1977. Applications of Lorenz Curves in Economic Analysis. *Econometrica* 45:719–728.

Kanbur, Ravi, and Matti Tuomala. 1994. Inherent Inequality and the Optimal Graduation of Marginal Tax Rates. *Scandinavian Journal of Economics* 96:275–282.

Kant, Immanuel. [1785] 1998. *Groundwork of the Metaphysics of Morals*. Translated and edited by Mary Gregor. Cambridge: Cambridge University Press.

Kaplow, Louis. 1986. An Economic Analysis of Legal Transitions. *Harvard Law Review* 99:509–617.

Kaplow, Louis. 1989. Horizontal Equity: Measures in Search of a Principle. *National Tax Journal* 42:139–154.

———. 1990. Optimal Taxation with Costly Enforcement and Evasion. *Journal of Public Economics* 43:221–236.

———. 1992a. Government Relief for Risk Associated with Government Action. *Scandinavian Journal of Economics* 94:525–541.

———. 1992b. Income Tax Deductions for Losses as Insurance. *American Economic Review* 82:1013–1017.

———. 1994a. A Note on Taxation as Social Insurance for Uncertain Labor Income. *Public Finance* 49:244–256.

———. 1994b. Taxation and Risk Taking: A General Equilibrium Perspective. *National Tax Journal* 47:789–798.

———. 1995a. A Fundamental Objection to Tax Equity Norms: A Call for Utilitarianism. *National Tax Journal* 48:497–514.

———. 1995b. A Note on Subsidizing Gifts. *Journal of Public Economics* 58:469–477.

———. 1996a. How Tax Complexity and Enforcement Affect the Equity and Efficiency of the Income Tax. *National Tax Journal* 49:135–150.

———. 1996b. On the Divergence between "Ideal" and Conventional Income-Tax Treatment of Human Capital. *American Economic Review (AEA Papers and Proceedings)* 86, no. 2:347–352.

———. 1996c. Optimal Distribution and the Family. *Scandinavian Journal of Economics* 98:75–92.

———. 1996d. The Optimal Supply of Public Goods and the Distortionary Cost of Taxation. *National Tax Journal* 49:513–533.

———. 1998a. Accuracy, Complexity, and the Income Tax. *Journal of Law, Economics, & Organization* 14:61–83.

———. 1998b. Tax and Non-tax Distortions. *Journal of Public Economics* 68:303–306.

———. 1998c. Tax Policy and Gifts. *American Economic Review (AEA Papers and Proceedings)* 88, no. 2:283–288.

———. 2001a. A Framework for Assessing Estate and Gift Taxation. In *Rethinking Estate and Gift Taxation*, edited by William G. Gale, James R. Hines, Jr., and Joel Slemrod, pp. 164–215. Washington, D.C.: Brookings Institution Press.

———. 2001b. Horizontal Equity: New Measures, Unclear Principles (Commentary). In *Inequality and Tax Policy*, edited by Kevin A. Hassett and R. Glenn Hubbard, pp. 75–97. Washington, D.C.: American Enterprise Institute Press.

———. 2003a. Concavity of Utility, Concavity of Welfare, and Redistribution of Income. Working Paper 10005, NBER Working Papers Series. Cambridge, Mass.: National Bureau of Economic Research.

———. 2003b. Transition Policy: A Conceptual Framework. *Journal of Contemporary Legal Issues* 13:161–209.

———. 2004. On the (Ir)relevance of Distribution and Labor Supply Distortion to Government Policy. *Journal of Economic Perspectives* 18, no. 4: 159–175.

———. 2005. Why Measure Inequality? *Journal of Economic Inequality* 3:65–79.

———. 2006a. Choosing Expensive Tastes. *Canadian Journal of Philosophy* 36:415–425.

———. 2006b. Myopia and the Effects of Social Security and Capital Taxation on Labor Supply. Working Paper 12452, NBER Working Paper Series. Cambridge, Mass.: National Bureau of Economic Research.

———. 2006c. On the Undesirability of Commodity Taxation Even When Income Taxation Is Not Optimal. *Journal of Public Economics* 90:1235–1250.

———. 2006d. Optimal Control of Externalities in the Presence of Income Taxation. Working Paper 12339, NBER Working Paper Series. Cambridge, Mass.: National Bureau of Economic Research.

———. 2006e. Public Goods and the Distribution of Income. *European Economic Review* 50:1627–1660.

———. 2007a. Capital Levies and Transition to a Consumption Tax. In *Institutional Foundations of Public Finance: Economic and Legal Perspectives*, edited by Alan J. Auerbach and Daniel Shaviro (forthcoming). Cambridge, Mass.: Harvard University Press.

———. 2007b. Discounting Dollars, Discounting Lives: Intergenerational Distributive Justice and Efficiency. *University of Chicago Law Review* 74:79–118.

———. 2007c. Non-optimizing Savings Behavior and Labor Supply. (Preliminary draft manuscript.)

———. 2007d. Optimal Income Transfers. *International Tax and Public Finance* 14:295–325.

———. 2007e. Optimal Policy with Heterogeneous Preferences. (Preliminary draft manuscript.)

———. 2007f. Primary Goods, Capabilities, . . . or Well-Being? *Philosophical Review* 116:603–632.

———. 2007g. Taxation. In *Handbook of Law and Economics*, edited by Mitchell Polinsky and Steven Shavell, vol. 1: 647–755. Amsterdam: North-Holland.

Kaplow, Louis, and Steven Shavell. 1994. Why the Legal System Is Less Efficient than the Income Tax in Redistributing Income. *Journal of Legal Studies* 23:667–681.

———. 2001. Any Non-welfarist Method of Policy Assessment Violates the Pareto Principle. *Journal of Political Economy* 109:281–286.

———. 2002. *Fairness versus Welfare*. Cambridge, Mass.: Harvard University Press.

Karlan, Dean, and John A. List. 2006. Does Price Matter in Charitable Giving? Evidence from a Large-Scale Natural Field Experiment. Working Paper 12338, NBER Working Paper Series. Cambridge, Mass.: National Bureau of Economic Research.

Keane, Michael, and Robert Moffitt. 1998. A Structural Model of Multiple Welfare Program Participation and Labor Supply. *International Economic Review* 39:553–589.

Kesselman, Jonathan R. 1993. Evasion Effects of Changing the Tax Mix. *Economic Record* 69:131–148.

Killingsworth, Mark R. 1983. *Labor Supply*. Cambridge: Cambridge University Press.

Killingsworth, Mark R., and James J. Heckman. 1986. Female Labor Supply: A Survey. In *Handbook of Labor Economics*, edited by Orley Ashenfelter and Richard Layard, vol. 1:103–204. Amsterdam: North-Holland.

King, Mervyn A. 1977. *Public Policy and the Corporation*. London: Chapman and Hall.

———. 1983. An Index of Inequality: With Applications to Horizontal Equity and Social Mobility. *Econometrica* 51:99–115.

Kleven, Henrik J. 2004. Optimum Taxation and the Allocation of Time. *Journal of Public Economics* 88:545–557.

Kleven, Henrik J., Claus T. Kreiner, and Emmanuel Saez. 2006. The Optimal Income Taxation of Couples. Working Paper 12685, NBER Working Paper Series. Cambridge, Mass.: National Bureau of Economic Research.

Kocherlakota, Narayana R. 1996. The Equity Premium: It's Still a Puzzle. *Journal of Economic Literature* 34:42–71.

———. 2005. Zero Expected Wealth Taxes: A Mirrlees Approach to Dynamic Optimal Taxation. *Econometrica* 73:1587–1621.

Kolm, Serge-Christophe. 1969. The Optimal Production of Social Justice. In *Public Economics: An Analysis of Public Production and Consumption and Their Relations to the Private Sectors*, edited by J. Margolis and H. Guitton, pp. 145–200. London: Macmillan.

Kondor, Yaakov. 1975. Optimal Deviations from Horizontal Equity: The Case of Family Size. *Public Finance* 30:216–221.

Konishi, Hideo. 1995. A Pareto-Improving Commodity Tax Reform under a Smooth Nonlinear Income Tax. *Journal of Public Economics* 56:413–446.

Kopczuk, Wojciech. 2003. The Trick Is to Live: Is the Estate Tax Social Security for the Rich? *Journal of Political Economy* 111:1318–1341.

———. 2005. Tax Bases, Tax Rates and the Elasticity of Reported Income. *Journal of Public Economics* 89:2093–2119.

Kopczuk, Wojciech, and Joseph Lupton. 2007. To Leave or Not to Leave: The Distribution of Bequest Motives. *Review of Economic Studies* 74:207–235.

Kopczuk, Wojciech, and Joel Slemrod. 2005. Denial of Death and Economic Behavior. *Advances in Theoretical Economics* 5, no.1: Article 5.

———. 2006. Putting Firms into Optimal Tax Theory. *American Economic Review (AEA Papers and Proceedings)* 96, no. 2:1330–1334.

Kopczuk, Wojciech, Joel Slemrod, and Shlomo Yitzhaki. 2005. The Limitations of Decentralized World Redistribution: An Optimal Taxation Approach. *European Economic Review* 49:1051–1079.

Kotlikoff, Laurence J., and Avia Spivak. 1981. The Family as an Incomplete Annuities Market. *Journal of Political Economy* 89:372–391.

Kotlikoff, Laurence J., Avia Spivak, and Lawrence H. Summers. 1982. The Adequacy of Savings. *American Economic Review* 72:1056–1069.

Koulovatianos, Christos, Carsten Schröder, and Ulrich Schmidt. 2005. On the Income Dependence of Equivalence Scales. *Journal of Public Economics* 89:967–996.

Kremer, Michael. 2001. Should Taxes Be Independent of Age? (Preliminary draft manuscript.)

Krishna, Aradhna, and Joel Slemrod. 2003. Behavioral Public Finance: Tax Design as Price Presentation. *International Tax and Public Finance* 10:189–203.

Krueger, Dirk, and Felix Kubler. 2006. Pareto-Improving Social Security Reform When Financial Markets Are Incomplete!? *American Economic Review* 96:737–755.

Krusell, Per, Burhanettin Kuruşçu, and Anthony A. Smith, Jr. 2000. Tax Policy with Quasi-geometric Discounting. *International Economic Journal* 14, no. 3:1–40.

Krusell, Per, Lee E. Ohanian, Jose-Victor Rios-Rull, and Giovanni L. Violante. 2000. Capital-Skill Complementarity and Inequality: A Macroeconomic Analysis. *Econometrica* 68:1029–1053.

Kuhn, Peter, and Fernando Lozano. 2005. The Expanding Workweek? Understanding Trends in Long Work Hours among U.S. Men, 1979–2004. Working Paper 11895, NBER Working Paper Series. Cambridge, Mass.: National Bureau of Economic Research.

Kydland, Finn E., and Edward C. Prescott. 1977. Rules Rather than Discretion: The Inconsistency of Optimal Plans. *Journal of Political Economy* 85:473–491.

Laibson, David I. 1996. Hyperbolic Discount Functions, Undersaving, and Savings Policy. Working Paper 5635, NBER Working Papers Series. Cambridge, Mass.: National Bureau of Economic Research.

———. 1997. Golden Eggs and Hyperbolic Discounting. *Quarterly Journal of Economics* 112:443–477.

Lam, David. 1997. Demographic Variables and Income Inequality. In *Handbook of Population and Family Economics,* edited by Mark R. Rosenzweig and Oded Stark, vol. 1B:1015–1059. Amsterdam: Elsevier.

Lambert, Peter J. 1999. Redistributional Effects of Progressive Income Taxes. In *Handbook of Income Inequality Measurement,* edited by Jacques Silber, pp. 485–509. Boston: Kluwer Academic Publishers.

———. 2001. *The Distribution and Redistribution of Income.* 3rd ed. Manchester: Manchester University Press.

Lancaster, Kelvin J. 1966. A New Approach to Consumer Theory. *Journal of Political Economy* 74:132–157.

Laroque, Guy. 2005. Indirect Taxation Is Superfluous under Separability and Taste Homogeneity: A Simple Proof. *Economics Letters* 87:141–144.

Lawrance, Emily C. 1991. Poverty and the Rate of Time Preference: Evidence from Panel Data. *Journal of Political Economy* 99:54–77.

Layard, Richard. 1980. Human Satisfactions and Public Policy. *Economic Journal* 90:737–750.

Leimer, Dean R. 1999. Lifetime Distribution under the Social Security Program: A Literature Synopsis. *Social Security Bulletin* 62, no. 2:43–51.

Lemieux, Thomas, Bernard Fortin, and Pierre Fréchette. 1994. The Effect of Taxes on Labor Supply in the Underground Economy. *American Economic Review* 84: 231–254.

Lerner, Abba P. 1944. *The Economics of Control: Principles of Welfare Economics.* New York: Macmillan.

Levine, Phillip B., and David J. Zimmerman. 2005. Children's Welfare Exposure and Subsequent Development. *Journal of Public Economics* 89:31–56.

Lewis, Clarence I. 1946. *An Analysis of Knowledge and Valuation.* La Salle, Ill.: Open Court.

Liebman, Jeffrey B. 2003. Should Taxes Be Based on Lifetime Income? Vickrey Taxation Revisited. (Preliminary draft manuscript.)

Liebman, Jeffrey B., and Richard J. Zeckhauser. 2004. Schmeduling. (Preliminary draft manuscript.)

Lind, Robert C., Kenneth J. Arrow, Gordon R. Corey, Partha Dasgupta, Amartya K. Sen, Thomas Stauffer, Joseph E. Stiglitz, J. A. Stockfisch, and Robert Wilson. 1982. *Discounting for Time and Risk in Energy Policy.* Washington, D.C.: Resources for the Future.

Lindahl, Erik. 1919. *Die Gerechtigkeit der Besteuerung: Eine Analyse der Steuerprinzipien auf der Grundlage der Grenznutzentheorie.* Lund: Gleerup and H. Ohlsson. (Chapter 4, "Positive Lösung," translated as "Just Taxation—A Positive Solution" in *Classics in the Theory of Public Finance,* edited by R. Musgrave and A. Peacock, pp. 168–176. London: Macmillan, 1958.)

Lindbeck, Assar. 1993. *The Welfare State,* vol. 2 of *The Selected Essays of Assar Lindbeck.* Aldershot, U.K.: Edward Elgar.

Lindbeck, Assar, and Jörgen W. Weibull. 1988. Altruism and Time Consistency: The Economics of Fait Accompli. *Journal of Political Economy* 96:1165–1182.

Lindsey, Lawrence B. 1987. Individual Taxpayer Response to Tax Cuts: 1982–1984, with Implications for the Revenue Maximizing Tax Rate. *Journal of Public Economics* 33:173–206.

Little, I. M. D. 1957. *A Critique of Welfare Economics.* 2nd ed. Oxford: Clarendon Press.

Low, Hamish, and Daniel Maldoom. 2004. Optimal Taxation, Prudence and Risk-Sharing. *Journal of Public Economics* 88:443–464.

Lucas, Robert E. B., and Oded Stark. 1985. Motivations to Remit: Evidence from Botswana. *Journal of Political Economy* 93: 901–918.

Luttmer, Erzo F. P. 2005. Neighbors as Negatives: Relative Earnings and Well-Being. *Quarterly Journal of Economics* 120:963–1002.

Mace, Barbara J. 1991. Full Insurance in the Presence of Aggregate Uncertainty. *Journal of Political Economy* 99:928–956.

MacKie-Mason, Jeffrey K. 1990. Some Nonlinear Tax Effects on Asset Values and Investment Decisions under Uncertainty. *Journal of Public Economics* 42:301–327.

MaCurdy, Thomas E. 1981. An Empirical Model of Labor Supply in a Life-Cycle Setting. *Journal of Political Economy* 89:1059–1085.

MaCurdy, Thomas, David Green, and Harry Paarsch. 1990. Assessing Empirical Approaches for Analyzing Taxes and Labor Supply. *Journal of Human Resources* 25:415–490.

Madrian, Brigitte C., and Dennis F. Shea. 2001. The Power of Suggestion: Inertia in 401(k) Participation and Savings Behavior. *Quarterly Journal of Economics* 116: 1149–1187.

Maital, Shlomo. 1973. Public Goods and Income Distribution: Some Further Results. *Econometrica* 41:561–568.

———. 1975. Apportionment of Public Goods Benefits to Individuals. *Public Finance* 30:397–416.

Marchand, Maurice, Pierre Pestieau, and María Racionero. 2003. Optimal Redistribution When Different Workers Are Indistinguishable. *Canadian Journal of Economics* 36:911–922.

Martinez-Vazquez, Jorge. 1982. Fiscal Incidence at the Local Level. *Econometrica* 50:1207–1218.

Masson, André, and Pierre Pestieau. 1997. Bequests Motives and Models of Inheritance: A Survey of the Literature. In *Is Inheritance Legitimate?*, edited by Guido Erreygers and Toon Vandevelde, pp. 54–88. Berlin: Springer.

Mayshar, Joram. 1991a. On Measuring the Marginal Cost of Funds Analytically. *American Economic Review* 81:1329–1335.

———. 1991b. Taxation with Costly Administration. *Scandinavian Journal of Economics* 93:75–88.

McAdams, Richard H. 1992. Relative Preferences. *Yale Law Journal* 102:1–104.

McCaffery, Edward J., and Joel Slemrod, eds. 2006. *Behavioral Public Finance*. New York: Russell Sage Foundation.

McLure, Charles E., Jr. 1979. *Must Corporate Income Be Taxed Twice?* Washington, D.C.: Brookings Institution.

Mead, Lawrence M. 2004. *Government Matters: Welfare Reform in Wisconsin*. Princeton: Princeton University Press.

Meerman, Jacob. 1978. Do Empirical Studies of Budget Incidence Make Sense? *Public Finance* 33:295–313.

Meghir, Costas, and Guglielmo Weber. 1996. Intertemporal Nonseparability or Borrowing Restrictions? A Disaggregate Analysis Using a U.S. Consumption Panel. *Econometrica* 64:1151–1181.

Menchik, Paul L. 1991. The Distribution of Federal Expenditures. *National Tax Journal* 44:269–276.

Messere, Ken, Flip de Kam, and Christopher Heady. 2003. *Tax Policy: Theory and Practice in OECD Countries*. New York: Oxford University Press.

Meyer, Bruce D., and Douglas Holtz-Eakin. 2001. Introduction. In *Making Work Pay: The Earned Income Tax Credit and Its Impact on America's Families*, edited by Bruce D. Meyer and Douglas Holtz-Eakin, pp. 1–12. New York: Russell Sage Foundation.

Meyer, Bruce D., and Dan T. Rosenbaum. 2001. Welfare, the Earned Income Tax Credit, and the Labor Supply of Single Mothers. *Quarterly Journal of Economics* 116:1063–1114.

Michael, Robert T., and Gary S. Becker. 1973. On the New Theory of Consumer Behavior. *Swedish Journal of Economics* 75:378–396.

Michalopoulos, Charles, Philip K. Robins, and David Card. 2005. When Financial Work Incentives Pay for Themselves: Evidence from a Randomized Social Experiment for Welfare Recipients. *Journal of Public Economics* 89:5–29.

Mill, John Stuart. 1859. *On Liberty*. London: J. W. Parker.

——. [1861] 1998. *Utilitarianism*. Edited by Roger Crisp. New York: Oxford University Press.

Milligan, Kevin. 2005. Subsidizing the Stork: New Evidence on Tax Incentives and Fertility. *Review of Economics and Statistics* 87:539–555.

Mirrlees, James A. 1971. An Exploration in the Theory of Optimum Income Taxation. *Review of Economic Studies* 38:175–208.

——. 1972. Population Policy and the Taxation of Family Size. *Journal of Public Economics* 1:169–198.

——. 1976. Optimal Tax Theory: A Synthesis. *Journal of Public Economics* 6: 327–358.

——. 1978. Arguments for Public Expenditure. In *Contemporary Economic Analysis*, edited by M. J. Artis and A. R. Nobay, vol. 1:273–299. London: Croom Helm.

——. 1982. The Economic Uses of Utilitarianism. In *Utilitarianism and Beyond*, edited by Amartya Sen and Bernard Williams, pp. 63–84. Cambridge: Cambridge University Press.

——. 1990. Taxing Uncertain Incomes. *Oxford Economic Papers* 42:34–45.

——. 1994. Optimal Taxation and Government Finance. In *Modern Public Finance*, edited by John M. Quigley and Eugene Smolensky, pp. 213–231. Cambridge, Mass.: Harvard University Press.

Moffitt, Robert A. 1989. Estimating the Value of an In-Kind Transfer: The Case of Food Stamps. *Econometrica* 57:385–409.

——. 2002. Welfare Programs and Labor Supply. In *Handbook of Public Economics*, edited by Alan J. Auerbach and Martin Feldstein, vol. 4:2393–2430. Amsterdam: Elsevier.

——, ed. 2003. *Means-Tested Transfer Programs in the United States*. Chicago: University of Chicago Press.

Moffitt, Robert A., and Mark O. Wilhelm. 2000. Taxation and the Labor Supply Decisions of the Affluent. In *Does Atlas Shrug? The Economic Consequences of Taxing the Rich*, edited by Joel B. Slemrod, pp. 193–234. New York: Russell Sage Foundation.

Moore, James F., and Olivia S. Mitchell. 2000. Projected Retirement Wealth and Saving Adequacy. In *Forecasting Retirement Needs and Retirement Wealth*, edited by Olivia S. Mitchell, P. Brett Hammond, and Anna M. Rappaport, pp. 68–94. Philadelphia: University of Pennsylvania Press.

Moulin, Hervé. 1987. Egalitarian-Equivalent Cost Sharing of a Public Good. *Econometrica* 55:963–976.

Mroz, Thomas A. 1987. The Sensitivity of an Empirical Model of Married Women's Hours of Work to Economic and Statistical Assumptions. *Econometrica* 55: 765–799.

Mueller, Dennis C. 1974. Intergenerational Justice and the Social Discount Rate. *Theory and Decision* 5:263–273.

Munro, Alistair. 1989. In-Kind Transfers, Cash Grants and the Supply of Labour. *European Economic Review* 33:1597–1604.

Musgrave, Richard A. 1959. *The Theory of Public Finance.* New York: McGraw-Hill.

———. 1990. Horizontal Equity, Once More. *National Tax Journal* 43:113–122.

Musgrave, Richard A., and Peggy B. Musgrave. 1973. *Public Finance in Theory and Practice.* New York: McGraw-Hill.

Musgrave, Richard A., and Tun Thin. 1948. Income Tax Progression, 1929–48. *Journal of Political Economy* 56:498–514.

Musgrave, Richard A., Karl E. Case, and Herman Leonard. 1974. The Distribution of Fiscal Burdens and Benefits. *Public Finance Quarterly* 2:259–311.

Myerson, Roger B. 1981. Utilitarianism, Egalitarianism, and the Timing Effect in Social Choice Problems. *Econometrica* 49:883–897.

Naito, Hisahiro. 1999. Re-examination of Uniform Commodity Taxes under a Non-Linear Income Tax System and Its Implication for Production Efficiency. *Journal of Public Economics* 71:165–188.

———. 2004. Endogenous Human Capital Accumulation, Comparative Advantage and Direct vs. Indirect Redistribution. *Journal of Public Economics* 88:2685–2710.

Nerlove, Marc, Assaf Razin, and Efraim Sadka. 1986. Some Welfare Theoretic Implications of Endogenous Fertility. *International Economic Review* 27:3–31.

Nerlove, Marc, Assaf Razin, Efraim Sadka, and Robert K. von Weizsäcker. 1993. Comprehensive Income Taxation, Investments in Human and Physical Capital, and Productivity. *Journal of Public Economics* 50:397–406.

Ng, Yew-Kwang. 1981. Bentham or Nash? On the Acceptable Form of Social Welfare Functions. *Economic Record* 57:238–250.

———. 1984a. Interpersonal Level Comparability Implies Comparability of Utility Differences. *Theory and Decision* 17:141–147.

———. 1984b. Quasi-Pareto Social Improvements. *American Economic Review* 74:1033–1050.

———. 1989. What Should We Do about Future Generations? Impossibility of Parfit's Theory X. *Economics and Philosophy* 5:235–253.

———. 2000a. *Efficiency, Equality, and Public Policy: With a Case for Higher Public Spending.* New York: St. Martin's Press.

———. 2000b. The Optimal Size of Public Spending and the Distortionary Cost of Taxation. *National Tax Journal* 53:253–272.

Nichols, Albert L., and Richard J. Zeckhauser. 1982. Targeting Transfers through Restrictions on Recipients. *American Economic Review (AEA Papers and Proceedings)* 72, no. 2:372–377.

Nisbett, Richard, and Lee Ross. 1980. *Human Inference: Strategies and Shortcomings of Social Judgment.* Englewood Cliffs, N.J.: Prentice-Hall.

Nishiyama, Shinichi, and Kent Smetters. 2005. Consumption Taxes and Economic Efficiency with Idiosyncratic Wage Shocks. *Journal of Political Economy* 113: 1088–1115.

Nordhaus, William D. 1994. *Managing the Global Commons: The Economics of Climate Change.* Cambridge, Mass.: MIT Press.

Nozick, Robert. 1974. *Anarchy, State, and Utopia.* New York: Basic Books.

Nussbaum, Martha, and Amartya Sen, eds. 1993. *The Quality of Life.* New York: Oxford University Press.

O'Donoghue, Ted, and Matthew Rabin. 2006. Optimal Sin Taxes. *Journal of Public Economics* 90:1825–1849.

O'Higgins, Michael, and Patricia Ruggles. 1981. The Distribution of Public Expenditures and Taxes among Households in the United Kingdom. *Review of Income and Wealth* 27:298–326.

Ordover, Janusz A., and Edmund S. Phelps. 1979. The Concept of Optimal Taxation in the Overlapping-Generations Model of Capital and Wealth. *Journal of Public Economics* 12:1–26.

Oswald, Andrew J. 1983. Altruism, Jealousy, and the Theory of Optimal Non-Linear Taxation. *Journal of Public Economics* 20:77–87.

Page, Benjamin I. 1983. *Who Gets What from Government.* Berkeley: University of California Press.

Parfit, Derek. 1984. *Reasons and Persons.* New York: Oxford University Press.

Parsons, Donald O. 1991. Self-Screening in Targeted Public Transfer Programs. *Journal of Political Economy* 99:859–876.

———. 1996. Imperfect "Tagging" in Social Insurance Programs. *Journal of Public Economics* 62:183–207.

Pauly, Mark V. 1973. Income Redistribution as a Local Public Good. *Journal of Public Economics* 2:35–58.

Peacock, Alan. 1974. The Treatment of Government Expenditure in Studies of Income Redistribution. In *Public Finance and Stabilization Policy: Essays in Honor of Richard A. Musgrave,* edited by Warren L. Smith and John M. Culbertson, pp. 151–167. Amsterdam: North-Holland Publishing Co.

Pencavel, John. 1986. Labor Supply of Men: A Survey. In *Handbook of Labor Economics,* edited by Orley Ashenfelter and Richard Layard, vol. 1:3–102. Amsterdam: North-Holland.

Persson, Torsten, and Guido Tabellini. 2002. Political Economics and Public Finance. In *Handbook of Public Economics,* edited by Alan J. Auerbach and Martin Feldstein, vol. 3:1549–1659. Amsterdam: Elsevier.

Phelps, Edmund S. 1973. Taxation of Wage Income for Economic Justice. *Quarterly Journal of Economics* 87:331–354.

Piggott, John, and John Whalley. 1987. Interpreting Net Fiscal Incidence Calculations. *Review of Economics and Statistics* 69:685–694.

Pigou, Arthur C. 1920. *The Economics of Welfare.* London: Macmillan.

———. 1928. *A Study in Public Finance.* London: Macmillan.

Pirttilä, Jukka, and Matti Tuomala. 1997. Income Tax, Commodity Tax and Environmental Policy. *International Tax and Public Finance* 4:379–393.

Plotnick, Robert. 1981. A Measure of Horizontal Inequity. *Review of Economics and Statistics* 63:283–288.

Plott, Charles R. 1978. Rawls's Theory of Justice: An Impossibility Result. In *Decision Theory and Social Ethics: Issues in Social Choice,* edited by Hans W. Gottinger and Werner Leinfellner, pp. 201–214. Dordrecht: D. Reidel Publishing Co.

Polinsky, A. Mitchell. 1974. Imperfect Capital Markets, Intertemporal Redistribution, and Progressive Taxation. In *Redistribution through Public Choice*, edited by Harold M. Hochman and George E. Peterson, pp. 229–258. New York: Columbia University Press.

Pollak, Robert A. 1985. A Transaction Cost Approach to Families and Households. *Journal of Economic Literature* 23:581–608.

Pollak, Robert A., and Terence J. Wales. 1979. Welfare Comparisons and Equivalence Scales. *American Economic Review (AEA Papers and Proceedings)* 69, no. 2:216–221.

Poterba, James M. 2001. Estate and Gift Taxes and Incentives for Inter Vivos Giving in the US. *Journal of Public Economics* 79:237–264.

———. 2002. Taxation, Risk-Taking, and Household Portfolio Behavior. In *Handbook of Public Economics*, edited by Alan J. Auerbach and Martin Feldstein, vol. 3:1109–1171. Amsterdam: Elsevier.

Powers, Elizabeth T. 1998. Does Means-Testing Welfare Discourage Saving? Evidence from a Change in AFDC Policy in the United States. *Journal of Public Economics* 68:33–53.

Prescott, Edward C. 2004. Why Do Americans Work So Much More Than Europeans? *Federal Reserve Bank of Minneapolis Quarterly Review* 28, no. 1:2–13.

Preston, Stephanie D., and Frans B. M. de Waal. 2002. Empathy: Its Ultimate and Proximate Bases. *Behavioral and Brain Sciences* 25:1–20.

Rabin, Matthew. 1998. Psychology and Economics. *Journal of Economic Literature* 36:11–46.

Ramsey, Frank P. 1927. A Contribution to the Theory of Taxation. *Economic Journal* 37:47–61.

Ravallion, Martin. 1994. *Poverty Comparisons*. Chur: Harwood Academic Publishers.

Rawls, John. 1955. Two Concepts of Rules. *Philosophical Review* 64:3–32.

———. 1971. *A Theory of Justice*. Cambridge, Mass.: Harvard University Press.

———. 1982. Social Unity and Primary Goods. In *Utilitarianism and Beyond*, edited by Amartya Sen and Bernard Williams, pp. 159–185. New York: Cambridge University Press.

———. 1993. *Political Liberalism*. New York: Columbia University Press.

Regan, Tom. 1983. *The Case for Animal Rights*. Berkeley: University of California Press.

Revesz, Richard L. 1999. Environmental Regulation, Cost-Benefit Analysis, and the Discounting of Human Lives. *Columbia Law Review* 99:941–1017.

Reynolds, Morgan, and Eugene Smolensky. 1977. *Public Expenditures, Taxes, and the Distribution of Income: The United States, 1950, 1961, 1970*. New York: Academic Press.

Robbins, Lionel. 1935. *An Essay on the Nature and Significance of Economic Science*. 2nd ed. London: Macmillan.

———. 1938. Interpersonal Comparisons of Utility: A Comment. *Economic Journal* 48:635–641.

Roberts, Kevin. 1984. The Theoretical Limits to Redistribution. *Review of Economic Studies* 51:177–195.

Robinson, James A., and T. N. Srinivasan. 1997. Long-Term Consequences of Population Growth: Technological Change, Natural Resources, and the Environment. In

Handbook of Population and Family Economics, edited by Mark R. Rosenzweig and Oded Stark, vol. 1B:1175–1298. Amsterdam: Elsevier.

Rogerson, William P. 1985. Repeated Moral Hazard. *Econometrica* 53:69–76.

Rose-Ackerman, Susan. 1982. Charitable Giving and "Excessive" Fundraising. *Quarterly Journal of Economics* 97:193–212.

Rosen, Harvey S. 1980. What Is Labor Supply and Do Taxes Affect It? *American Economic Review (AEA Papers and Proceedings)* 70, no. 2:171–176.

Rosen, Sherwin. 1979. Wage-based Indexes of Urban Quality of Life. In *Current Issues in Urban Economics,* edited by Peter Mieszkowski and Mahlon Straszheim, pp. 74–104. Baltimore: Johns Hopkins University Press.

Roth, Jeffrey A., John T. Scholz, and Ann D. Witte, eds. 1989. *Taxpayer Compliance:* vol. 1, *An Agenda for Research;* vol. 2, *Social Science Perspectives.* Philadelphia: University of Pennsylvania Press.

Ruggles, Patricia. 1990. *Drawing the Line: Alternative Poverty Measures and Their Implications for Public Policy.* Washington, D.C.: Urban Institute Press.

———. 1991. The Impact of Government Tax and Expenditure Programs on the Distribution of Income in the United States. In *Economic Inequality and Poverty: International Perspectives,* edited by Lars Osberg, pp. 220–245. Armonk, N.Y.: M. E. Sharpe, Inc.

Ruggles, Patricia, and Michael O'Higgins. 1981. The Distribution of Public Expenditure among Households in the United States. *Review of Income and Wealth* 27:137–164.

Runkle, David E. 1991. Liquidity Constraints and the Permanent-Income Hypothesis: Evidence from Panel Data. *Journal of Monetary Economics* 27:73–98.

Russek, Frank S. 1996. CBO Memorandum: Labor Supply and Taxes. Washington, D.C.: Congressional Budget Office.

Sadka, Efraim. 1976. On Income Distribution, Incentive Effects and Optimal Income Taxation. *Review of Economic Studies* 43:261–267.

Saez, Emmanuel. 2001. Using Elasticities to Derive Optimal Income Tax Rates. *Review of Economic Studies* 68:205–229.

———. 2002a. The Desirability of Commodity Taxation under Non-Linear Income Taxation and Heterogeneous Tastes. *Journal of Public Economics* 83:217–230.

———. 2002b. Optimal Income Transfer Programs: Intensive versus Extensive Labor Supply Responses. *Quarterly Journal of Economics* 117:1039–1073.

———. 2004a. Direct or Indirect Tax Instruments for Redistribution: Short-Run versus Long-Run. *Journal of Public Economics* 88:503–518.

———. 2004b. The Optimal Treatment of Tax Expenditures. *Journal of Public Economics* 88: 2657–2684.

———. 2004c. Reported Incomes and Marginal Tax Rates, 1960–2000: Evidence and Policy Implications. In *Tax Policy and the Economy,* edited by James M. Poterba, vol. 18:117–173. Cambridge, Mass.: MIT Press.

Sala-i-Martin, Xavier. 2002. The Disturbing "Rise" of Global Income Inequality. Working Paper 8904, NBER Working Paper Series. Cambridge, Mass.: National Bureau of Economic Research.

Salanié, Bernard. 2003. *The Economics of Taxation.* Cambridge, Mass.: MIT Press.

Sammartino, Frank, and David Weiner. 1997. Recent Evidence on Taxpayers' Response to the Rate Increases in the 1990's. *National Tax Journal* 50:683–705.

Sammartino, Frank, Eric Toder, and Elaine Maag. 2002. Providing Federal Assistance for Low-Income Families through the Tax System: A Primer. Discussion Paper No. 4. Washington, D.C.: Urban-Brookings Tax Policy Center.

Samuelson, Paul A. 1954. The Pure Theory of Public Expenditure. *Review of Economics and Statistics* 36:387–389.

———. 1956. Social Indifference Curves. *Quarterly Journal of Economics* 70:1–22.

———. 1975. Optimum Social Security in a Life-Cycle Growth Model. *International Economic Review* 16:539–544.

Sandmo, Agnar. 1976. Optimal Taxation: An Introduction to the Literature. *Journal of Public Economics* 6:37–54.

———. 1993. Optimal Redistribution When Tastes Differ. *Finanzarchiv* 50:149–163.

Sarkar, Shounak, and George R. Zodrow. 1993. Transitional Issues in Moving to a Direct Consumption Tax. *National Tax Journal* 46:359–376.

Schelling, Thomas C. 1984. *Choice and Consequence*. Cambridge, Mass.: Harvard University Press.

Scholz, John Karl, Ananth Seshadri, and Surachai Khitatrakun. 2006. Are Americans Saving "Optimally" for Retirement? *Journal of Political Economy* 114:607–643.

Schroyen, Fred. 2003. Redistributive Taxation and the Household: The Case of Individual Filings. *Journal of Public Economics* 87: 2527–2547.

Schultz, T. Paul. 1994. Marital Status and Fertility in the United States: Welfare and Labor Market Effects. *Journal of Human Resources* 29:637–669.

Scitovsky, Tibor. 1951. *Welfare and Competition: The Economics of a Fully Employed Economy.* Chicago: Richard D. Irwin, Inc.

———. 1976. *The Joyless Economy: An Inquiry into Human Satisfaction and Consumer Dissatisfaction.* New York: Oxford University Press.

Seade, J. K. 1977. On the Shape of Optimal Tax Schedules. *Journal of Public Economics* 7:203–235.

Seidman, Laurence S. 1997. *The USA Tax: A Progressive Consumption Tax.* Cambridge, Mass.: MIT Press.

Sen, Amartya. 1970. The Impossibility of a Paretian Liberal. *Journal of Political Economy* 78:152–157.

———. 1973a. *On Economic Inequality.* Oxford: Clarendon Press.

———. 1973b. On Ignorance and Equal Distribution. *American Economic Review* 63: 1022–1024.

———. 1976. Poverty: An Ordinal Approach to Measurement. *Econometrica* 44:219–231.

———. 1977. On Weights and Measures: Informational Constraints in Social Welfare Analysis. *Econometrica* 45:1539–1572.

———. 1979. Utilitarianism and Welfarism. *Journal of Philosophy* 76:463–489.

———. 1985a. *Commodities and Capabilities.* Amsterdam: North-Holland.

———. 1985b. Well-being, Agency and Freedom: The Dewey Lectures 1984. *Journal of Philosophy* 82:169–221.

Sen, Amartya. 1997. *On Economic Inequality*. Enlarged ed. Oxford: Clarendon Press.

Sen, Amartya, and Bernard Williams, eds. 1982. *Utilitarianism and Beyond*. Cambridge: Cambridge University Press.

Shavell, Steven. 1981. A Note on Efficiency vs. Distributional Equity in Legal Rulemaking: Should Distributional Equity Matter Given Optimal Income Taxation? *American Economic Review (AEA Papers and Proceedings)* 71, no. 2:414–418.

Shaviro, Daniel. 1999. *Effective Marginal Tax Rates on Low-Income Households*. Washington, D.C.: Employment Policies Institute.

———. 2000. *When Rules Change: An Economic and Political Analysis of Transition Relief and Retroactivity*. Chicago: University of Chicago Press.

———. 2004. Rethinking Tax Expenditures and Fiscal Language. *Tax Law Review* 57:187–231.

Sheshinski, Eytan. 1989. Note on the Shape of the Optimal Income Tax Schedule. *Journal of Public Economics* 40:201–215.

Sheshinski, Eytan, and Yoram Weiss. 1982. Inequality within and between Families. *Journal of Political Economy* 90:105–127.

Shiller, Robert J. 1999. Social Security and Institutions for Intergenerational, Intragenerational, and International Risk-Sharing. *Carnegie-Rochester Conference Series on Public Policy* 50:165–204.

Shore, Miles F. 1997. Psychological Factors in Poverty. In *The New Paternalism: Supervisory Approaches to Poverty*, edited by Lawrence M. Mead, pp. 305–329. Washington, D.C.: Brookings Institution Press.

Shoven, John B., and Sita N. Slavov. 2006. Political Risk versus Market Risk in Social Security. Working Paper 12135, NBER Working Paper Series. Cambridge, Mass.: National Bureau of Economic Research.

Showalter, Mark H., and Norman K. Thurston. 1997. Taxes and Labor Supply of High-Income Physicians. *Journal of Public Economics* 66:73–97.

Sidgwick, Henry. [1907] 1981. *The Methods of Ethics*. Reprint of 7th ed. Indianapolis: Hackett Publishing Co.

Silber, Jacques, ed. 1999. *Handbook of Income Inequality Measurement*. Boston: Kluwer Academic Publishers.

Sillamaa, Mary-Anne, and Michael R. Veall. 2001. The Effect of Marginal Tax Rates on Taxable Income: A Panel Study of the 1988 Tax Flattening in Canada. *Journal of Public Economics* 80:341–356.

Silver, Morris. 1980. Money and Happiness?: Towards "Eudaimonology." *Kyklos* 33: 157–160.

Simons, Henry C. 1938. *Personal Income Taxation*. Chicago: University of Chicago Press.

Singer, Peter. 1975. *Animal Liberation: A New Ethics for Our Treatment of Animals*. New York: New York Review/Random House.

———. 1988. Reasoning towards Utilitarianism. In *Hare and Critics: Essays on Moral Thinking*, edited by Douglas Seanor and N. Fotion, pp. 147–159. Oxford: Clarendon Press.

———. 2004. *One World: The Ethics of Globalization*. 2nd ed. New Haven: Yale University Press.

Sinn, Hans-Werner. 2000. Why a Funded Pension System Is Useful and Why It Is Not Useful. *International Tax and Public Finance* 7:389–410.

Slemrod, Joel. 1988. Effect of Taxation with International Capital Mobility. In *Uneasy Compromise: Problems of a Hybrid Income-Consumption Tax*, edited by Henry J. Aaron, Harvey Galper, and Joseph A. Pechman, pp. 115–148. Washington, D.C.: Brookings Institution.

———. 1990a. The Economic Impact of the Tax Reform Act of 1986. In *Do Taxes Matter? The Impact of the Tax Reform Act of 1986*, edited by Joel Slemrod, pp. 1–12. Cambridge, Mass.: MIT Press.

———. 1990b. Optimal Taxation and Optimal Tax Systems. *Journal of Economic Perspectives* 4, no. 1:157–178.

———. 1996a. High-Income Families and the Tax Changes of the 1980s: The Anatomy of Behavioral Response. In *Empirical Foundations of Household Taxation*, edited by Martin Feldstein and James M. Poterba, pp. 169–189. Chicago: University of Chicago Press.

———. 1996b. Which Is the Simplest Tax System of Them All? In *The Economic Effects of Fundamental Tax Reform*, edited by Henry J. Aaron and William G. Gale, pp. 355–391. Washington, D.C.: Brookings Institution Press.

———. 2000. The Economics of Taxing the Rich. In *Does Atlas Shrug? The Economic Consequences of Taxing the Rich*, edited by Joel B. Slemrod, pp. 3–28. New York: Russell Sage Foundation.

———. 2001. A General Model of the Behavioral Response to Taxation. *International Tax and Public Finance* 8:119–128.

Slemrod, Joel, and Wojciech Kopczuk. 2002. The Optimal Elasticity of Taxable Income. *Journal of Public Economics* 84:91–112.

Slemrod, Joel, and Shlomo Yitzhaki. 1987. The Optimal Size of a Tax Collection Agency. *Scandinavian Journal of Economics* 89:183–192.

———. 2001. Integrating Expenditure and Tax Decisions: The Marginal Costs of Funds and the Marginal Benefit of Projects. *National Tax Journal* 54:189–201.

———. 2002. Tax Avoidance, Evasion, and Administration. In *Handbook of Public Economics*, edited by Alan J. Auerbach and Martin Feldstein, vol. 3:1423–1470. Amsterdam: Elsevier.

Slemrod, Joel, Shlomo Yitzhaki, Joram Mayshar, and Michael Lundholm. 1994. The Optimal Two-Bracket Linear Income Tax. *Journal of Public Economics* 53: 269–290.

Sloan, Frank A., and Edward C. Norton. 1997. Adverse Selection, Bequests, Crowding Out, and Private Demand for Insurance: Evidence from the Long-term Care Insurance Market. *Journal of Risk and Uncertainty* 15:201–219.

Smart, J.J.C. 1973. An Outline of a System of Utilitarian Ethics. In *Utilitarianism: For and Against*, by J.J.C. Smart and Bernard Williams, pp. 3–74. Cambridge: Cambridge University Press.

Smetters, Kent. 2005. Social Security Privatization with Elastic Labor Supply and Second-Best Taxes. Working Paper 11101, NBER Working Papers Series. Cambridge, Mass.: National Bureau of Economic Research.

Smith, Sarah. 2006. The Retirement-Consumption Puzzle and Involuntary Early Retirement: Evidence from the British Household Panel Survey. *Economic Journal* 116, no. 510:C130–C148.

Snow, Arthur, and Ronald S. Warren, Jr. 1983. Tax Progression in Lindahl Equilibrium. *Economics Letters* 12:319–326.

Stark, Oded. 1995. *Altruism and Beyond: An Economic Analysis of Transfers and Exchanges within Families and Groups.* Cambridge: Cambridge University Press.

Stern, Nicholas H. 1976. On the Specification of Models of Optimum Income Taxation. *Journal of Public Economics* 6:123–162.

———. 1982. Optimum Taxation with Errors in Administration. *Journal of Public Economics* 17:181–211.

Steuerle, Gene. 2003. Can the Progressivity of Tax Changes Be Measured in Isolation? *Tax Notes* 100:1187–1188.

Stigler, George J., and Gary S. Becker. 1977. De Gustibus Non Est Disputandum. *American Economic Review* 67:76–90.

Stiglitz, Joseph E. 1976. Simple Formulae for Optimal Income Taxation and the Measurement of Inequality. Technical Report No. 215, The Economics Series. Stanford, Calif.: Institute for Mathematical Studies in the Social Sciences.

———. 1982a. Self-Selection and Pareto Efficient Taxation. *Journal of Public Economics* 17:213–240.

———. 1982b. Utilitarianism and Horizontal Equity: The Case for Random Taxation. *Journal of Public Economics* 18:1–33.

———. 1985. Inequality and Capital Taxation. Economics Series, IMSSS Technical Report No. 457. Stanford, Calif.: Institute for Mathematical Studies in the Social Sciences.

———. 1987. Pareto Efficient and Optimal Taxation and the New New Welfare Economics. In *Handbook of Public Economics,* edited by Alan J. Auerbach and Martin Feldstein, vol. 2:991–1042. Amsterdam: North-Holland.

———. 2000. *Economics of the Public Sector.* 3rd ed. New York: W. W. Norton & Company.

Stiglitz, Joseph E., and Partha Dasgupta. 1971. Differential Taxation, Public Goods, and Economic Efficiency. *Review of Economic Studies* 38:151–174.

Strawczynski, Michel. 1998. Social Insurance and the Optimum Piecewise Linear Income Tax. *Journal of Public Economics* 69:371–388.

Strnad, Jeff. 2004. The Progressivity Puzzle: The Key Role of Personal Attributes. Working Paper No. 293, Stanford Law School, John M. Olin Program in Law and Economics. Stanford, Calif.: John M. Olin Program in Law and Economics.

Strotz, Robert H. 1958. How Income Ought to Be Distributed: A Paradox in Distributive Ethics. *Journal of Political Economy* 66:189–205.

Suits, Daniel B. 1977. Measurement of Tax Progressivity. *American Economic Review* 67:747–752.

Summers, Lawrence. 1986. Comment on Hubbard and Judd, "Liquidity Constraints, Fiscal Policy, and Consumption." *Brookings Papers on Economic Activity* 1986, no. 1:53–57.

Sumner, L. W. 1978. Classical Utilitarianism and the Population Optimum. In *Obligations to Future Generations*, edited by R. I. Sikora and Brian Barry, pp. 91–111. Philadelphia: Temple University Press.

———. 1996. *Welfare, Happiness, and Ethics*. New York: Oxford University Press.

Surrey, Stanley S. 1973. *Pathways to Tax Reform: The Concept of Tax Expenditures*. Cambridge, Mass.: Harvard University Press.

Surrey, Stanley S., and Paul R. McDaniel. 1985. *Tax Expenditures*. Cambridge, Mass.: Harvard University Press.

Tarkiainen, Ritva, and Matti Tuomala. 1999. Optimal Nonlinear Income Taxation with a Two-Dimensional Population; A Computational Approach. *Computational Economics* 13:1–16.

Taubman, Paul. 1996. The Roles of the Family in the Formation of Offsprings' Earnings and Income Capacity. In *Household and Family Economics*, edited by Paul L. Menchik, pp. 5–45. Boston: Kluwer Academic Publishers.

Tax Foundation. 1981. *Allocating Tax Burdens and Government Benefits by Income Class, 1972–73 and 1977*. Washington, D.C.: Tax Foundation.

Tiebout, Charles M. 1956. A Pure Theory of Local Expenditures. *Journal of Political Economy* 64:416–424.

Triest, Robert K. 1990. The Effect of Income Taxation on Labor Supply in the United States. *Journal of Human Resources* 25:491–516.

Trostel, Philip A. 1993. The Effect of Taxation on Human Capital. *Journal of Political Economy* 101:327–350.

Tuomala, Matti. 1990. *Optimal Income Tax and Redistribution*. Oxford: Clarendon Press.

U.S. Department of the Treasury. 1992. *Report of the Department of the Treasury on Integration of the Individual and Corporate Tax Systems: Taxing Business Income Once*. Washington, D.C.: Department of the Treasury.

Varian, Hal R. 1980. Redistributive Taxation as Social Insurance. *Journal of Public Economics* 14:49–68.

Veblen, Thorstein. 1899. *The Theory of the Leisure Class: An Economic Study in the Evolution of Institutions*. New York: Macmillan Company.

Veenhoven, Ruut. 1991. Is Happiness Relative? *Social Indicators Research* 24:1–34.

Vickrey, William. 1939. Averaging of Income for Income-Tax Purposes. *Journal of Political Economy* 47:379–397.

———. 1945. Measuring Marginal Utility by Reactions to Risk. *Econometrica* 13:319–333.

———. 1947. *Agenda for Progressive Taxation*. New York: Roland Press Company.

Viscusi, W. Kip. 1995. Discounting Health Effects for Medical Decisions. In *Valuing Health Care*, edited by Frank A. Sloan, pp. 125–147. Cambridge: Cambridge University Press.

Wane, Waly. 2001. The Optimal Income Tax When Poverty Is a Public "Bad." *Journal of Public Economics* 82:271–299.

Weisbach, David A. 2004. The (Non)Taxation of Risk. *Tax Law Review* 58:1–57.

Weisbach, David A., and Jacob Nussim. 2004. The Integration of Tax and Spending Programs. *Yale Law Journal* 113:955–1028.

Weisbrod, Burton A. 1968. Income Redistribution Effects and Benefit-Cost Analysis. In *Problems in Public Expenditure Analysis*, edited by Samuel B. Chase, Jr., pp. 177–209. Washington, D.C.: Brookings Institution.

Weizsäcker, Carl Christian von. 1971. Notes on Endogenous Change of Tastes. *Journal of Economic Theory* 3:345–372.

West, Sarah E. 2004. Distributional Effects of Alternative Vehicle Pollution Control Policies. *Journal of Public Economics* 88:735–757.

Westen, Peter. 1990. *Speaking of Equality: An Analysis of the Rhetorical Force of "Equality" in Moral and Legal Discourse*. Princeton: Princeton University Press.

Westermarck, Edward. 1932. *Ethical Relativity*. New York: Harcourt, Brace and Company.

Weymark, John A. 1991. A Reconsideration of the Harsanyi-Sen Debate on Utilitarianism. In *Interpersonal Comparisons of Well-Being*, edited by Jon Elster and John Roemer, pp. 255–320. Cambridge: Cambridge University Press.

Whittington, Leslie A., James Alm, and H. Elizabeth Peters. 1990. Fertility and the Personal Exemption: Implicit Pronatalist Policy in the United States. *American Economic Review* 80:545–556.

Wicker, Bruno, Christian Keysers, Jane Plailly, Jean-Pierre Royet, Vittoria Gallese, and Giacomo Rizzolatti. 2003. Both of Us Disgusted in *My* Insula: The Common Neural Basis of Seeing and Feeling Disgust. *Neuron* 40:655–664.

Wierzbicka, Anna. 2004. "Happiness" in Cross-Linguistic & Cross-Cultural Perspective. *Dædalus* 133, no. 2:34–43.

Williams, Bernard. 1973. A Critique of Utilitarianism. In *Utilitarianism: For and Against*, by J.J.C. Smart and Bernard Williams, pp. 75–150. Cambridge: Cambridge University Press.

Wilson, Edward O. 1980. *Sociobiology*. Abridged ed. Cambridge, Mass.: Harvard University Press.

Wilson, Paul, and Robert Cline. 1994. State Welfare Reform: Integrating Tax Credits and Income Transfers. *National Tax Journal* 47:655–676.

Wolff, Edward N. 2003. The Impact of Gifts and Bequests on the Distribution of Wealth. In *Death and Dollars: The Role of Gifts and Bequests in America*, edited by Alicia H. Munnell and Annika Sundén, pp. 345–377. Washington, D.C.: Brookings Institution Press.

Yaari, M. E. 1965. Uncertain Lifetime, Life Insurance, and the Theory of the Consumer. *Review of Economic Studies* 32:137–150.

Yitzhaki, Shlomo. 1979. A Note on Optimal Taxation and Administrative Costs. *American Economic Review* 69:475–480.

Zeckhauser, Richard J. 1981. Using the Wrong Tool: The Pursuit of Redistribution through Regulation. Washington, D.C.: Chamber of Commerce of the United States.

Zeldes, Stephen P. 1989. Consumption and Liquidity Constraints: An Empirical Investigation. *Journal of Political Economy* 97:305–346.

Index